For Mr and Mrs Bodek,
With warmest Regards
Richard J. Wattenmaker
Philadelphia March 17, 1995

THE LIBRARY OF AMERICAN ART

MAURICE PRENDERGAST

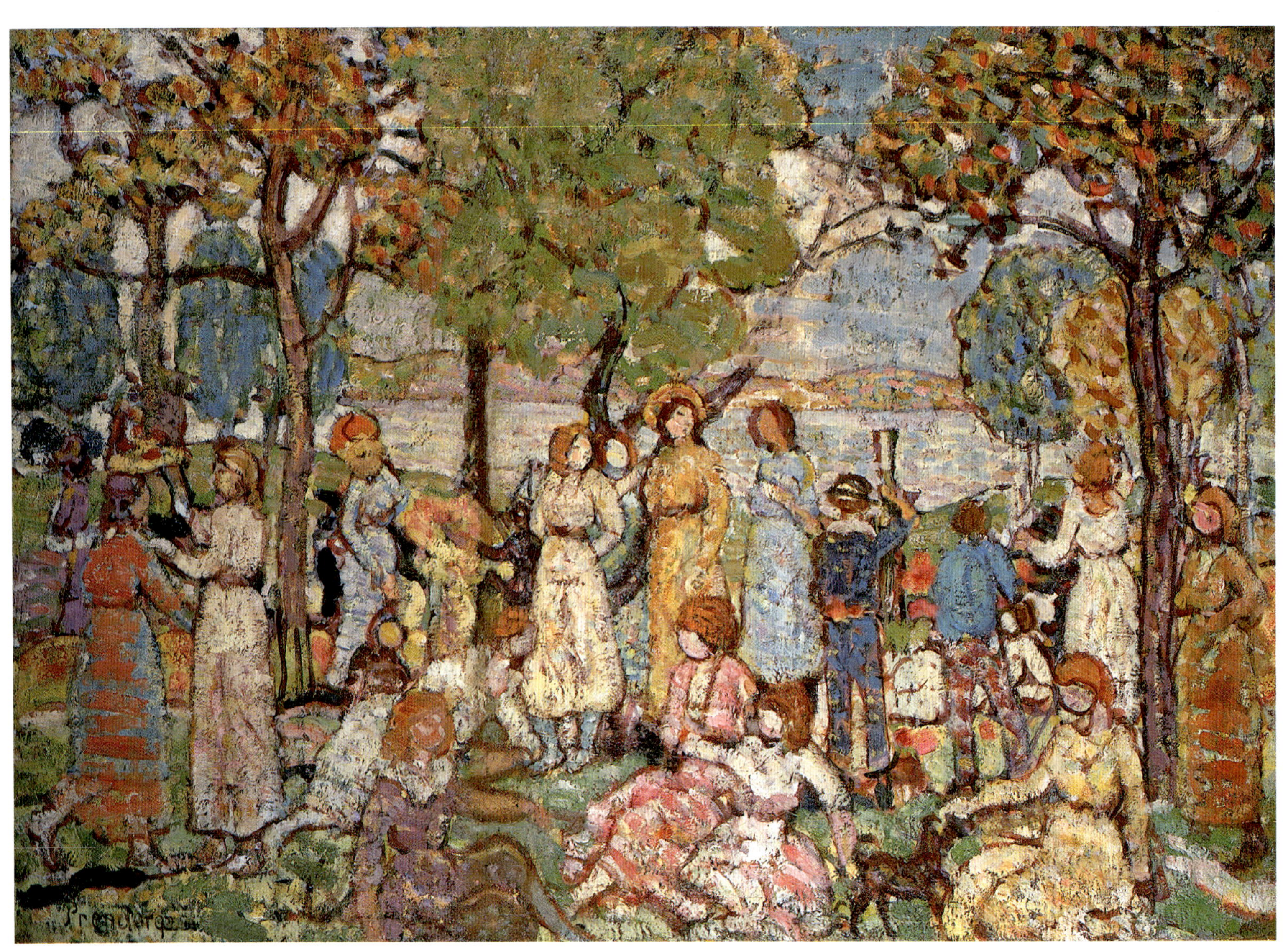

Maurice Prendergast

RICHARD J. WATTENMAKER

Harry N. Abrams, Inc., Publishers
IN ASSOCIATION WITH
The National Museum of American Art, Smithsonian Institution

For Eva, Adrian, and Barnaby

Series Director: Margaret L. Kaplan
Editor: Lory Frankel
Designer: Ellen Nygaard Ford
Photo Research: Catherine Ruello

Library of Congress Cataloging-in-Publication Data

Wattenmaker, Richard J.
Maurice Prendergast / by Richard J. Wattenmaker.
p. cm.—(Library of American art)
Includes bibliographical references (p.) and index.
ISBN 0–8109–3726–3
1. Prendergast Maurice Brazil, 1858–1924—Criticism and interpretation. I. Prendergast, Maurice Brazil, 1858–1924. II. Title. III. Series: Library of American art (Harry N. Abrams, Inc.)
N6537.P38W38 1994
760′.092—dc20 93–46816
CIP

Frontispiece: *Holidays*
c. 1915–18. Oil on canvas, 30 x 43¼″
Minneapolis Institute of Arts.
The Julia B. Bigelow Fund by John Bigelow
(see pl. 122)

Published in 1994 by Harry N. Abrams, Incorporated, New York
A Times Mirror Company

Printed and bound in Japan

Contents

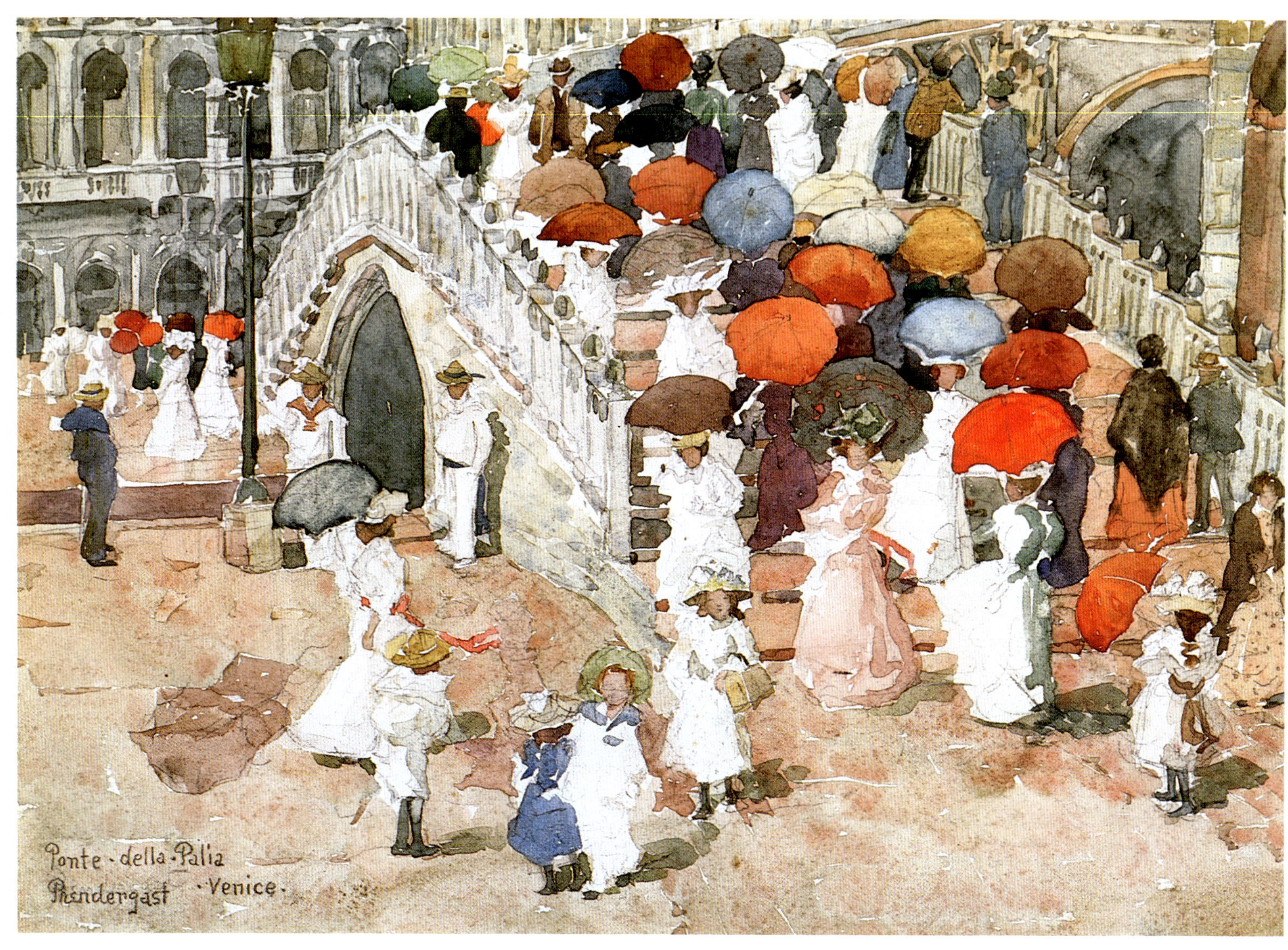

Ponte della Paglia

Preface and Acknowledgments

Until recent years, many well-worn but misleading tales about Maurice Prendergast were uncritically accepted and endlessly repeated. They were all drawn from the same sources. Even his place and date of birth were uncorroborated. The recollections of devoted and well-intentioned friends, the vignettes of colleagues, critics, dealers, and collectors, the often one-dimensional impressions of those who met him in his later years and not surprisingly sometimes misconstrued his hearing-impaired reactions, as well as the suppositions of writers who unwittingly transmitted confused versions of these stories—all these enshrouded Prendergast in a form of generalized hagiography. Gradually, the myth of a poverty-stricken, otherworldly naïf, solitary, critically neglected or misunderstood, is, under fresh examination, being superseded by an increasing body of verifiable facts that reveal more accurately Maurice's background, education, personality, values, opinions, and tastes, as well as the chronology of his oeuvre, its sources, and its critical reception. Progressive reexamination of the known available documents has permitted scholars to clear away long-standing impediments and to fashion a synthesis of the fragmentary data, sufficient to understand more fully the pictures themselves. Maurice's known surviving personal and business correspondence, the voluminous notations found throughout his eighty-eight surviving sketchbooks, as well as collateral manuscript and photographic materials provide reliable sources and intimate, even poignant glimpses into the complex mind of this singularly creative American artist. These documents pose a challenge to interpretation for students of his art and will surely form the basis in the future for specialized studies. More of Prendergast's correspondence will be located and published, to be read and reread, as are Cézanne's letters, not because they are great literature but because they provide deeper insights into the ultimately unknowable mysteries of the artist's creative vision.

My quest to understand Maurice and his brother Charles began in 1959, with an unparalleled opportunity to study the definitive collection of paintings, watercolors, panels, and frames by both the brothers Prendergast in the collection of the Barnes Foundation, Merion Station, Pennsylvania. In 1968, I had the privilege of organizing a comprehensive exhibition, "The Art of Charles Prendergast," presented at the Museum of Fine Arts, Boston, the Rutgers University Art Gallery, New Brunswick, New Jersey, and the Phillips Collection, Washington, D.C., which, for the first time, revealed the creative scope of this unique artist-craftsman, the fragility of whose work had made it relatively inaccessible to the general public. Charles's carved and gilded gesso panels as well as his frame designs are now accorded their full due as works of art, highly prized and copied, whereas twenty-five years ago they were still being discarded in favor of imitation European frames, which were thought to make pictures look more imposing. The frames that Charles carved for paintings owned by such astute

Ponte della Paglia

1898–99. Watercolor on paper, 10¼ x 14¾"
Hirschl & Adler Galleries, Inc., New York

For commentary, see page 45.

collectors as Isabella Stewart Gardner, Lillie P. Bliss, John Quinn, Albert C. Barnes, and many others were often the result of collaboration with Maurice, who sought out motifs on his European travels and recorded several hundred of them in his sketchbooks. Some of these frames were signed by both brothers and dated. Although Maurice's important contribution to frame design and fabrication is not the subject of the present study, research has intensified on this lesser-known aspect of the Prendergasts' work.

In the course of developing this project, so many persons have assisted me that it would be impossible to express adequately to all of them my gratitude for their contributions to this publication.

Foremost are Mrs. Charles Prendergast and the board members of the Eugénie Prendergast Foundation, John W. Boyd, Joseph T. Butler, Harold and Catherine Genvert, for their support of Prendergast research through the Prendergast Archive and Study Center at the Williams College Museum of Art.

Garnett McCoy, Curator Emeritus and Editor, *Archives of American Art Journal,* generously made me the beneficiary of his uniquely comprehensive knowledge of the Archives and guided me to many sources I would otherwise have overlooked. His reading and dispassionate commentary of the first draft of the manuscript was enormously helpful and appreciated.

Ellen Glavin, S.N.D., Associate Professor, Emmanuel College, distinguished scholar, friend, and colleague, has graciously shared with me the fruits of her own ongoing Prendergast research. She has provided an enlightened sounding board for many of my ideas and interpretations.

Nancy Mowll Mathews, Prendergast Curator, Williams College Museum of Art, has been unfailingly generous in making available to me the resources of the Prendergast Archive and Study Center at Williams. Especially worthwhile has been the opportunity to discuss aspects of Prendergast's career with Dr. Mathews.

At the Archives of American Art, my associates have been steadfastly supportive. My warmest thanks are extended to Judith E. Throm, Reference Archivist, who went out of her way to help me on innumerable occasions, and Darcy N. Tell, Managing Editor, *Archives of American Art Journal,* who made order out of my draft bibliography and notes. Susan A. Hamilton, Deputy Director; Stephen C. Polcari, Director, New York Regional Center; Robert F. Brown, New England Regional Center; Arthur J. Breton, Curator of Manuscripts; Elizabeth A. Kirwin, Southeast Regional Collector; Susan Grant, Coordinator, Paris Survey Project; Barbara J. Dawson, Chief, Collection Management and formerly Archivist, the Corcoran Gallery of Art; Catherine J. Stover, Supervisory Archivist; Peggy A. Feerick, Archives Specialist; Christine Murphy, Archival Technician; Brinah M. White, Administrative Specialist; and Karen B. Weiss, Catalogue Database Manager have all provided essential assistance.

Cecilia H. Chin, Librarian, National Museum of American Art/National Portrait Gallery Library, and her staff were resourceful in locating even the most obscure publications, which they did with surpassing good nature. I want to underscore my lively appreciation to Martin Kalfatovic, Circulation/Interlibrary Loan Librarian; Pat Lynagh, Assistant Librarian; Kathryn A. Trillas, Serial Librarian; and L. Kimball Clark, Catalogue Librarian for their energetic professionalism.

At the Smithsonian, Tom L. Freudenheim, Assistant Secretary for Arts and Humanities, and Robert S. Hoffmann, Assistant Secretary for Science, made it possible for me to devote myself in the summer of 1991 exclusively to the book.

Elizabeth Broun, Director, National Museum of American Art, first suggested to Harry N. Abrams, Inc., that I author a study of Maurice Prendergast for the Library of American Art in association with the National Museum of American Art, Smithsonian Institution. I am most indebted to Betsy for her advocacy and goodwill.

To the following who facilitated my work, my sincerest appreciation: William Adair, Gold Leaf Studios; Jeremy E. Adamson, Curator, Renwick Gallery of the National Museum of American Art; Ingrid Marr Adamson, Curator of Exhibitions, Library of Congress; William C. Agee, Professor, Hunter College, New York; the trustees of the Barnes Foundation; Carol Clark, Associate Professor, Amherst College, Massachusetts; Roy Davis; the late Ira Glackens; Ann Greenwood, Administrator, Prendergast Archive and Study Center, Williams College Museum of Art; Charles C. Hill, Curator of Canadian Art, National Gallery of Canada; Bette A. Holloway, Williams College Museum of Art; Melissa Hough, Director, CIGNA Museum and Art Collection, Philadelphia; Alain Joyaux, Director, Ball State University Museum of Art, Muncie, Indiana; Katherine Kaplan, Kraushaar Galleries, New York; Evelyn A. Kassouf; Hilton Kramer, Editor, and Roger Kimball, Managing Editor, *The New Criterion*; Cecily Langdale; Cheryl Leibold, Archivist, Pennsylvania Academy of the Fine Arts, Philadelphia; Sue Levy, Curator, CIGNA Museum and Art Collection, Philadelphia; Thelma and Melvin Lenkin; Bob and Sandy London; Lillian Morris, S.N.D., Professor, Emmanuel College, Boston; Gwendolyn Owens; Carole M. Pesner, Director, Kraushaar Galleries; Victoria Jennings Ross, Department of American Painting and Sculpture, the Metropolitan Museum of Art, New York; Linda Shearer, Director, Williams College Museum of Art; David M. Sokol, Professor, University of Illinois at Chicago; Esther Van Sant; and Cheryl Wagner, Archivist, the Detroit Institute of Arts.

Margaret L. Kaplan, Senior Vice President and Executive Editor; Lory Frankel, Senior Editor; Catherine Ruello, Photo Researcher; Ellen Nygaard Ford, Designer, Joan Siebert; and Joanna Cypis of Harry N. Abrams, Inc., Publishers, made important contributions to this enterprise.

I am particularly indebted to Barton Church, friend and teacher, for years of conversations during which he shared his rich store of knowledge, encouraging me to expand my own. I treasure his forceful insights and wise counsel. Barton and Mary Jane Church have my heartfelt thanks for their enlightened support.

RICHARD J. WATTENMAKER, DIRECTOR
ARCHIVES OF AMERICAN ART, SMITHSONIAN INSTITUTION

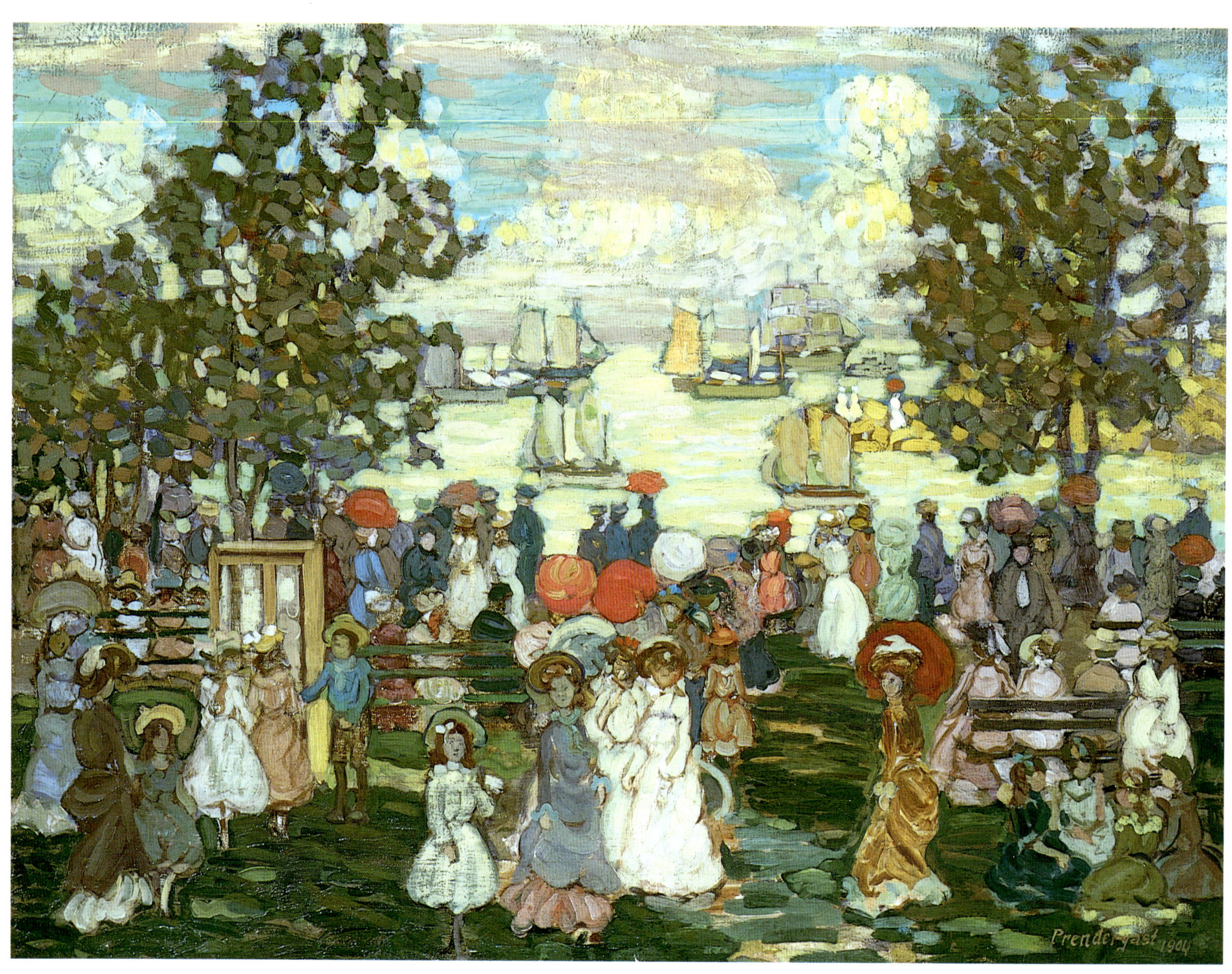

Salem Willows

Introduction

Maurice Prendergast worked in the last decade of the nineteenth century and the early decades of the twentieth perfecting a personal style that earned him a worthy place in the history of modern art. Out of the transient scenes of everyday life that were his primary repertoire of motifs, he created an abundant legacy. Prendergast expressed his joyous response to humanity with a breadth of observation firmly rooted in concrete reality, with no narrative overlay, no deflection into the realm of the sentimental; he was never interested in the unadventurous illustrative naturalism that confined the Impressionism of so many Americans at the end of the last century. His was a deeply inquiring mind, persevering in wide-ranging investigations into the traditions and the discoveries of his contemporaries, both at home and abroad.

The essential constituent of Prendergast's vision is its multiple harmonies of color. He explored, expanded, and deepened the color relationships through his chosen mediums, progressively mastering and polishing each of them. Ideas that emerged from his watercolors and monotypes were adapted and purposefully transformed into the subtler, more elaborate, and unpredictable colors of his oils on panel and canvas. The breadth of Prendergast's color sensitivity cannot be overstated; his unique perception endowed his sensuous experiments in pattern and texture, atmosphere and light with a stature achieved by few artists of his generation.

In 1910 Maurice was characterized by Charles Hovey Pepper, one of his colleagues of oldest acquaintance, who had known and exhibited with him since the 1890s, as a "short, white-haired, slight man, shut into his own world in a measure by his deafness, wiry, enthusiastic, strong in his likes and dislikes, indefatigable worker. . . ."[1] Daphne Dunbar, a painter who was a friend in Boston during the early years of the century, recalled, "Mr. Maurice painted every day, but about five o'clock he and Charlie liked to go out. Most nights we'd walk from Mt. Vernon Street across the Common and go to Jake Wirth's for pigs knuckles and potato salad. Then we would walk around, generally to Chinatown and see the lights. Mr. Maurice loved that. Mr. Maurice took us all to a burlesque show once . . . [he] liked to watch the lights and the flicker. . . . We had such good times. They were odd and wonderful people, Mr. Maurice and Charlie. They always looked so clean and jaunty."[2] Dunbar also attested to his keen intellect: "Maurice read and thought a great deal. He read French easily and could get along conversationally when in France. He knew the work of the Russian novelists."[3] Max Weber recounted a discussion with Prendergast in 1912: "We talked about modern art, about Cézanne, the great instigator and prophet, the great archaics, the ancients and the primitives. Conversation on art on this level or plane was rare and far between in those days. Mr. Prendergast was a lovable and unusually gentle and sensitive man."[4] Jerome Myers observed that "Maurice Prendergast . . . had no envy, only a deep interest in what others did."[5]

Salem Willows

1904. Oil on canvas, 26 x 34″
Terra Museum of American Art, Chicago.
Daniel J. Terra Collection

For commentary, see page 73.

During the winter of 1908–9, Marsden Hartley visited the Prendergasts' Boston studio:

> *I got to know Maurice & Charles Prendergast. . . . I . . . remember this place on Mt Vernon Street—a frame shop really—where Charles made his frames and Maurice painted in one corner.*
>
> *There was always this sense of fluttering gold in the air of that room. Maurice weaving through it all his curiously involved tapestry patterns in paint. . . .*
>
> *Maurice was a person of fiery enthusiasms as regards painting. It was the one thing worth doing in life—it was the means of life for him.*
>
> *His extreme deafness didn't seem to matter much to him. If people really wanted him to hear they talked loud enough. If not, he went on painting and any other painting that looked sincere to him sent something like flames of joy over him. He became ecstatic.*
>
> *Maurice had served a certain apprenticeship in Paris as everyone did at that time. He had learned much from impressionism. He loved Cézanne devoutly—and anything that he thought good must be spoken of to the world at once. He liked my pictures & wrote letters down to Glackens and Davies & gave me introductions to them. . . .*[6]

In a sketch written in 1955, Forbes Watson depicted one of his last visits to the Prendergasts in their studio at 50 Washington Square South, New York:

> *My memories of Maurice Prendergast are few but vivid. The most vivid, by far, is of a sunny day in Maurice's south painting room in which he was slowly improvising while his brother Charles and William Glackens and I spasmodically looked on. Maurice was then deaf. He had put aside his hearing aid purposely I thought as if he liked the sociability of our presence but felt that the sound of our voices would be distracting. Actually we spoke little. Charles, as usual, did most of the talking. He was a gay spirit and his long financial struggle had developed his native canniness. He loved to tell stories, not always documented but always touched with comedy, about collectors, dealers, museum officials and other artists. But Glackens had undoubtedly heard all of his stories and I had heard a good proportion of them. Every few minutes Maurice turned and smiled at us and we smiled back. And the painting proceeded in silence. Some painters whom I know won't tolerate being watched. Others can't. Still others, like the late George Luks, loved an audience. I have seen George fail and succeed. . . . But Maurice never indulged in pyrotechnics. One could not know him for a day and imagine his ever showing off. He was extremely modest but perfectly confident and strong-minded.*
>
> *Some artists thought that painting and patriotism mixed in equal shares made the best art. Prendergast had no affiliation with this school of thought. He was broadly cultivated in art and enjoyed the association of other artists who were cultivated. I gained the impression that he hated the praise of the ignorant more than their insults. But he liked best of all the understanding of his cultivated equals and did not lower himself as some less confident artists do, to seek the praise of his inferiors.*

While we were talking painting Maurice was doing painting. And that, I think, might be said to be the keynote of Maurice's career. He did and let others talk.[7]

William Glackens's son Ira, who knew the Prendergast brothers, portrayed Maurice as reserved in demeanor, unpretentious, intensely absorbed in his art, observant, and sociable. He saw him not as the naive, otherworldly hermit, as he is often presented, but as a man full of wonder and curiosity. "Whenever they appeared the news spread through the community, 'The Prendies are in town!' [New York] for they were much loved, and all their friends made haste to wine and dine them. Then, after a few days of festivities and visiting the galleries to see what was going on in the way of art, the Prendergasts could return to the peace of Mount Vernon Street."[8] Dinner in New York at Mouquin's Restaurant or Petitpas with his friends, many of them painters much younger than himself, a bottle of wine, and a cigar recalled the times with his comrades in Paris and Florian's in the Piazza San Marco, Venice, which Maurice found so congenial. "There was always an unquenchable youthfulness in the man himself," said Walter Pach, who knew Maurice from 1907 until the very end of his life. Pach stressed the serious dimension to Prendergast's personality: "'The best painting isn't done by boys,' Mr. Prendergast said one time, 'it's the work of mature men.'"[9]

The human dimension is revealed by Maurice's diarylike account summarizing his passage on board *La Gascogne,* bound for Le Havre, France:

Dear Charlie, Sunday May 19, 1907, First night out—had an excellent dinner. . . .
May 20th: I am commencing to feel much Jollier and recovering my old Self.
May 22: 4th night . . . The dinners are very Jolly affairs the wine sets them all talking together and it is great fun . . . on this boat travelling is a pleasure again.
Thursday 23rd May fifth day out: . . . The critical sense leaves one completely on these boats. I will make up my mind to eliminate that and that and this but when I sit down to the Table I devour everything that comes along. I seem to be all right afterwards and hungry again for the next meal. I noticed a library of french books I tried to get one out but seems they are for sale.
Friday 24th: To day we had real French Dejeuner 1st Radish, Sardines, Butter. 2nd tete de Veau—oil great. 3 codfish baked with tomatoes & Potatoes 3 lamb chop des pommes frites 4 cheese & cake 5th apples & nuts 6 cafe . . . so far my appetite is très bon and I am commencing to sleep well.
Saturday 25th I have no fault to find with the boat. . . . Opposite me at the table sit three Germans each try to out do the other to see who can drink the most and I am the referee. There is great fun at the table every body drinks one another's health.
Monday 27th: The dinner to night was a grand affair and wine flowed like water, the three Germans that sat opposite tried to drink me off my feet, but they caught a tartar. The dinner was first class. They had little paper caps . . . laid at the Side of Each plate, coloured helmets Miters, Etc. When everybody had a cap on their head the effect was quite gay. . . . [The French] found out I am an artist and I am quite a popular man. . . .

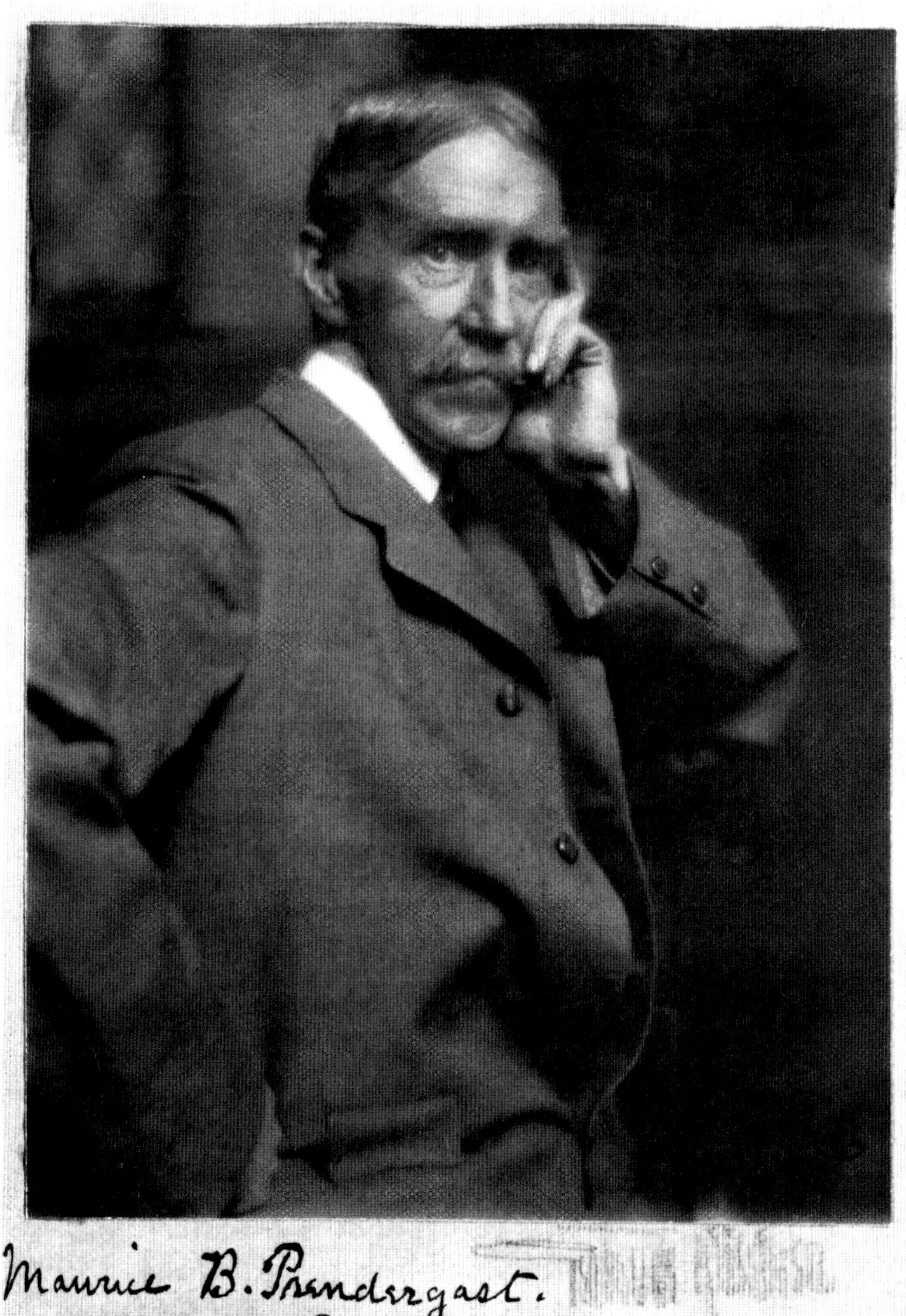

1. Gertrude Käsebier (1852–1934). *Portrait of Maurice B. Prendergast*

I. The Early Years 1858–90

MAURICE BRAZIL PRENDERGAST WAS BORN IN the British Crown Colony of Newfoundland on October 10, 1858. His father, Maurice Prendergast, Sr., and his mother, Mary Malvina Germaine, married in Saint John's in 1857. Maurice was baptized in Saint John's Basilica in the parish of Saint John's. Charles James (later changed to Edward or E.) Prendergast was baptized in Saint John's in 1863. Mary Prendergast's father, Thomas H. Germaine, was a physician, and her brother, Charles Napoleon (after whom Charles was named), received his M.D. from Harvard Medical School in 1850. Maurice's godfather was Patrick Brazil, thus accounting for his unusual surname.[10]

Information about the Prendergasts' early life is sparse. At the time of the brothers' birth, Maurice senior was proprietor of a grocery store or trading post in Saint John's. Young Maurice undoubtedly received his early schooling there, possibly in a parish school or in a school operated by the Benevolent Irish Society, established by Irish immigrants, in which his father's family was active.[11] In 1868, the Prendergasts emigrated to Boston, where Maurice, age ten, entered the Boston public school system.[12] It is not recorded where the Prendergast family lived from 1868 to 1872. From 1872 until the late 1870s they resided on West Dedham Street, the center of which divided the Rice and Dwight school districts. As the records of both the Rice and Dwight schools no longer exist, it cannot be ascertained which grammar school Maurice attended, although he could have gone to Rice. His South End neighbor, the future architect Louis Sullivan (1856–1924), exactly two years Prendergast's senior, attended the Rice Grammar School for Boys from 1866 to 1870. He has left an account of the milieu in which both boys were raised, in families where their respective fathers—Sullivan's as a "teacher of dancing," Prendergast's as a "laborer" or "confectioner"—had little or no success in establishing themselves. In 1868, the Rice school had just moved to a new building on Dartmouth Street in the Back Bay district. According to Sullivan's autobiography, the structure was "up to date in all respects," although he did not esteem the teachers' conventional ideas and open anti-Irish bias.[13]

After leaving grammar school around 1872, Maurice was employed wrapping packages at the dry-goods store Loring and Waterhouse. Notwithstanding the reduced circumstances in which each was raised, Prendergast, like Sullivan, seems not to have suffered any cultural deprivation or lack of confidence. Boston, the presumptive capital of American culture and learning in literature and science, nurtured a devotion to intellectual pursuits in the future artists. Both were lifelong readers of literature, poetry, and philosophy; both became

1. Gertrude Käsebier (1852–1934). *Portrait of Maurice B. Prendergast*

1907. Platinum print, 8 x 6" Signed and dated: "Maurice Prendergast 1913"
Archives of American Art, Smithsonian Institution, Washington, D.C. Macbeth Gallery Records

Francophiles who were conversant in French. Exaggerated portrayals of the Prendergast brothers as poverty-stricken arose as Charles embellished the Horatio Alger image of their no doubt far from luxurious but nevertheless not desperately poor early life. Each had relatives on his mother's side who were capable of providing financial sustenance at difficult moments. Dr. Charles Germaine, Maurice's uncle, was a prominent physician in Westfield, Massachusetts, and Maurice went there on visits, where he sketched out of doors.[14] Stories about walking miles to save carfare and other economies, while probably true, have a distinctly Lincolnesque cast.

Ellen Glavin has greatly expanded our knowledge of Prendergast's early art training, documenting that Maurice participated in classes instituted to teach mechanical and industrial drawing in the public schools.[15] That curriculum stressed drawing freehand from a model or object as well as from memory and, in addition, geometrical and perspective drawing. Glavin also discovered that during the 1870s Maurice studied at one of several Free Evening Drawing Schools established in Boston, where he followed a comprehensive curriculum in all aspects of industrial draftsmanship as well as drawing from models and historical ornament and passed examinations there in 1873 and 1877.[16]

After working for Loring and Waterhouse, Maurice is said to have been apprenticed in lettering show cards, or "store cards" used as advertising signs in shops.[17] By 1879, he is listed in the Boston directory as a "designer," in the 1880 United States census as a "painter," and in 1882 as a "decorator." Nothing specific is known about his work and no examples have been identified. In 1877, Charles, five years Maurice's junior, became an errand boy for the Doll & Richards Gallery in Boston, where he worked for three years. From 1880 to 1893, the family resided in Roxbury, and in 1886 Maurice gave his business address as the firm of Peter Gill, designer of show cards. This work called for a sophisticated knowledge of color mixtures as well as layout and lettering skills.

From what we know of Maurice's subsequent career, it is certain that he spent time looking at the growing collections of the Museum of Fine Arts, which had opened on Copley Square in 1876. Society shows of contemporary Boston painters, many of whom became early adherents of Impressionism, gallery exhibitions of every conceivable type from Barbizon landscapists to the French Impressionists provided Maurice with more than ample opportunity to form a personal perspective of contemporary painting during the 1880s. The watercolors of Winslow Homer and John La Farge, James McNeill Whistler, and the full spectrum of illustrators reproduced in journals and magazines were well known to him. If his later custom is any guide, he also must have taken the boat to New York from time to time to see the collections in the Metropolitan Museum of Art.

According to Charles's recollections, Maurice was engrossed in sketching the countryside around Boston, indicating a desire to hone his skills as a draftsman by direct observation, along the lines of painters like Jean-François Millet, whose student and admirer, William Morris Hunt (1824–1879), had popularized the Barbizon painters and Camille Corot in Boston. Around this time

Charles made the first of two trips to England, traveling on a cattle boat. On the second trip Charles was accompanied by Maurice, who made sketches in watercolor and pencil of cottages in Hawarden, Wales, several of which survive, dated August 1886.[18] Conventional, careful renderings, they record the prosaic facts of the motif. Some writers have surmised that Maurice first visited Paris during this 1886 trip, but there is no evidence to support this speculation. In any event, trips to Europe, even on a cattle boat, do not bespeak financial deprivation.

Maurice's earliest sketchbook also contains drawings of landscapes with cattle and houses, several of which are dated April and May 1887, when he was in Everett, Massachusetts. This sketchbook was carried on his trip to England and Wales, as indicated by addresses noted therein. Drawings touched with subdued gray-blue and tan washes done at Brook's Cove, Westport, Maine, in 1889, boats and shacks and a fisherman on the dock by the waterside with a dory, as well as a watercolor dated 1889 of a schooner with sails reflected in the water suggest the Barbizon–Hague school style seen in the sketches done in Wales. These, plus a drawing of cows and one of sheep in a field, dated July 1890, are all that remain of Maurice's early experiments in watercolors.[19]

Arthur H. Jameson, who owned three of the 1889 sketches, had met Maurice at age eighteen in Brook's Cove and reported to Hedley Rhys in 1951 that Maurice already at that time had "a definite dullness of hearing—not deaf."[20]

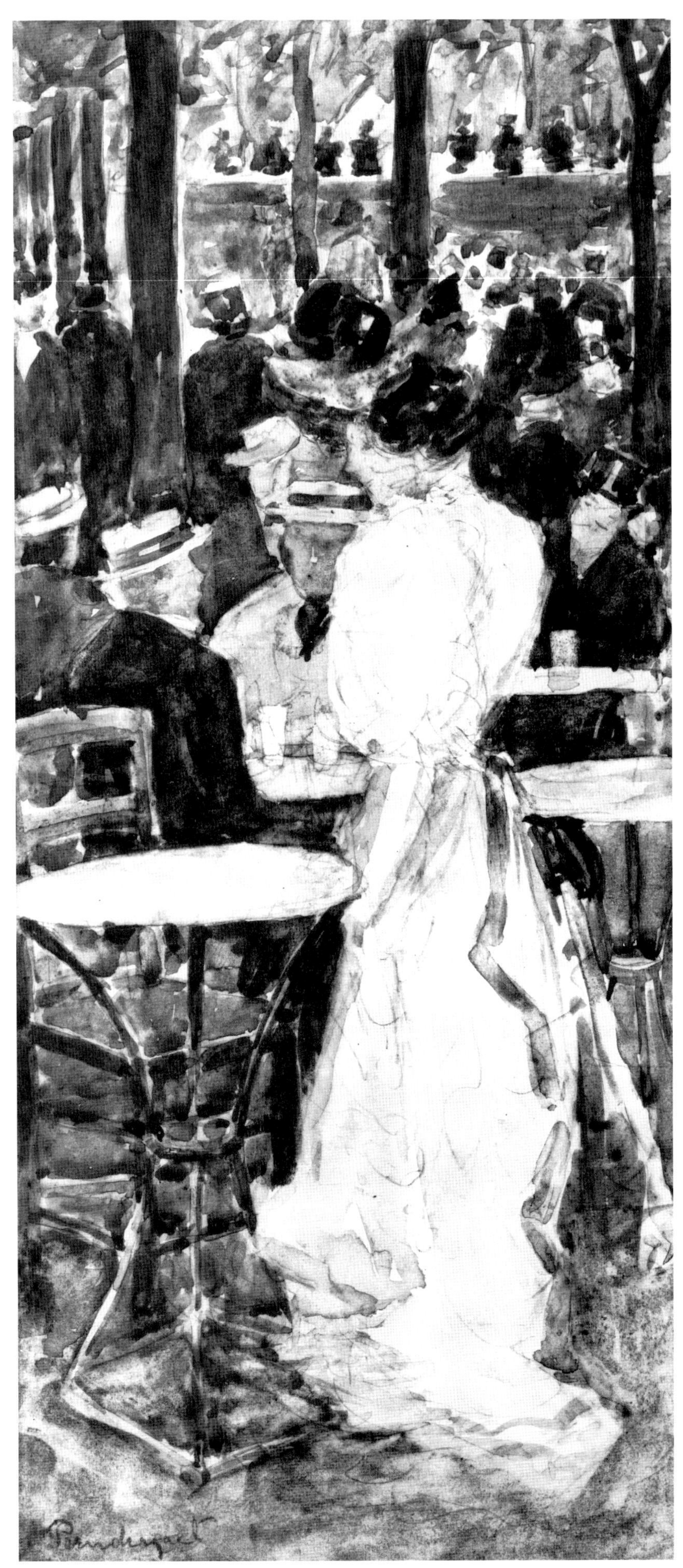

2. *Park Scene, Paris*

II. France 1891–94

IT IS FROM THIS MOMENT THAT WE TRACE MAURICE'S development as an artist. By the latter part of 1890, the brothers had saved enough money to make another trip to France. Charles accompanied Maurice and they both enrolled at the Atelier Colarossi by January 1891, where the classes were presided over by Gustave Courtois (1853–1923).

The seedy atmosphere at Colarossi is described in a contemporary article:

> *Near the juncture of the Boulevard Raspail and the Boulevard Montparnasse is a little street leading Seine-ward . . . with the pretentious title of "La Grande-Chaumière." Midway, on this little street, between the Boulevard Montparnasse and the Rue Notre Dame des Champs . . . is situated the Académie Colarossi. One could pass it a dozen times and never realize that he was in the neighborhood of a great art school—so modest in appearance is the little portal that admits one into its dingy interior, or rather the dingy, small corridor that takes him back to the Academy proper. As one emerges from this sooty corridor . . . he finds himself on a curious open stair-landing of worn brick that looks down over the courtyard of the Academy . . . a steep flight of impossible steps leads to the room above, and another flight, of broken ones, conducts into the yard below. Vines and shrubbery grow in great profusion everywhere, and among them is scattered about a variety of antique and broken statuary. A more interesting or picturesque spot it would be hard to find in the city of Paris.*[21]

In October, Maurice entered the Académie Julian, 31 rue du Dragon, where his instructors were Jean-Paul Laurens (1838–1921) and Joseph-Paul Blanc (1846–1904).[22] Many years later, in 1914, when asked to provide information on his formal art training, Maurice responded: "I studied in Paris several years at various schools, Julians, the Beaux arts, etc. and was a pupil of Joseph Blanc."[23] Carefully rendered watercolors, several dated January 1891, were made from the models at Colarossi and are all that remain from the work in the academies.

Charles Hovey Pepper (1864–1950) studied at Julian's in the mid-1890s, just after Maurice, and first saw his work there in the studio of a mutual friend. He provided a terse firsthand description of the chaotic atmosphere in the studio: "Monday morning, early to the school—choosing a model—wrangling for places—figure put in—change—the action—get that action. Tuesday, at it again—whooping choruses . . . noisy. Wednesday . . . Silvia y Fernandez swells out his chest because Laurens has said '*Pas mal.*' This familiar art mill. Essential, but . . . leaving a good deal to get out of the system."[24]

2. *Park Scene, Paris*

c. 1893–94. Watercolor and pencil on paper, 11 5/8 x 5 1/8"
Collection Mrs. Malim Harding

A firm linear gridwork is established by the supports of the foreground table and the chair behind it, moving to the figures in straw hats, then to the trees beyond, with a gallery of uniformed musicians across the background. Prendergast frequented both the outdoor cafés and the indoor salles de danse, *such as the Bal Bullier, favorite haunts of American tourists and artists in search of motifs.*

3. Ladies in the Rain

c. 1893–94. Watercolor and pencil on paper, 13¾ x 5¾"
Permanent Collection Museum of Art, Fort Lauderdale, Florida. Bequest of Ira Glackens

Charles FitzGerald of the New York Sun *described Prendergast's watercolors on exhibit at the New York Water Color Club from November 7 through 20, 1897: "the parasols and gowns are much more gayly colored than they are in real life, nowadays, they are good examples of a free and sketchy handling of transparent washes. . . . Each carries in itself something that's personal and prepossessing" (November 14, 1897).*

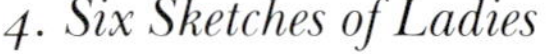

4. Six Sketches of Ladies

c. 1893–94. Monotype on paper with pencil additions, 14 x 10¾"
Courtesy of The Fogg Art Museum, Harvard University, Cambridge, Massachusetts. Collection of Katharine S. Goodman, on loan at the Fogg Art Museum

This is the only instance where Maurice employed the screen motif. However, Charles brought it into play much later; the reverse of his 1916–17 Screen *has three single figures, blue, pink, and gold, each 75 inches high, on a gold background.*

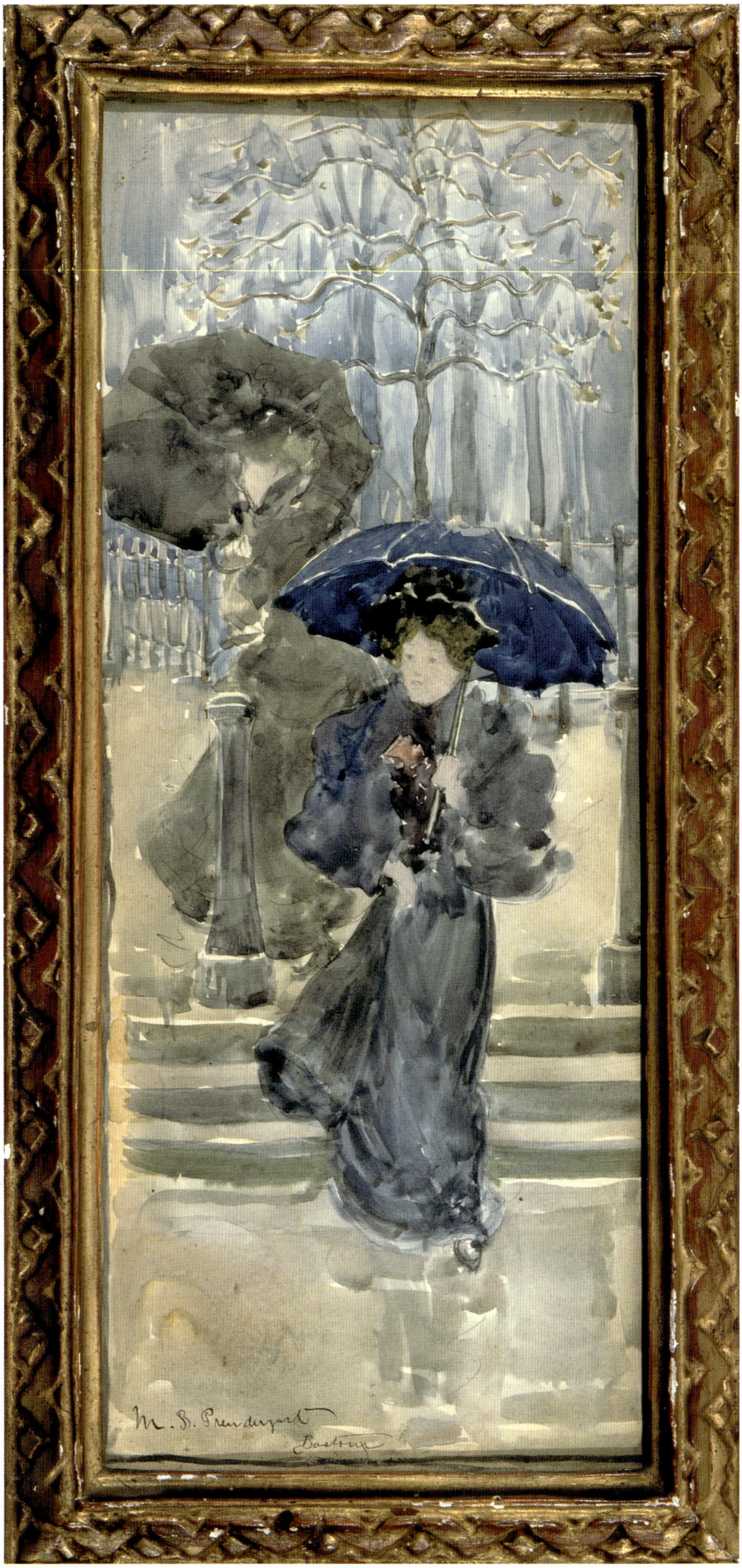

3. Ladies in the Rain

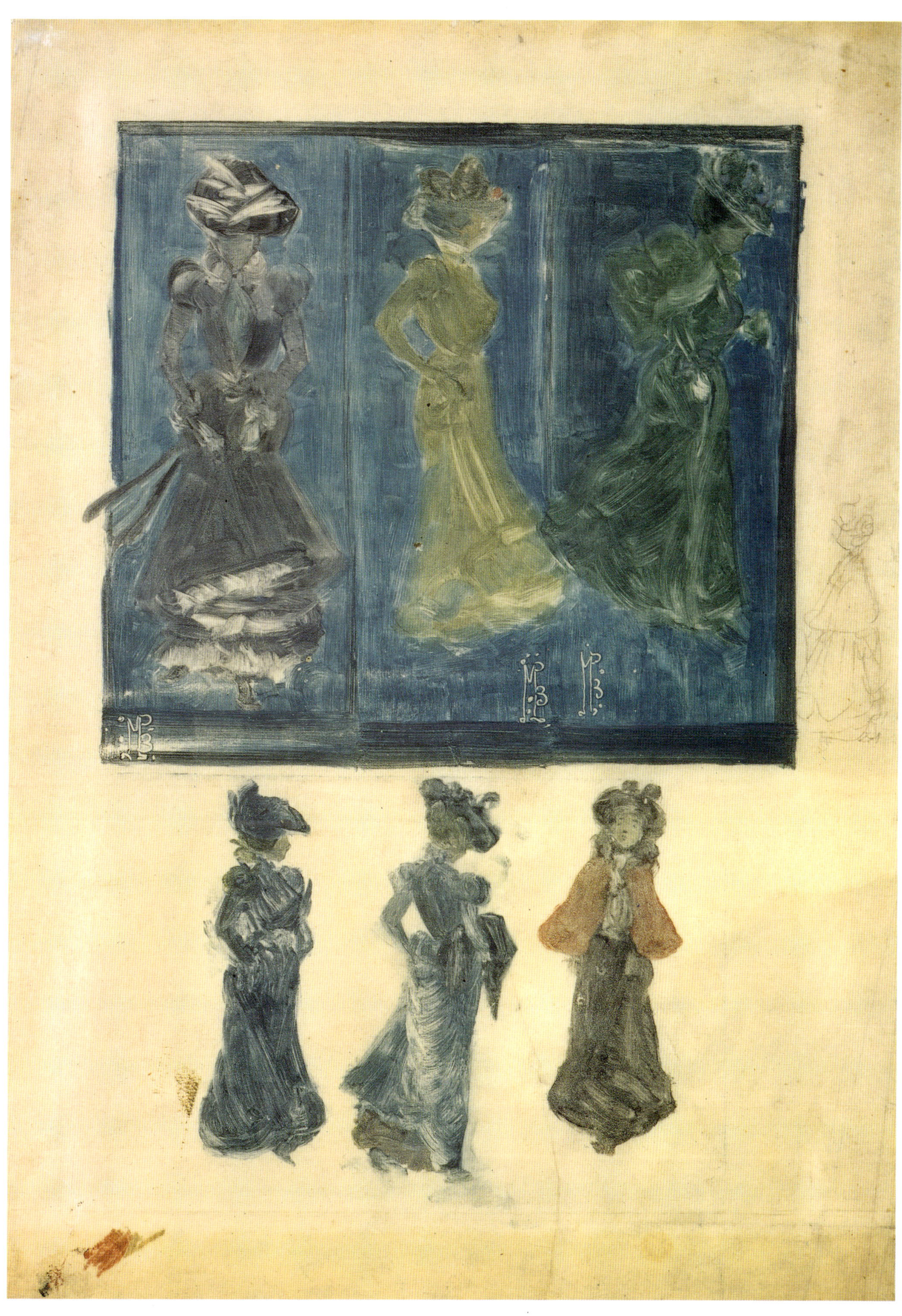

4. Six Sketches of Ladies

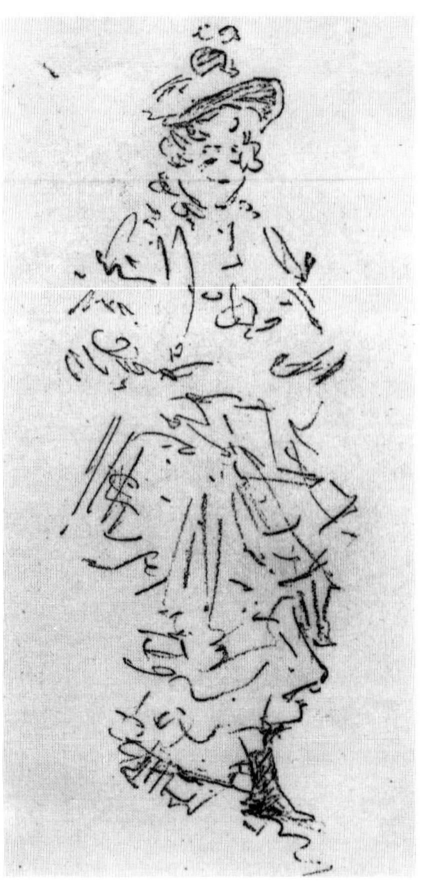

5. *Untitled*

Reproduced in The Studio, vol. 1 (1893)

These poised figures are reminiscent of the loosely constructed linear strokes of Whistler's lithographs. These pencil sketches were stolen and reproduced in The Studio. *George Thompson, the author of one of three articles, remarked, "With a decided prepossession for grace, they show much daintiness and skill in rendering action."*

According to Pepper, Prendergast spent each morning for two years following a routine of drawing and painting under the casual tutelage of these teachers. He added:

> *The afternoons Prendergast spent with notebook in the cafés and the gardens, in the river, in the Bois, constantly sketching. Cabs, nursemaids,* sergents de ville, *boats—everything passes through his grist. Drawing moving life. Developing keen observation and memory of form and movement. He had found it of great value. It is, in fact, one of the bases of his art.*[25]

Our most concrete evidence of Prendergast's drawing style during this extended French sojourn is given by the drawings reproduced in *The Studio* magazine in 1893, the fortuitous result of a theft of these sketches of Prendergast's and their subsequent publication under the name of one Michael Dignam (pl. 5).[26] These lively rapid pencil notations, done from life, are the first manifestations of the artist's personal style and bear out Pepper's remarks. They delineate both the outlines and the gestures of the women as they are caught in motion, emphasizing not detail or verisimilitude, as in an illustration, but rather their generalized activity. Drawing in the studio from casts in pursuit of a career as an academic painter was not Maurice's objective. The drawings published in *The Studio* are concurrent with watercolors and monotypes that evince an identical animation and linear flourishes. Prendergast's preponderant subject motifs were women in their fashionable finery—elaborate hats, muffs, capes, and boas, all of which stimulated the liveliness of his crayon or brush. Van Wyck Brooks later recounted: "When short skirts came into fashion . . . he spoke of the beautiful movement that women had made when, at a street-corner, they turned round to lift up their skirts before they scurried across the street: 'That's a lost art,' he said."[27]

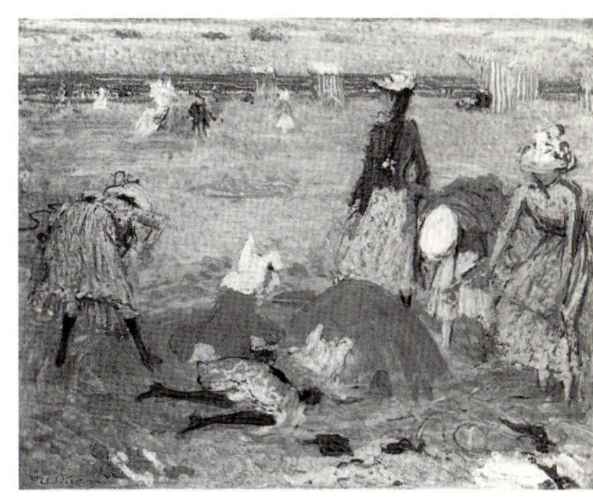

6. Philip Wilson Steer (1860–1942)
Boulogne Sands

1888–91 (dated 1892). Oil on canvas, 24 x 30 1/8"
The Tate Gallery, London

Prendergast associated with the young English-speaking artists in Paris. James Wilson Morrice (1865–1924), from Montreal, became a lifelong acquaintance; similarities in style have long been noted between the small oils on panel of Morrice and Prendergast. Morrice introduced Prendergast to Charles Conder (1868–1909), and the three painted together on the Normandy and Brittany coasts. Pepper wrote: "In the summers with Morrice, [Charles C.] Curran . . . and others, he went to Dinard and St. Malo where the same work [drawing] was followed together with sketching in oil. *Pochades* and more *pochades*."[28] Prendergast also worked at Dieppe and Le Tréport, and there are watercolors, several of which are signed M. Brazil Prendergast,[29] done in Paris and en route to the coast. (Maurice was peripatetic in his quest for picturesque motifs, establishing a pattern that he would follow throughout his career.) Morrice owned at least seven of Prendergast's early watercolors.[30] Prendergast was also familiar with the work of Walter Sickert (1860–1942) and Philip Wilson Steer (1860–1942), whose *Boulogne Sands* (pl. 6), 1888–89, epitomizes the images that he found appealing as prototypes for his own work.

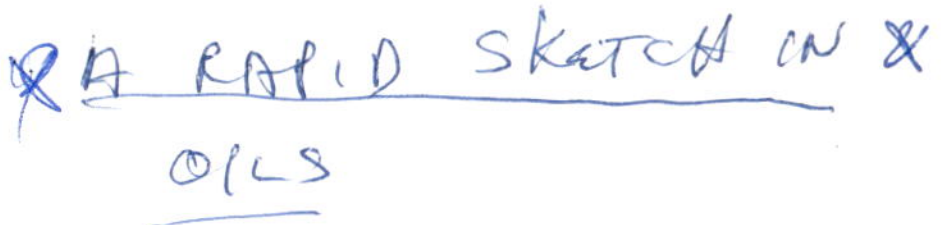

All of these fledgling painters shared a common devotion to the work of Whistler, his delicate use of grays and loose linear fluency, particularly in his small oils, watercolors of beaches, and panels of city streets, as well as his lithographs. They also shared an alternate source for their *pochades* in the small oil panels of Constable, whose sketches from nature had been an important stimulus for both Delacroix and the Impressionists. Best known for delicate, neo-rococo fans painted in watercolors on silk, Conder had been working on small nine-by-five-inch cigar box lids in the late 1880s in Australia and had exhibited his colorful oil sketches in Melbourne in 1889 prior to leaving for France, where he arrived at Julian's by October 1890. Prendergast knew Conder's Impressionist work of this period, which predates the paintings on silk begun in 1892–93. By means of these associations Prendergast was introduced to the work of at least some of the French avant-garde.

The animation of the pencil sketches is directly carried over to watercolors done at the same time. *Park Scene, Paris* (pl. 2) of c. 1893–94 depends on the brisk pencil notations that underlie the delicacy of the watercolor touches laid over them. At this early stage, Maurice already maintained the freshness of his color, without sacrificing spontaneity. While he was absorbed in exploring the Impressionist discoveries of light and color, his sketchbooks and watercolors disclose knowledge of Manet and Delacroix watercolors as well as their paintings. In fact, Maurice's constant use of sketchbooks is akin to Delacroix's methods of careful color annotations.

8. James Wilson Morrice (1865–1924)
Untitled (A Paris Café Scene)

Oil on panel, 6 x 5"
Permanent Collection, Museum of Art, Fort Lauderdale, Florida. Bequest of Ira Glackens

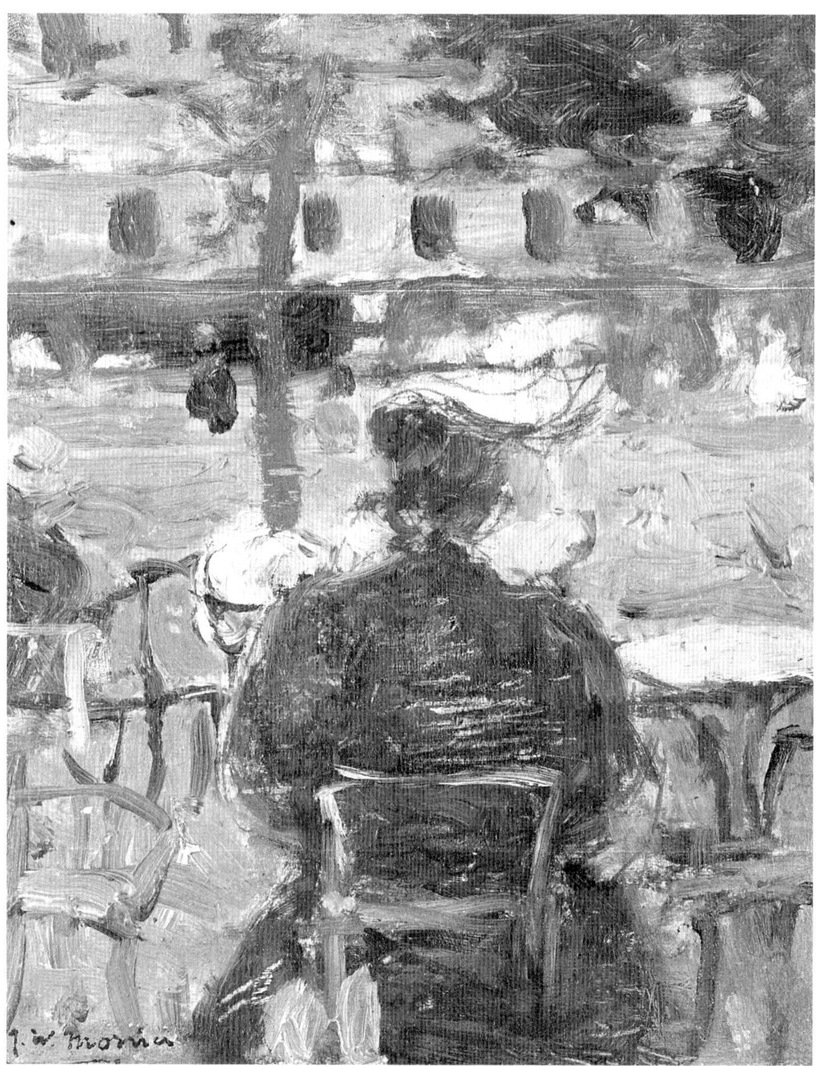

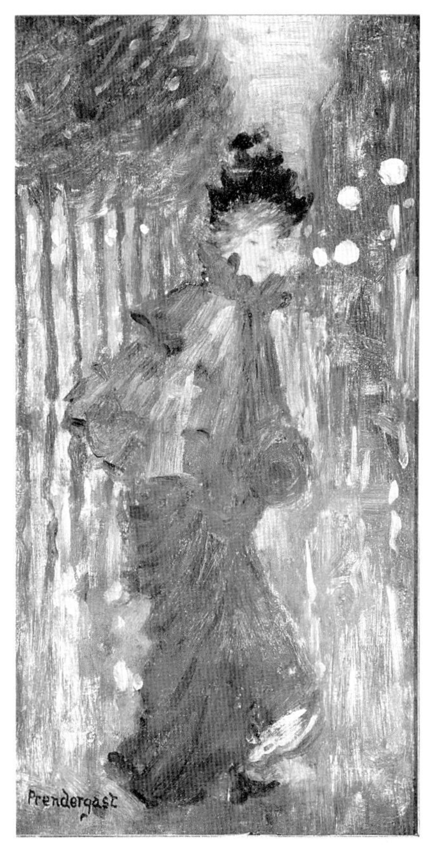

7. Lady on the Boulevard (The Green Cape)

c. 1892–94. Oil on panel, 13½ x 7"
Terra Museum of American Art, Chicago. Daniel J. Terra Collection

Distinctly Japanese in effect, with lights and their reflections in the wet street approximating Japanese lanterns, this oil on panel shares its brisk brushwork with the artist's contemporary pencil sketches, watercolors, and monotypes.

Ladies in the Rain (pl. 3), c. 1893–94, has a motif that also shares the elongated shape of a woman raising her dress as she descends a short flight of steps, grasping an umbrella in her other hand. The pencil notations are replaced by deft strokes of the watercolor brush, which create both the pattern of the dress and the space within the umbrella. A second figure walking behind a stanchion at the top of the stairs, less detailed and dramatic, functions as an echo or reflection of the woman in the foreground. The rippling, sinuous horizontal lines of the tree branches and trunks in the background create a candelabra-like foil for the figures. With no hesitancy, Maurice already demonstrated mastery over the elusive technique of painting in watercolors.

Both the drawing by means of touches of color and the motifs of the watercolors are maintained in Maurice's monotypes made contemporaneously in Paris. Around the time Prendergast studied there, monotypes were "the rage" among students in the Latin Quarter. The American Art Association held "monotype parties," where it was reported that "judging from the enthusiasm with which everyone takes to it and the fascination there always is in work or

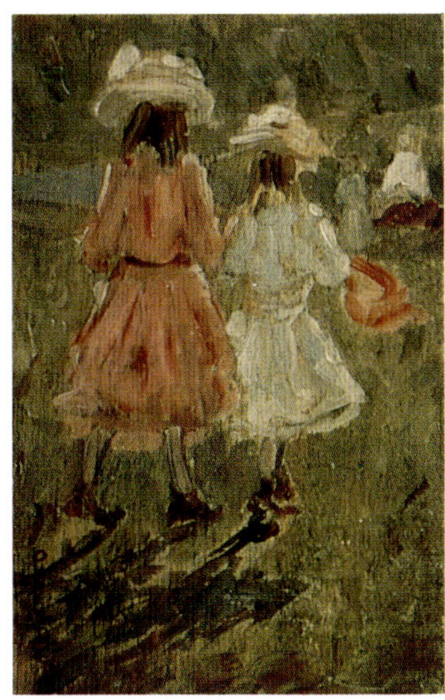

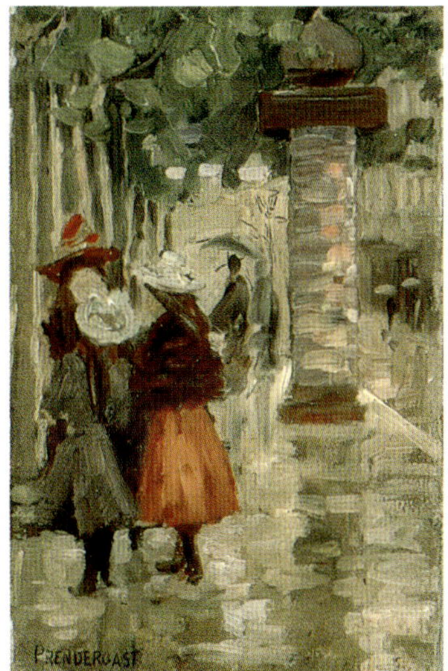

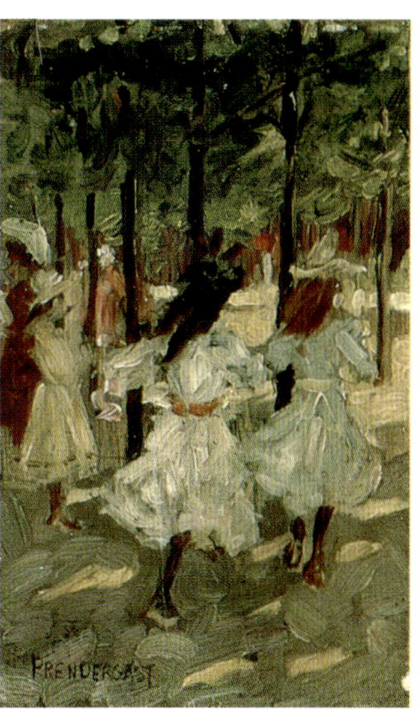

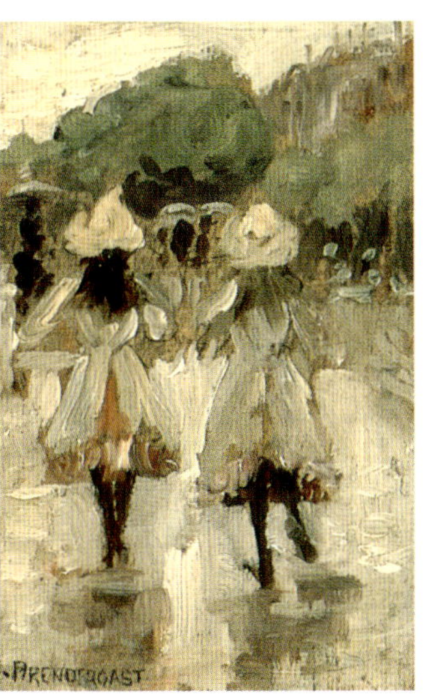

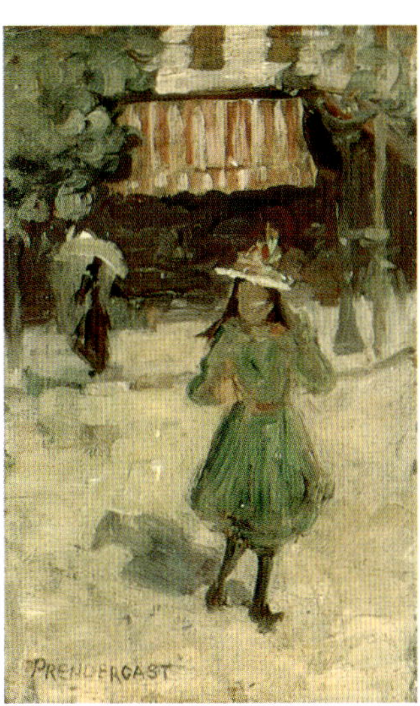

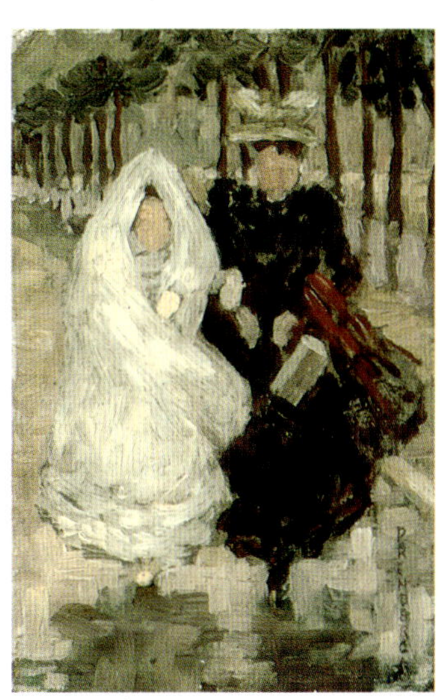

play of any kind where much depends on 'luck' . . . meetings have been devoted to little else since."[31]

The technical procedure Maurice followed in making his monotypes was recorded by Mrs. Oliver E. Williams (1867–1964), his friend and student: "Paint on copper in oils, wiping parts to be white. When [the] picture suits you, place it on Japanese paper and either press in a press or rub with a spoon till it pleases you. Sometimes the second or third plate is the best."[32] They were frequently heightened with pencil and/or additional touches of color, to reinforce or add a summary detail such as a facial feature or pattern or to strengthen a color area or contrast between two adjacent units. Some of them exist in two variant images taken from the plate, which might have been augmented by selective repainting between "pulls." The prints reflect careful observation of the monotypes of Degas and Pissarro. Pissarro, who was, among the Impressionists, the most pervasive influence on Maurice, included his monotypes in at least two exhibits held at the Durand-Ruel gallery while Maurice was in Paris in the early 1890s.

9. Sketches in Paris.

c. 1892–94. Oil on panel, each 6¼ x 3¾"
Addison Gallery of American Art,
Phillips Academy, Andover, Massachusetts

Although flat, the figures in these small oil panels, or pochades, *emerge distinctly from their screenlike backgrounds. The crisp patterns of dress and skirt, kiosk and striped awning create firm spatial relations, making each vignette a coherent composition in itself. The seven panels were assembled and framed by Charles in the early 1930s.*

Six Sketches of Ladies (pl. 4), also c. 1893–94, reversed the process of some of the watercolors in that the figures were drawn in color on the plate and then, after the paper was removed from the plate, additions in pencil were made to reinforce the images. The tripartite screen device, wherein the central figure's dress sweeps into the adjacent vertical frame, is a bold variation on Japanese screens. The figures replicate in color the animation of the pencil strokes seen in *The Studio* drawings. Another unusual effect is the trio of figures in the lower section of the print, who seem to have stepped out of the screen and struck different poses. There can be no doubting Prendergast's debt to the pervasive influence of Japanese prints and screens, to which he had been exposed both in Paris and in Boston's Museum of Fine Arts.[33] The oil on panel *Lady on the Boulevard (The Green Cape)* (pl. 7), c. 1892–94, is closely related to these Japanese themes. Among the twenty works Maurice exhibited in the spring of 1897 in Boston, from their titles presumably watercolors, some of them French subjects, was one forthrightly entitled *Japanese Study*.[34] The following year, when he showed his work in the "Eighteenth Exhibition of the Boston Art Students' Association," a reviewer reacted: "One scarcely knows whether to class . . . Prendergast's paintings, so Japanesque in their feeling, among the landscapes or figure-pieces."[35]

In specific instances Prendergast would inscribe a title, signature or monogram, and, rarely, a date into the colors on his monotype plates. In nearly all of these sheets at least one letter is written backward, thus adding, surely intentionally, a charming puzzle to the print. An example is *Bastille Day (Le Quatorze Juillet 1892)* (pl. 10), wherein the J is reversed. The keynote to these images is spontaneity. A reviewer in 1901 caught the essence of these colorful miniatures: "They remind one of water colors and are most quaint and dainty, full of life and motion."[36]

Prendergast's diminutive oils on wood panel, painted during his more than three and a half years in France, demonstrate that from the outset he was intent on exploring the discoveries in light and color of the Impressionists, especially Manet, Pissarro and Degas. Much of his perception of the French Impressionists, however direct his contact with their work may have been, was filtered through the young English-speaking artists with whom he associated and whose responses to contemporary French art he shared. The seven diminutive (6¼ by 3¾ inches) *Sketches in Paris* (pl. 9), c. 1892–94, park views with women and/or children on pipe-stem legs, reveal his awareness of Whistler and Steer, among the expatriate Anglophones in Paris, and recall as well Manet and Pissarro. They also resemble Morrice's *pochades;* for example, *Untitled (A Paris Café Scene)* (pl. 8), virtually identical in size and format, exemplifies the type of multidirectional color strokes and decorative textures Maurice saw and admired.[37] Although flat, the figures in Prendergast's *pochades* are somewhat more distinctly set off against their screenlike backgrounds.

In Paris Maurice was exposed to an enormous variety of styles, from the posters of Toulouse-Lautrec, Pierre Bonnard, Jules Chéret, and their contemporaries to the watercolors of Constantin Guys and Johan Barthold Jongkind

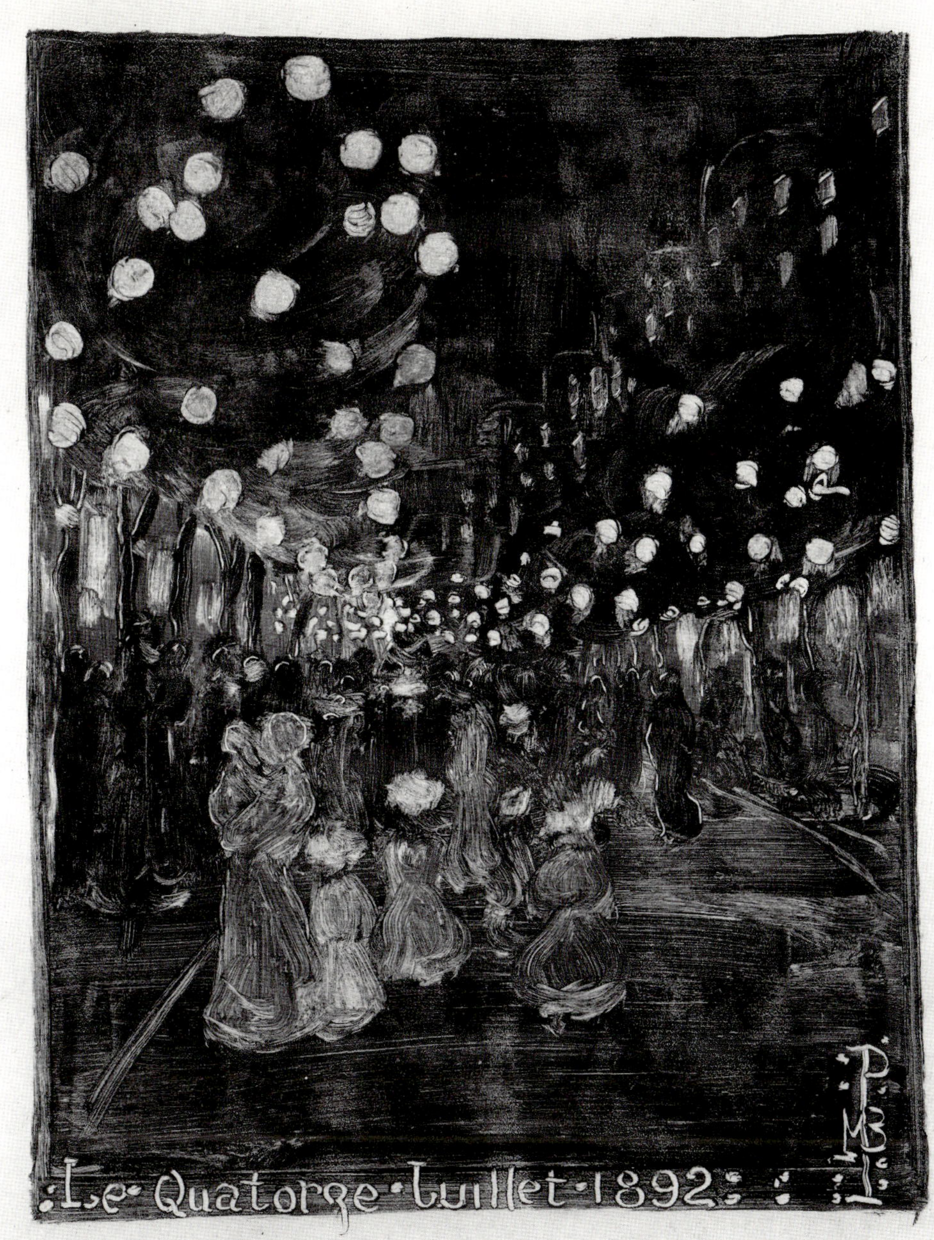

10. Bastille Day (Le Quatorze Juillet 1892)

1892. Monotype on paper, 6⅞ x 5⅛"
The Cleveland Museum of Art.
Gift of the Print Club of Cleveland

Prendergast's fascination with lights, emphasized in this early monotype, was evident in many subsequent prints and watercolors.

and the drawings of Degas's followers such as Jean-Louis Forain, Jean-François Raffaelli, and Théophile Steinlen. Prendergast's style was an amalgam of his personal observations and a distillation of all he saw around him—major and minor—from the academics, whom he quickly dismissed, to the Whistlerian Englishmen, as well as the great Frenchmen from whom their work ultimately derived.

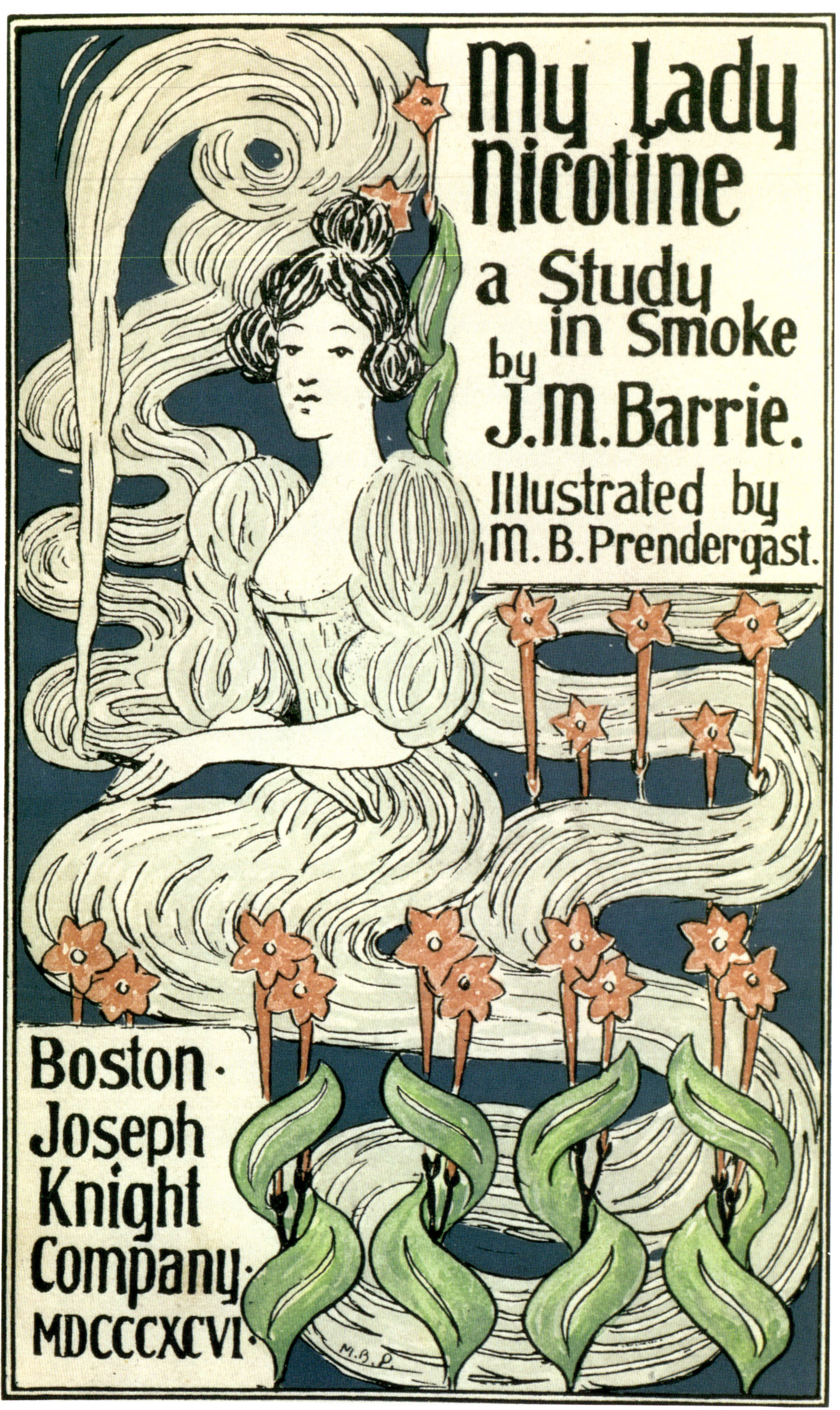

11. Title page from *My Lady Nicotine: A Study in Smoke*

III. Interlude: My Lady Nicotine

MAURICE RETURNED TO BOSTON VIA ENGLAND on September 1, 1894, his education in art—the experience of working in the thick of the Parisian ateliers and most of all on the boulevards, in the parks and cafés, and on the seacoast—confidently commenced, with a body of work in an emerging personal manner to show for it. Although the anecdotal tradition claims that Maurice had saved for years to raise the one thousand dollars for his extended sojourn in France, a tantalizing detail is provided by the catalogue of an auction sale of Prendergast's work in May 1897, whose brief text, "Rising Painters," states, "Prendergast, when a student in Paris, was the most popular man in his class, and his fellows always bought everything he painted, paying from twenty-five francs upward for his sketches. Since his return to Boston he has been unable to keep pace with the demand."[38]

Maurice took on several graphic design commissions—posters, book covers, and illustrations—for the Joseph Knight Company, a Boston firm. His designs show a skillful application of contemporary conventions of Art Nouveau, Japanese prints, Walter Crane (1845–1915), English book designer and decorator, and the Boston graphic designer Will H. Bradley (1868–1962) in controlled linear outlines, sinuous shapes, and dramatic silhouettes. However, the firm's tightly prescribed formats ran counter to Prendergast's inclinations and his cultivation in his own drawings, watercolors, and monotypes of the loose, free application of color washes over spontaneous pencil notations.

A singularly delightful exception to the enforced control of line and pattern seen in Maurice's posters are the 138 drawings and marginal embellishments and watercolors, all reproduced in black and white, with color cover and title page, for Knight's 276-page pirated edition of James M. Barrie's *My Lady Nicotine: A Study in Smoke,* which the artist executed in 1895. A cigar smoker himself—Barrie never smoked one in his life—Prendergast employed ingenious devices to disperse the drawings on the page and in the margins and integrate them in endless asymmetrical sequences within the text. The cover image of a woman somewhat provocatively holding a cigar, enveloped in a sinuous boalike garland of smoke and placed behind a row of flowering tobacco plants is adapted from similar book covers and posters by the Frenchman Eugène Grasset (1841–1917).

The title page (pl. 11), a close variant of the cover but with azure background, pale green leaves, and pink flowers, gives a freer rendition of the tight sinuosity of the outer cloth. The half-title page, a full-length figure demurely grasping with both hands a box of cigars lettered "Arcadia Mixture," is set

11. Title page from *My Lady Nicotine: A Study in Smoke*

by James M. Barrie. Boston: Joseph Knight Company, 1895
Collection Alain Joyaux

212 MY LADY NICOTINE.

"From that evening the face haunted me. I do not mean that it possessed me to the exclusion of everything else, but at odd moments it would rise before me, and then I fell into a revery. You must have noticed my thoughtfulness of late. Often I have laid down my paper at the club and tried to think back to the original. She was probably better known to Jack Goring than to myself. All I was sure of was that she had been known to both of us. Jack and I had first met at Cambridge. I thought over the ladies I had known there, especially those who had been friends of Goring's. Jack had never been a 'lady's man' precisely; but, as he used to say, comparing himself with me, 'he had a heart.' The annals of our Cambridge days were searched in vain. I tried the country house in which he and I had spent a good many of

PRIMUS. 161

tyrant Poppy, and they practised walking the plank at Scrymgeour's window. The plank was pushed nearly half-way out at the window, and you walked up it until it toppled and you were flung into the quadrangle. Such was the romance of William John that he walked the plank with his arms tied, shouting scornfully, by request, "Captain Kidd, I defy you! ha, ha! the buccaneer does not live who will blanch the cheeks of Dick, the Doughty Tar!" Then William John disappeared, and had to be put in poultices.

While William John was in bed slowly recovering from his heroism, the pirate captain and Johnny Fox got me into trouble by stretching a string across the square, six feet from the ground, against which many tall hats struck, to topple in the dust. An improved sling from the Lowther Arcade kept the glazier constantly in the inn. Primus and Johnny Fox strolled into Holborn, knocked a bootblack's cap off, and returned with lumps on their foreheads. They

12. Page 212 from *My Lady Nicotine: A Study in Smoke*

by James M. Barrie. Boston: Joseph Knight Company, 1895

13. Page 161 from *My Lady Nicotine: A Study in Smoke*

by James M. Barrie. Boston: Joseph Knight Company, 1895

against a long tobacco leaf. Many of the watercolors reproduced as illustrations appear to have been taken directly from Maurice's Parisian watercolors. A typical example is the seated figure on page 212 (pl. 12), which incorporates a table identical to that seen in *Park Scene, Paris* (pl. 2). Maurice drew on Degas's work for the informal, caught-in-the-act poses and dramatically cropped silhouettes of some of the figures. He also borrowed from the striking black-and-white patterns of Aubrey Beardsley. On page 161, for example, he let his fancy run free, with top hats spilling down the center of the page, and on page 230 a jaunty musical notation of pipes appears against the white page (pls. 13 and 14). The illustration on page 115 (pl. 15) pays unmistakable homage to the Japanese in the trails of smoke from the pipes of five seated men at the bottom rising upward through and even slightly above the type, entwining the printed type in a subtly composed calligraphy resembling a musical score.

A contemporary reviewer caught the spirit of Prendergast's work:

> *This is a new and attractive edition of Mr. J. M. Barrie's book. The difficulty of illustrating a book of this kind, which does not offer endless variety of subjects for the*

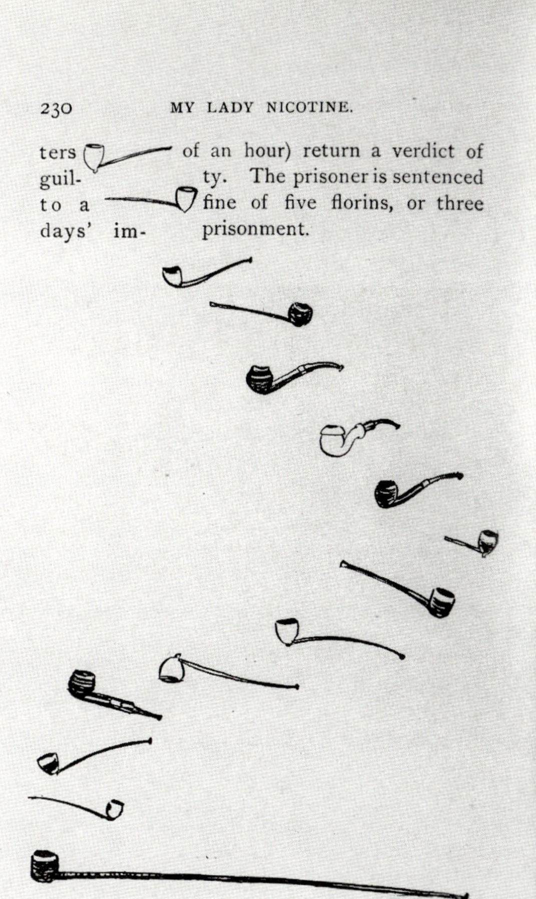

230 MY LADY NICOTINE.

ters of an hour) return a verdict of guil- ty. The prisoner is sentenced to a fine of five florins, or three days' im- prisonment.

THE GRANDEST SCENE IN HISTORY. 115

placid, for he does not know that the tobacco Ned is handing him is the Arcadia Mixture. I love Ned Alleyn, and like to think that Shakespeare got the Arcadia from him.

For a moment let us turn from Shakespeare at this crisis in his life. Alleyn has left him and is paying the score. Marlowe remains where he fell. Nash has forgotten where he lodges, and so sets off with Peele to an ale-house in Pye Corner, where George is only too well known. Kempe and Cowley are sent home in baskets.

Again we turn to the figure in the corner, and there is such a light on his face that we shade our eyes. He is smoking the Arcadia, and as he smokes the tragedy of Hamlet takes form in his brain.

This is the picture that Scrymgeour will never dare to paint. I know that there is no mention of tobacco in Shakespeare's plays, but those who smoke the Arcadia tell their secret to none, and of other mixtures they scorn to speak.

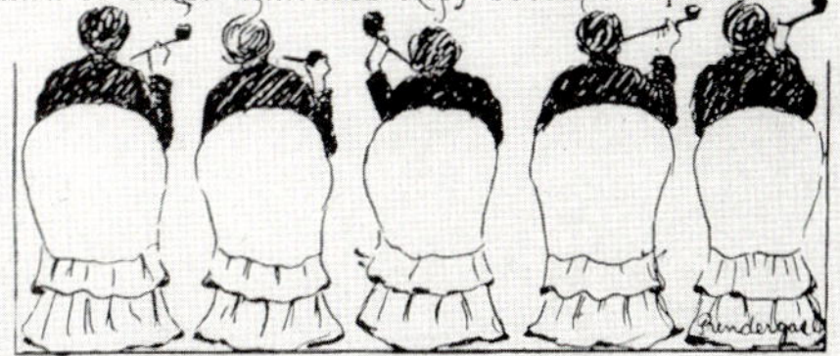

artist's pencil has been very successfully overcome by Mr. Maurice B. Prendergast, who has decorated almost every page with spirited sketches, which possess the merit of being quite in keeping with the character of the book itself.

. . . his illustrations to My Lady Nicotine *make it evident that he possesses the qualities of a true artist. Among those that show the greatest originality and artistic feeling are his little sketches of women some of which appear to have been taken directly from the artist's sketch book.*[39]

14. Page 230 from *My Lady Nicotine: A Study in Smoke*

by James M. Barrie. Boston: Joseph Knight Company, 1895

15. Page 115 from *My Lady Nicotine: A Study in Smoke*

by James M. Barrie. Boston: Joseph Knight Company, 1895

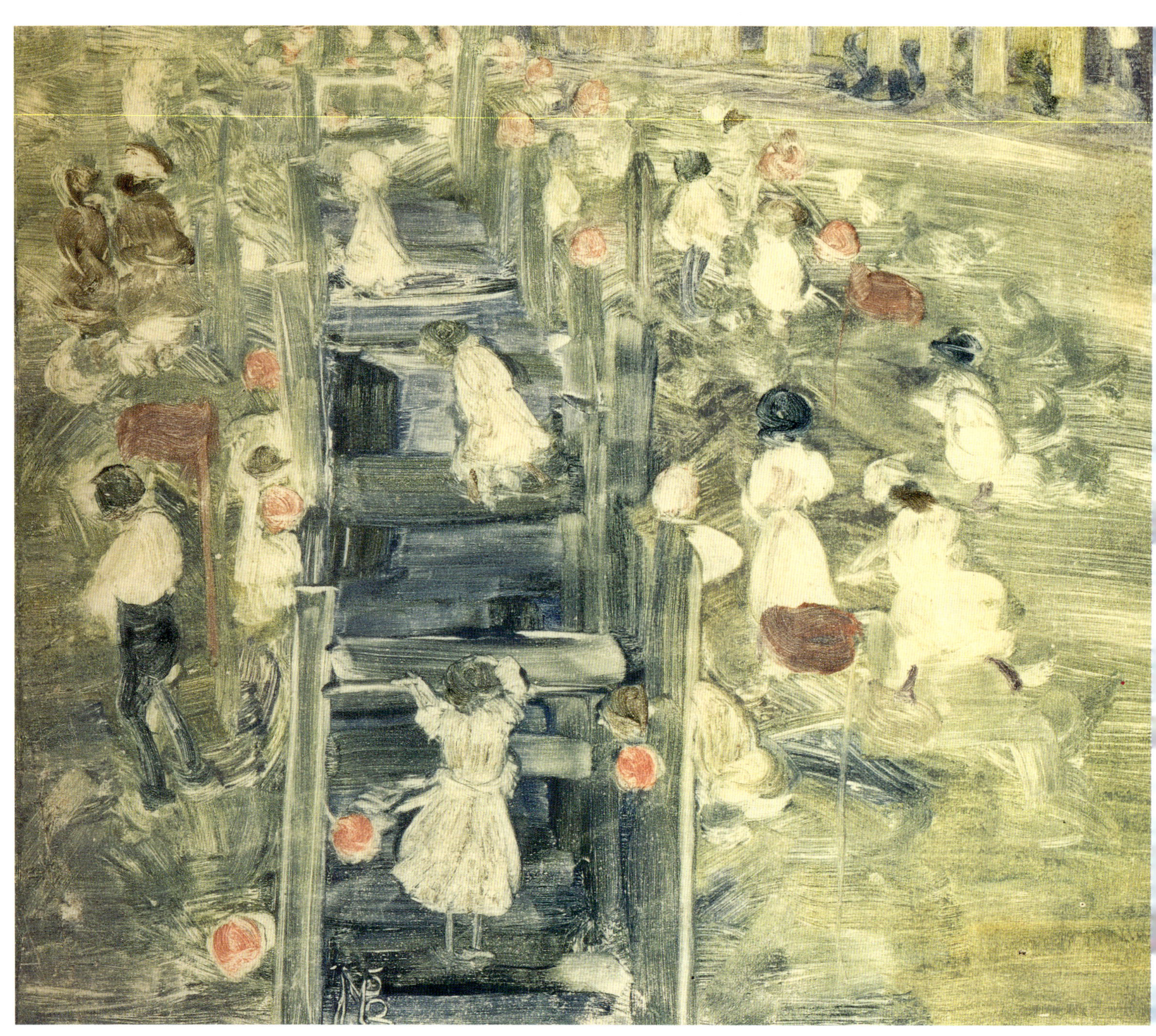

16. The Race

IV. *Boston 1895–98*

CONCURRENTLY WITH THE BOOK ILLUSTRATIONS, which must have taken up a considerable amount of time immediately following his return from abroad, Prendergast established a consistent pattern of placing his work before the public. He entered watercolors and monotypes in group shows in Boston, Philadelphia, and New York, subsequently assembling solo exhibitions in both private galleries and museums across the country, gaining a reputation as a serious colorist to be watched and followed and, important for him, bought. He assiduously maintained this approach throughout his life. The myth of neglect and isolation that grew up and was fostered by numerous modern critics is a misapprehension of the frequent and preponderantly positive critical reception accorded Prendergast's work from the mid-1890s onward.

In his first documented public exhibition, Prendergast entered two watercolors in the spring annual of 1895 at the Boston Art Club. Despite a generally unfavorable assessment of the more than one hundred and fifty exhibits as an "unattractive collection" with a "sort of 'job lot' appearance," the writer for the *Boston Sunday Herald* remarked on "Maurice Prendergast, who has lately returned to Boston from his studies in Paris. His *Fishing Boats—Tréport, France* and his *Porte St. Denis* [CR 542] show a finely disciplined sense of pure and brilliant color, subordinated to a vivacious and accurate style of description."[40] William H. Downes, future biographer of Homer and Sargent and reviewer for the *Boston Evening Transcript*, described the former watercolor as a "sparkling piece of daring color, lively in style and action, but a trifle too frank about showing its technique. Better still . . . *Porte St. Denis* which depicts a bit of the boulevards on a heavy grey day and has every aspect of variety and animation. This is a first-rate street scene worthy of the best painters who have made such themes their specialities."[41]

Beginning in 1896, Prendergast became a regular entrant not only to exhibitions in and around Boston but at the Pennsylvania Academy of the Fine Arts, Philadelphia, the Art Institute of Chicago, the New York Water Color Club, and the Society of American Artists, New York. His April 1897 watercolor entry in the "Fifty-sixth Exhibition of the Boston Art Club" elicited the following encomium from Downes:

> People on the Beach *[pl. 17] by Maurice Prendergast. This is without peer for brilliance in the exhibition. There is a point of excellence at which color and light in a painting fill the vision with such a deep sensation of satisfaction that it would be wicked to ask for more, or different, excellence. There is a poetry in color not less than in design, and there is a poetry of rich color not less than that of low tones.*[42]

16. The Race

c. 1895–97. Monotype on paper, $7\frac{7}{8} \times 9''$
Terra Museum of American Art, Chicago.
Daniel J. Terra Collection

The field of pale grayish blues and greens, enlivened by circular and spherical patterns of pink and rose, creates a breathtaking sweep of upward motion whose compositional ambiguities intrigue rather than confuse as the eye is drawn over the surface and back into space.

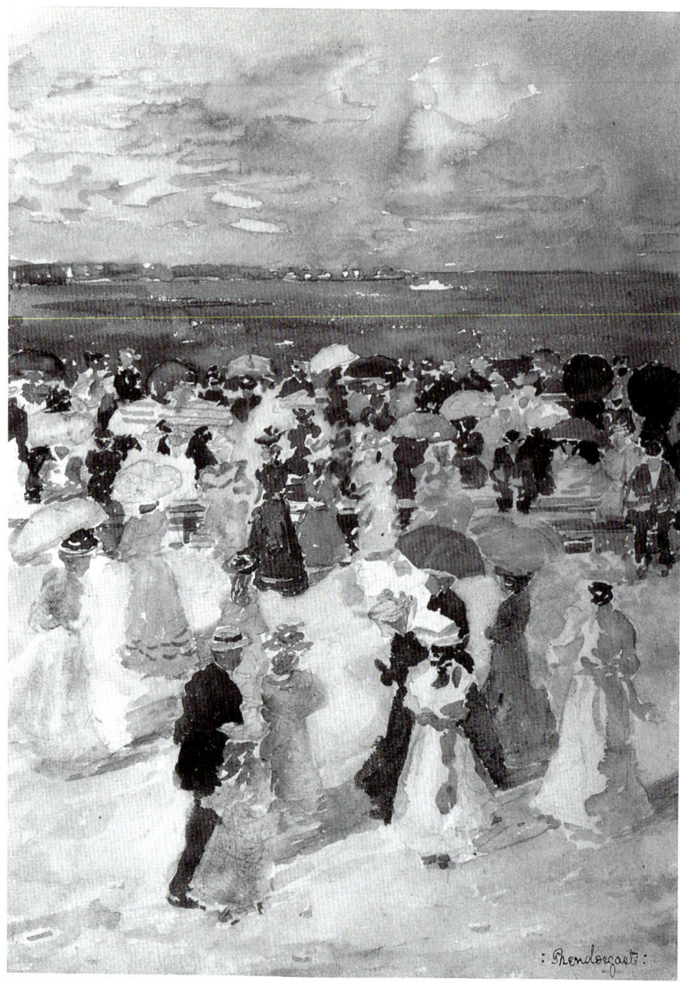

17. People on the Beach

c. 1896. Watercolor and pencil on paper, 13½ x 9¼"
Private collection

William H. Downes, in the Boston Evening Transcript, *responded enthusiastically to this picture: "A splendid bouquet of flowers or a cluster of radiant jewels. It glows. It flashes" (April 3, 1897).*

The critics were nearly unanimous in their enthusiastic reactions to Prendergast's debut in the art world of Boston, where his work was acclaimed and his position as a new creative force assured. The reviews of his entries in shows across the country likewise served to reinforce his growing reputation.

In the work accomplished from 1895 through the first half of 1898, Maurice concentrated on extending the expressive depth of his color, primarily by means of watercolors and monotypes. The few paintings of this period are, for the most part, renditions of the effects found in his monotypes, both in their subjects and their pervasively subdued Whistlerian color harmonies. Maurice ambitiously began to expand the single and multiple figure motifs of the Parisian watercolors and monotypes into complex, multifigure arrangements, almost all of them scenes by the seashore.

In a group of watercolors done in 1896 at Revere Beach, Nahant, and other sites in the vicinity of Boston, his work assumed a gentle lightness. The figures have the weight of those in Conder's painted fans or Whistler's watercolors and are clustered like Eugène Boudin's. *Revere Beach* (pl. 18), dated 1896, with its gray, beige, and pale green touches, uses a central band of figures and a diminutive second file in the distance at the water's edge. The composition is firmly fixed by the dramatic red parasol in the center that sets surrounding units in

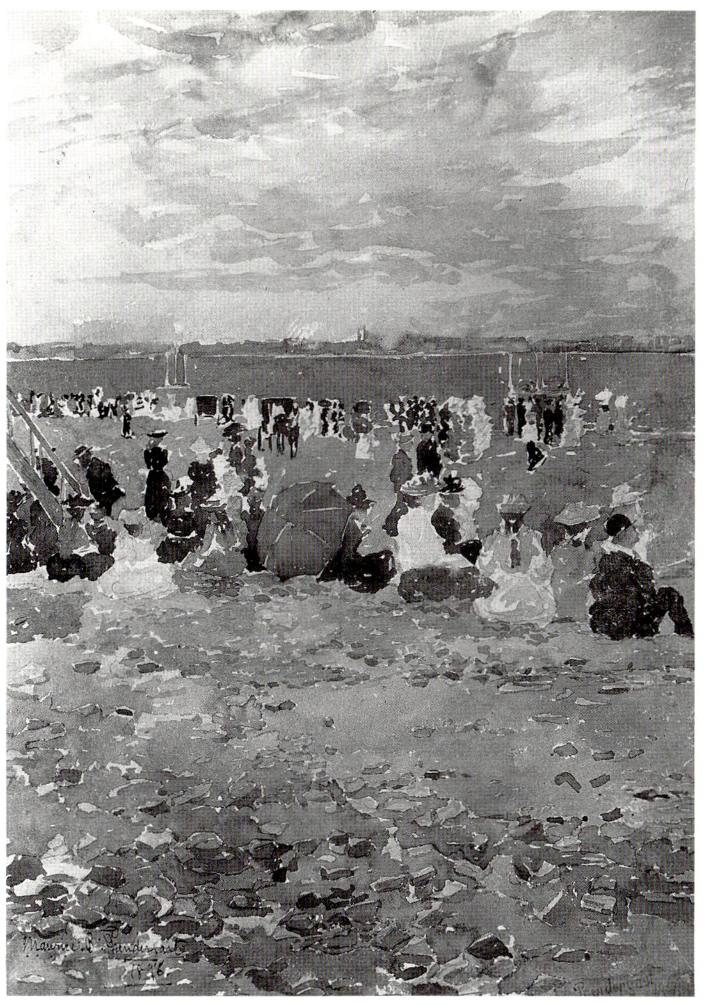

18. Revere Beach

1896. Watercolor and pencil on paper, 13⅝ x 9⅞"
The Saint Louis Art Museum. Museum Purchase

Maurice created a deep thrusting space by sandwiching the central band of horizon, water, and figure groups between the sparkle of foreground beach and diagonal sweep of sky.

space. This concision of detail and pervasive colorfulness is evidence of Prendergast's increased proficiency with the watercolor medium. *Handkerchief Point* (pl. 19), 1896, enlarges on this compositional intricacy while maintaining the delicacy of individual figures. Its lateral extension, with raft, bathers, and sailboats, creates a sweep into space that completely surpasses the tentative seaside watercolors done at Tréport several years earlier. *On the Beach* (pl. 20), c. 1896–97, takes the motif of *Revere Beach* to a more complex level, with the two seated women and two children in the foreground and surrounding figures of varied scale filling the foreground and middle ground with a sequence of colorful patterns. The device used in the Parisian watercolors of girls reflected in wet streets here becomes a silhouetted man reflected in a pool in the middle ground. In this work, instead of using single figures, Maurice opened a pocket of space on the left that plays against a densely patterned crowd on the right. The placement of the man's head is notable as it rises above the water's edge and joins with the small distant perspective patterns of that edge, helping to link the large foreground women and the tiny figures on the shoreline. The transparency of color is heightened by the paper showing through, which intensifies the sparkle of the color patches and binds them together in a loosely knit fabric across the surface.

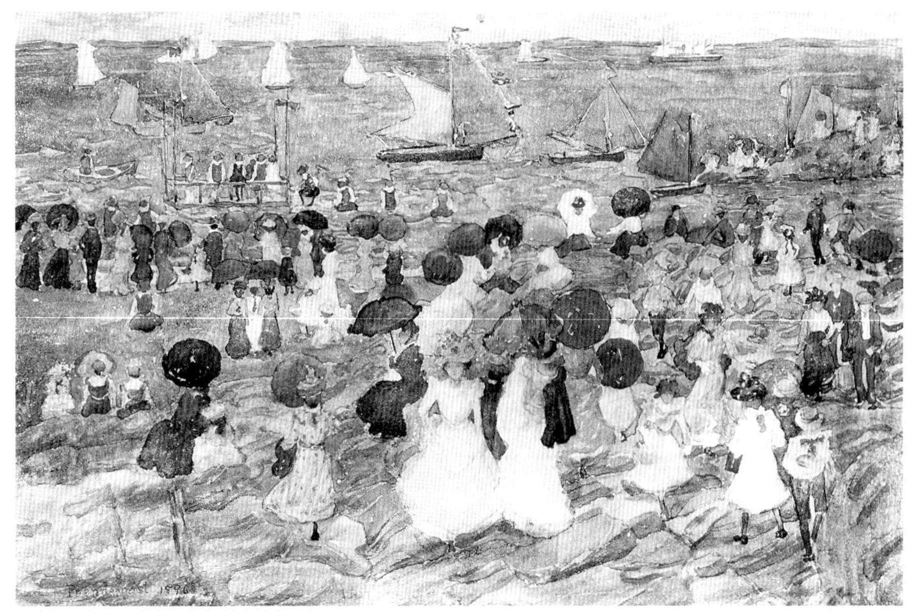

19. Handkerchief Point

1896. Watercolor and pencil on paper, $13\frac{1}{4}$ x $20\frac{1}{4}$"
Collection Mr. and Mrs. Meyer P. Potamkin

Prendergast here displayed his mastery over complex multifigure groupings in which the composition is layered with dresses, parasols, raft, boats, and sails that sweep from side to side, foreground to background, toward the horizon. This type of watercolor led to his subsequent polyphonic compositions in oils.

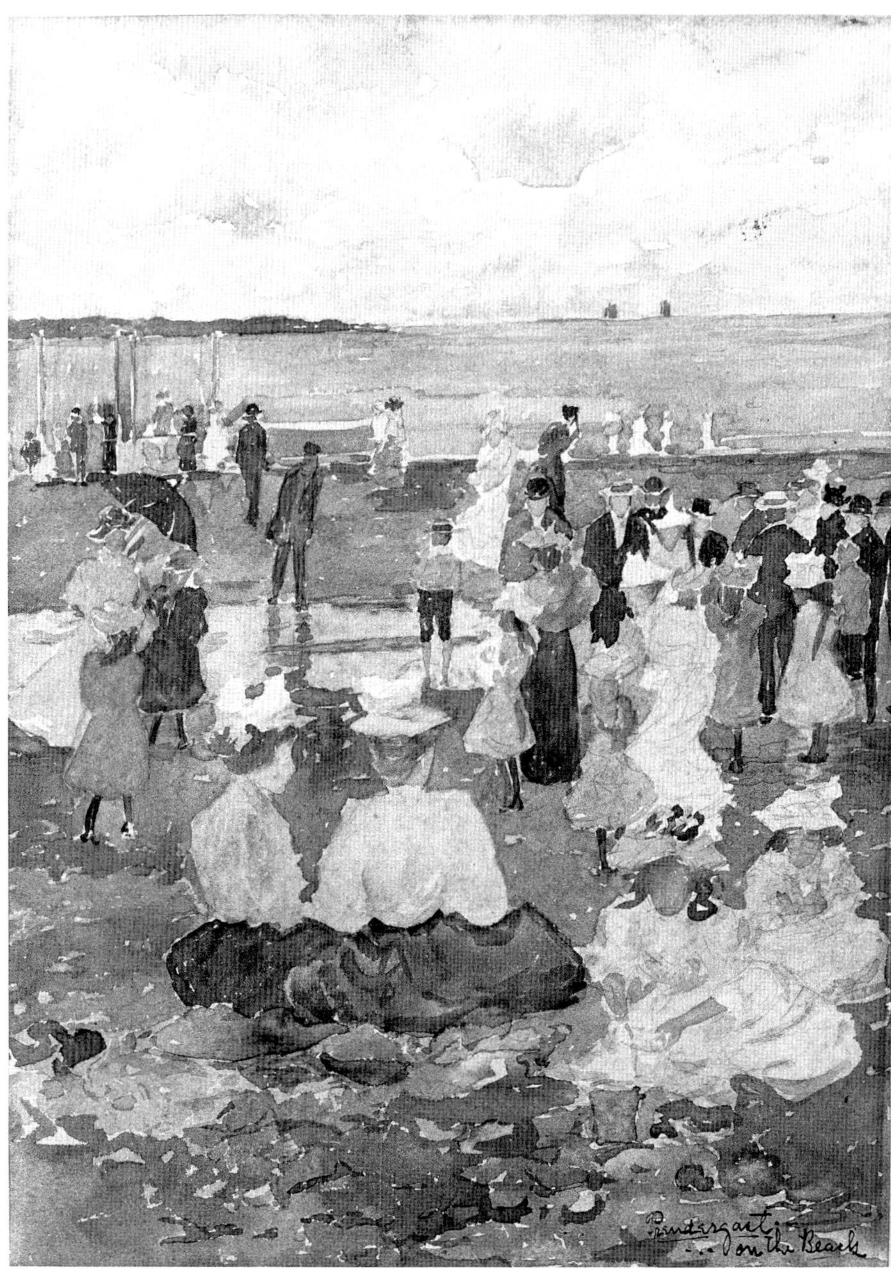

20. On the Beach

c. 1896–97. Watercolor and pencil on paper, 13 x $9\frac{1}{2}$"
The Barnes Foundation, Merion Station, Pennsylvania

In this vertical format the zigzag of figures through the beach area provides striking silhouette patterns that hold the eye in the shimmering lights and reflections.

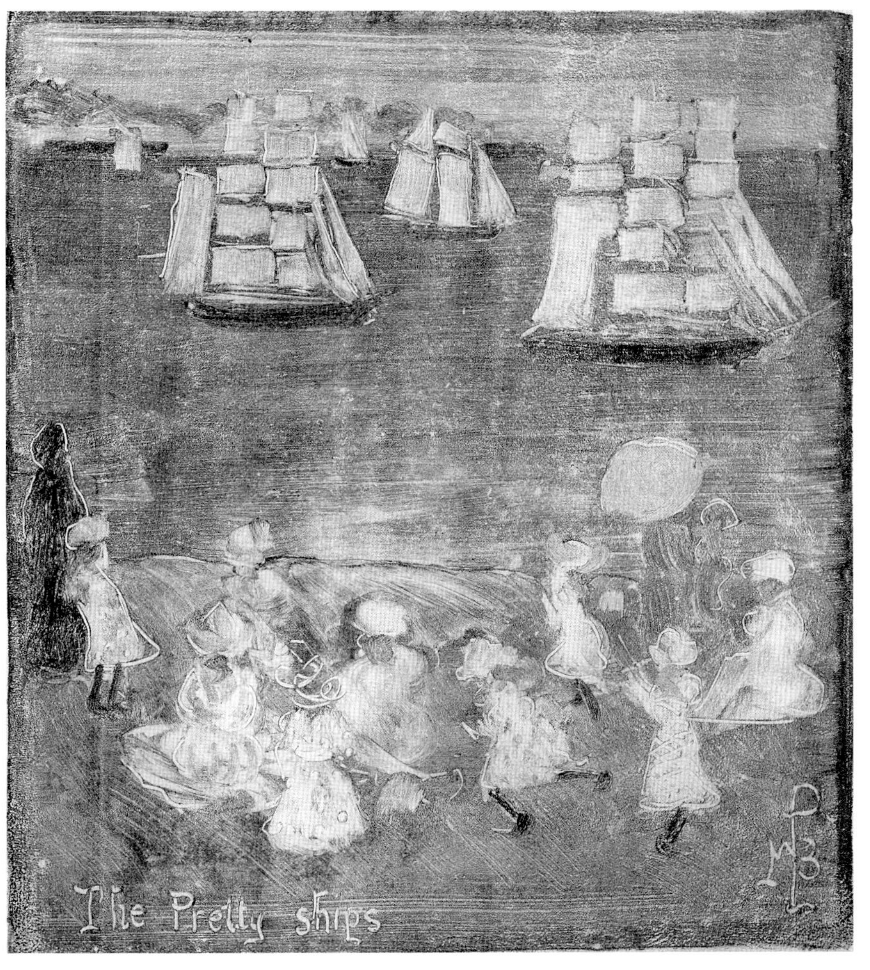

21. The Pretty Ships

c. 1895–97. Monotype on paper, 7 x 6⅛″
Courtesy, Museum of Fine Arts, Boston.
George P. Gardner Fund

Prendergast frequently used the wooden end of the brush to gain a linear accent in the monotypes and found it a means of increasing the spontaneity of expression.

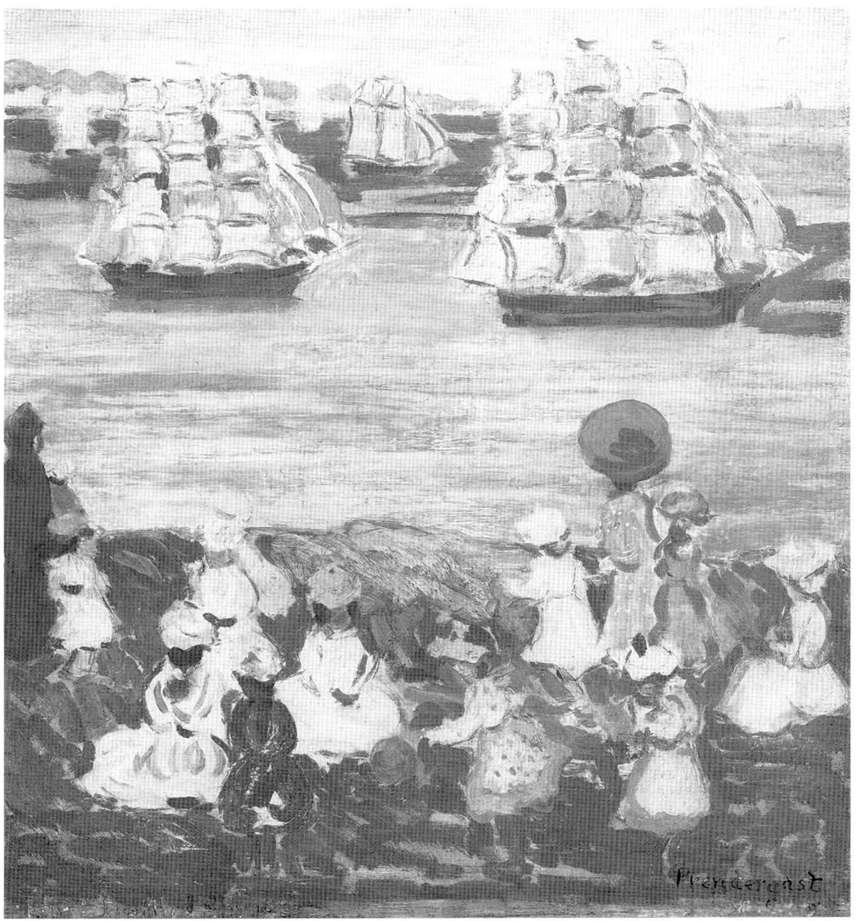

22. The Pretty Ships.

c. 1895–97. Oil on panel, 13 x 13½″
Courtesy, Museum of Fine Arts, Boston.
Gift of the Estate of Harriet C. Weed, 1971

This is an example of a small oil on panel that is either derived from or the source for the monotype of the same composition.

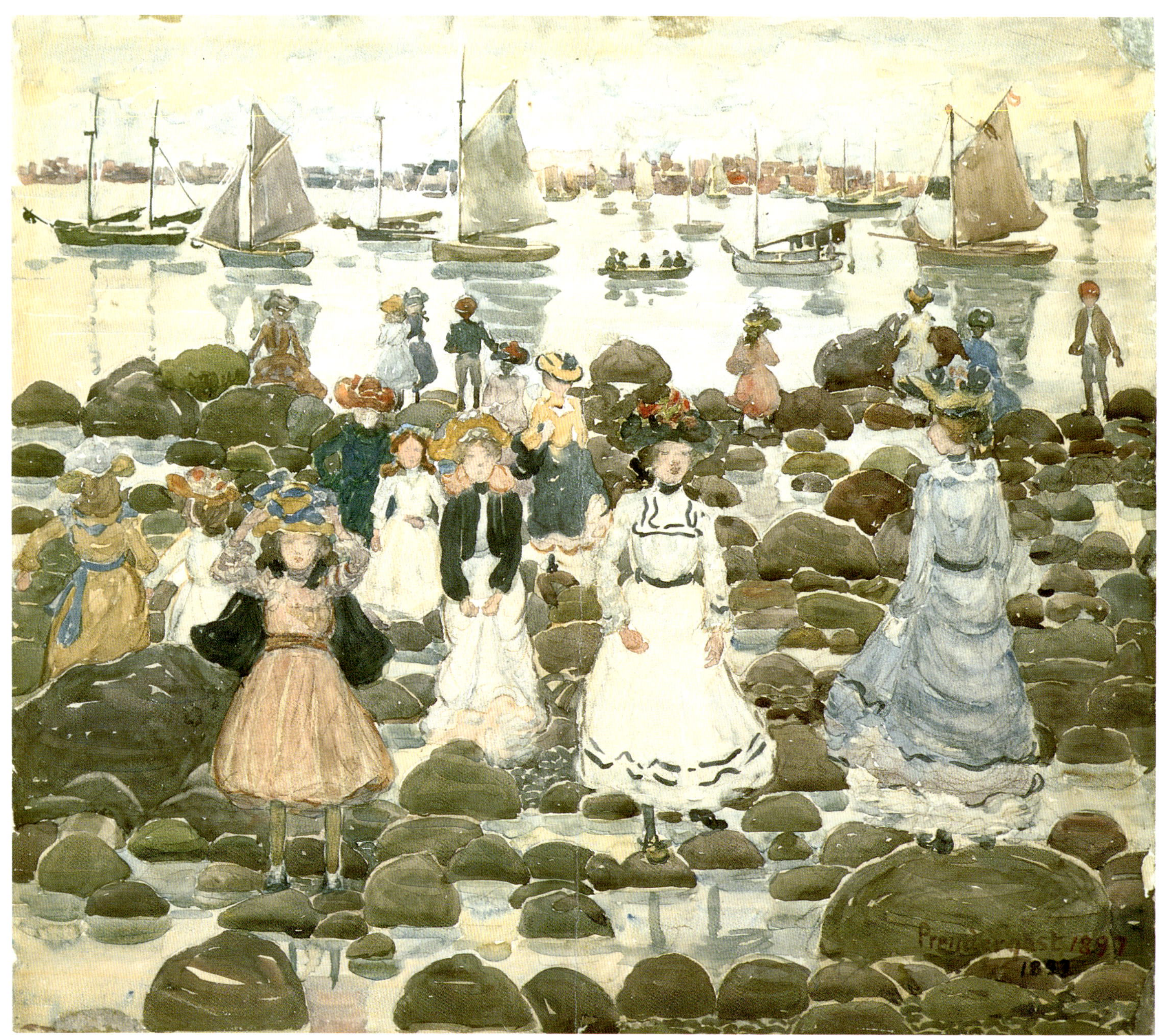

23. Low Tide, Beachmont

c. 1897. Watercolor and pencil on paper, $19\frac{1}{2}$ x $22\frac{1}{8}$″
Worcester Art Museum, Massachusetts

The row of children spaced intermittently in the background suggests the work of Winslow Homer. The boats, their masts, and especially their sails convey an impression of Oriental junks and provide background reverberations of the shapes of the ladies' dresses and the corresponding verticals of legs and their shadows.

24. The Stony Beach

c. 1897. Watercolor and pencil on paper, $20\frac{7}{8}$ x 14″
Collection Mr. and Mrs. Arthur G. Altschul

Prendergast here achieved full command of the watercolor medium. A pleasant outing at a New England beach, Nahant, Massachusetts, has been transformed into a captivating arrangement of magical colorfulness without any trace of the tentative visible in its antecedents.

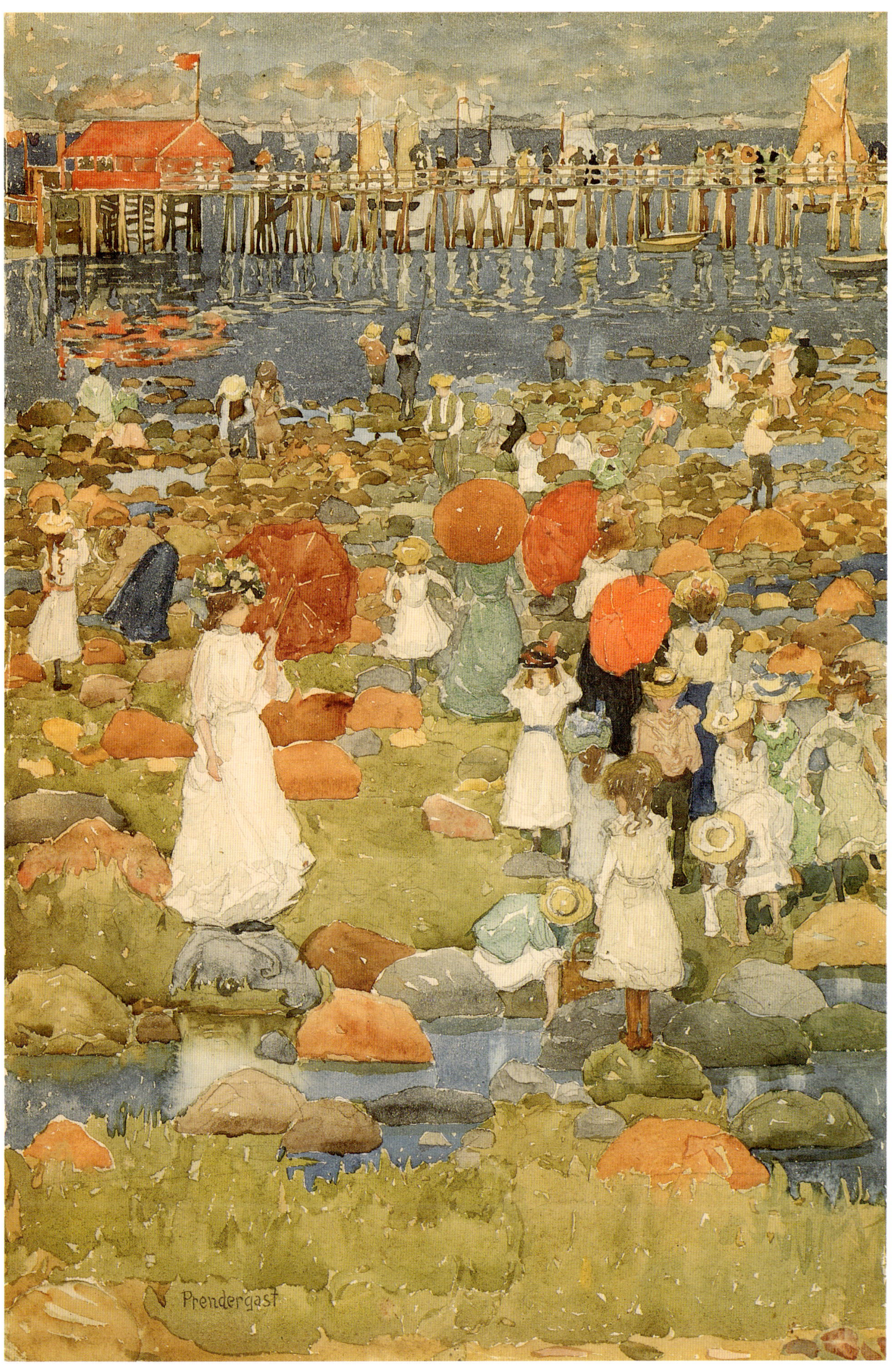

24. *The Stony Beach*

There is a conscious interplay between the monotypes, watercolors, and oils done in the years 1895 to 1898 (pls. 21 and 22). Color in the prints is usually restrained. On the other hand, contrary to the minute control of the brush exercised by Prendergast in order to maintain overall consistency of color freshness in the watercolors, the monotypes are executed with vigorous Whistlerian brushstrokes. Their silken veil of colors have been fluidly brushed and wiped and incised over the plates' surfaces, however small, creating broad patterns and textures that enhance their muted harmonies. This freedom and directness in the monotypes was progressively transferred to some of the watercolors as their patterns became larger and more dramatic than the daintier 1896 *Revere Beach* and related series. The monotypes therefore functioned as stimuli for Maurice to clarify and expand his expressive range. In a monotype such as *The Race* (pl. 16), c. 1895–97, the composition is divided into sections, an ingeniously asymmetrical variant on the earlier screen device of *Six Sketches of Ladies* (see pl. 4), in which the beams of the children's jungle gym diminish as the structure moves from bottom to top and simultaneously into space from foreground to background. There are areas wiped almost clean, saturating the surface with light. At the same time, the firm color strokes treat the distinctive subject in summary shorthand painting, approaching the abstract. Nonetheless, there is a decisive grasp of the activity portrayed—the girl with arms outstretched in the foreground reaching for a beam, another at the right running.

In *Low Tide, Beachmont* (pl. 23), c. 1897, the mossy grayish brown stones, resembling a patch of outsize mushrooms, provide the setting for a sequence of women and girls in the foreground and middle ground, most of them posed with frontal stances. The stones establish a pitter-patter rhythmic beat, with the pale water interspersed so as to emphasize the shapes of the stones. While the scene is subdued rather than bathed in sunlight, the overall grayish tonalities are no less colorful than the wan Whistlerian harmonies of many contemporary monotypes. At this point, Maurice was often increasing the size of his watercolors. Not infrequently, as in *Low Tide,* he experimented with a large, nearly square format as a container for his color patterns.

In *The Stony Beach* (pl. 24), c. 1897, Prendergast took a step in a new direction, from the predominant daintiness of previous watercolors to a large-scale color ensemble of both delicacy and power, in which the irregular patterns of rocks, figures, umbrellas, water, and sky are interspersed and tilted like a page from a Persian miniature. Prendergast left pencil notations visible throughout the sheet in a manner similar to the added pencil and scratched-out markings that indicate in a generalized fashion the units in his monotypes. The flattened mustard-colored proscenium across the foreground sets up a recession into space composed of stones of slightly varying chromatic shades of orange and tan, which dominate the left half of the composition. On a mottled gray rock, a tall woman in white, wearing a flowered bonnet and holding a russet umbrella with its ribs clearly defined, is silhouetted against orange and brown boulders. On the right side of the composition, figures seen from the front and back, standing, sitting, bending, three carrying parasols, are massed and balanced against the white figure and the boulders. The pattern of the three parasols seen from different angles create a broad diagonal recession that creates a link with the red shack on the pier and its multicolored red and blue reflections in the water. The corresponding half of this broad crisscross moves from lower left to the blotted pale orange sailboat in the top right corner. The hub of this crisscrossed X in space is the round orange umbrella seen near the center of the composition. It is this hub that permits the warm foreground and the cool distant colors to open into the depth of space so effectively while at the same time retaining the two-dimensional miniature pattern over the surface that zigzags along the diagonals. Tiny pristine figures at the water's edge and on the pier beyond fill the surface with sparkling reverberations of the top border of the horizontal foreground pattern. While these shapes establish the recession into space along these lines, they set up a frame for the diverse illustrative incidents to occur in a tranquil, impersonal drama.

Prendergast was bouyed by the flood of approbation that his colorful pattern and line organizations elicited from the critics. His watercolors charmed and seduced writers, inspiring them to flights of fanciful rhetoric surprising for reserved Boston. Thus celebrated, enjoying a *succès d'estime,* the forty-year-old artist found these heady days. His decision eight years earlier to forsake the drudgery of commercial art to study in Paris had been clear-sighted, and he had worked hard to make the most of what he had learned there. In the summer of 1898, Maurice departed for sixteen months in Italy.

Pepper relates the general itinerary:

> *In 1898 he went to Venice. He spent the first week studying the galleries. He was most forcibly impressed by Tintoretto and Carpaccio. Much of the time was also spent in studying the architecture of the city's old palaces and churches. He soaked up Venice. Then saturated, he worked . . . he found his work and did it. All day long, day after day. Evenings burned pictures on his memory, to be painted in the morning. This for six or eight months. Then to Padua with its Giottos. . . . After this constant application he went to Florence "for to behold and to see" the paintings, the frescos, the galleries, the churches. Not much painting done here. . . . At Siena two months, then to Orvieto and Rome. Here the fever attacked him. The fever for work, and he painted in and about Rome during the winter. . . . After a short rest in Naples and Capri, he returned for the summer and fall to Venice.*[43]

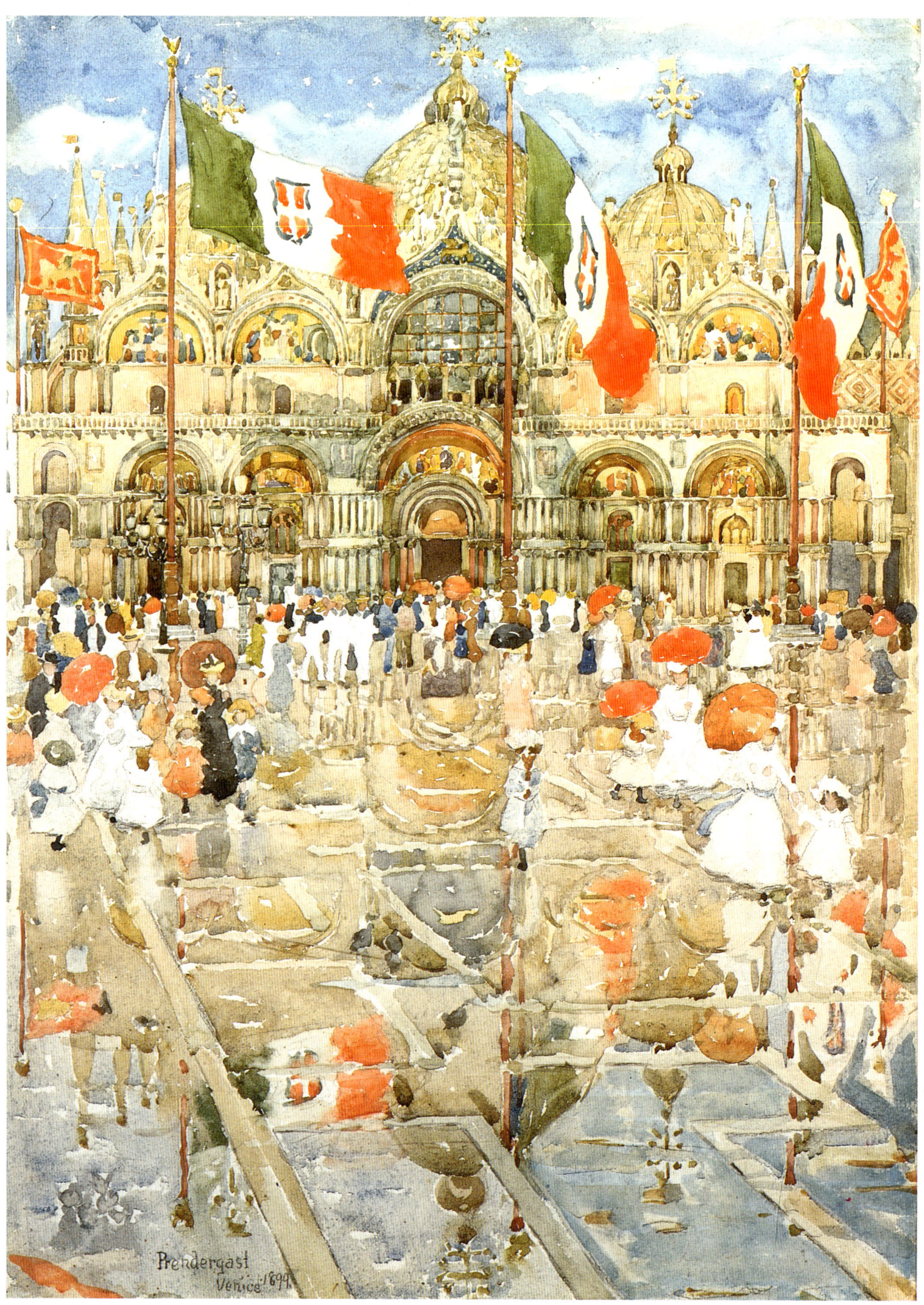

25. *Splash of Sunshine and Rain*

V. Venice 1898–99

THE WATERCOLORS AND MONOTYPES PAINTED IN ITALY have an expansive brilliance and pervasive color sparkle reminiscent of Delacroix and Manet. Prendergast saw Venice in glorious decay, its canals with their weathered stuccoed walls and crumbling bricks, a picturesque backwater in tranquil enchanting decrepitude, which had lured and enticed painters and writers, including many Americans—Whistler, Sargent, Frank Duveneck, William Dean Howells, Henry James, Herman Melville—for generations. He undoubtedly was acquainted with Howells's *Venetian Life,* originally published in 1866 and again in a two-volume edition with watercolor illustrations by Childe Hassam in 1892.[44] Maurice was fascinated by the splendor of Venice and recorded the illusive drama of its bridges, church facades and interiors, bustling piazzas, the panoply of its human activity. He was drawn to its festivals, exotic *palazzi,* glimmering canals, and mysterious nocturnal evanescence.

Building on the subtle color adjustments of the New England coastal series, the Italian watercolors maintain their level of richness and complexity, assuming a luminosity and transparency that in sheet after sheet simply dazzle in their vibrant, airy, shimmering sweep. The proficiency that had expanded following Maurice's return from Paris in 1894, absorbing the spontaneity of the monotypes, blossomed as a consequence of the boundless allure of Venice. *Splash of Sunshine and Rain* (pl. 25), dated 1899, typifies Maurice's exhilaration as he reanimated the lambent puddles and tidal pools of Nahant in the gossamer watery pavements of the Piazza San Marco. Limpid reflections of flags and the profile of Saint Mark's transfer the eddies and smooth stones of *The Stony Beach* (see pl. 24), c. 1897, to the engaged columns of the church's facade, which then become the equivalent of the latticed patterns of the pier in the background of that glowing composition. Prendergast's flags recall Delacroix's use of banners in his 1826 Venetian drama *Execution of Doge Marino Faliero.*[45]

Easter Procession, St. Mark's (pl. 26), 1898–99, has the appeal of a bejeweled Byzantine book cover. A smoky atmospheric resonance illuminates this large-scale interior; the red processional banner in the foreground is effective as a space-defining device, as were the red umbrellas in the seaside watercolors, while the chandelier suspended at the left and the crucifix in the center serve similar roles. Maurice captured the exotic opulence of inlaid marble, gilded statues surmounting the screen leading to the altar, and the repeated arch motifs of the vaults, baldachin, semicircular steps in the center, and arcade at the lowest register of the screen. These convey a dense, layered, organizational echo of the irregular geometry of the basilica's exterior. *St. Mark's Square (The*

25. *Splash of Sunshine and Rain*

1899. Watercolor and pencil on paper, 19⅜ x 14½″
Collection Alice M. Kaplan

Certain Venetian watercolors, such as this one, display a careful delineation of the pencil and a sophisticated control of perspective, over and around which Maurice constructed his enchanting improvisations. It is possible that some of these sheets were commenced on the site and completed—or adjusted—in the solitary atmosphere of his pensione.

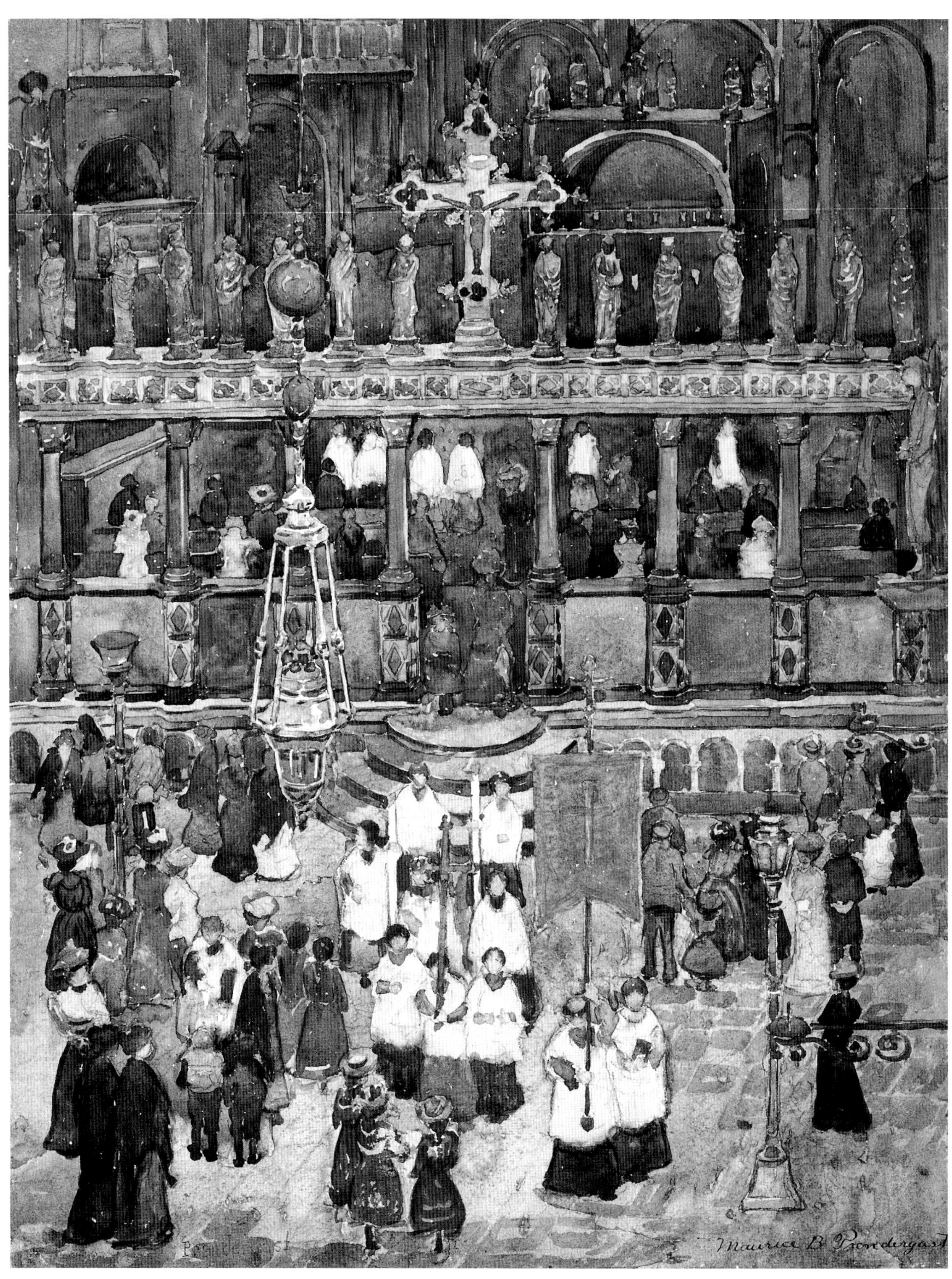

26. Easter Procession, St. Mark's

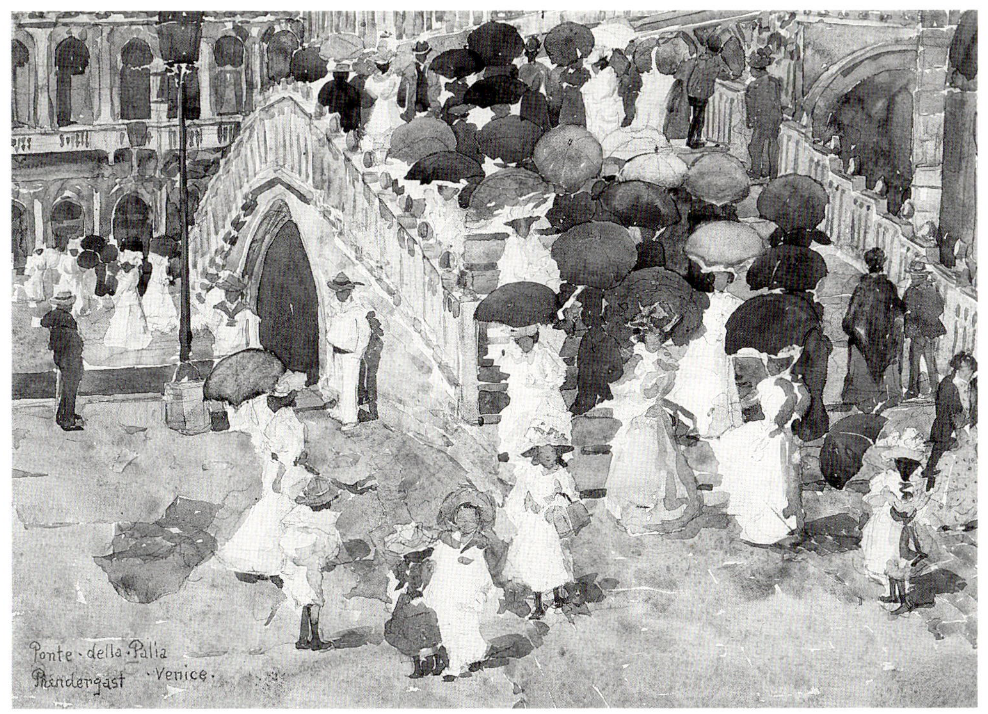

27. Ponte della Paglia

1898–99. Watercolor on paper, 10¼ x 14¾″
Hirschl & Adler Galleries, Inc., New York

The composition is a variant of both Ponte della Paglia (Marble Bridge) *(pl. 31) and* Umbrellas in the Rain *(pl. 29) from a vantage point that shows in the upper left corner a small section of the facade of the Library of San Marco designed by Jacopo Sansovino (1486–1570). Prendergast lettered the inscription, "Ponte della Palia," in script, characteristically misspelling the word* paglia.

Clock Tower) (pl. 28), 1898, exemplifies the scintillating colorfulness of the Venetian watercolors: the glowing parasols, the background with its gold leaf–like flecks on a field of blue that serves as a foil for the lion of Saint Mark's and the Madonna and child. These elements, plus the columns and minuscule details, are masterfully fitted into a most unusual vertical format. Maurice's finesse as a draftsman is revealed by the cluster of figures and umbrellas, an ensemble recalling Daumier's children spilling out of the school doorway. A sheet closely related in its fresh delicate touch, *Ponte della Paglia* (pl. 27 and p. 6), 1898–99, reconfigures the children of *The Clock Tower* composition, with an exceptional degree of color nuance in the umbrellas played against the firm irregular geometry of the marble bridge. *Umbrellas in the Rain, Venice* (pl. 29), 1898–99, with the faint, generalized abstraction of the balusters reflected in a broad arc below, approaches this horizontal treatment by means of the loosest possible washes of the multitoned grays and beiges in the pavement of the embankment. Its cluster of sensuous color notes, consisting almost exclusively of umbrellas, is set against the carefully delineated tracery of the arcade of the Doges' Palace. A frontal approach to this theme is provided in *Sunlight on the Piazzetta, Venice* (pl. 30), 1898–99, in which the Gothic arches provide a luscious foil for the promenade of poised costumed figures in a stagelike setting reminiscent of Prendergast's predecessor Canaletto, who treated identical motifs a century and a half earlier. A particularly subtle touch is the variation on the russets between the ground level arcade and the ocher reflections of the quatrefoil patterns cut from the stone tracery.

In *Ponte della Paglia (Marble Bridge)*, 1898–99 (pl. 31), shown from an elevated vantage point on the upper balcony of the Doges' Palace, Prendergast sus-

26. Easter Procession, St. Mark's

1898–99. Watercolor and pencil on paper, 18 x 14″
Collection Erving and Joyce Wolf

Prendergast's capacity to float patterns of color over the surface of the paper—a majestic Persian carpet of color—and yet retain the painting's architectural coherence and perspective is notable in this unorthodox composition.

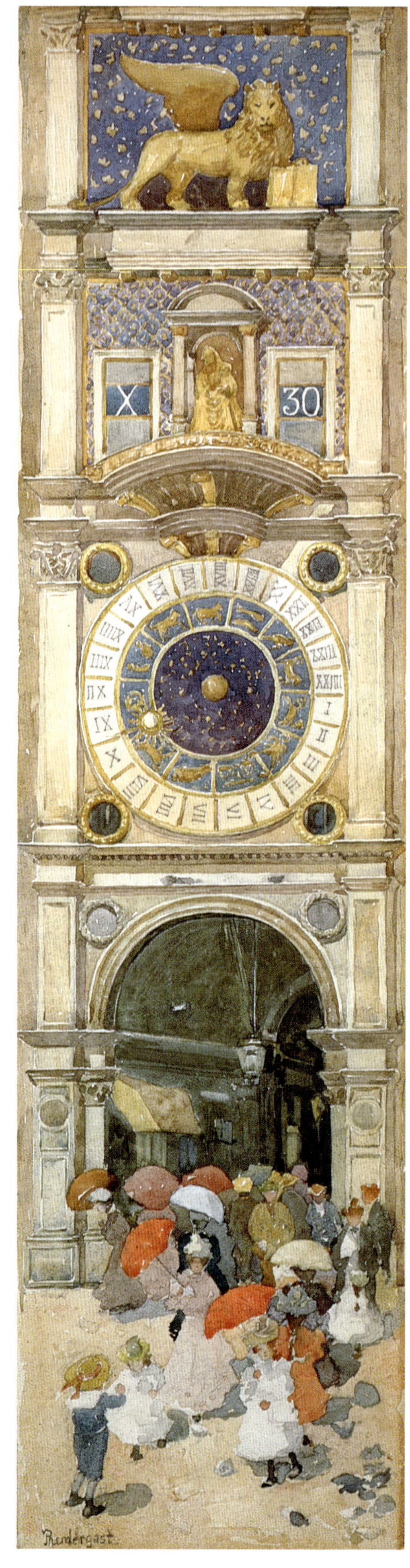

28. St. Mark's Square
(The Clock Tower)

1898. Watercolor and pencil on paper, 26 x 6"
Collection, William A. Farnsworth Library and Art Museum, Rockland, Maine

Prendergast's show-card lettering and early design experience may be discerned in the control of the brush and terse precision with which the "X 30" of the clock calendar, the signs of the zodiac, and the calendar were rendered.

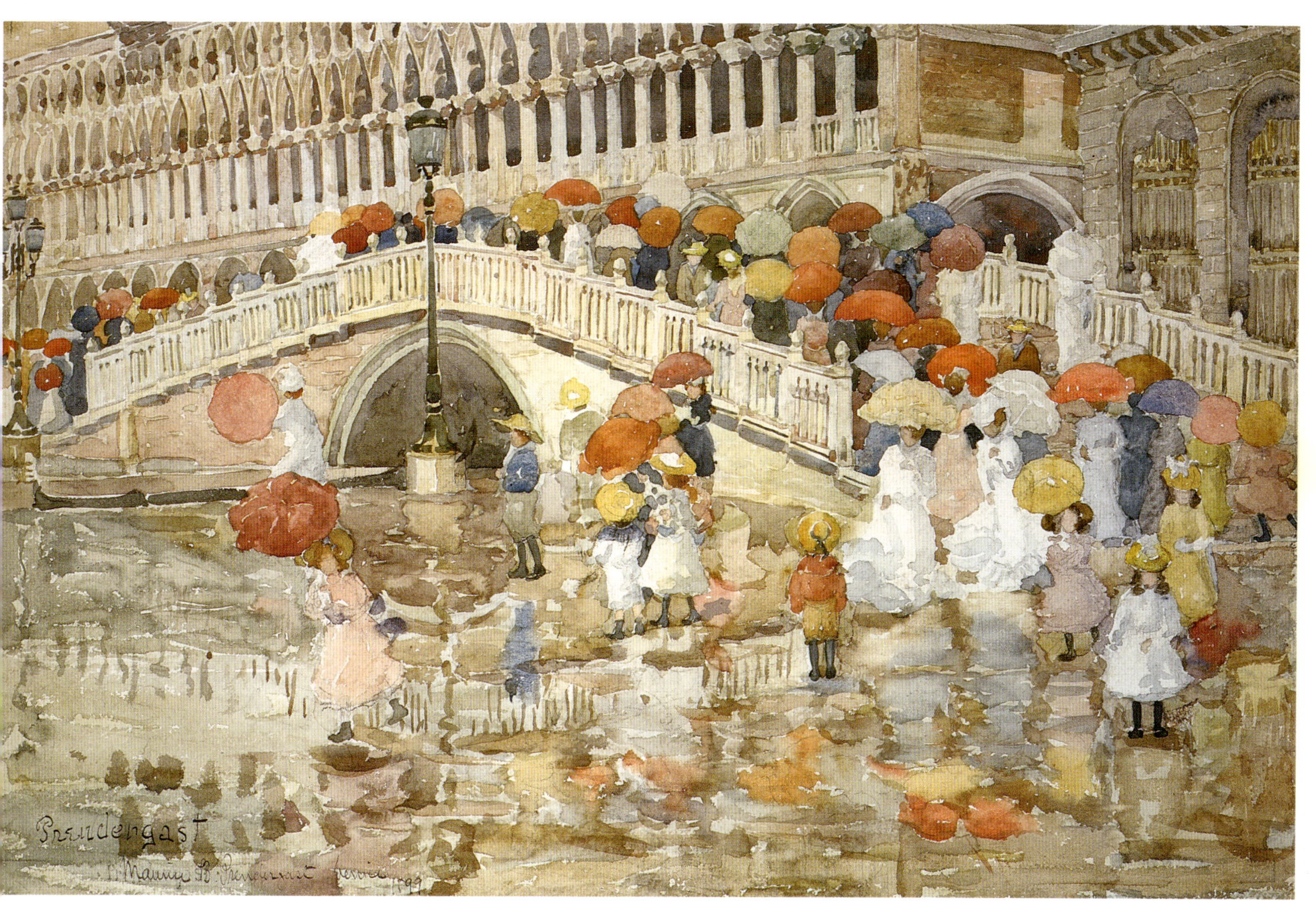

29. Umbrellas in the Rain, Venice

1898–99. Watercolor and pencil on paper, 14 x 20⅞″
Courtesy, Museum of Fine Arts, Boston.
Charles Henry Hayden Fund

This composition is a particularly Impressionist exploration of color and light reflections, with loose wet touches of color contrasting with the firm geometry of bridge and columns of the facade of the Doges' Palace in the upper half of the composition.

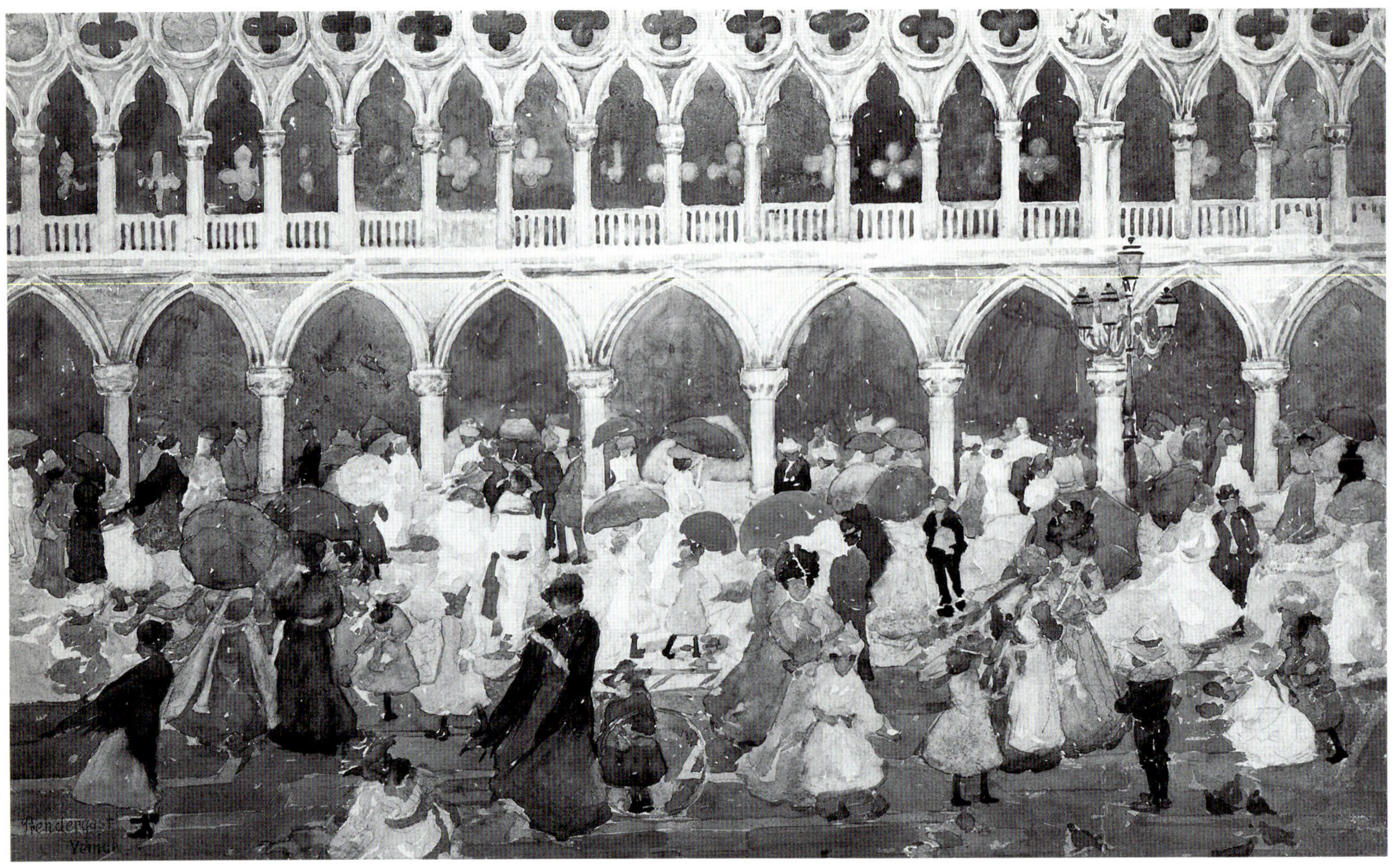

30. Sunlight on the Piazzetta, Venice

1898–99. Watercolor and pencil on paper, 12⅜ x 20⅝"
Courtesy, Museum of Fine Arts, Boston.
Gift of Mr. and Mrs. William T. Aldrich, 1961

The regular patterns of the repetitive archways of the ground-level arcade stabilize the shifting irregular patterns of the throng of figures in sunlight and shadow.

31. Ponte della Paglia (Marble Bridge)

1898–99. Watercolor and pencil on paper, 17¼ x 14⅛"
Collection Mr. and Mrs. Arthur G. Altschul

Here, Prendergast reveled in the complex patternings that create a broad and deep spatial container rather than the rising perspective common to so many of his New England and previous Venetian scenes.

tained the pervasive atmospheric colorfulness of the previous watercolors. The Marble Bridge is opened out to encompass nearly all of the foreground with the side closest to the Doges' Palace in perspective. Marble pommellike newels punctuate the rapid progression of the balusters up and across the steps. The red umbrellas and white dresses succinctly delineate the foot traffic in both directions across the bridge, with a zone of smaller, equally colorful figures in the middle ground, while in the distance, minuscule specks of color echo the vivacious harmonies of the foreground. The setting for this distant reverberation is a sequence of architecture curving along the length of the waterfront.

The inclusion of conspicuous architectural motifs coupled with the low horizon of Venice itself incline some of these compositions toward increased spaciousness. This is clearly evident in such a composition as *The Grand Canal, Venice* (pl. 32), 1898–99, in which the scene is bifurcated between the figures on the embankment and gondolas on the water, each side framed by architecture. The sweep to a distant vanishing point is charged with observed figures—a gondolier in white raising his oar to bring his jewellike red and green boat to rest among four knobbed pilings, a boy with blue trousers sitting on the base of a tall light standard, talking with a young girl, the elevated lantern itself silhouetted in front of the distant buildings. The blue water is loosely brushed and combined with purple shadows from the gondolas, and the multicolored dresses of the figures—mainly strolling women and children—replace the parasols of

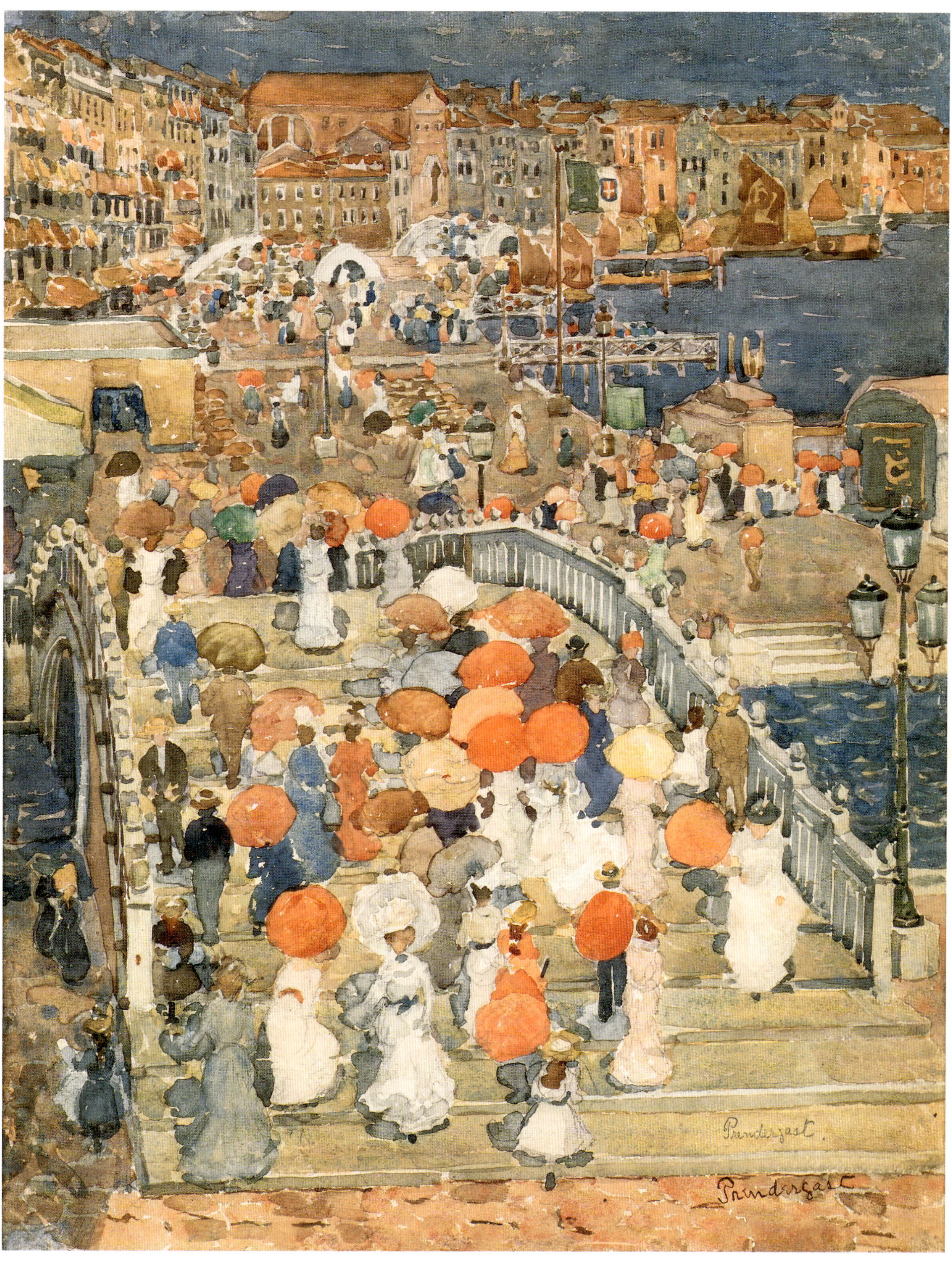

31. Ponte della Paglia (Marble Bridge)

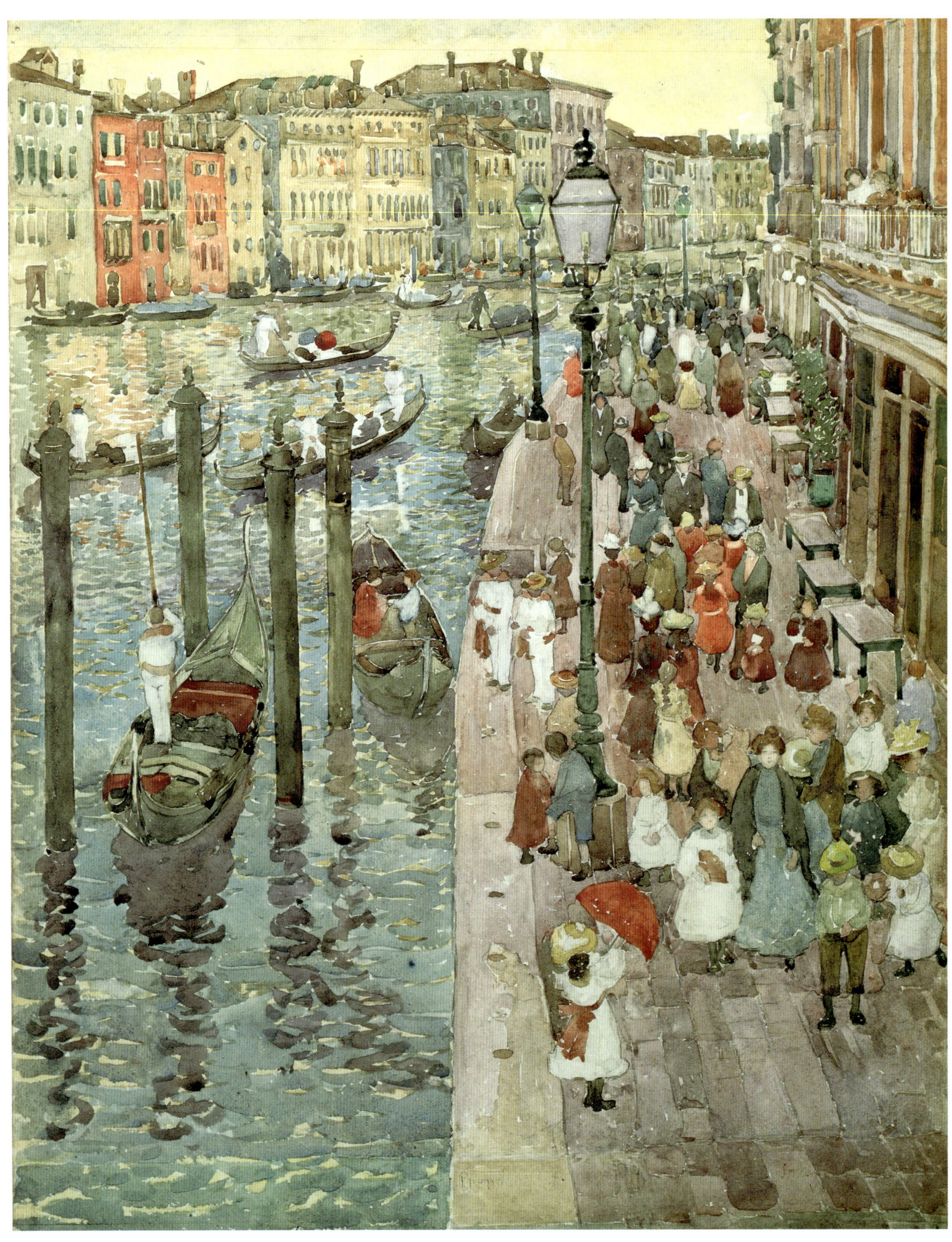

32. *The Grand Canal, Venice*

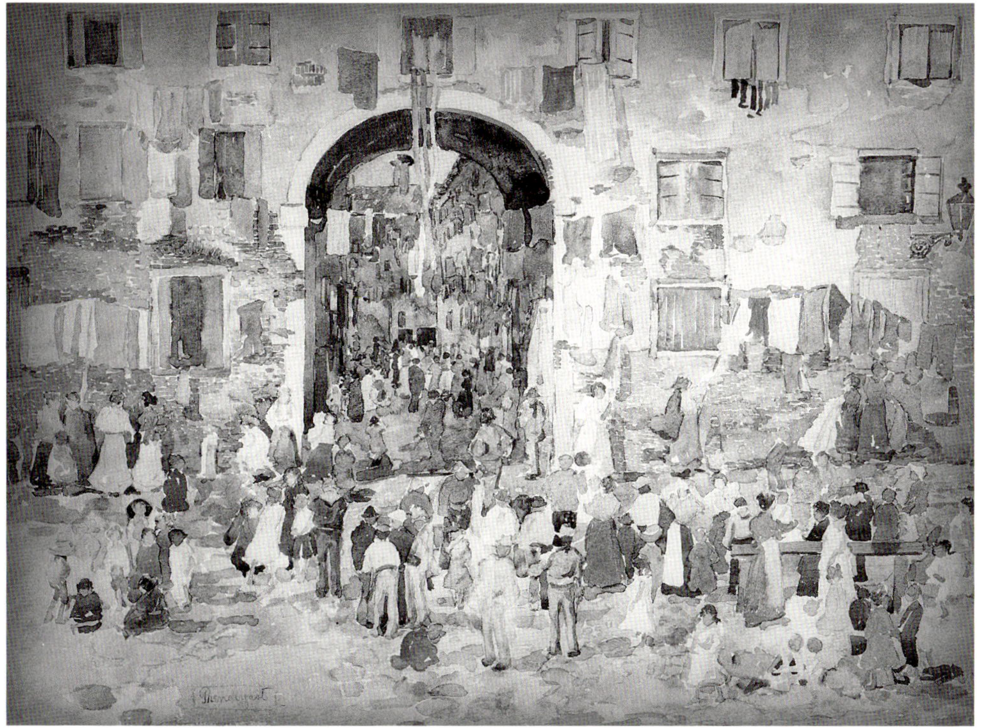

33. Riva degli Schiavoni, Castello (Venice)

1898–99. Watercolor and pencil on paper, $14^{1}/_{2}$ x 19″
Thyssen-Bornemisza Foundation, Lugano, Switzerland

To Prendergast's eye, nothing in Venice was plain or ordinary. Here, the large dark entrance to the Arsenal provides an off-center hub that anchors the laundry and figures spread over the surface.

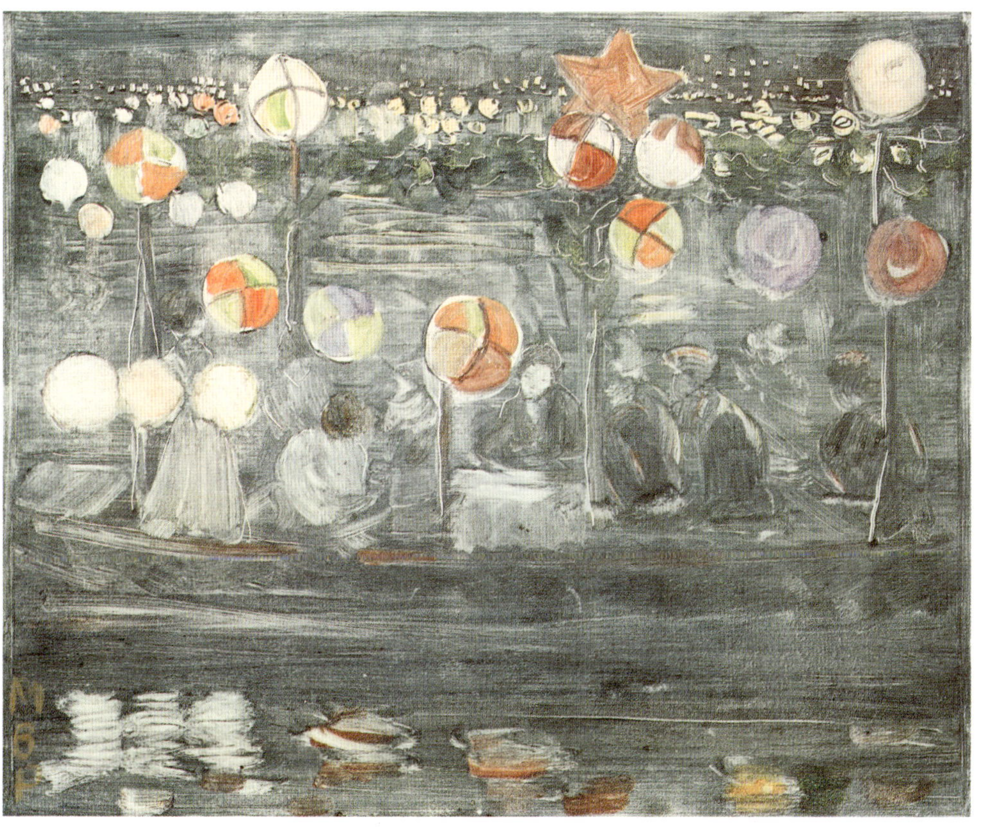

34. Festa del Redentore, Venice

1899. Monotype on paper, $7^{1}/_{2}$ x $9^{3}/_{4}$″
University of Iowa Museum of Art.
Collection of John J. Brady, Estate

Night scenes gave Maurice the opportunity to deploy a wide variety of tonal colors to create effects of lights against the darks.

32. The Grand Canal, Venice.

1898–99. Watercolor and pencil on paper, $7^{1}/_{4}$ x $13^{3}/_{4}$″
Terra Museum of American Art, Chicago.
Daniel J. Terra Collection

This watercolor is one of a series of a half-dozen similar compositions in which the elevated vantage point, in this instance, a view from the Rialto Bridge, is employed to survey a long vista down the Grand Canal.

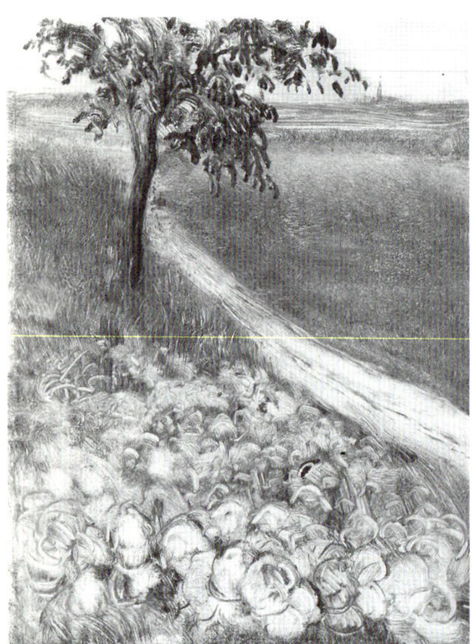

35. Camille Pissarro (1830–1903)
Road by a Field of Cabbages

c. 1880. Color monotype, 8⅛ x 6"
National Gallery of Art, Washington, D.C.
Print Purchase Fund (Rosenwald Collection)

Ponte della Paglia. In his Italian watercolors, Maurice used walls as natural grids; among their intervals he packed the spaces full of picturesque activity, a tradition that Carpaccio, the Bellinis, and the eighteenth-century Venetian view painters, especially Canaletto, followed in their large-scale set pieces, choreographing the activity with a precision and elegant calligraphic notation that Maurice doubtlessly scrutinized at every opportunity in the Galleria dell' Accademia.

Facades, especially in smaller canals and backwaters, their variegated surfaces and shuttered windows often draped with colorful banners and laundry stretched on lines from one side of the embankment to the other, constitute a frequent motif. In *Riva degli Schiavoni, Castello (Venice)* (pl. 33), 1898–99, windows, shutters, sills, and lines draped with laundry produce an effect of multicolored flags. It was in the Scuola di San Giorgio dei Schiavoni, as well as in the Accademia, that Maurice discovered the masterful processions and complex interiors of Vittore Carpaccio.

Like the eighteenth-century Venetians—and Whistler—Prendergast tried his hand at limning the nighttime pageants on the canals. *Festa del Redentore, Venice* (pl. 34), a monotype of 1899, represents the Festival of the Redeemer, which is held on the third Sunday in July. Prendergast was sufficiently intrigued to create the only mosaic of his career of the same nocturnal subject.[46]

Orange Market (pl. 36), 1898–99, eschews the wan color schemes of many of the Venetian subjects in favor of a field of golden ocher-oranges, reinforced with pencil, specifically recalling such color monotypes by Pissarro as *Road by a Field of Cabbages* (pl. 35), c. 1880. Its figures and umbrellas also drew inspiration from Degas's monotypes. It is known that Maurice was aware of Pissarro from the early 1890s, as his paintings provided the underlying Impressionist base for Maurice's *Sketches in Paris* (see pl. 9), but he related years later to Walter Pach, "I was much influenced by Pissarro but with the watercolors it was nature pure and simple. Some effects I would see would really drive me frantic."[47]

During the spring of 1899, following travels to Florence and Siena to study the early primitives, Prendergast installed himself in Rome, where, in addition to visiting museums and churches, he created approximately a half-dozen watercolors and an equal number of monotypes. *Afternoon, Pincian Hill* (pl. 37), 1898–99, a grouping of figures inserted within a broad zigzag of beige, russet, and terra-cotta–colored walls, is yet another of Prendergast's variations on the Persian miniature. The color has a pervasive warm glow, consisting predominantly of reds and terra-cottas, and the figures have a lilting grace. The foreground quartet at the wall is drawn with consummate delicacy, as is the woman with flowing streamers on her headdress pushing a red baby carriage. The red spokes of the carriage wheels in the foreground and those half-concealed by the wall in the middle ground provide a subtle repetition of the angled fifteen-degree alignment of the walls. This same thematic material is taken up again in the monumental *Monte Pincio, Rome* (pl. 38), 1898–99, one of two closely related horizontal versions. *Monte Pincio* has the dry, weathered look of an early fresco, with a zestful profusion of variously hued figures, a Carpaccio-inspired

36. *Orange Market*

1898–99. Monotype, printed in color with pencil additions, composition 12⅙ x 9⅛"
Collection, The Museum of Modern Art, New York. Gift of Abby Aldrich Rockefeller

The briskly stroked figures and the rapid wipes of the plate used to define the ribs of the umbrellas demonstrate a directness rare even for Prendergast.

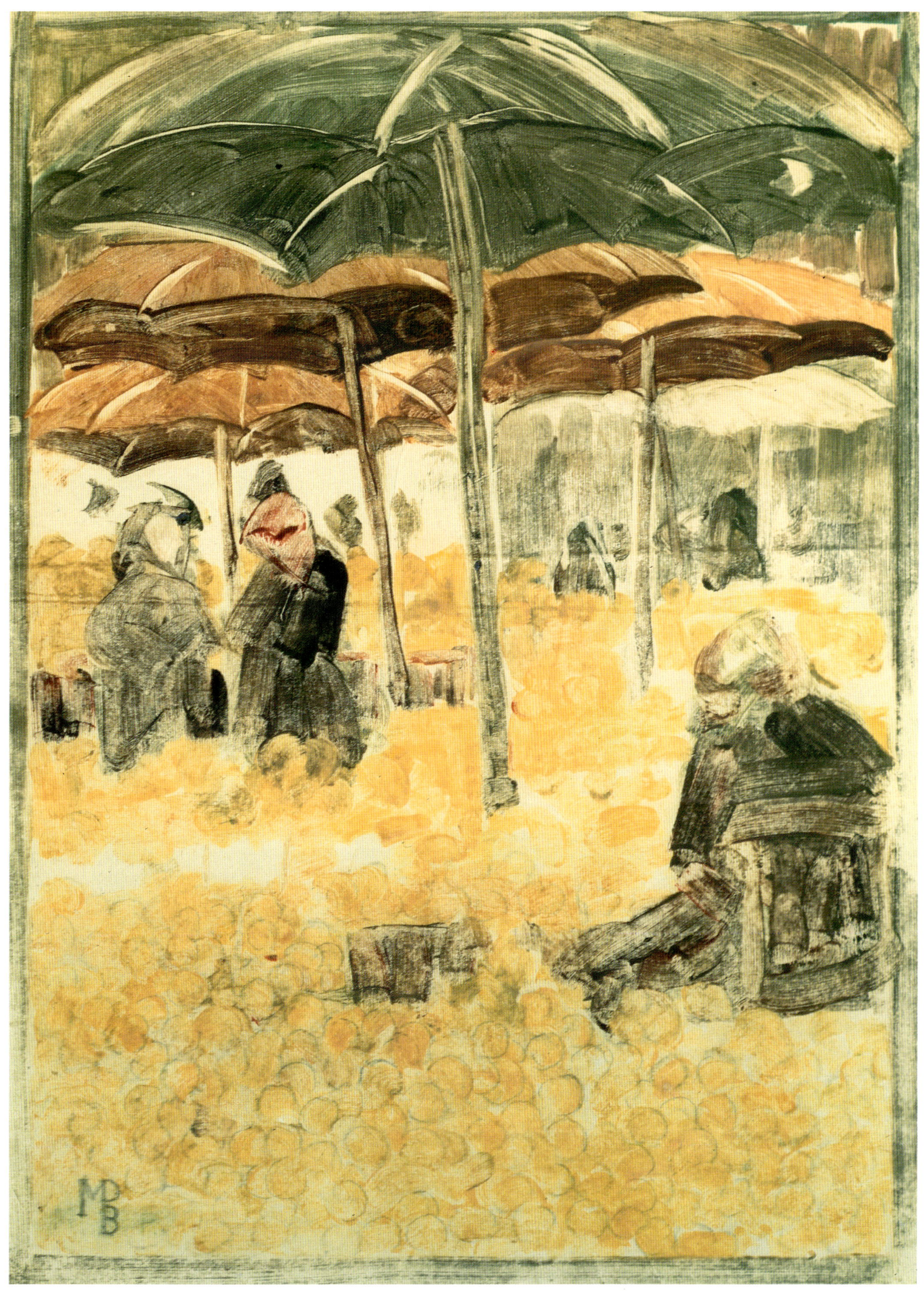

36. Orange Market

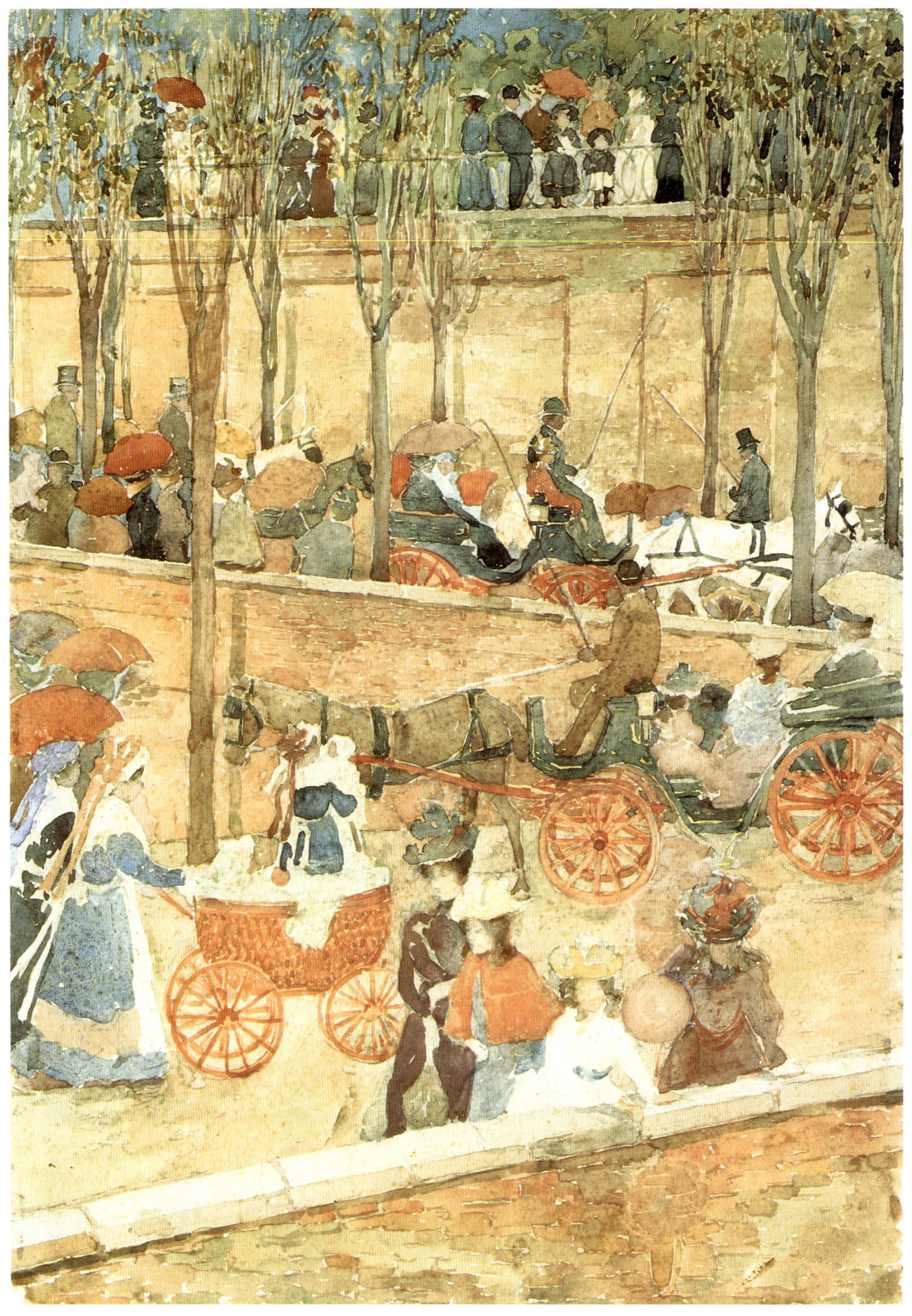

37. *Afternoon, Pincian Hill*

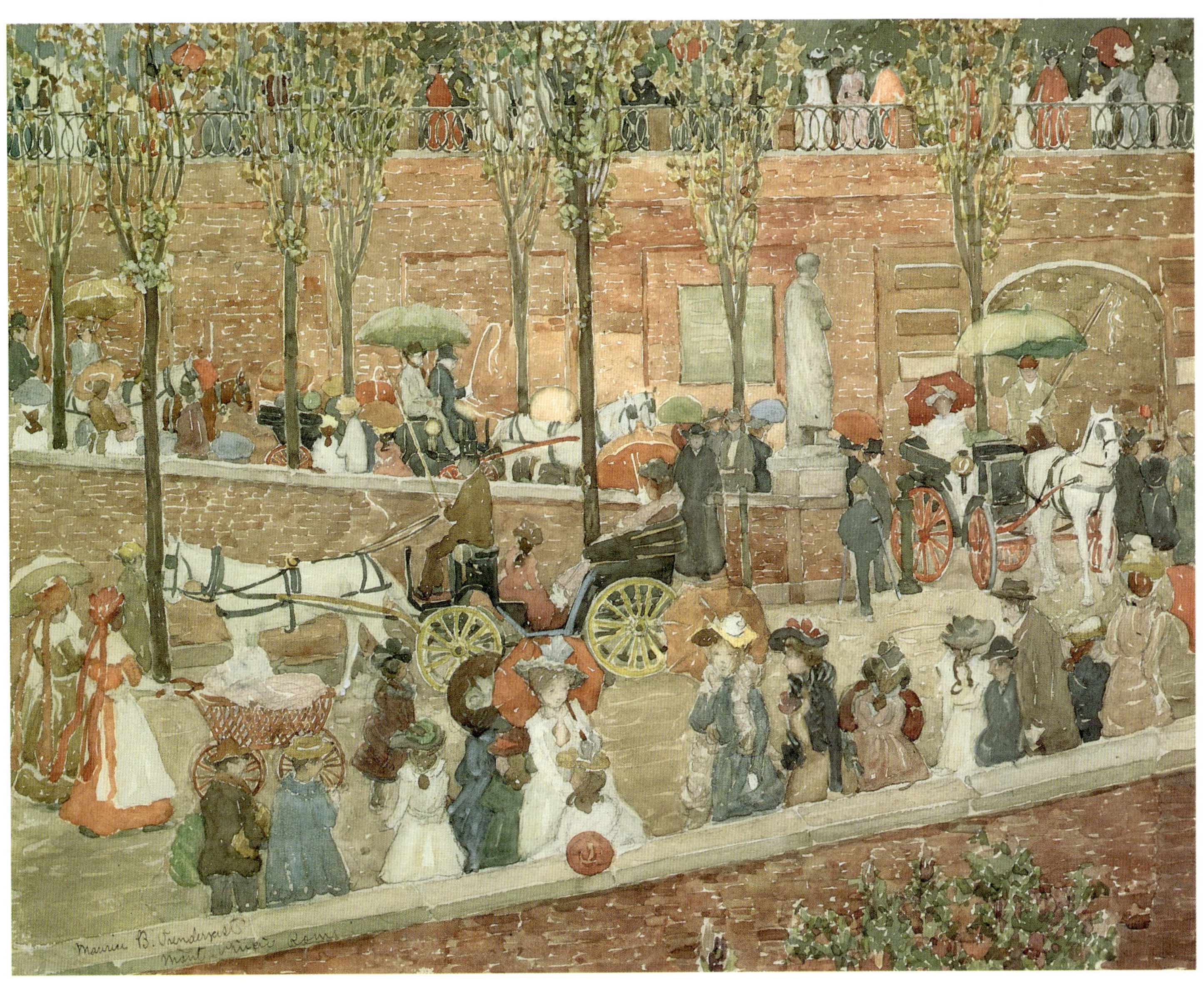

38. Monte Pincio, Rome

1898–99. Watercolor and pencil
on paper, 15½ x 19¼″
Terra Museum of American Art, Chicago.
Daniel J. Terra Collection

It would appear that the inspiration of the frescoes Prendergast was studying throughout his Italian journey led him to depart from the standard formats of his watercolors and monotypes and work on a larger scale.

37. Afternoon, Pincian Hill

1898–99. Watercolor and pencil
on paper, 15⅛ x 10⅝″
Honolulu Academy of Arts.
Gift of Mrs. Philip E. Spaulding, 1940

The small units across the top of the composition, a lacy filigree made up of figures, the branches and shadows of the slender trees, and overlapping ovals of the railings, form a variant on the di sotto in su *(seen from below) vantage point found in old master frescoes from Mantegna to Goya.*

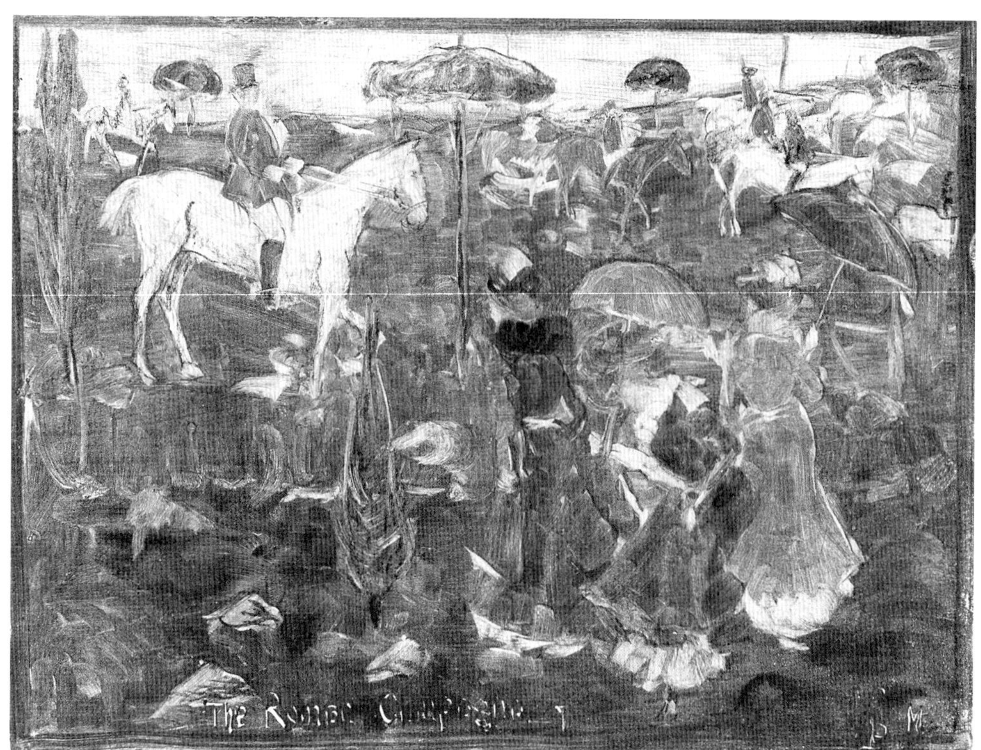

39. The Roman Campagna

c. 1899. Monotype on paper, 9⅛ x 12⅞"
Des Moines Art Center. Purchased with funds from the Truby Kelly Kirsch Memorial Fund, 1953

A deft wipeout on the plate created a stately horse and rider, which was used as a foil to set off the three women with parasols in the right foreground.

procession wherein the carriages proceed down and around the pathway, one in the process of actually turning the corner. The slender tree trunks open out the space, serving an architectonic function related to the flagpoles and pilings in the Venetian compositions. Carriage drivers with whips in hand, families strolling in their finery, a priest in his long cassock, a one-legged boy on crutches, and an impassive marble statue—all play their respective roles in an outdoor theatrical worthy of Gozzoli or Pinturicchio.

Horseback Riders (pl. 40), c. 1900, with its conspicuous pencil additions to elements such as the horse pulling the red carriage and the very dots on the dress of the girl on the left, adapted from the preliminary sketch, brings into play the motifs Maurice was inserting into his Pincian Hill watercolors and monotypes such as *The Roman Campagna* (pl. 39), c. 1899.

40. Horseback Riders

c. 1900. Monotype on paper with pencil additions, 9⅛ x 12¼"
Ball State University Museum of Art, Muncie, Indiana. Elisabeth Ball Collection, permanent loan from the George and Frances Ball Foundation

En route home after a brief stopover in Berlin, Prendergast spent a few days in London. There he sketched a street scene with a girl in a patterned dress (CR 1479), a Whistlerian motif that he went on to use in a series of monotypes, including Horseback Riders.

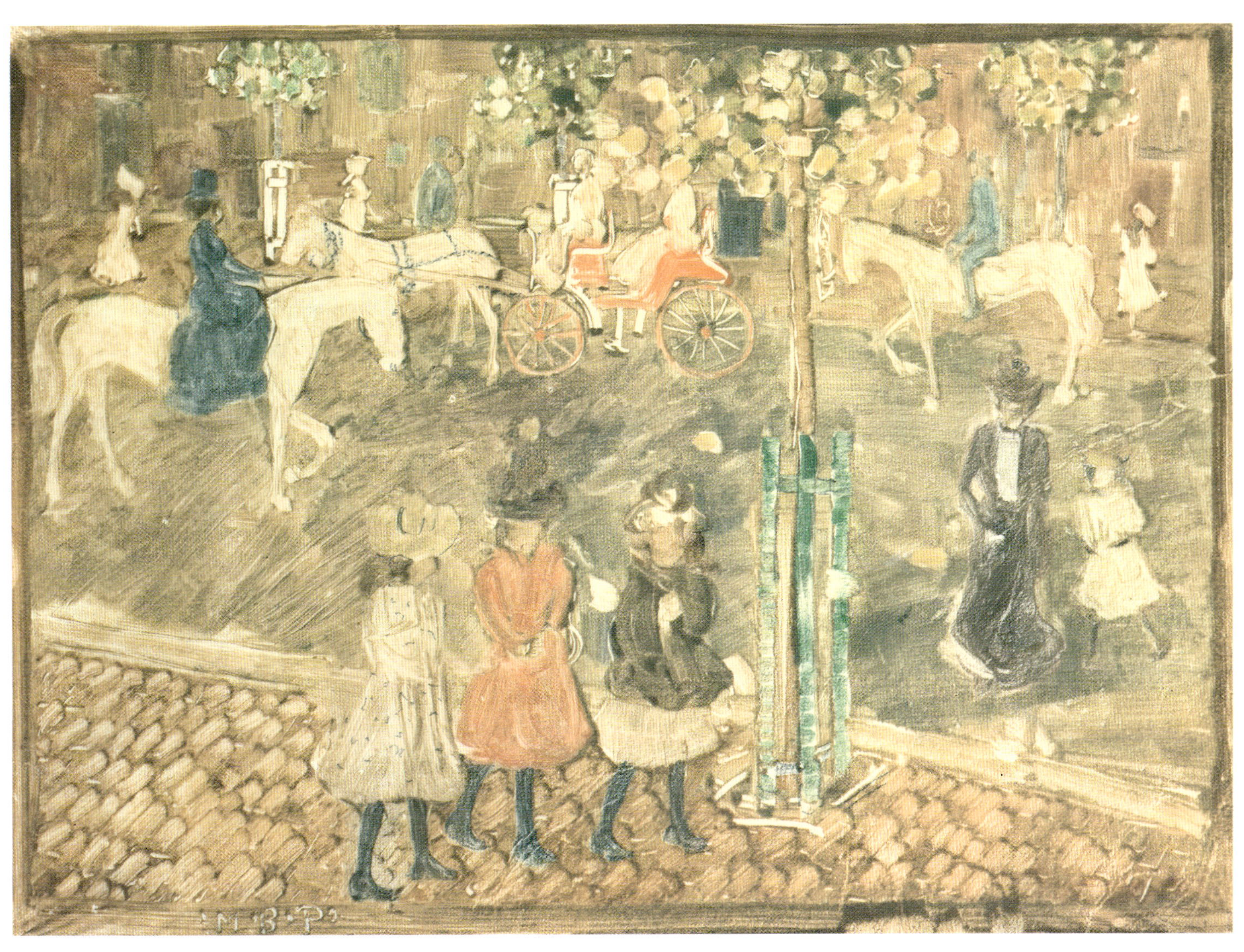

40. Horseback Riders

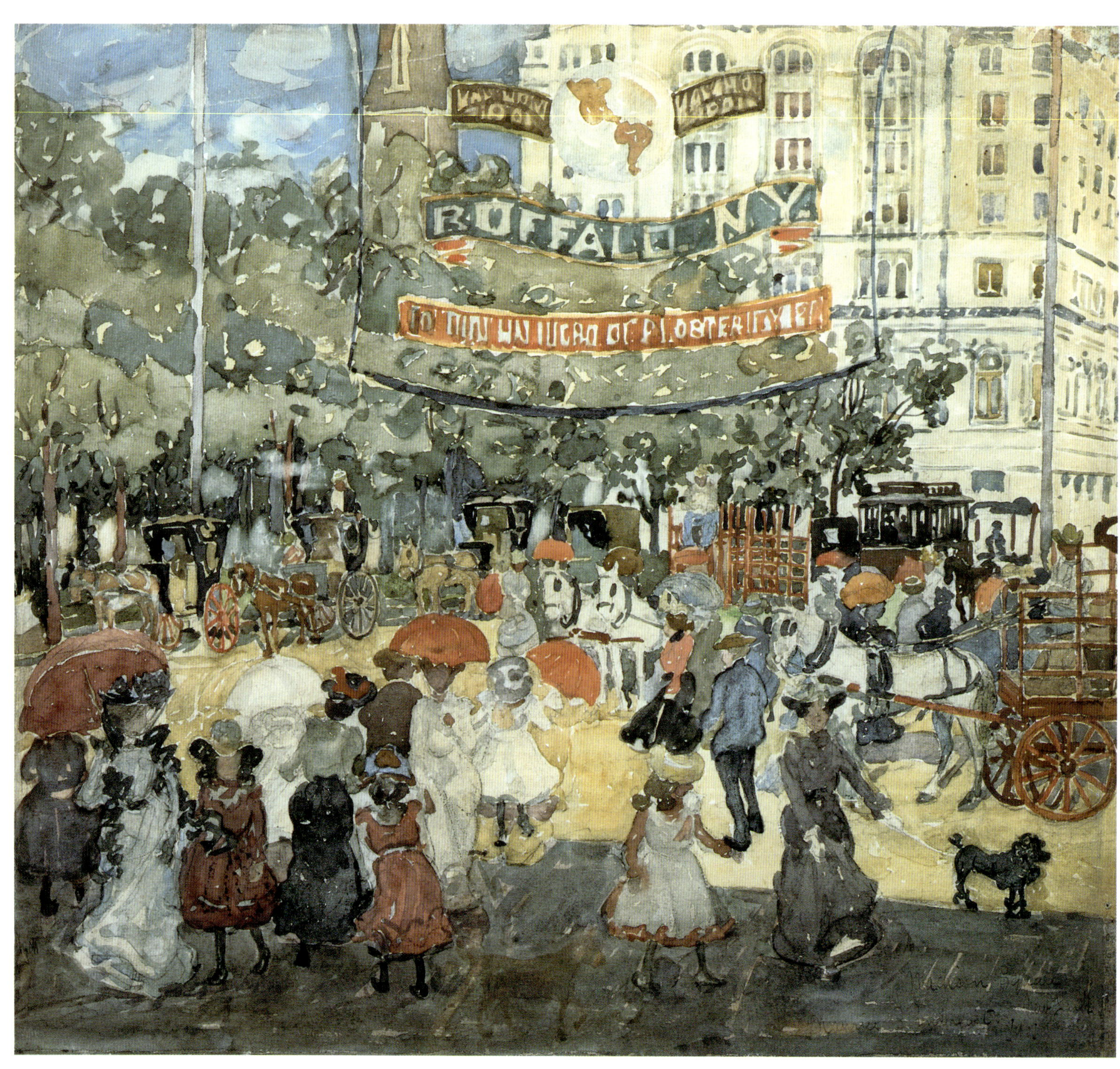

41. Madison Square

VI. *Boston and New York 1900–1907*

ITALY, PARTICULARLY VENICE, WAS THE FULCRUM Maurice's subsequent career rests upon. There he made a discovery and a decision. The discovery was the variety, complexity, and colorful depth of the Venetian tradition, especially the love of pageantry, the monumental scale and luminosity of Trecento and Quattrocento frescoes, and the bold color and striking pattern of Byzantine mosaics. As he was preparing to depart in November 1899, Maurice wrote in a sketchbook, "I am bidding good[by] to Italie this week . . . it has been the visit of my life. I have been here almost a year and a half. I have seen so many beautiful things it almost makes me ashamed of my profession today."[48] The decision was to master oil painting and explore its manifold potentialities.

Inspired rather than intimidated, immediately after his return Maurice brought to bear on his work the capacity for clear organization that he had demonstrated in the practical sphere and turned what Barbara Novak has called his "formidable intelligence" to painting.[49] The critical success he enjoyed did not turn his head or seduce him to coast through a career of satisfying the cautious public by giving it what it had been led to expect. Failing to comprehend Prendergast's real objectives, the Boston critics henceforth gradually diminished their praise and reduced their support. Despite this, Prendergast never changed course. His newly acquired deeper insights convinced him to set his standards higher. Impressionism, in the hands of his Boston contemporaries, had become a thoroughly insipid style. He had learned in Italy what the Post-Impressionists had learned in the Louvre—that Impressionism, in all its gloriously colorful aspects, was an insufficiently broad foundation for an artist. He knew, as he studied the achievements of the Italian masters, that the ease and control over the medium of watercolor that he had so mastered was merely a point of departure for the new and more difficult tasks that he would set for himself. With the determination that was integral to his personality, he began to approach painting in the same spirit.

He gave up making monotypes; the last dated prints were pulled in 1902. Until around 1902 he continued to paint watercolors in the same spirit as the Italian and earlier New England sheets, notably the sparkling and typically engaging multifigure holiday scenes in Central Park made on his frequent spring and fall trips to New York.

West Church, Boston (pl. 42), c. 1900–1901, was among at least six closely related variants. The autumn scene includes many of Prendergast's familiar motifs: the screenlike cast-iron fence, the vertical framework of tree trunks and figures, especially children, set on the brick sidewalk in a way identical to the

41. Madison Square

1901. Watercolor and pencil on paper, 15 x 16¼"
Collection, Whitney Museum of American Art, New York. Joan Whitney Payson Bequest

This work provides an example of Maurice's early show-card lettering skills put to good use. He chose the frontal pattern of the banner, so reminiscent of similar motifs in the Italian watercolors, in order to set off the diverse human activity below.

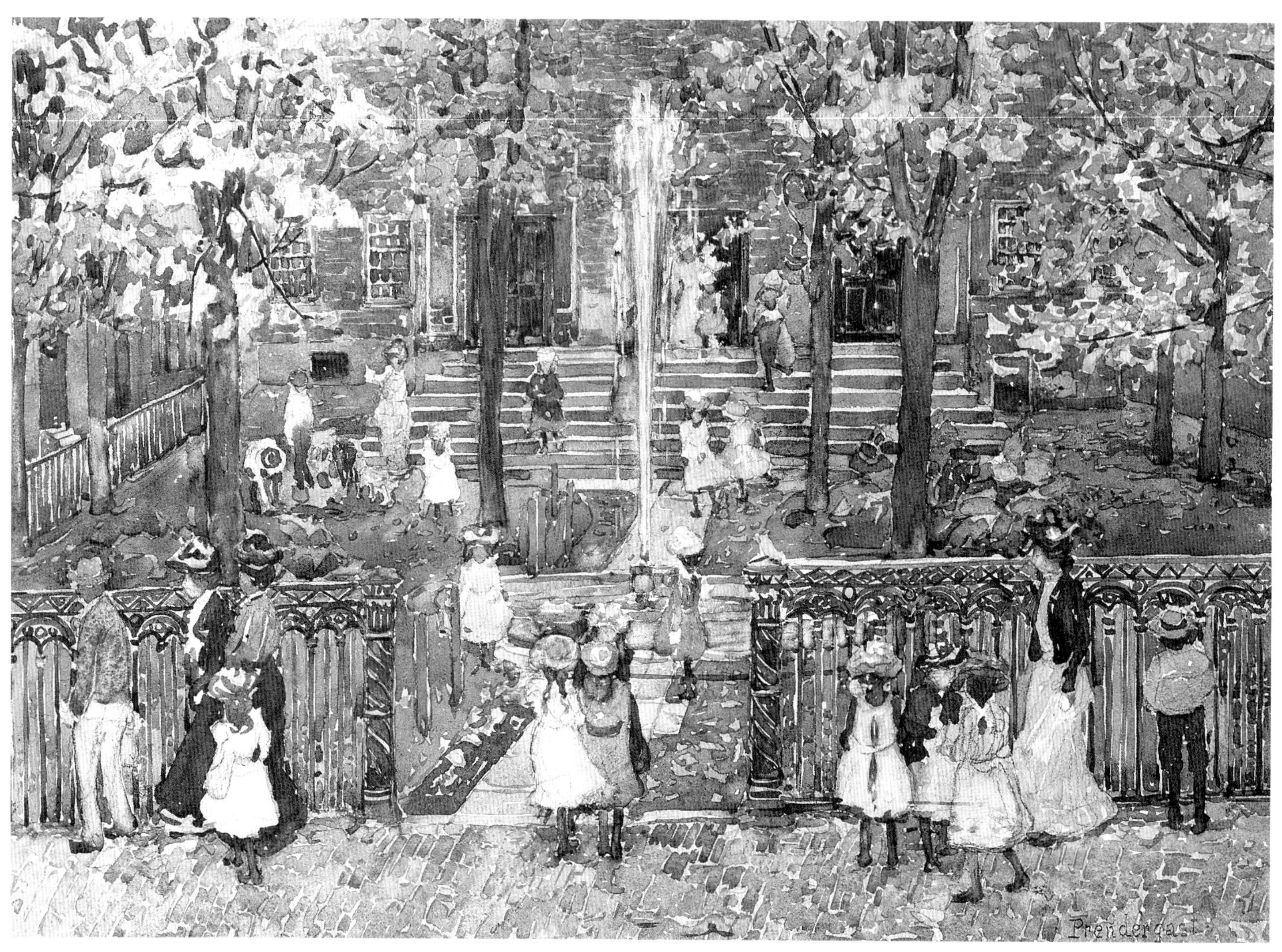

42. West Church, Boston

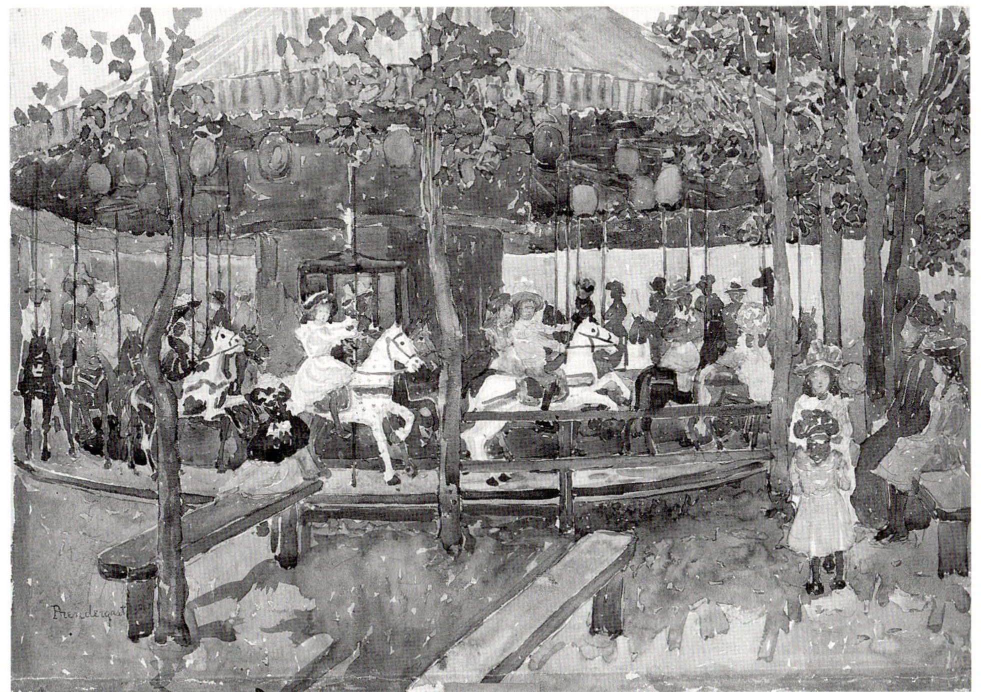

43. Merry-Go-Round, Nahant

c. 1900–1901. Watercolor and pencil on paper, 13¼ x 19″
Museum of Fine Arts, Springfield, Massachusetts. The Horace P. Wright Collection

The whole sweep of the merry-go-round is explored here from the bright foreground figure to the distant silhouetted hats. Prendergast's eye for the picturesque is exemplified by the striking blue of the benches.

contemporaneous monotypes of London and Boston. *Merry-Go-Round, Nahant* (pl. 43), c. 1900–1901, subsequently the basis for an oil several years later, again demonstrates Prendergast's eye for the picturesque. The blue benches, like the red carriage wheels on the Pincian, form striking patterns that catch the eye and lead one into the activity on the carousel, a colorful arena containing horses with their multicolored trappings, the figures and silhouettes of the riders, the pink-rose roundhouse, and the Japanese lanterns, all typical Prendergast details.

Several years later, on June 5, 1904, Maurice wrote to his New York dealer, William Macbeth (1851–1917), thus providing us with insight into his sheer delight in his favorite outdoor subjects. "I received your considerate post card and got out to Prospect Park in good time and was lucky enough to see the procession from the grand stand. It was a great sight; thousands of little children marching with their banners and flags waving. I tried to discover Mr. Macbeth among the mass of white clouds but gave up the attempt. I am glad that I saw it and that they had such a glorious day."[50] Macbeth, who was very active in the affairs of the Brooklyn Sunday Schools Anniversary Parade, was happy to oblige "his" artist with a ready-made motif.

Madison Square (pl. 41), 1901, with its graphic banners and achitectural details, horses and wagons, carriages and streetcar, is a reprise of the Italian themes. The play of shadow and sunlight, the delicious multicolor shapes of figures, umbrellas, and poodle eloquently assert Prendergast's command of the medium. *The East River* (pl. 44), 1901, has a gray-over-blue and dusty rose color scheme underlying its diagonal grid composition. *The Mall, Central Park* (pl. 45), 1901, employs an elaborate and substantial architectural framework, drawing

42. West Church, Boston

c. 1900–1901. Watercolor, pencil, and opaque white on paper, 10⅞ x 15⅝″
Courtesy, Museum of Fine Arts, Boston. Charles Henry Hayden Fund

Prendergast had to repeat this watercolor, a commission from Cyrus Bartol, minister of the West Church when it served as a branch of the Boston Public Library, because the clergyman felt the church was not prominent enough in the composition. Van Wyck Brooks ("Anecdotes of Maurice Prendergast") recounted that while Prendergast was working on the second version, housepainters repainted the "beautiful old greeny blue" of the doors a more intense blue, which was faithfully recorded for the finicky patron.

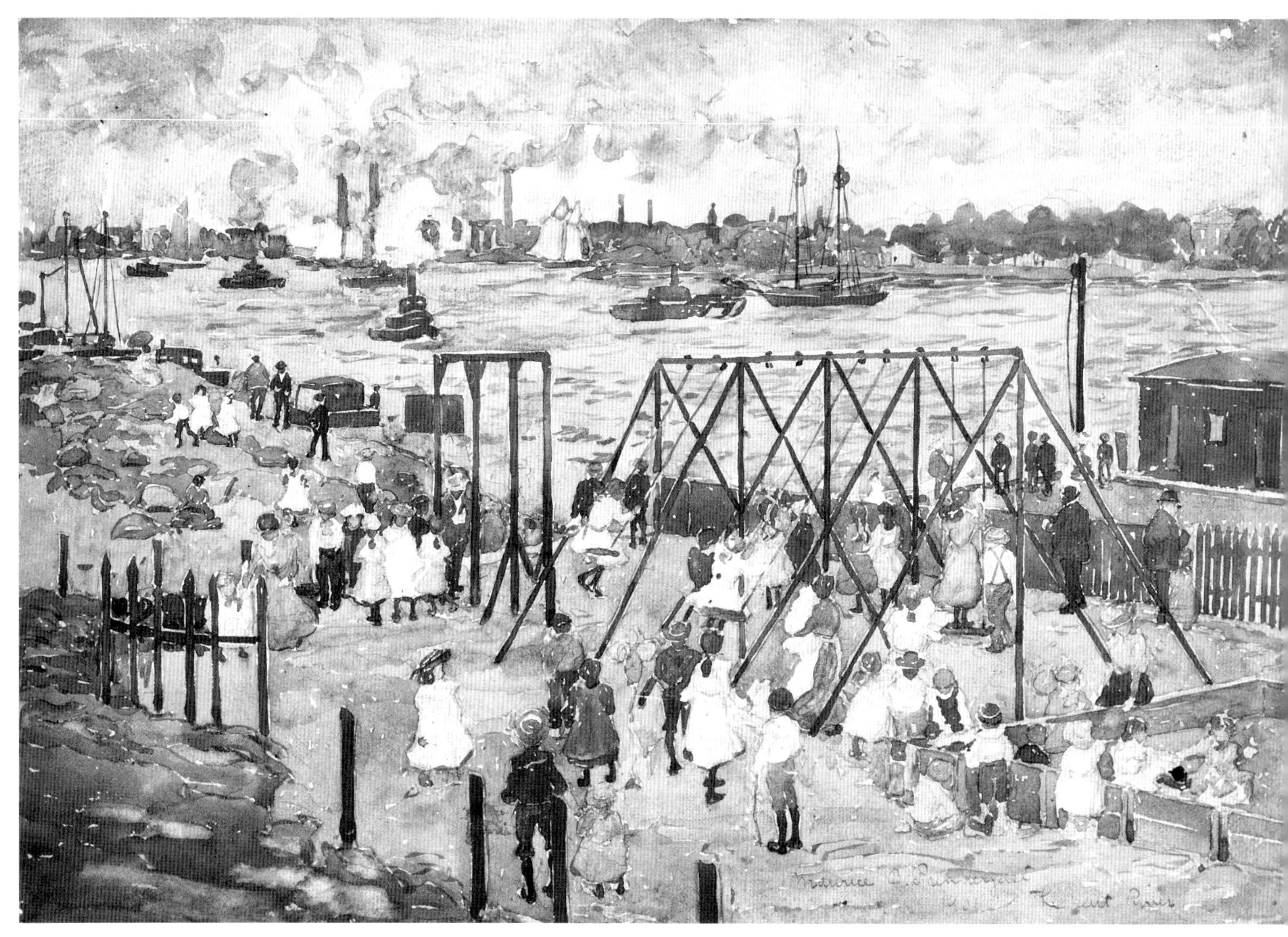

44. The East River

1901. Watercolor and pencil on paper, $13^{3}/_{4}$ x $19^{3}/_{4}$"
Collection, The Museum of Modern Art, New York. Gift of Abby Aldrich Rockefeller

Not all of Prendergast's New York motifs were Central Park subjects. This view of the East River is reminiscent of Pissarro's quayside vistas, especially those done in Rouen, which were surely known to Maurice.

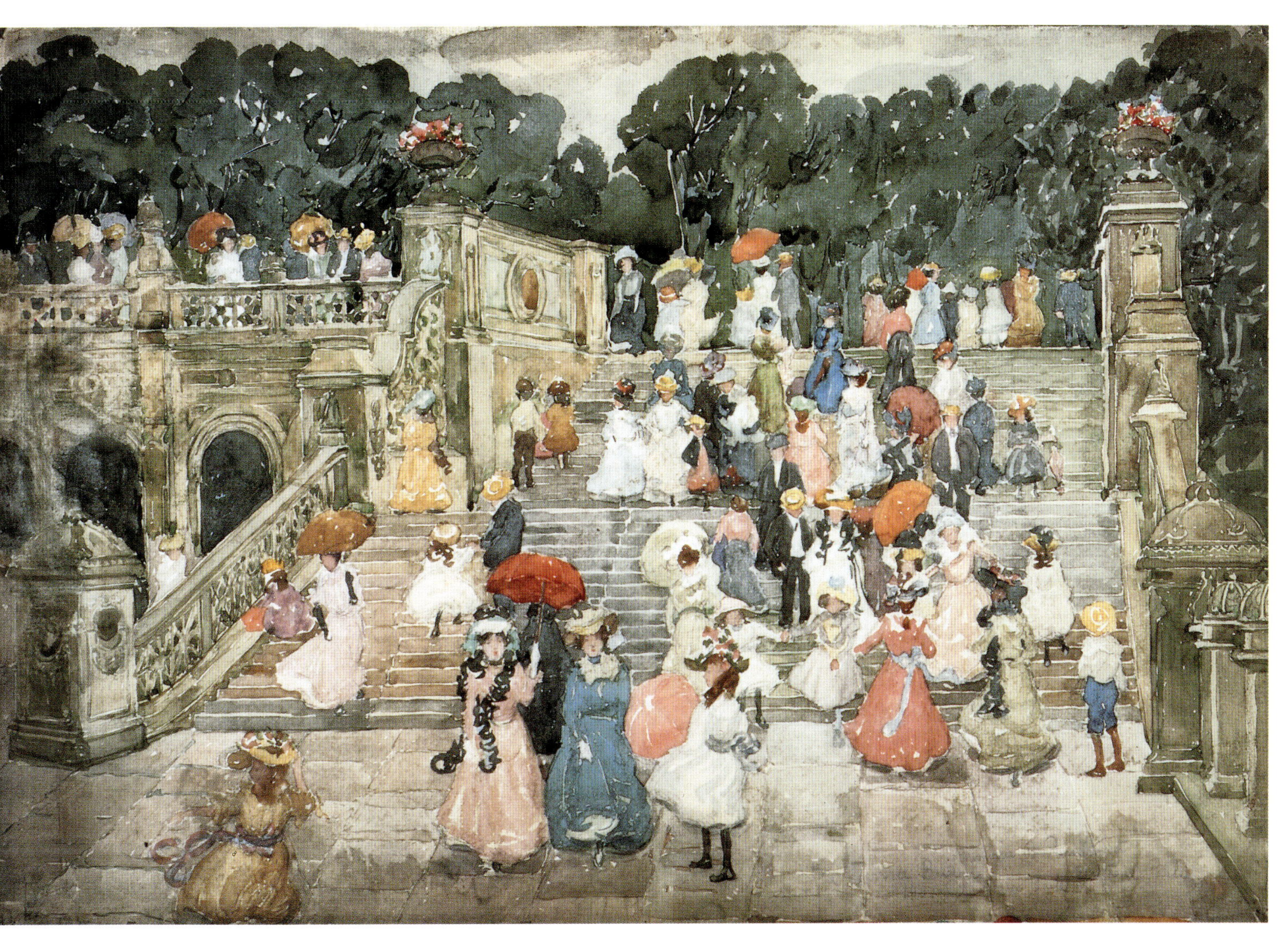

45. The Mall, Central Park

1901. Watercolor and pencil
on paper, 15¼ x 22½″
The Art Institute of Chicago.
The Olivia Shaler Swan Memorial Collection

Prendergast's capacity to build up intricate perspective detail with no loss of spontaneity and freshness heightened the pyramidal organization of the figures from the lower corners to the top center of the composition.

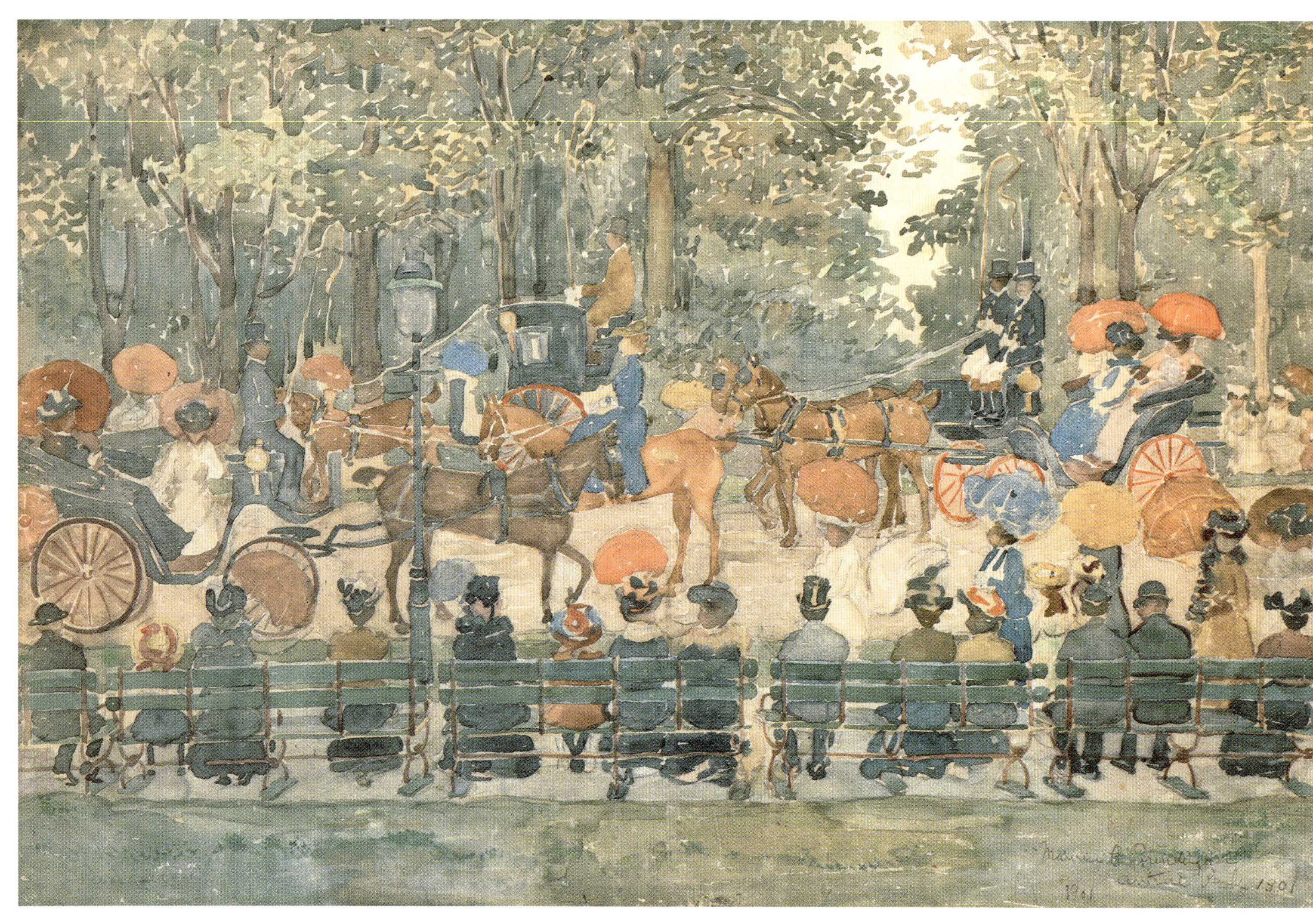

46. Central Park

on the *Ponte della Paglia* compositions (see pls. 27 and 31), and its simplified screen of subdued greenery provides a backdrop for the ornate Beaux-Arts staircase. In another of his variations, *Central Park* (pl. 46), 1901, Prendergast had different color sequences in mind as he reworked the familiar motifs. In this composition, so reminiscent of such images as the monotype *The Roman Campagna* (see pl. 39), 1899, the illustrative specificity of horse and rider is extended to a complex alignment of crisscrossing horses, riders, carriages, coachmen, and passengers in a friezelike arrangement. The foreground is augmented with touches of pastel; the figures are subtly enriched successors to those at the bottom of page 115 in *My Lady Nicotine* (see pl. 15). The open unpainted areas that define the reins of the horsemen constitute a particular tour de force. Years later, Maurice paid very careful attention to this very feature of Cézanne's work, pointing it out.[51]

The maypole theme was explored in such watercolors as *May Day, Central Park* (pl. 47), 1901, whose sprightly streamers recall those three hanging from a window above the center of the archway in the Venetian *Riva degli Schiavoni, Castello (Venice)* (see pl. 33), 1898–99. *Central Park* (pl. 48), c. 1901–2, is a monotype variation on the spontaneous rhythms of this happy theme. In *May Day, Central Park* (pl. 49), c. 1902, a broad filigree screen is held in place by dense foreground shadows, continuing the ideas of such Venetian compositions as *Sunlight on the Piazzetta* (see pl. 30), 1898–99. The importance of the maypole is diminished and made coequal with the densely packed pattern of the crowd.

In *Maypole* (pl. 50), 1902, the multiplicity of colors and patterns, the complexities of spatial interaction presented a challenge that Prendergast investigated systematically. Freely drawn pencil outlines establish the overall composition rather than its details. The lines are then covered with pale watercolor tones in such a way that the lines beneath, not rigorously adhered to, are still visible. Prendergast first toned the surface of the larger figures in the foreground and the maypole with its dangling ribbons, leaving areas, as was his custom, uncovered. Large strokes of grayish green were then floated in the foreground and simultaneously in the large tree. These accents were very strong in relation to the large figures, with their pale, Whistlerian delicacy. Prendergast reworked with broad strokes the umbrella-shaped unit of the maypole and retouched the pole itself in a deeper rose than the original pink, which shows through in spots, making it a stronger feature. He did not, however, rework the ribbons. Patches of color were added to several of the figures, including the girl in the foreground with upraised arms tying a bow in her hair. Her dress, which had originally been pale pink with grayish white polka dots, was made a rosier hue with grayish undertones. The girl to the right of the figure in pink was strengthened by bands of pale tan, and the blue patterns on her dress, around the waist and bodice, were added to provide a crisp linear accent to the lower center of the picture. The leaves, in their density, form one of Prendergast's classic screen devices, found throughout this group of Central Park watercolors. These minute adjustments were essential to achieve the harmonies of a unified ensemble that Prendergast sought. Structure, balance, and poised movement

46. Central Park

1901. Watercolor, pencil, ink, and pastel on paper, 14⅜ x 21⅝"
Whitney Museum of American Art, New York. Purchase

The composition consists of a horizontal band of seated men and women with variously shaped hats, several holding umbrellas subtly tilted at different angles. These colorful shapes correspond to the umbrellas above and behind the figures in the carriages, punctuating and opening up the space between the foreground, the middle ground, and the background foliate screen.

were the result of careful planning and deft technical execution, a freedom always under the control of a firmly conceived picture idea.

Unlike many of the Italian watercolors of 1898–99, *Maypole* and its related group of Central Park watercolors painted from 1900 to 1902 emphasize a contrast of light and dark that recalls Manet. As opposed to the brilliance of the earlier scenes, the muted sparkle is characteristic of many, but not all, of Maurice's watercolors of this period. They represent not so much dramatic evidence of growth but, rather, a consolidation, a refinement, a perfection of the framework that he was comfortable with, and within these bounds Prendergast, a master of depicting gesture, exercised maximum flexibility and confident control.

Prendergast had not neglected his business affairs when he was in Italy in 1898–99. In April 1899, sixteen watercolors, some of which he had shipped home, were shown at the J. Eastman Chase Gallery, Boylston Street. As usual, the reviews were full of unqualified praise. At the Boston Water Color Club in March, 1899, eleven Venice works were displayed. Downes wrote, "Mr. Prendergast was born to paint fetes, and he carries a whole Fourth of July in his color-box. What an irresistible spirit of happy holiday activity pervades his scintillating and Watteau-like scenes! Flags fluttering, waves rippling, sun shining over all, brilliantly dressed throngs of men, women and children, all moving, here and there, in a veritable kaleidoscope of life!"[52] During his absence he was also included in shows at the Art Institute of Chicago, the New York Water Color Club, and the Pennsylvania Academy of the Fine Arts. No break is discernible in his established custom. Indeed, while he was still abroad, plans were set in motion for its intensification.

On September 29, 1899, Charles responded to a letter from William Macbeth: "I have no doubt he would be willing for you to handle some of his work." Soon thereafter Macbeth heard from Hermann Dudley Murphy, a friend who had shared a successful exhibition of monotypes with Maurice two years earlier and who had recently learned frame making under Charles's tutelage: "I will send you two or three Prendergasts in a few days as his brother tells me you wanted some. All his pictures are in my studio and until his return I am taking charge of them for him."[53] Murphy and Prendergast shared a two-man show at the Art Institute of Chicago, which opened January 3, 1900. Murphy arranged the exhibition and received top billing in the catalogue, showing sixty-five works, while Maurice displayed fifteen Venice watercolors and the same number of monotypes. Reviews by Boston critics who visited the show were unrestrained in their praise. However, the Chicago critics were notably sour. Lorado Taft derided, "They are the queerest things I have ever seen for many a day. . . ."[54] Downes, who was ecstatic in his review,[55] took the extraordinary step of publishing a rejoinder: ". . . the expression of a man who is not easily pleased," he wrote two weeks later, ". . . if we may use a figurative phrase he tears them all to pieces. One reserves the right to differ from it emphatically."[56] Contrary to later legend, Boston, at the turn of the century, was defending its own, and this could only have pleased Prendergast and reinforced his confidence. Many buyers of his watercolors were prominent members of Boston society.

Maurice's first letter to Macbeth, of January 10, 1900, is typically straightforward: "I should be glad to have you make a selection from my pictures to sell on commission. I don't see how I can let you see anything at present as I have a lot of pictures on exhibition at the Institute in Chicago which I will not get back until the end of this month. Then I have to send a group to the water color club which will run till the twentieth of February. After that I can have something for you to select from if not too late in the season. . . . Will you please let me know if you give single exhibitions in your galleries." On February 12, Prendergast wrote to Macbeth: "I shall have all my things on to you by the first of March. I am not charging very high prices for the sketches. . . ."

"Exhibition of Water Colors and Monotypes in Color" opened at Macbeth's on March 9 and included about a dozen of the sheets shown in Chicago among the twenty-six watercolors and about ten of the seventeen monotypes. The show was welcomed by the New York press, and seven works were sold before it closed on March 24. It was at this time that Charles FitzGerald, editor of the *Sun*, introduced Prendergast to William Glackens (1870–1938) and other members of the Realist group, including George Luks (1866–1933). After the show's close on March 24, Maurice wrote to Macbeth, "I must thank [you] very much for the way you treated [me] and I don't think you will lose anything by me in the long run. I wish if not too much trouble you would send some of the papers with the criticisms." On March 27, Maurice wrote Macbeth, "Three of the water colors I should like to send to Chicago . . . if not sold." These were destined for another show at the Art Institute, which opened April 29. Macbeth also shipped a selection to San Francisco, where for two weeks in May they were put on view at the Vickery Gallery. The reviewer could not restrain himself: "A collection of water colors by Maurice B. Prendergast is on exhibition . . . and its coming marks an epoch in the art records of the West. This is, in fact, the first time that the stay-at-home local painters . . . have had an opportunity to study . . . the legitimate impressionist. Mr. Prendergast . . . has been in every important exhibition in the East." He concluded, "A 'Prendergast,' in a living room would be the next best thing to a trip abroad. His mission is one of good cheer."[57] The highest price for a single work, including two dealers' commissions, was $110. On June 30, Prendergast wrote Macbeth, "I shall be preparing for an exhibition here in the fall. Many thanks for the enclosed check for it was contrary to my expectations. I am not prospering outside of the check but I am hammering away steadily to work which is a great satisfaction." And on July 17, 1900, "I am about starting on a sketching trip tomorrow and expect not to be back before the middle of Sept and will try and get some new things into shape—good stuff to show you."

Preparations for exhibitions continued. On February 24, 1901, Maurice wrote to Macbeth, "As I am invited to send a group of water colors to [the] Buffalo Exposition so if Mr. Budworth sends for those two bad water colors of mine you have please deliver them to him. . . . [P.S.] Very soon you will have the pleasure or agony to see some very bad oil paintings of mine, M.B.P." Apparently, referring to his "bad" works was a figure of speech Prendergast used with some of his close associates, and it referred to works he considered especially impor-

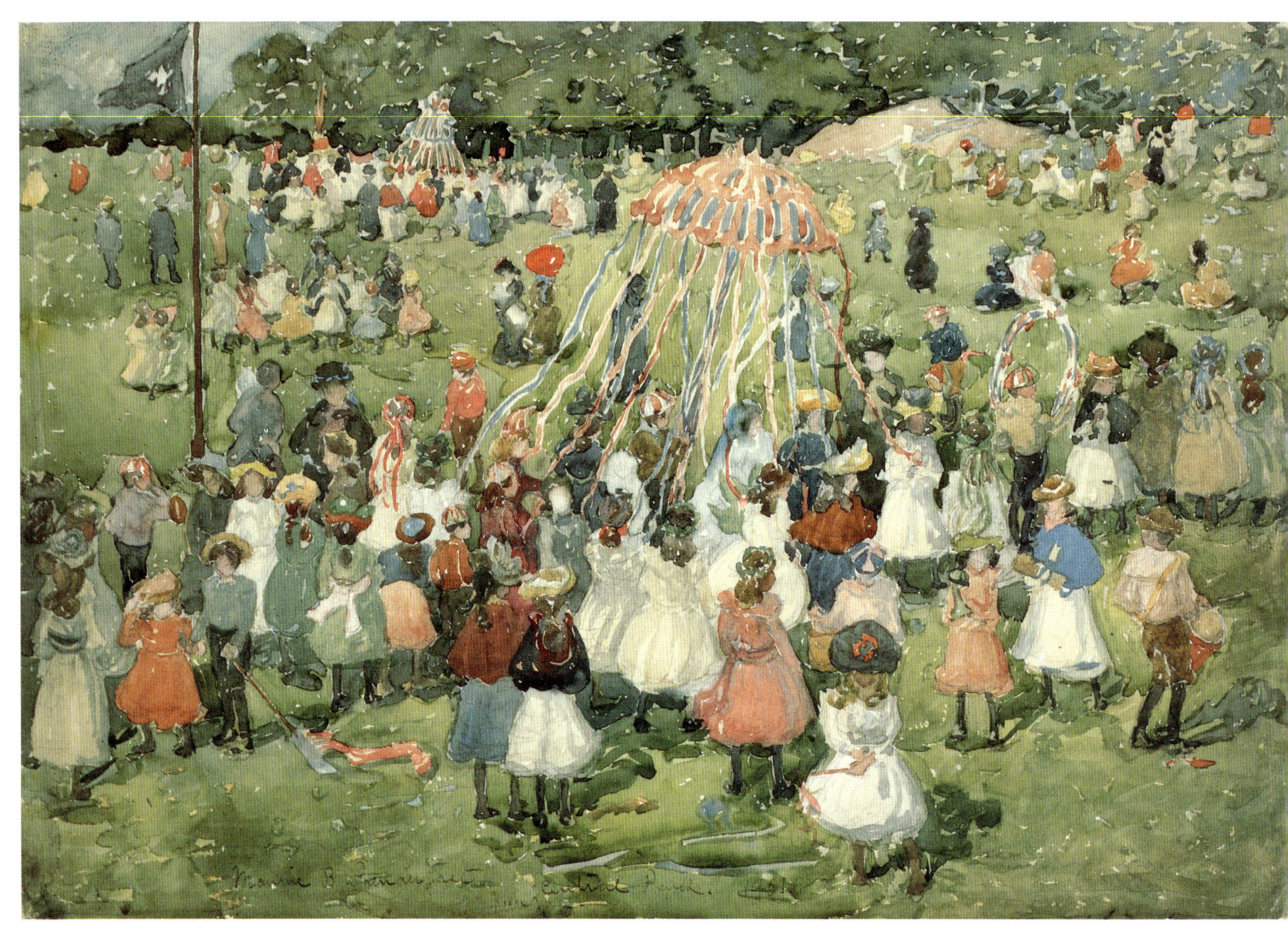

47. May Day, Central Park

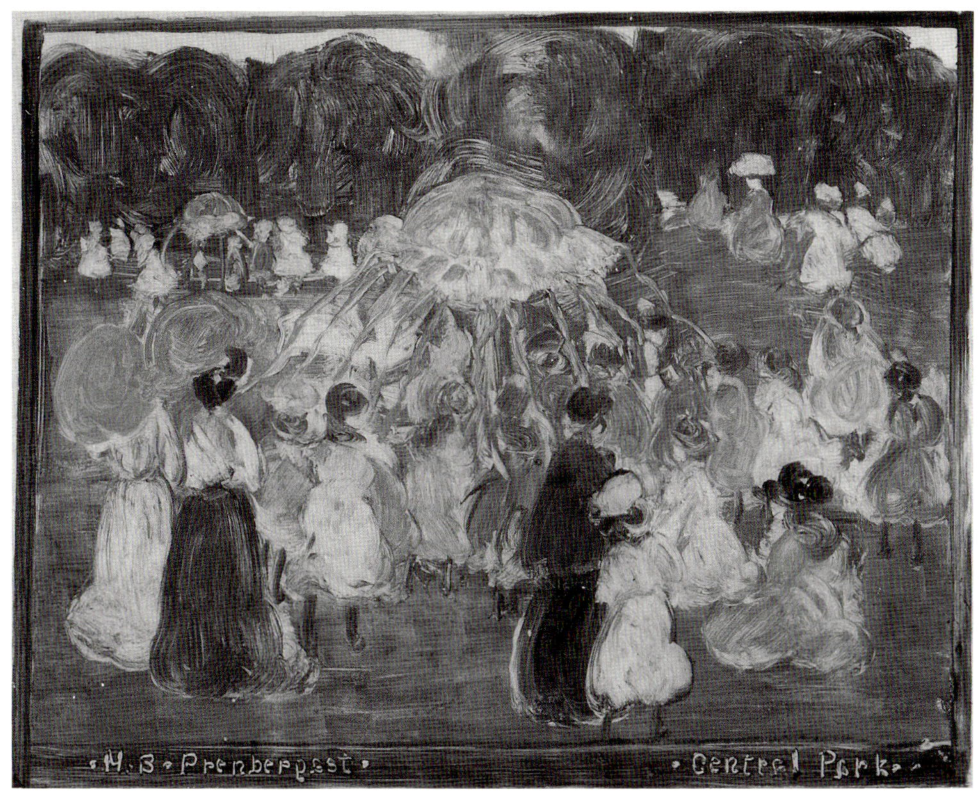

48. Central Park

c. 1901–2. Monotype on paper, 7⅞ x 10″
Private collection

Instead of looking down on the field as in the related watercolor May Day, Central Park *(pl. 47), this monotype opens up a depth of space, demonstrating why Boston critics likened Maurice to Watteau.*

tant. At the Pan-American Exposition in Buffalo, held May through November, Prendergast exhibited four New England watercolors. *The Stony Beach* (see pl. 24), c. 1897, won a bronze medal. Charles Caffin reviewed the show. "There are several brilliant pictures by Prendergast, such as his *Crescent Beach, a Holiday* [792], a *parterre* of bright color. . . ."[58]

In June 1901 Prendergast wrote to the director of the Detroit Museum of Art, A. H. Griffith, "My Dear Sir, Can you give me an exhibition and sale sometime during the late fall or early winter . . . Mr. Macbeth has referred me to you." By June 24, Griffith having agreed, Prendergast wrote, "I shall have about or between 50 or 60 water colors and colored monotypes . . . and they will be framed. Your arrangements would be extremely satisfactory to me and especially sending them to Chicago or Cleveland afterwards." July 16: "I have already directed Messrs Vickery Atkins & Torrey . . . San Francisco to send you one of the cases. . . . I shall also direct . . . the Cincinnati Museum to send a water color of the Church of St. Marks which was on exhibition there." On September 30, Prendergast wrote both to Griffith and also to Macbeth. "Dear Mr. Griffith: I am busy with the water colors and expect to get them into shape . . . (I could have started them before only for sickness in the family). . . ." (Maurice's father died in September). He asked Macbeth to send two watercolors to Griffith. On October 16 he wrote to Griffith, "Accompanying is the list of water colors. . . . Enclosed is my photograph which you have asked for and please send it back when you get through with it. . . ." On November 8, after receiving a newspaper, the *Detroit Journal* of October 26, 1901, with a reproduction of Maurice's *On the Grand Canal* (with the caption "A watercolor by Prendergast of New York"), he

47. May Day, Central Park

1901. Watercolor and pencil on paper, 13⅞ x 19¾″
The Cleveland Museum of Art. Gift of J. H. Wade

A bright, mellow sparkle of color and light pervades this park scene viewed on high from almost a Pissarro cityscape perspective. As he did in The East River *(pl. 44) and* Riva degli Schiavoni, Castello (Venice) *(pl. 33), Prendergast approached the Brueghelian with his multifigure theme.*

told Griffith, "I am delighted with the newspaper reproduction. I am so pleased I wish you would do me the great favor to send me four of the newspapers. The Harpers tried to reproduce some for their weekly and went all to pieces over it. I like your plan to have them go to Cincinnati next . . . the Museum Association wrote me some time ago stating he would like to have some work for an exhibition. . . ." November 14: "Enclosed are the prices which I have marked on the catalogue."[59] On November 18 he sent a priced list of twenty-four watercolors to J. H. Gest. On December 3 he wrote to Griffith, "I have lately received a letter from Mr. Gest Cincinnati Museum telling [me] he has room at my disposal for an exhibition. . . ." Prendergast wrote to Griffith, December 8, "I thank you very much for the use of the gallery and I hope I shall have the pleasure [of] meeting you in New York. . . . Please send back the photo. . . ."[60] On December 21 he wrote to Gest: "Enclosed is a list of the prices for the monotypes. . . . I thank you and all the artists connected with the School for your kind appreciation and Mr. Duveneck [of] whom I am a great admirer." Prendergast continued to exhibit at Vickery, writing to Macbeth on March 18, 1902, "Can you do me a favor. Will you take the *Church of St. Marks* of mine out of the frame roll it up and send it by post to Messrs. Vickery. . . . I will be in New York early next week."

Clearly, Maurice Prendergast was not an innocent or passive bystander in the practical matters of the exhibition circuit. He was in no way isolated from the give and take, the mechanics, as it were, indispensable to building a national reputation in the world of art. Correct, even courtly in many instances, he was punctilious in his relations with exhibition officials, often calling to their attention misdirected shipments or damaged frames. Unlike many of his confreres, Prendergast rarely turned down a request to enter a picture. He liked to have his work seen, and he consistently priced it to sell. Writing to A. H. Griffith of the Detroit Museum of Art in 1901, he said, "The prices on the monotypes are within the reach of anybody and I hope you will clear them out." Prices in this instance were as low as ten dollars; only a single print out of thirty-nine reached forty dollars.

In 1903, Charles joined Murphy to establish a company, Carrig-Rohane, in Winchester, Massachusetts, employing a Swedish craftsman, Walfred Thulin, to collaborate in creating frames, but he did not play an active role in the venture after its formation. The brothers continued to accept commissions from artists and collectors for their own custom-designed frames, and this work consumed a portion of Maurice's time. A 44-by-82-inch frame commissioned by the speculator-financier Thomas W. Lawson for a portrait of his prized bulldogs was decorated in the panel area with Maurice's incised and punched drawings of the bulldogs and four young girls holding them on a leash.[61] Signed by both brothers and dated 1903, the elaborate frame, surmounted by a medallion with a carved-relief Pegasus, brought enough money for the Prendergasts to move from Winchester into Boston, where they took a studio at 56 Mount Vernon Street no later than April 1903.[62]

Obliged by circumstance and accustomed by years of frugality, the brothers adopted a practical routine that allowed Maurice the maximum freedom to

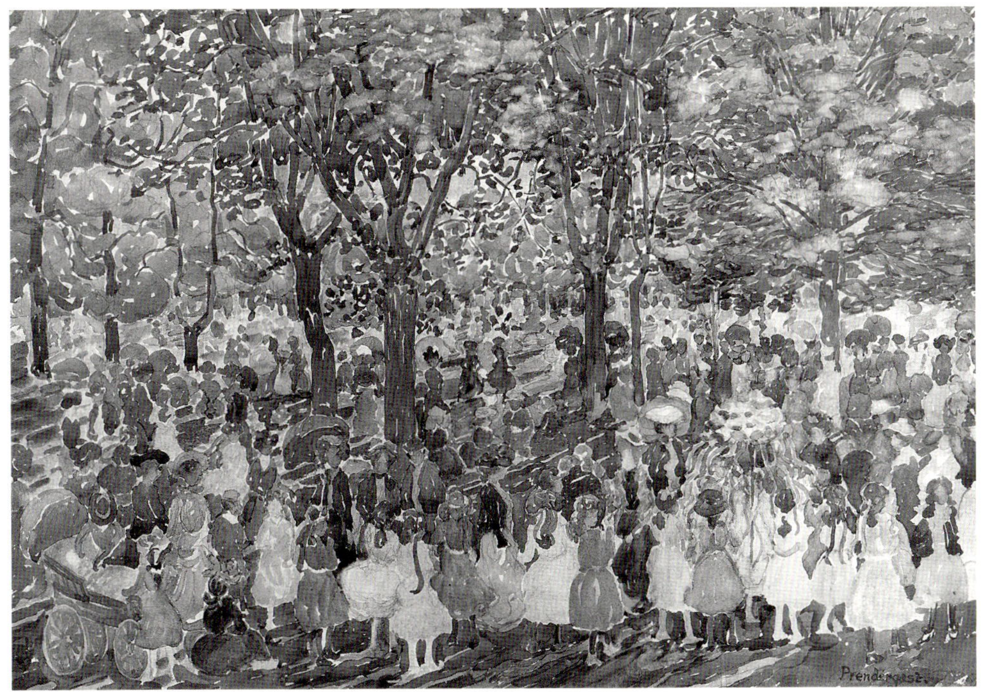

49. May Day, Central Park

c. 1902. Watercolor and pencil on paper, 14½ x 21⅝"
Collection, Whitney Museum of American Art, New York. Exchange

In this watercolor, Prendergast proposed a lacy variation on Manet's Music in the Tuileries *of 1862 (National Gallery, London).*

paint while Charles carried on the frame-making enterprise—often with Maurice's participation when a deadline for an order had to be met. It is not unusual to read in a letter to a friend or museum official that he cannot attend an opening in which one of his pictures was featured because "I am helping my brother in some work which will take seven or eight days to finish up. . . ." There was nothing haphazard in Prendergast's approach; he was focused, even intense in channeling his energies. Having been interrupted, he wrote: "I am working. My mind is virtually set to compose, to which everything else is secondary, that is, which interferes with my work."[63] He was deliberate and could not be prodded or hurried to accelerate his pace.

Time was set aside each summer for extended holidays, during which Maurice painted along the beaches and parks of New England. Favorite motifs in the immediate vicinity of Boston included Gloucester, Annisquam, Marblehead, Salem, Nahant, Revere Beach, Beachmont, Boston Harbor, Nantasket, and Cohasset. He worked farther north along the coast to Maine and in the mountains of New Hampshire, returning again and again to explore their limitless variations. The painting expeditions, which also took place in the spring and autumn, were purposeful. One year (about 1915) Maurice wrote in a sketchbook, "I am awfully absorbed in painting this summer so much that I do not like to leave it."[64] And, in a sense, he never had to, for his and Charles's life was consciously organized to preserve his one necessity, the time to devote himself to painting. These coastal expeditions in search of motifs provided the basis for the intensive work carried on in the studio throughout the winter months. There he deliberately realigned and patiently readjusted picture ideas that had long intrigued him. He aimed now to integrate the subtle color experiences of the watercolors and transfer these effects to his new experiments in oils. According to Pepper, "He was accustomed to do water-colors of scenes that caught his

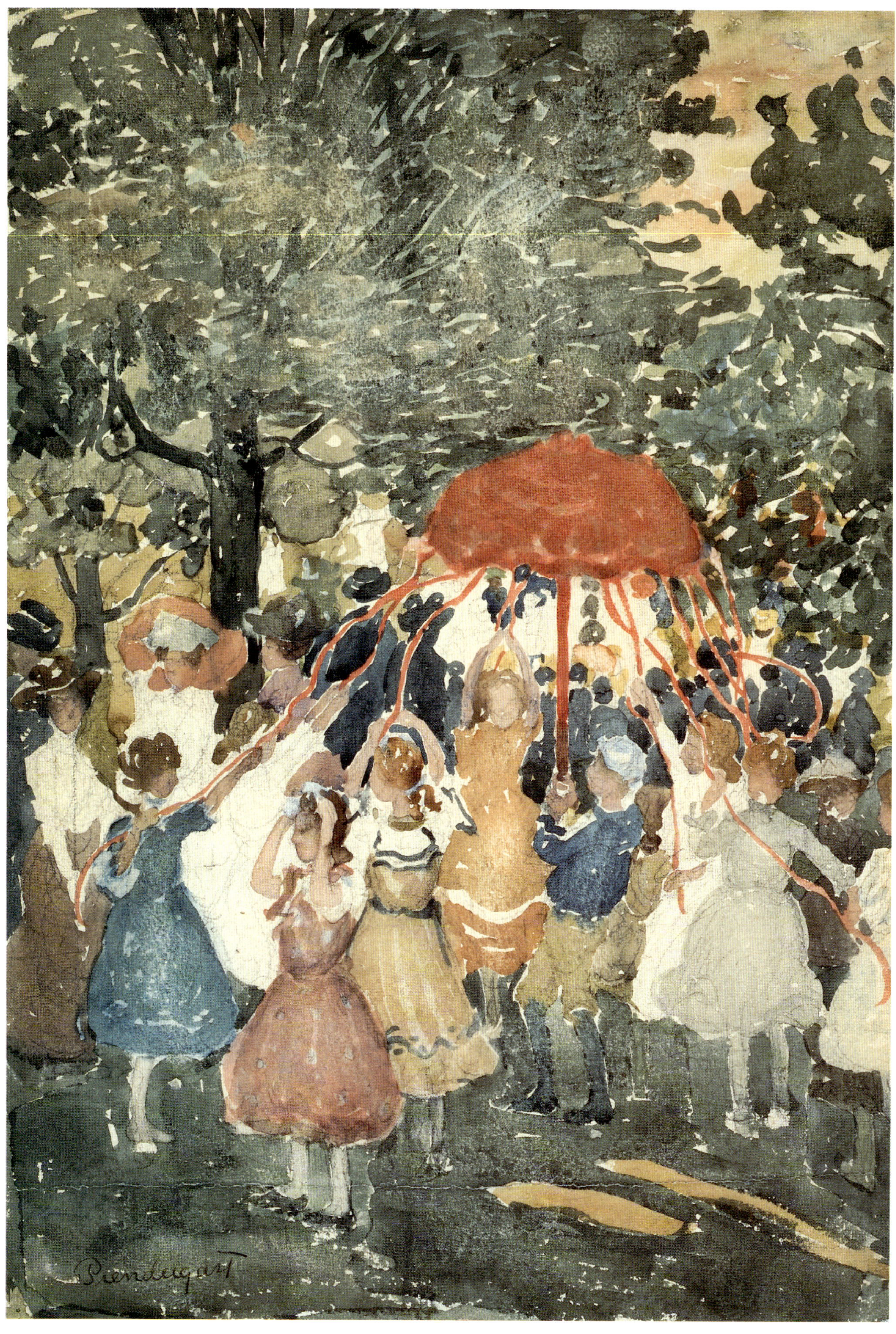

50. *Maypole*

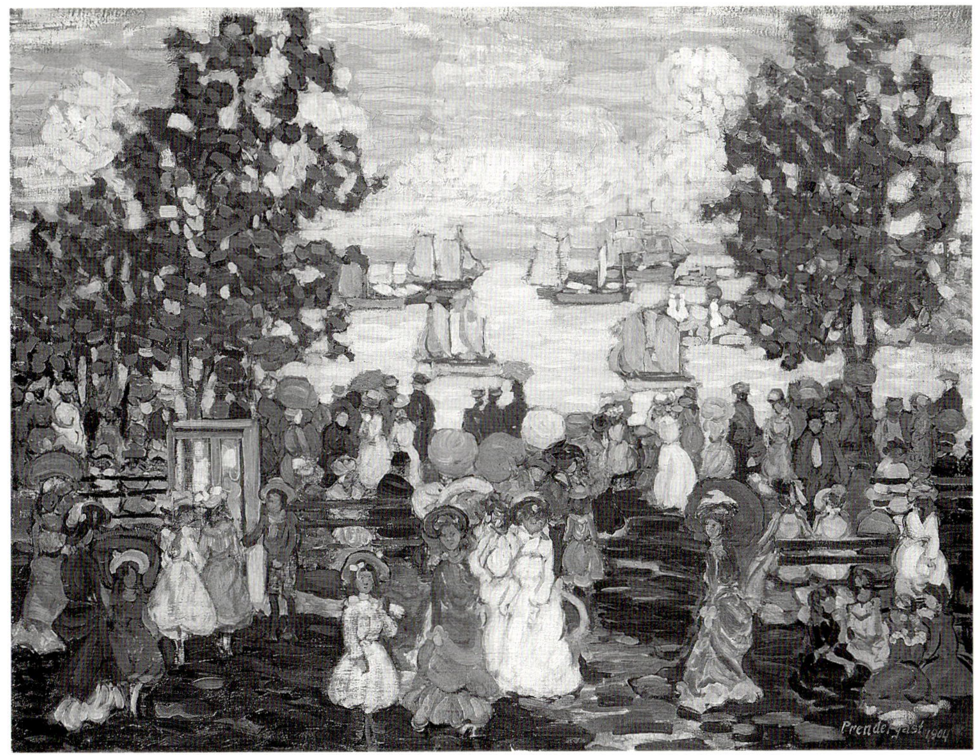

51. Salem Willows

1904. Oil on canvas, 26 x 34"
Terra Museum of American Art, Chicago.
Daniel J. Terra Collection

The color organization of this canvas lays stress on a gentle but decisive contrast within the context of an overall pale tonality—white, beige, shades of grayish green—with freely applied beige strokes in the sky, left and center, as the sky meets the water. The water around the boats is painted in pale tan-greens.

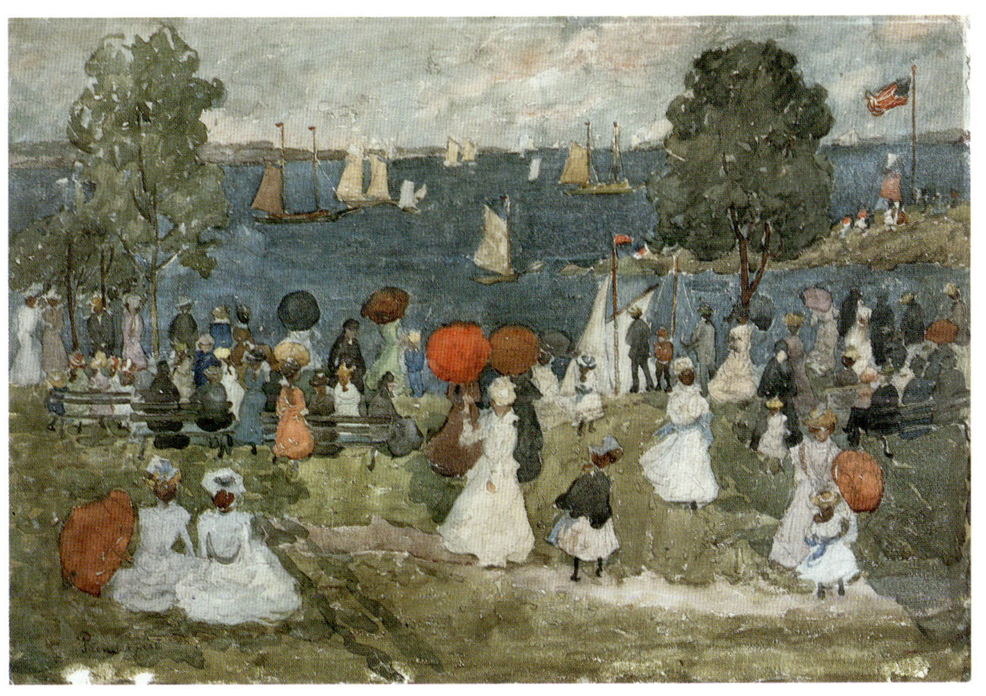

52. The Yacht Race

c. 1897/reworked c. 1900
Watercolor and pencil on paper, 14 x 20⅞"
The Art Institute of Chicago. Watson F. Blair Purchase Prize

The Yacht Race, *probably done at Salem and retouched following the artist's return from abroad, is characteristic of the subdued color scheme of the watercolors painted between 1900 and 1902. Its expansive composition served as the model for* Salem Willows *and, through that canvas, many of Prendergast's subsequent oils.*

50. Maypole

1902. Watercolor and pencil on paper, 16½ x 11¼"
Allen Memorial Art Museum, Oberlin College, Ohio. Gift of Mrs. Chauncey B. Smythe

What appears in a reproduction as abrasion across the surface, particularly in the upper section of trees and leaves, is an intentional blotting and/or rubbing, created when Prendergast adjusted the values of his color application from area to area. In the large tree, this rubbing or intentional abrading achieves a silvery effect.

fancy—rather complete little pictures in themselves—and then compose his larger canvases from these in the studio."[65] Maurice never copied the old masters in his own paintings, although countless sketches of their work, based directly on the pictures themselves as well as reproductions in books and periodicals, began to appear consistently in his sketchbooks.

Salem Willows (pl. 51 and p. 10), a 26-by-34-inch canvas dated 1904 but started in 1900 or 1901,[66] is an important culminating point of Prendergast's experimentation, containing within its composition and rich color ensemble the embryo of the artist's subsequent multifigure panoramas. Considerably reworked over a period of several years before the artist relinquished it in the fall of 1905, this signal composition extends many of the color features found in the watercolors of 1896 through 1902, recasting Prendergast's understanding of Carpaccio and early Italian frescoes, together with Impressionism, particularly that of Pissarro, and the vivid processional park scenes of Adolphe Monticelli (1824–1886). The brushstroke is already broken and woven into mosaiclike patterns, a dovetailing of light and dark, as Maurice explored a distinctly colorful space. Stressed is the muted sparkle of red and orange parasols, vivid blues, greens, and lavenders in the figures' clothes, a variegated spectrum of chalky greens, grays, and tans in the flattened trees, and the subdued pale tonalities of water, sails, and clouds. He leaned toward the decorative; although the figures are solid, the emphasis is on gentle but decisive contrast rather than on weight or power. It is the first of innumerable personal variations on the *fête galante*[67] that Prendergast developed from the lessons of the masters.

Salem Willows is based compositionally on a watercolor, *The Yacht Race* (pl. 52), c. 1897 (reworked c. 1900), closely related to *Handkerchief Point* (see pl. 19) of 1896. *The Yacht Race* shares features in common with *The East River* (see pl. 44) of 1901, especially the background and pink-gray sky, as well as with *May Day, Central Park* (see pl. 49) and *The Mall, Central Park* (see pl. 45), in the handling of the trees and the diagonal strokes in green, right and left in the foreground, retouches of the type already noted in *Maypole* (see pl. 50), 1902. Even the two flattened disks of the red and russet parasols in the center, which were transferred from *The Yacht Race* to *Salem Willows,* have been reworked. The composition has been compressed in the painting, but the primary alignment is close to the watercolor. The sequence of green benches and trees at the left, the boats themselves, the jetty on the right behind a single bifurcated tree trunk and bench—all indicate that this watercolor was preparatory to the monumental canvas. As the canvas was developed and repainted intermittently over a period perhaps as long as five years, the water changed from blue to chalky white and pale ocher, the clouds became a prominent architectonic feature of the composition, and the foreground was heightened by large, horizontal strokes in the manner of Manet. The trees are tightly constructed of smaller, subdued gray-green and beige strokes with bright blue touches.

In this work, with its frank geometric patterning and silhouettes, its deep recession into space in the center, Prendergast translated the wall-size pageantlike decorations in the churches and palaces of Italy into a format that was comfortable and accessible to him. The painting thus represents a milestone, a fusion of his perfected watercolor brilliance and fluency with the newly found complexity that the Italians had revealed to him in wall after wall, a complexity accomplished with an ease and inventiveness that virtually stopped Maurice in his tracks and turned him in a new direction—one that would occupy all of his energies for the rest of his life.

Mrs. Oliver E. Williams, who had known the Prendergast brothers since the

1890s, worked with Maurice in his studio and became a devoted friend. Maurice's letters to Esther Baldwin Williams constitute one of the most valuable sources we have about him. Although in his letters he never addressed her by her first name, he was not the slightest bit reticent or prudish in expressing himself to his fellow painter. Prendergast visited the Williamses at their summer home at Annisquam and painted there as well as at their home nearby at 92 Mount Vernon Street. Mrs. Williams had purchased a Venetian watercolor, *Riva San Biagio,* in May 1899 from the Chase Gallery, and Maurice painted her portrait around 1902.[68] On April 27, 1904, Maurice wrote from New York to Mrs. Williams, "Charley has wrote me saying how much you and Mr. Williams admire the 'Salem Willows' and would like to possess it. It is immensely encouraging for me (for you are hardly aware how much respect I have for your opinion on all art matters) that you like it enough to buy it. Of course I will make a big concession to you and Mr. Williams but I do not like to decide anything about it now as I would like to have it around me during the summer. So if you care to let the matter rest until next fall...."[69] In a sketchbook of 1905, he recorded, "received $400 from Mrs. Williams for 'The Promenade.' She expresses everything I felt when painting it.... *Getting up steam again for painting, it is a great profession.*"[70]

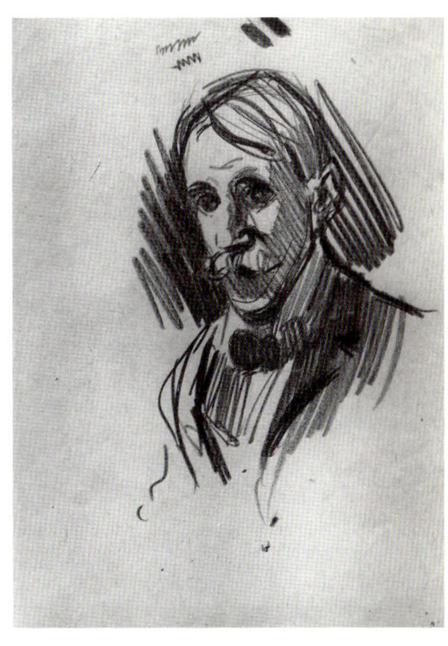

53. George Luks (1866–1933)
Maurice B. Prendergast

c. 1904. Pencil on paper, 10 x 6¾"
Courtesy, Whitney Museum of American Art, New York. Gift of Mr. and Mrs. Edward W. Root

On January 17, 1904, Maurice wrote to Macbeth to ask him to receive seven unsold paintings from an exhibition he shared with Robert Henri, Glackens, Arthur B. Davies, John Sloan, and Luks at the National Arts Club, New York: "I am sending... 7 small oil panels... for our exhibition.... I have named them 'Promenades on the Sea Shore' Nos. 1.2.3.4.5.6.7 as I have marked on the backs. As Glackens tells me you are going to have them in your galleries afterwards I wish you every success."[71] The show was reviewed by Charles DeKay, founder of the National Arts Club, three days later in the *New York Times:*

> *They furnish a very lively half-hundred of pictures in all the stages of impressionism from a full-length portrait... to a vivid little memorandum for a landscape, slapped on a canvas in thick welts of paint.... They represent the vigorous school of picture-making which tries to get the objects on the canvas before the enthusiasm that caused their selection has had time to evaporate and the red-hot impression time to cool.... [Prendergast's] spotty little pictures reveal a sense for color schemes that is very uncommon; they are like memoranda for large pictures.... Mr. Prendergast should be an ideal man for mosaics, since it is rare to find anyone with such a delicate feeling for the relations of colors and so true a sense for composition.*[72]

After the Storm (pl. 55) and *By the Seashore* (pl. 56), both c. 1901–3, are representative of the type of small panel in the show. *After the Storm* is a scene of figures by the seashore, a motif carried over from numerous watercolors and monotypes painted by Prendergast from around 1897 to the early 1900s. Instead of the compact spatial rhythms that weave figures around a maypole and recede to a midline horizon, this striking panel stacks figures over its entire surface from the horizon at the top down to the bottom in steady horizontal and diagonal bands. The almost checkerboard movement of figure groups dramat-

54. Rocks, Waves and Figures

c. 1902–4. Watercolor and pencil on paper, 10½ x 15″
The Barnes Foundation, Merion Station, Pennsylvania

This composition pertains to a group of watercolors with surf breaking on the rocky shoreline similar to the motif found in After the Storm *(pl. 55). The looser handling of the watercolor medium gradually increased as the watercolors became more closely related to the oils instead of, as earlier, to the artist's monotypes.*

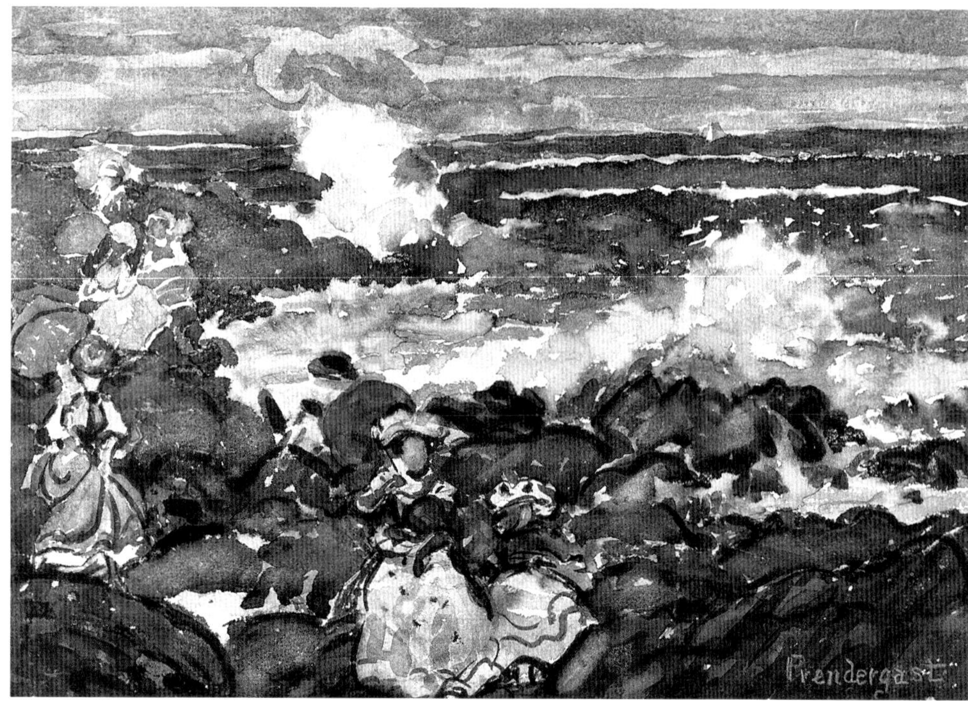

ically points to similar areas in *Salem Willows* and Prendergast's future compositional interests. The figures are painted in a direct manner resembling Manet and Morrice, the broad sketchy patchwork of brushstrokes resulting in a dynamic surface. Several strokes, especially those at the left, were laid in thinly and rapidly worked while the paint was still wet; the turpentine in the medium caused the fluid pigment to run in drips. Other figures in both the foreground and water areas are thicker in texture.

The character of this small panel has an immediacy strongly reminiscent of Prendergast's monotypes. The artist also adopted motifs that he had repeatedly employed in his watercolors, further indicating that during this period Prendergast relied on his watercolors as a point of departure for his oils. For example, the girl in tan with hat bending over in the foreground center of the composition is found in both watercolors and monotypes ranging in date from about 1897 to about 1902. Prendergast, in a sketchbook entry of April 28, 1902, noted, "Palette Manet!! ivory black, flake white, venetian red, vermilion, yellow ocher, red sienna."[73] The struggle to consolidate and transfer the color and compositional ideas from the watercolors to his painting, to the medium that was to absorb him for the rest of his life, was already apparent by April 1902, at which time FitzGerald observed, "Prendergast['s] . . . color clears up as he grows more practiced in the use of oils, maintaining the charm and brilliancy of his wonderful little water-colors."[74]

On the closing day of the show, DeKay wrote a negative article in the *New York Times:* "Luks, Prendergast and Davies appear to regard the vulgar yearning for realism in the human figure . . . with the greatest indifference. . . . None of them, unless it be Mr. Prendergast, touches the sphere of the French neo-impressionists."[75] Maurice declined an offer of fifty dollars for the panels, writ-

55. After the Storm

c. 1901–3. Oil on panel, 10⅝ x 13⅝″
Allen Memorial Art Museum, Oberlin College, Ohio. Gift of Mrs. Chauncey B. Smythe

The white froth of the waves, painted in a vigorous impasto akin to Winslow Homer's churning water, dramatically silhouettes the figures to the left of he composition and provides, as in Homer's work, a foil for the boat breasting the waves.

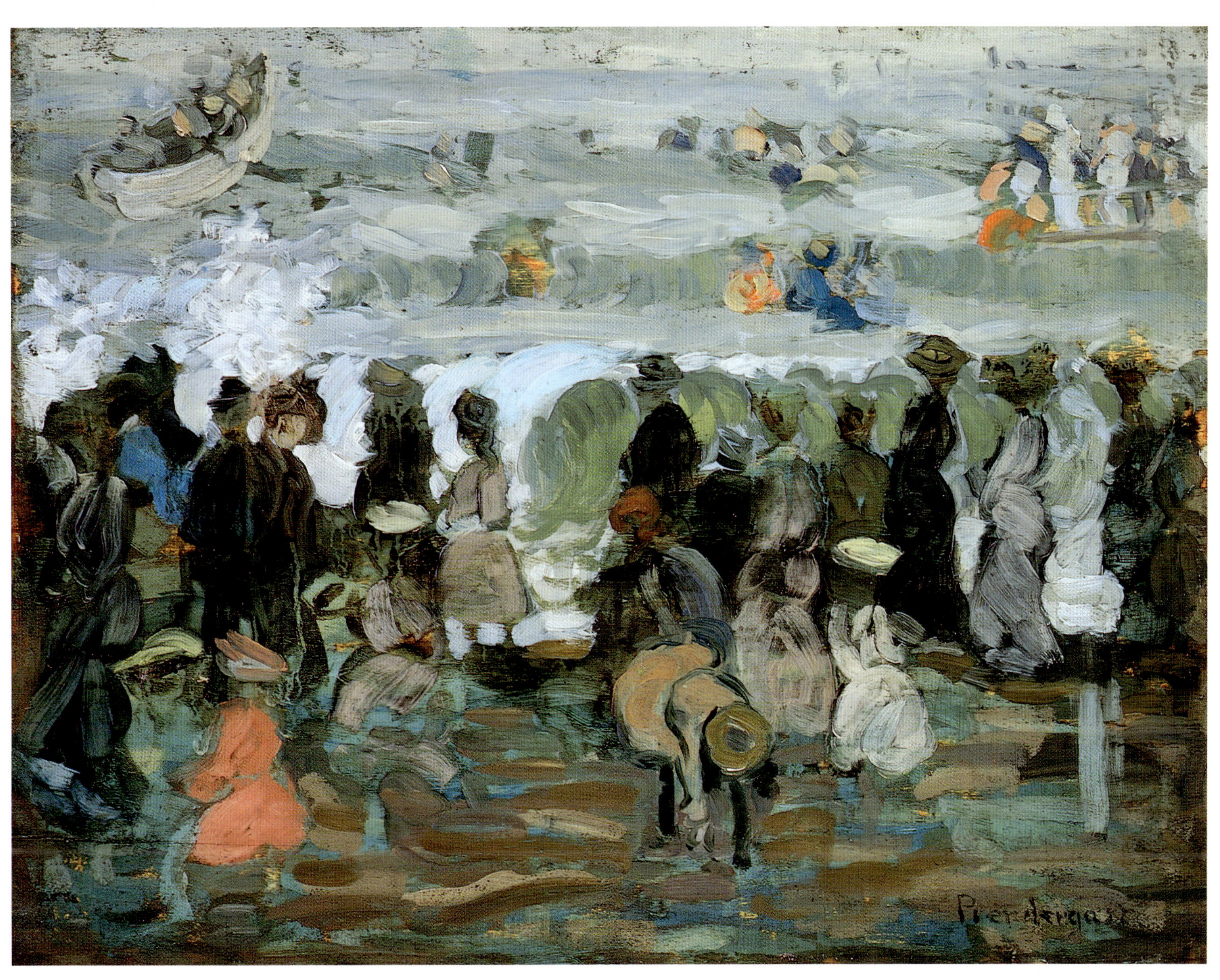

55. *After the Storm*

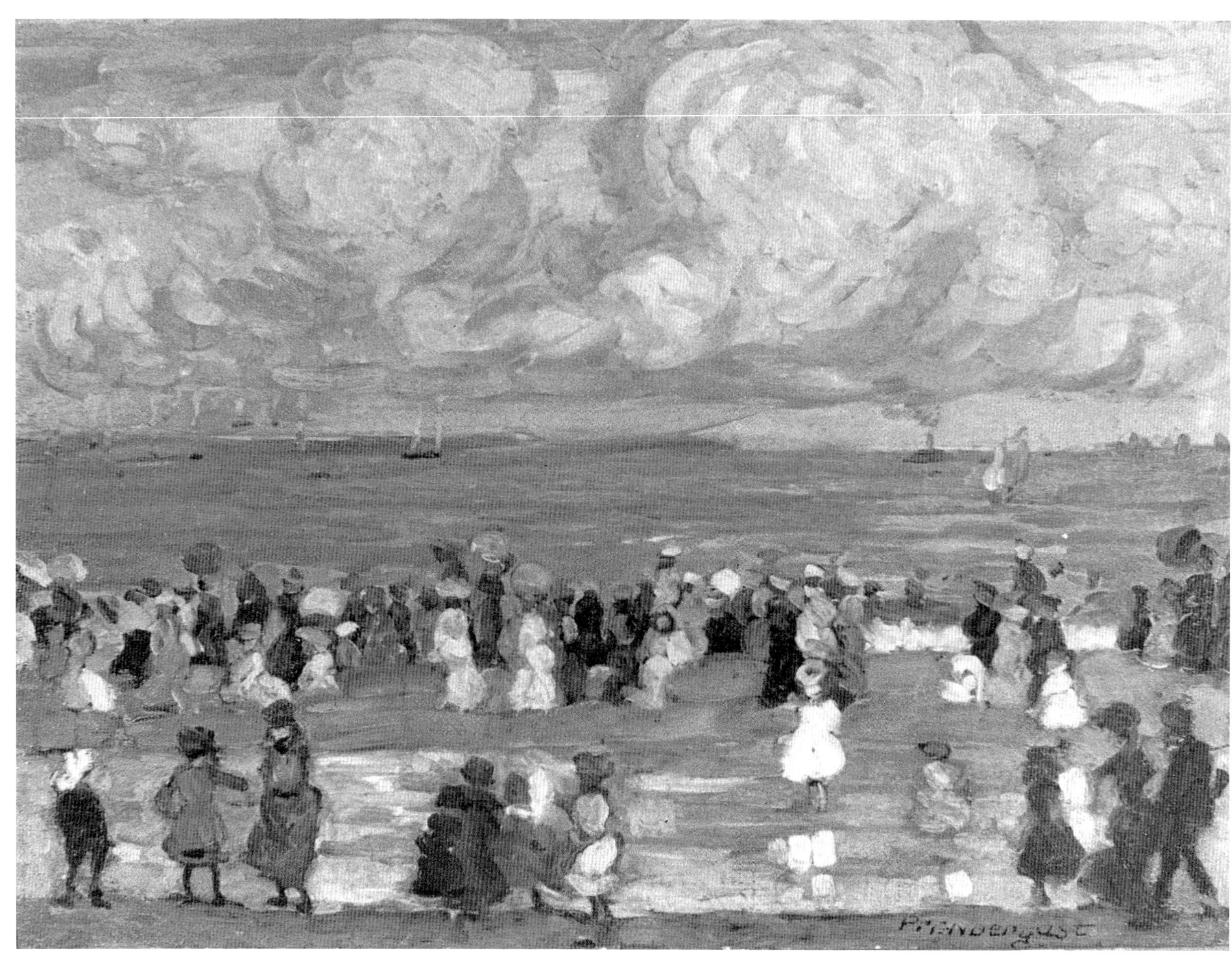

56. By the Seashore

ing to Macbeth on March 10, "Fifty dollars a piece for the panels is not encouragement enough for me and I really think I ought to get a little more for them. With all honor to Mr. [Hugh H.] Breckenridge as a friend of Mr. FitzGerald, Mr. Henri and Mr. Luks and for his *good appreciation*."[76]

Around 1902, Prendergast also explored simplified, summary, boldly drawn watercolors in a limited tonal range, in which color application became less dainty and more diffused and the dark-light contrast was stressed. In the sea drama *Rocks, Waves and Figures* (pl. 54), c. 1902–4, showing a Homer-like scene with a spume of waves breaking on the rocks, he approximated the broad strokes of the small oil panels such as *After the Storm* and monotypes such as *Summer Day* (pl. 57), c. 1901. *April Snow, Salem* (pl. 59), c. 1902, with its worn weathered surface effect and animated flourishes of linear outlines, also recalls the free brushwork of Prendergast's later monotypes. In panels such as *Rainbow* (pl. 60), c. 1905, and *Beach Scene No. 4* (pl. 58), c. 1905, Maurice reduced the dark-light contrast in favor of a brisk Impressionist/Neo-Impressionist application of color patches.

The years 1905 and 1906 saw a falling off of Maurice's productivity. His hearing problems, which were noticeable even before 1890, worsened dramatically. By 1902, he was consulting ear doctors in Boston, but with no results. By early 1905, he resolved to pursue alternate methods, joining an outdoor swimming group called the L Street Brownies, a male bathhouse, which he described in a letter of May 14 to Mrs. Williams: "I was so bothered about my ears, the doctors and one thing and another. . . . I am painting every day but two hours and a half are [given] to the open air cure. . . . Whether it be a cure or not remains to be seen." He declined to exhibit at the Carnegie Institute, writing the director, John W. Beatty, on September 12, 1905, "Regret I have nothing completed in time for Pittsburg exhibition this year." The problems were not ameliorated by this cure, and Maurice reiterated his preoccupation in a letter he wrote to Mrs. Williams on November 10 to thank her for the four hundred dollars for *Salem Willows*: "I still keep up the swimming and some of the mornings I find the water very cold but I am getting inured. I have not got back my hearing yet but I am getting used to it like Sir Joshua Reynolds with his ear trumpet."

Other complaints interrupt his work: on November 5 he confided to Mrs. Williams, "I started to paint [in children's heads]. Two hours sketching every morning with an artist friend. Was getting along fine when I strained my eyes. Had to give up painting for the rest of the summer and fall. I should like to take it up again this winter. . . ."

On November 16, 1905, Prendergast recorded in a sketchbook, "You must make yourself a strong man. You are on the threshold as an artist. Be firm and determined."[77] By January 1906, he wrote in the same notebook, "A beautiful warm day, almost summery. Don't work enough . . . doing no work." He wrote to Macbeth on January 21, 1906, "Give my regards to Mr. Davies. Tell him I am in splendid condition but, alas! have [not] recovered my hearing as yet." In his sketchbook: "Had my first swim on the 28th of March. The temperature of the water was 38 and the temperature of the day 32 fahrenheit. Doing no work." On

56. By the Seashore

c. 1901–3. Oil on panel, 11¾ x 16″
The Mitchell Museum, Mount Vernon, Illinois. Gift of John R. and Eleanor R. Mitchell

This work and After the Storm *(pl. 55) typify the horizontal layered composition that Prendergast would repeat with progressively intensified color in his numerous small beach scenes from about 1904 through about 1908 or 1909.*

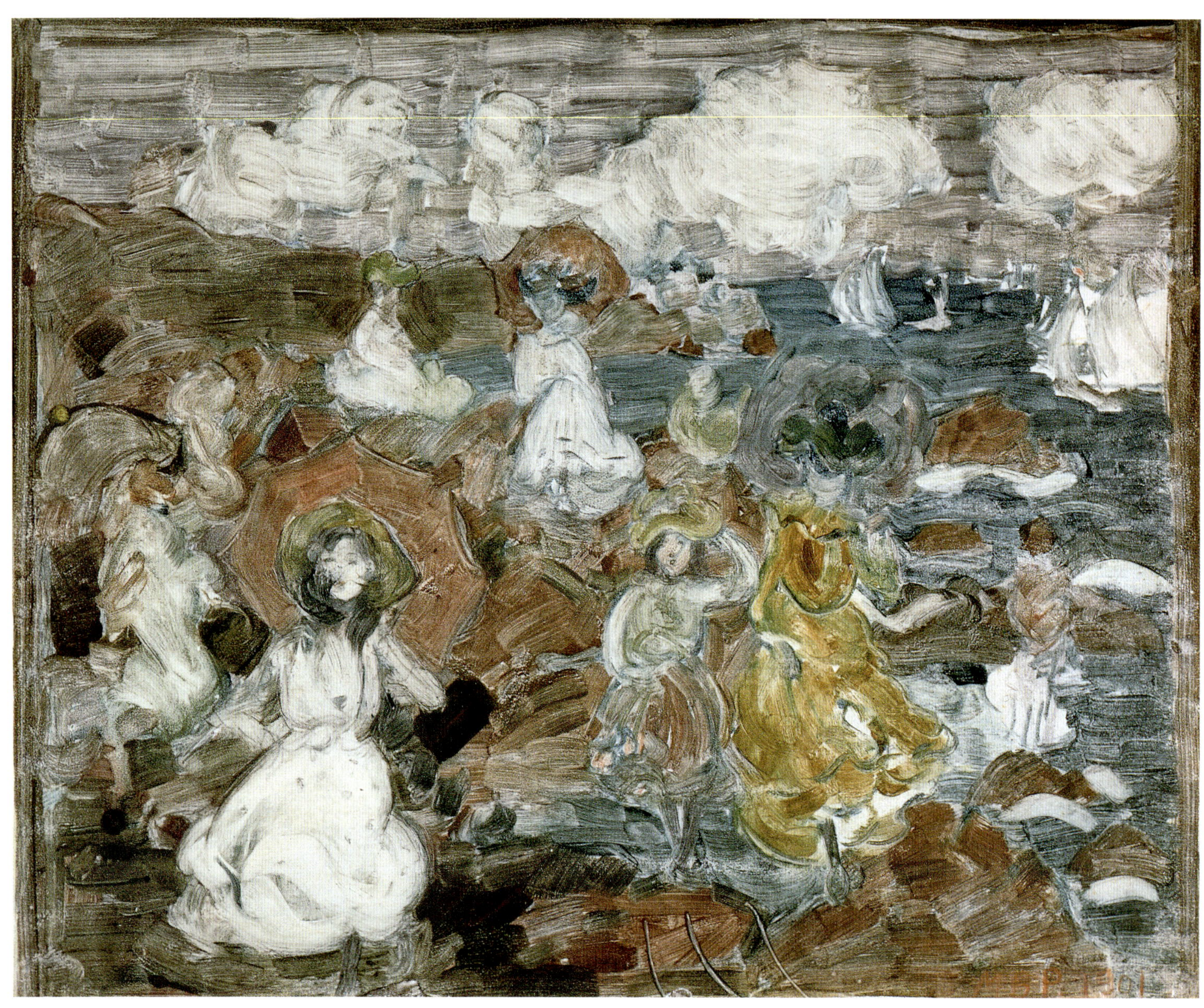

57. *Summer Day*

c. 1900–1902. Monotype on paper
with pencil additions, 11¼ x 13¾"
Terra Museum of American Art, Chicago.
Daniel J. Terra Collection

The broadly brushed spontaneity of the late monotypes led Prendergast into the more complex structure of oil painting.

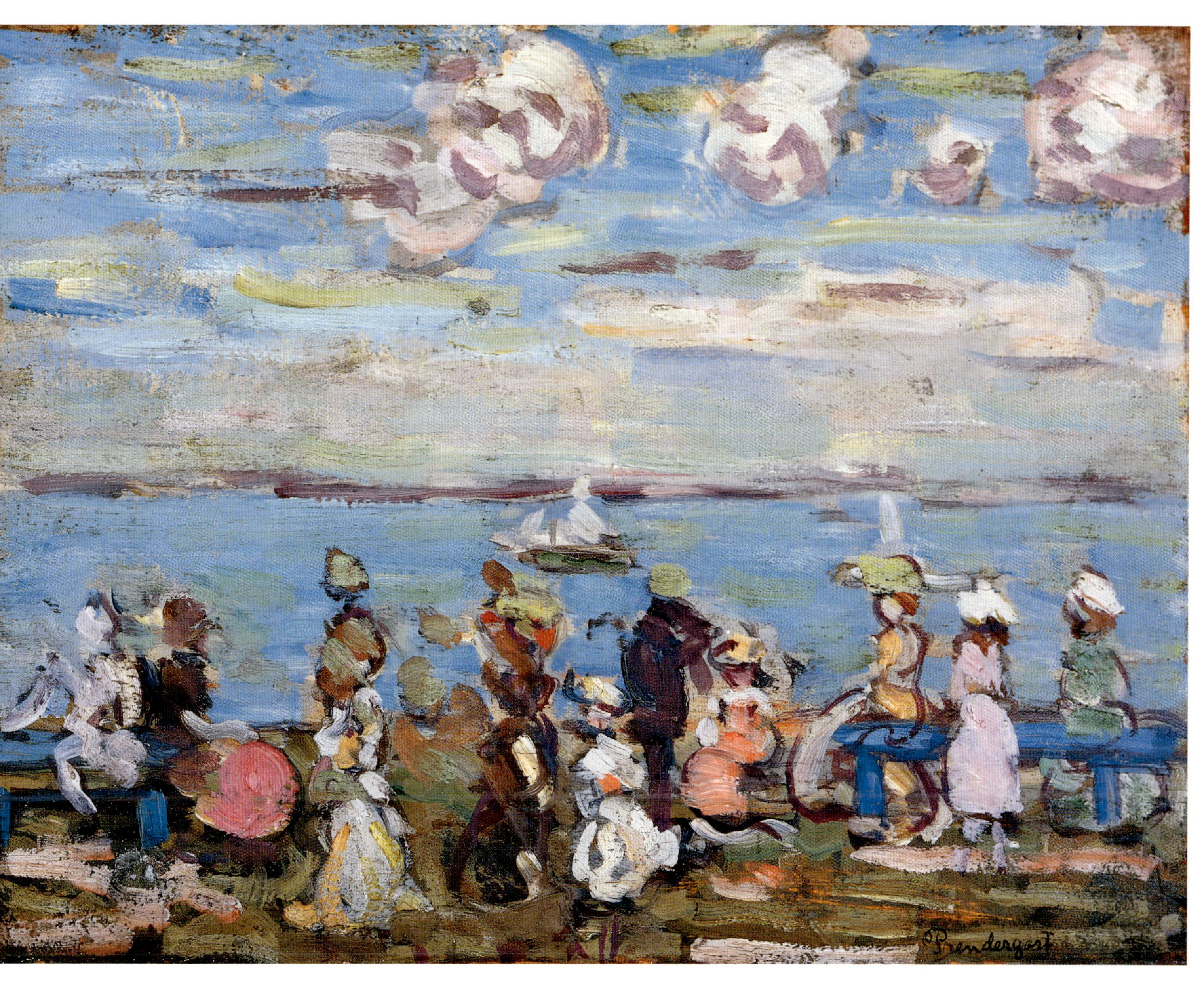

58. Beach Scene No. 4

c. 1905. Oil on panel, 10 3/8 x 13 5/8″
Williams College Museum of Art.
Gift of Mrs. Charles Prendergast

This is one of a small group of panels, painted prior to Maurice's 1907 trip to France, in which small strokes of bright color are pervasive.

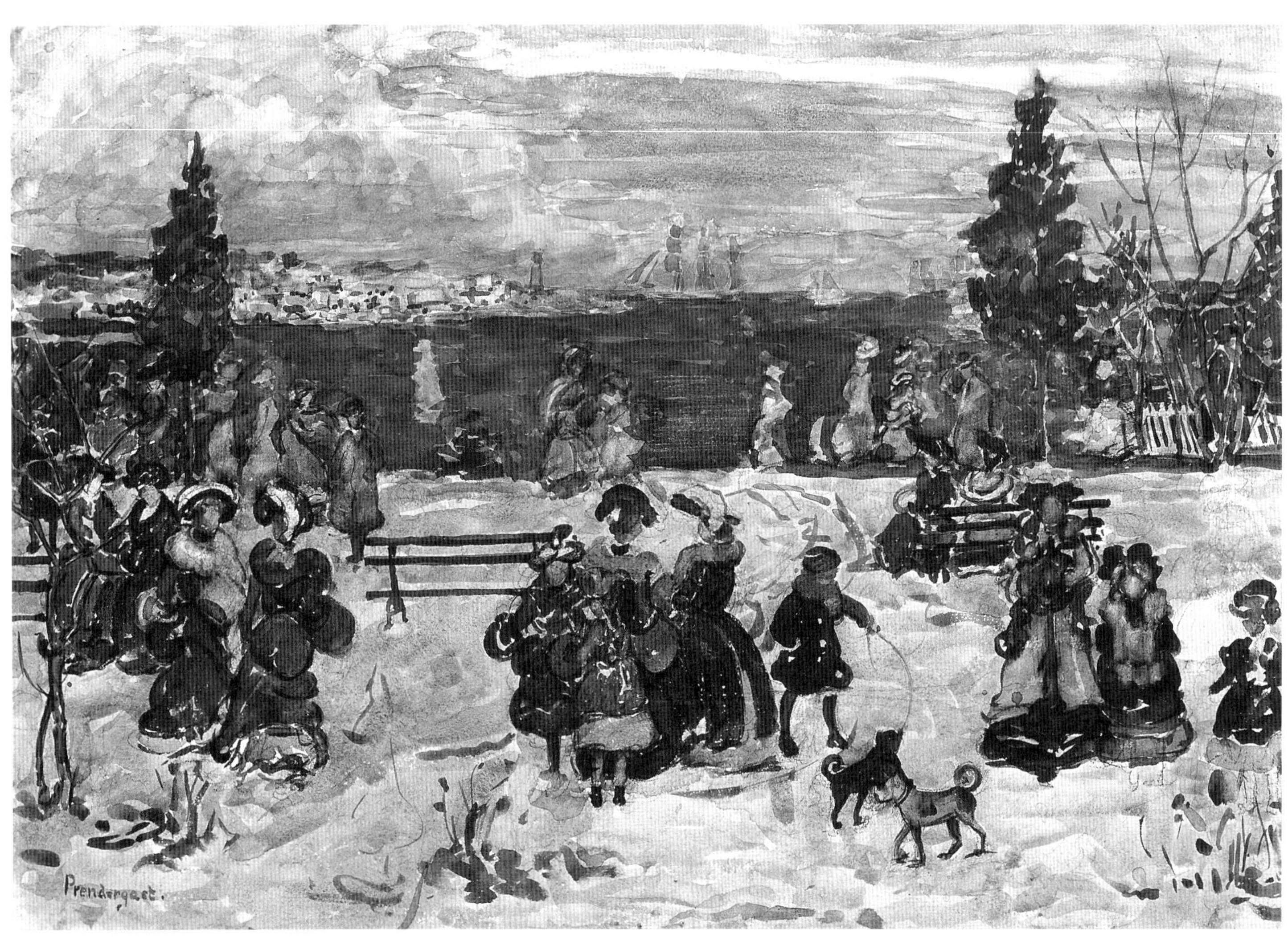

59. April Snow, Salem

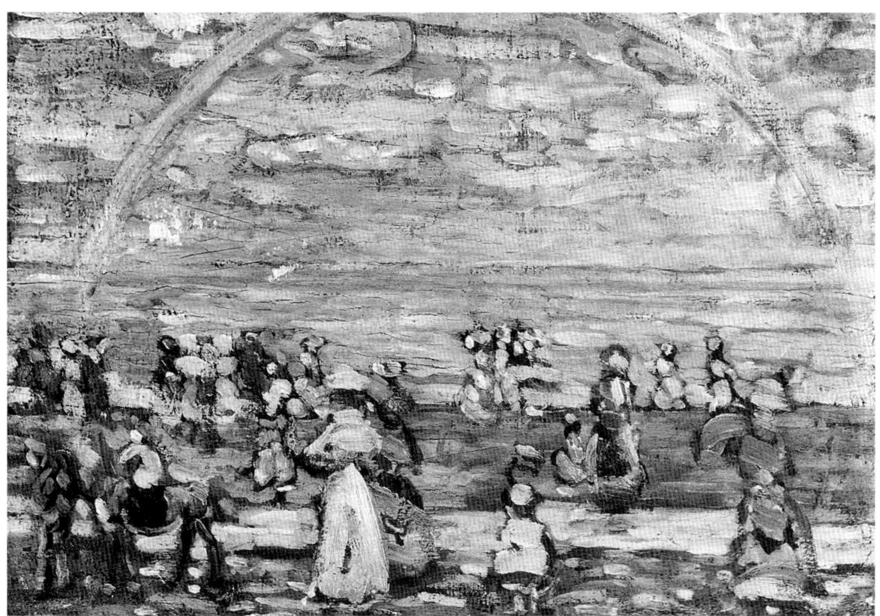

60. Rainbow

c. 1905. Oil on panel, 10¾ x 15"
Private collection

This oil panel, bearing a frame signed and dated "Prendergast 1905," is one of a group of small beachside compositions painted subsequent to the completion in 1904 of Salem Willows *(pl. 51). Its bright color and staccato paint applications demonstrate that Maurice had moved beyond a color scheme primarily based on Manet before he visited Paris and Saint-Malo in the summer and fall of 1907.*

May 19, he jotted down, "Accustom yourself to master things which you seem to despair of"—advice he had already written some eight years earlier. He inscribed below this exhortation, "Doing no work and it causes me a lot of bother. Time flies and . . ." Although he exhibited in 1905, 1906, and the first half of 1907, his response to an invitation from E. D. Trask, secretary, to exhibit at the Pennsylvania Academy of the Fine Arts annual watercolor exhibition in 1906 sums up his predicament: "I am deeply sensible of your kind offer to send a group of water colors to the exhibition. Unfortunately, I will not be able to take advantage of it as I have not done any to speak of during the last year. The two which I have done I am sending to the [Boston] Art Club if I knock them into shape owing to a previous invitation."

We shall never know what, if anything, in addition to his health problems, was troubling Maurice. He was nearing fifty and his was a life devoted to his art. The solitary concentration that it demanded required a kind of constancy that was bound to falter from time to time. Maurice was bent on a program of self-improvement that would serve to fortify his resolve to paint. The sketchbooks contain lists of authors—Blake, Byron, Dostoyevski, Emerson, Goethe, Heine, Ibsen, Machiavelli, Pater, Rabelais, La Rochefoucauld, Stendhal, Swift, Whitman, Wilde. He read philosophers—Schopenhauer, William James ("The Powers of Men," 1907), and, above all, Nietzsche—as well as novelists, playwrights, and essayists as diverse as Tolstoy, a personal favorite, Strindberg, Gerhart Hauptmann, Havelock Ellis, and John Muir. He copied passages, often inspirational in tone, particularly in the years between 1899 and about 1910. He also read biographies of artists, memoirs such as *Reminiscences of the South Seas* by John LaFarge, scholarly articles in specialized art journals, van Gogh's letters, and such works in French as *Greco ou le secret de Tolède* by Maurice Barrès. All of these merely hint at the intellectual curiosity of a creative personality determined to acquire knowledge and reason things out for himself.

59. April Snow, Salem

c. 1902. Watercolor, pencil, and colored pencil on paper, 15¼ x 22⅛"
Collection, The Museum of Modern Art, New York. Gift of Abby Aldrich Rockefeller

Traditionally dated about 1905–7, this winter motif has more in common compositionally, especially in the sky-cloud area, with The Yacht Race *(pl. 52) and* Salem Willows *(pl. 51). It resembles such monotypes as* Lighthouse, *c. 1900–1902 (Daniel J. Terra Collection, CR 1762).*

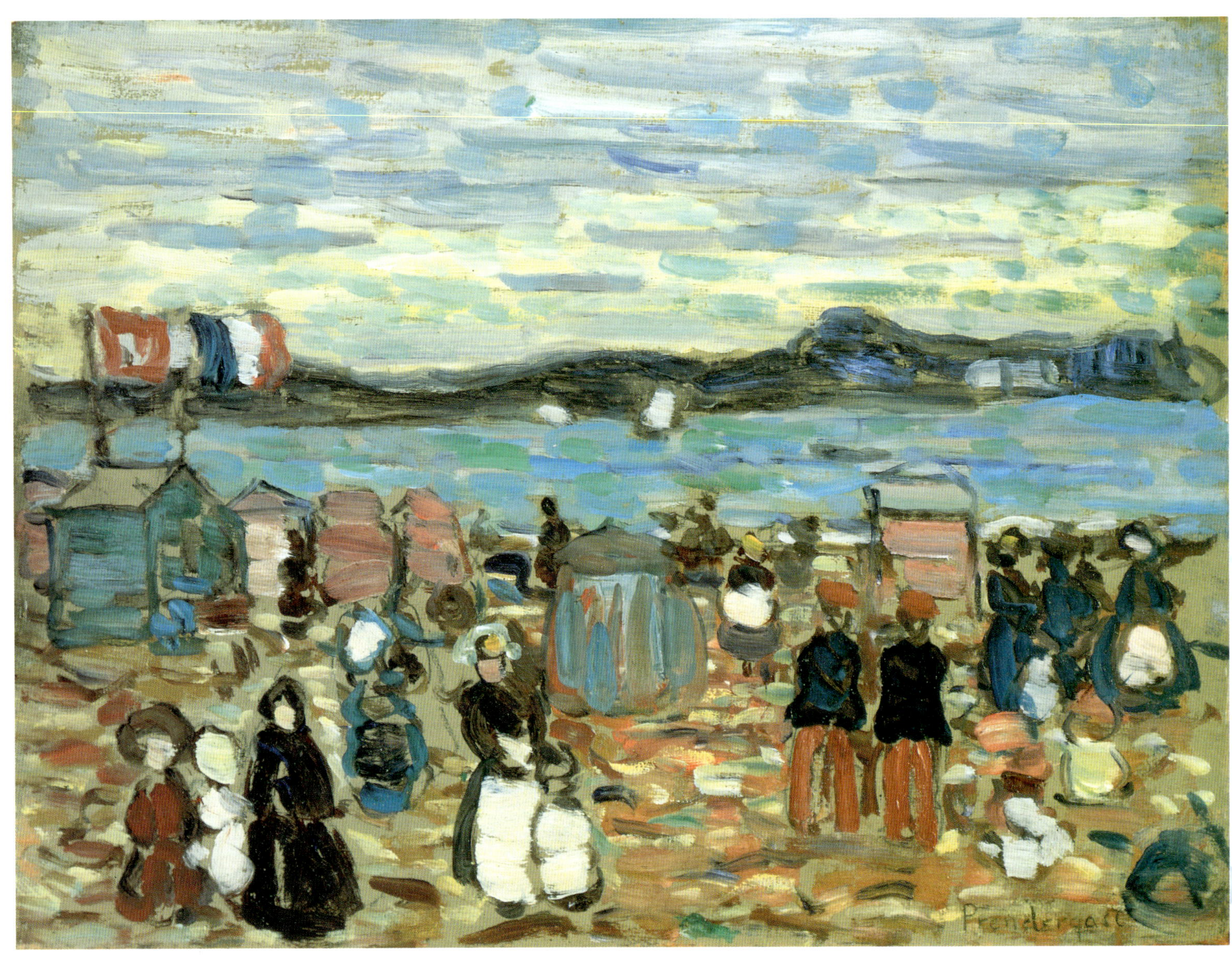

61. Bathing Tents, St. Malo

VII. France 1907

By early 1907, his health having improved enough for a canoe trip in April, Maurice decided after a thirteen-year absence to travel to France. Had he been stung by critics who had implied that he was in a rut? "[Prendergast] is doing exactly the same kind of things with which he began a few years ago. He should widen his range, lest his style harden."[78] Maurice made arrangements to depart in mid-May. Perhaps he thought the trip abroad would be good for his morale. In any case, he wanted to paint at Saint-Malo and be in Paris to speak French once again, visit the museums, sit in the cafés, and rekindle his creative energies.

Just before his departure, the newspapers announced the organization of "a group of eight painters who have been . . . referred to often as 'the apostles of ugliness' . . . have formed themselves into a body, it was announced last evening, without leader, president or formal organization of any kind. . . . The eight will give their first exhibition next winter, perhaps in February, at the galleries of William Macbeth. . . ."[79] No friend of the genteel tradition, Prendergast admired the Realists with whom he had exhibited four years earlier at the National Arts Club. As he had written on April 27, 1904, to Mrs. Williams: "New York is gayer than ever. The centre of the society exhibition is Sargent's The Three Miss Hunters. . . . One can cut it all to pieces but it is still tremendously clever. Luks had a portrait that created quite a stir when it was before the jury. It was a full length portrait of a teamster. All the jury laughed when it came before them. One of them, a man named [Bryson] Burroughs, stood up and said you can well laugh for it is a sad laugh for I think that [it] has more artistic qualities than the Sargent which you are all howling over. They passed a vote but it was chucked." Invited by Arthur B. Davies to participate, Maurice was in sympathy with the group's aims and fully entered into the spirit of the Eight project.

Prendergast arrived on May 28 in Le Havre after a lively crossing. His spirits and health revived, he concluded his daily shipboard record of the trip by assuring Charles, "All the way across I have had a splendid appetite and have enjoyed first class health and I am full of the fighting fit" (see p. 13). Around May 31, he wrote to Charles:

> *I have at last arrived in Paris. . . . I shall probably stay around Paris until the season opens at St. Malo about the end of June. . . . I have just seen the Champ de Mars exhibition and it was worth travelling 100,000 miles to see and to spend all [the] money one could afford. When I landed at Havre I got quite homesick and regretted coming over but once at the Champ de Mars [it] made me feel like an artist once again. One thing [that] made a great impression on me were the beautiful colors*

61. Bathing Tents, St. Malo

1907. Oil and pencil on panel, 10½ x 13¾"
Allen Memorial Art Museum, Oberlin College, Ohio. Gift of Mrs. Chauncey B. Smythe

Painted on a panel with tan ground on which rough preliminary pencil sketching is clearly visible, Bathing Tents, St. Malo *has a color glow and saturation heretofore found only in a lighter vein in the artist's watercolors. While the other compositional essentials of beach, water, and horizon line correspond to those of* Beach at St. Malo *(pl. 66), Prendergast simplified the patterning of the sky, shifting attention to the weightier figures, dispersed the cabanas, and employed bolder tricolor flags.*

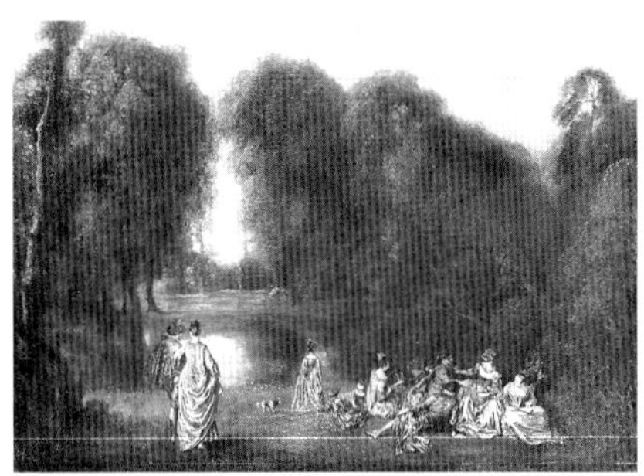

62. Antoine Watteau (1684–1721)
Gathering in a Park

c. 1716–17. Oil on canvas, 12⅝ x 18⅛"
The Louvre, Paris

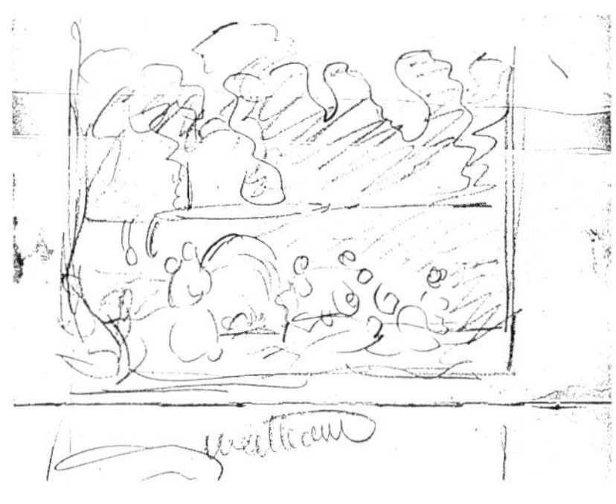

63. Sketch after Watteau's
Gathering in a Park

1907. Pencil on paper, 6½ x 4⅜"
Courtesy, Museum of Fine Arts, Boston.
Gift of Mrs. Charles Prendergast in honor of Perry T. Rathbone, 1972, "Sketchbook #38" (CR 1486)

which they got and in wonderful taste, all have that, whatever color they are. There is a beautiful quality of grey in them. And I tell you I was kept busy between looking at the frames and the pictures. I got in at eight in the morning and I happened to look at my watch and it was four o'clock in the afternoon. I forgot [hunger], I forgot I was in Paris, I was so absorbed. Of course there is a lot of rot and so many and many charming and delightful, so much, so much in my own temperament. I never got such a shake-up and it made me feel glad I have that quality. And there are so many others [it] made Paris feel so homelike. It is the real home of the artists. There is no thinking of yourself like alas—Boston.

Morrice has 5 delightful things all hung together. He has that Whistler quality but his color is more luminous and he is all right with his frames too. . . .

You have no idea what a novelty it is for me to see all those stunning little artistic things on exhibition.

You ought to see the Luxembourg Garden now, it is in full swing—the Band playing and the children romping about and women talking, sewing and embroidering. I see pictures in every direction, and I am dam[n] glad I did [not] stay at Havre. It would pay any artist just to come over for a couple weeks and look around. . . .

I have not seen anyone yet but I suppose I will [be] running across someone sooner or later.

He wrote again to Charles on June 13: "To day . . . I thought I['d] run out and have a look at Versailles. This morning was magnificent and everyone was pouring pell mell for the country. . . . My time is so short and every day counts. . . . I have seen the Champ de Mars. It gave me the impression I was working all right. Morrice's things are sloughy in their execution but he gets fine color and compositions something like my color prints. He is much talked about. The exhibitions are the great things here. They are wonderfully interesting. I learn more from them than anything." A few days later Maurice visited the show of seventy-nine Cézanne watercolors held at the Bernheim-Jeune gallery from June 16 through 29. In a letter written in Paris but mailed from Saint-Malo, Maurice wrote to Charles, "I have started in to work doing both watercolors and oils but the weather has been awful. . . . I see Morrice about every other night. . . ." He saw the Chardin–Fragonard exhibition at the Georges Petit gallery and copied Watteau's *Gathering in a Park* (pls. 62 and 63) in the Louvre, reinforcing an interest in eighteenth-century French painting already noted by critics of Prendergast's work at the turn of the century.[80]

He spent the summer working at Saint-Malo, where, despite foul weather, he painted thirty-five oils on panel and canvas, most of these small studies, some based on watercolors and pencil sketches of the same motifs. Some were done on the spot and others probably in his studio after his return home. He also painted a series of about a dozen oil panels of figures in the Luxembourg and Tuileries gardens when he returned from the coast at the end of September. More than sixty watercolors of the same subjects were carried out during the five-month stay. He remained long enough to visit the Salon d'Automne, which opened on October 1 and included fifty-six paintings by Cézanne. He sketched Matisse's *Le Luxe I* (pls. 64 and 65) as well as frames on the Cézannes. His rapturous letter to Mrs. Williams of October 10 sums up his experiences.

You will be disappointed when I tell you I never went to Dinan after all. I was so busy at St. Malo and when the time arrived late in September I concluded to go up. I found the boats had stopped for the season so that settled it. During July and August the season was very brilliant. During September it did not interest me quite so well so I bid good bye to St. Malo with its high tides and ramparts and fled to Paris. . . . I have been extremely fortunate in regard to the exhibitions, not only in the Spring with the Salons, but Chardins, Fragonard etc. and the delightful fall exhibitions which last during the month of October. They [all have] Paul Cézannes, Berthe Morisots and Eva Gonzales. Cézanne gets the most wonderful color, a dusty kind of a grey and he had a water color exhibition late in the Spring which was to me perfectly marvelous. He left everything to the imagination. They were great for their simplicity and suggestive qualities.

I am delighted with the younger Bohemian crowd. They outrage even the Byzantine and our North American Indians with their brilliant colors would not be in the same class with them. Vallotton, Félix is one of the younger men and Vuillard paints on cardboard which by the way seems to be popular among them. Vuillard is a rare exception, he paints interiors, quaint and old fashioned, with the most delightful greys. All those exhibitions worked me up so much that I had to run up and down the Boulevards to work off steam.

Then there is another crowd here, the independents, who Paul Adam says paints for notoriety. Can you imagine a picture which is called Maternity, the mother surrounded by her children, an interior. The Mother has a brick red face and arms, with a Prussian blue dress, the baby has a vermillion face with a green dress and the other children in ratio. The furniture is indian red, the whole backed with a cadmium yellow wall. The faces are outlined in black eye brows, black shadows etc. The effect is startling but there is something I like about them. I wish we had some [of] it in Boston or New York. Our exhibitions are so monotonous.

I intend starting for home on the 26th. Then, good bye Paris, it is the same fascinating Paris.

I have not done anything important, that is, anything large—mostly all sketches. But I got what I came over for, a new impulse. I was somewhat bewildered when I first got over here, but I think Cézanne will influence me more than the others. I think so now.

Cézanne died about six months ago and they had some photographs taken of some decorations on his studio walls somewhere in the country and they were done under Chinese influence. One can easily detect it and it came to me quite as a surprise.

When I was in New York Mrs. Kasebier took several [photographs] of me. . . . She had photos taken of all of us whom they call the Red Hots.

I am so chocked full of the exhibitions here I don't know what influence it will have after I am once more home.

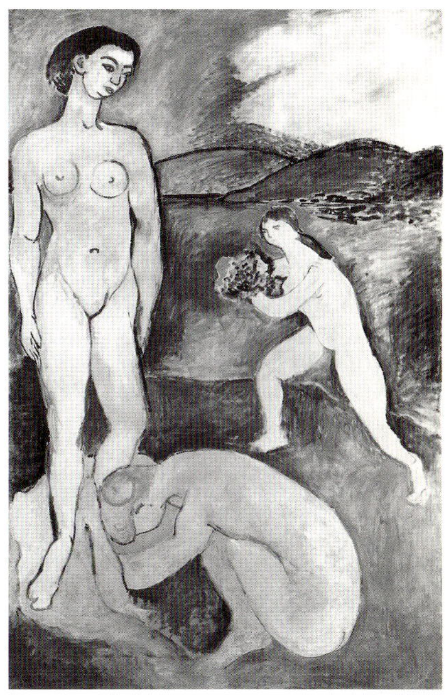

64. Henri Matisse (1869–1954)
Le Luxe I

1907. Oil on canvas, 82¾ x 54½″
Musée National d'Art Moderne, Centre Georges Pompidou, Paris

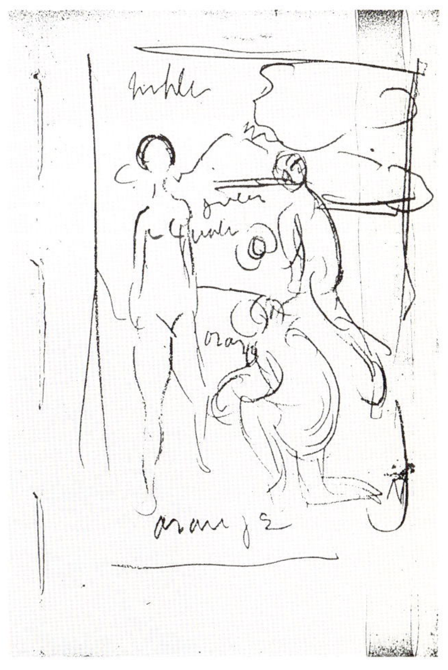

65. Sketch after Matisse's
Le Luxe I

1907. Pencil on paper, 6½ x 4⅜″
Courtesy, Museum of Fine Arts, Boston.
Gift of Mrs. Charles Prendergast in honor of Perry T. Rathbone, 1972, "Sketchbook #38" (CR 1486)

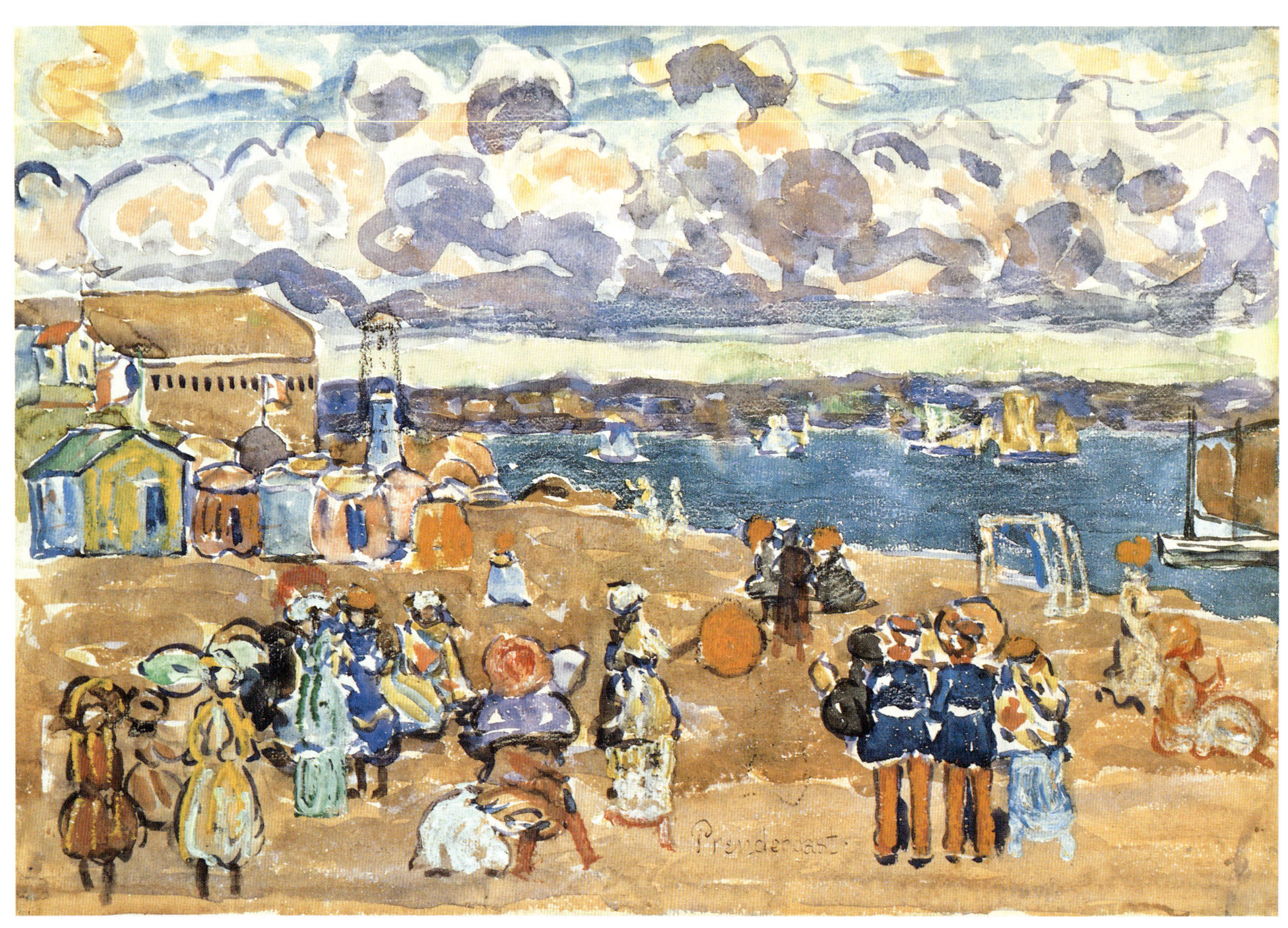

66. Beach at St. Malo

In addition to the more than one hundred pictures and a storehouse of impressions, Maurice brought home his own forty-six-page, handwritten translation of Emile Bernard's article "Paul Cézanne," published in *L'Occident* in 1904.[81]

Cézanne's watercolors and paintings, the bright Neo-Impressionist and Fauve works Prendergast saw in Paris, along with the many other old and new masters, were but a verification of the direction in which he was already headed. After he had seen the Champ de Mars Salon, but before the Cézanne watercolor show opened, he wrote to Charles, "it [the Salon] gave me the impression I was working all right." What he had found when he got to Paris was that other artists were thinking along lines he was already pursuing, and this contact, immersion one might term it, reinforced rather than caused his orientation. His conception of painting matured as a result of his fusing the Paris experience of 1891–94 and Italy in 1898–99 with his own ideas and receptive outlook. What Prendergast perceived in 1907 in Cézanne's work, both the watercolors and oils, was that pictures could be made of color, without concessions to academic tricks of the sort he had spent more than fifteen years successfully avoiding in the genteel art societies of Boston and New York. It was his own method and independence that he saw reflected, and for all his appreciation of the French artist's achievement, which he grasped immediately, Maurice's work never assumed the appearance of a Cézanne acolyte.

Bathing Tents, St. Malo (pl. 61), painted during Prendergast's visit to Saint-Malo in the summer of 1907, continues the direction indicated by *Salem Willows* (see pl. 51) and reveals the transformation that had taken place since the painting of *After the Storm* (see pl. 55). The echoes of Homer and Whistler's pale simplifications are gone. The bolder brushwork of Manet and Morrice is further modified into a vigorous set of color chords. Although the traces of Manet and Morrice are still present—indeed, Maurice painted at least six 6-by-9-inch *pochades* at Saint-Malo that summer—he absorbed their brushwork into a brilliant array of colors—a vivid Morse code of red, green, blue, and white dots and dashes. Prendergast used the warm, yellow-ivory off-white of the ground to harmonize the contrasts of his spontaneous brushstrokes of strong colors in a manner analogous to the use of white areas in the watercolors, which help create space around figures and heighten the drama of the watercolor strokes. Indeed, a watercolor extensively touched up with oil and pastel, *Beach at St. Malo* (pl. 66), was derived from the same motif. The two uniformed soldiers standing on the beach at the right, each in red cap, deep blue coat, and trousers heightened with orange paint, indicate Prendergast's freedom in reorganizing stock figures, much as he adjusted and redeployed the bending girl in *After the Storm.* The use of stock figures permitted Maurice to concentrate on the distinctly different color harmonies each picture contains—which was, after all, his main objective.

In *Seascape (St. Malo)* (see pl. 73), 1907, compositionally divided into four distinct quadrants, the foreground figures become a dense screen instead of the directly painted figures found in *Bathing Tents.* The right upper quadrant is strongly reminiscent of Seurat's small seascape *pochades.*

Larger-format watercolors such as *Le Port, St. Malo, Brittany* (pl. 67) reveal

66. Beach at St. Malo

1907. Watercolor, oil, crayon, and pastel on paper, 13½ x 19⅝"
Hirshhorn Museum and Sculpture Garden, Smithsonian Institution, Washington, D.C.
Gift of the Joseph H. Hirshhorn Foundation, 1966

The fact that this watercolor is touched up with oils, crayon, and pastel indicates the extent to which Maurice had shifted his emphasis toward painting. This sheet is actually larger than the corresponding oil panel, Bathing Tents, St. Malo *(pl. 61), and is rendered equally vivid by the conspicuous heightening of its forthright color in several mediums.*

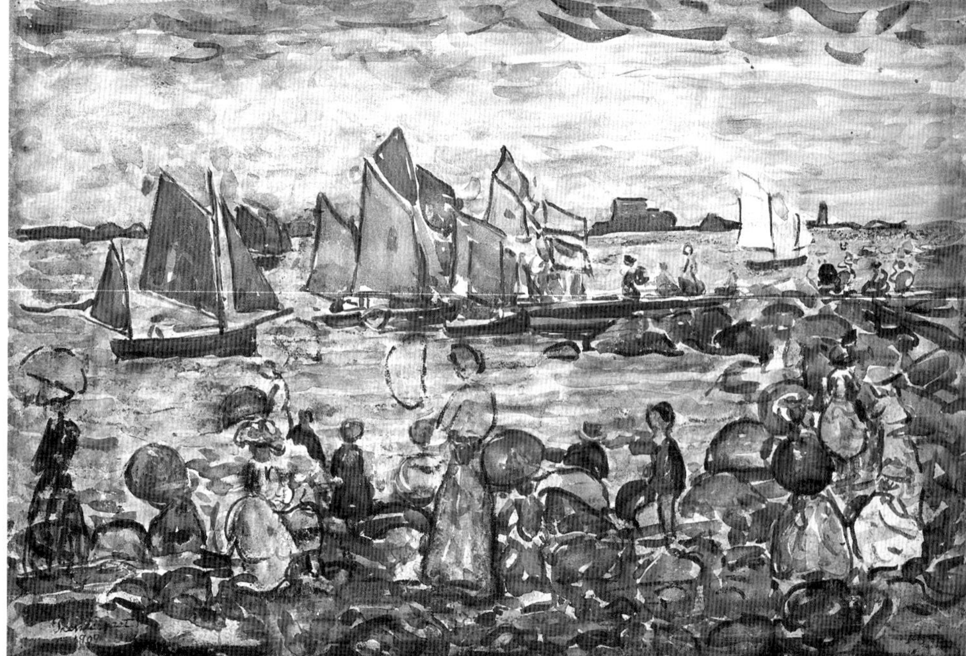

67. Le Port, St. Malo, Brittany

1907. Watercolor on paper, 13⅝ x 19⅞″
Allen Memorial Art Museum, Oberlin College, Ohio. Gift of Mrs. Anna Konoff, 1981

The spacing of the figures in this watercolor takes on a stately, measured cadence. In its free-flowing fluidity, luminosity, and color intensity, Le Port, St. Malo, Brittany *has moved far beyond the subtle, restrained lyricism of Maurice's New England and New York watercolors of about 1900–1902.*

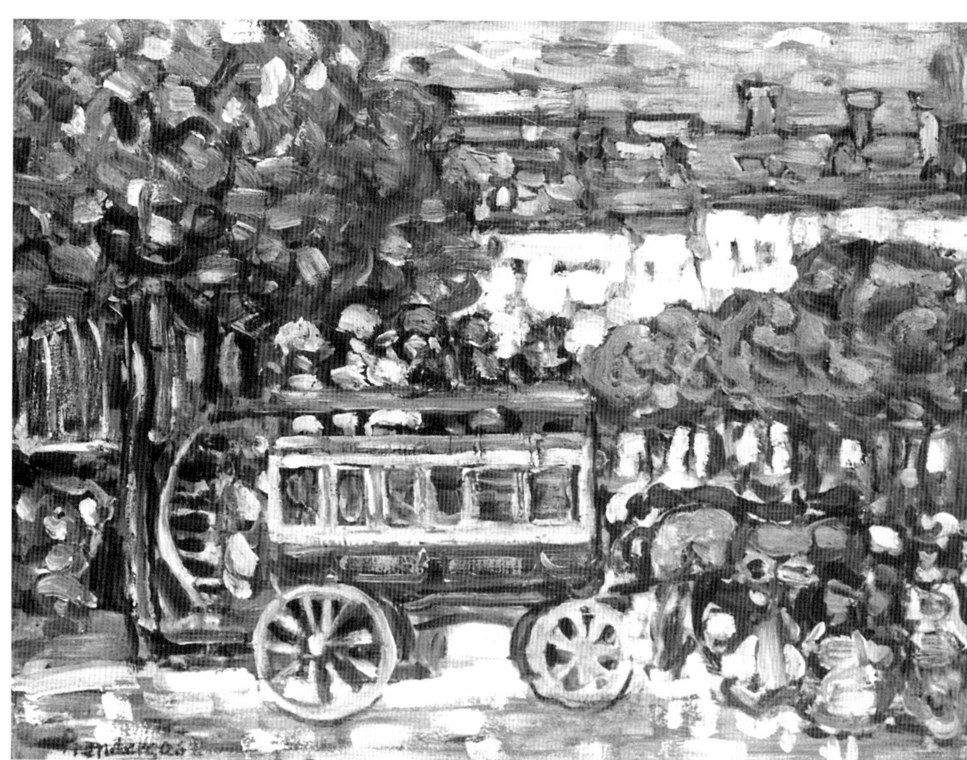

68. Paris Omnibus

1907. Oil on panel, 10¼ x 13⅝″
Center Gallery, Bucknell University, Lewisburg, Pennsylvania

Paris Omnibus *was preceded by a pencil sketch (CR 1487) and paralleled by a watercolor,* The Paris Omnibus *(CR 922), with considerably more illustrative detail than the oil displays.*

that Maurice was impressed with the watercolor port scenes of Paul Signac, for small, square, bright strokes that seem to pattern randomly the sails and rocks are frankly derived from that source. The figures and boats are drawn directly with a flowing blue outline. This outlining of figures in color, a color not necessarily corresponding to the local color of the unit of apparel denoted, takes into account Cézanne's technique of broken rhythmic color outlines, which Prendergast had intently studied in June. The loose and blobby brushwork serves to

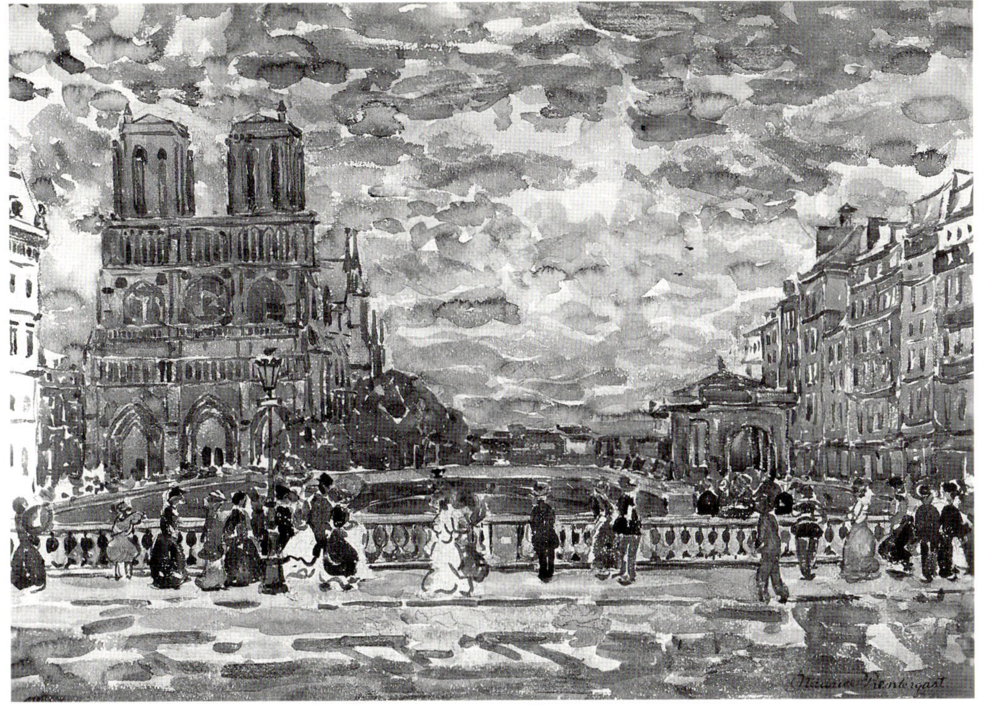

69. Notre-Dame, Paris

1907. Watercolor and pencil on paper, $13\frac{7}{8}$ x 20"
Worcester Art Museum, Massachusetts

The muted strokes of grayish brown in the foreground and sky areas, setting off the diminutive band of figures on the Pont Saint-Michel, are a tangible response to Prendergast's observations that "Cézanne gets . . . a dusty kind of a grey. . . . He left everything to the imagination. [Cézanne's watercolors] were great for their simplicity and suggestive qualities" (letter to Esther Williams, October 10, 1907).

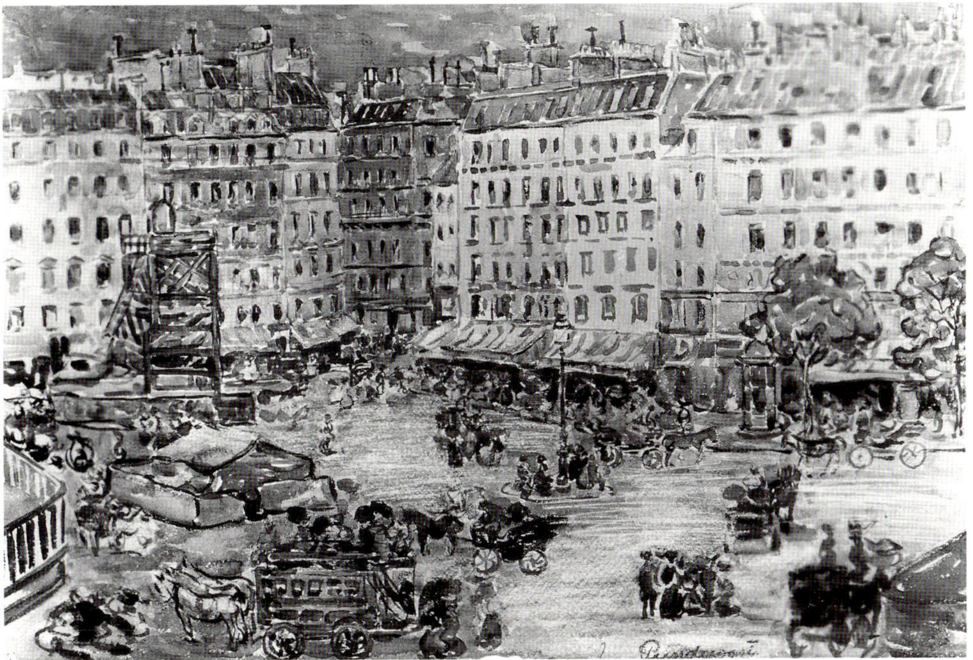

70. Montparnasse

1907. Watercolor and pastel on paper, $14\frac{3}{8}$ x $20\frac{1}{2}$"
Collection Mr. and Mrs. Meyer P. Potamkin

Maurice not only explored elaborate architectural settings in the Italian watercolors of 1898–99, particularly those done in Venice, but also painted similar motifs in watercolors of Boston (CR 858 and 859) in the years 1905 to 1907 prior to his 1907 trip to France.

heighten the seemingly casual placement of the various colors. Instead of the dense overlapping found in corresponding compositions of figures on the seashore dating from the late 1890s, broad linear arabesques open the space around the figures. The larger, simplified color units, flattened and disposed across the picture plane, foreshadow Prendergast's large oil compositions.

Having refocused his energies to emphasize oil painting, with its increased depth, weight, and texture, and to extend the color experimentation that in his watercolors and monotypes he had so skillfully brought to a state of resolution, Prendergast opened himself to inspiration from new sources. In this one trip

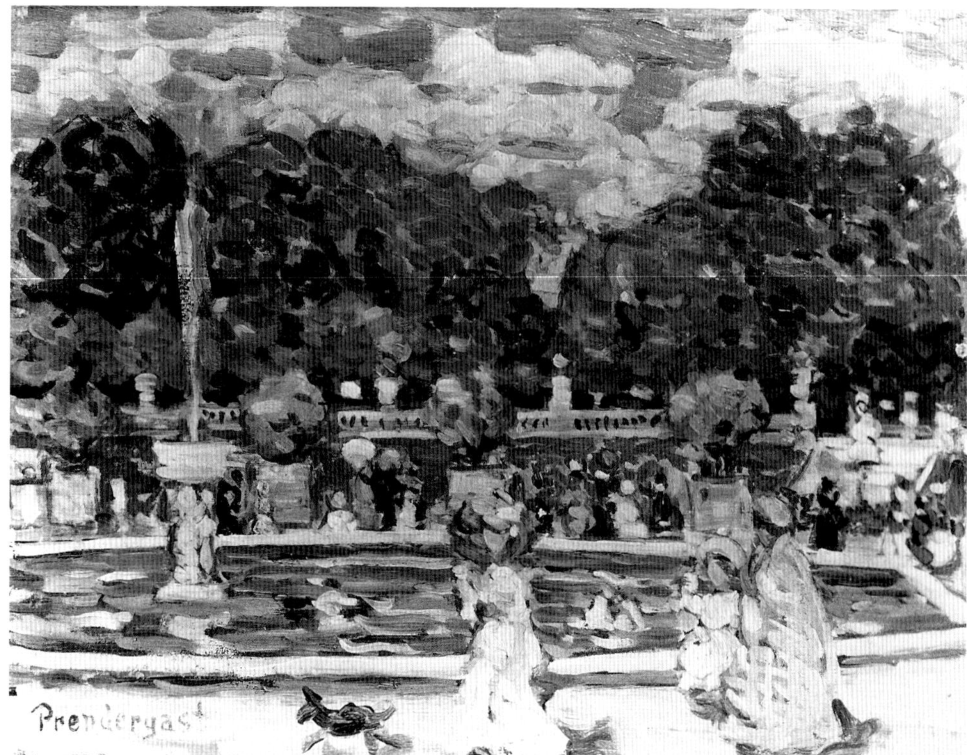

71. Luxembourg Gardens

1907. Oil on panel, 10½ x 13½"
Collection Mr. and Mrs. Meyer P. Potamkin

In this colorful vignette, compositionally reminiscent of Maurice's earlier watercolor park scenes, the Luxembourg Gardens succeeded the Boston Public Garden and Central Park as a point of departure for the artist's vivacious Impressionist pochades.

Prendergast, already thoroughly conversant with the vocabulary of the Impressionists, came into contact with a new world of values: the Fauves, the Neo-Impressionists, and, among the older generation, the work of van Gogh, Gauguin, and Odilon Redon.

In the Luxembourg Gardens (pl. 72), *Luxembourg Gardens* (pl. 71), and *Paris Omnibus* (pl. 68), all of 1907, are an outgrowth of Prendergast's earlier post-card-size panels, Seurat's *pochades,* and the Neo-Impressionism of such contemporaries as Signac and Louis Valtat. Expressive color experiments in which the intermediate pale tonalities of *Salem Willows* were forsaken intensify the Impressionist color and the modified Manet brushwork of earlier oils. Pigment was applied in overlapping strokes of varying size and direction, their unctuosity amplified by the sheen of the wood surfaces, with a resultant glow not previously found in the oils. These small vignettes, of which Prendergast produced at least twelve while he was in Paris in addition to the panels painted at Saint-Malo, are an important step toward his later oils.

72. In the Luxembourg Gardens

1907. Oil on panel, 10¾ x 14"
Private collection

This panel retains essential compositional features already found in Salem Willows *(pl. 51), 1904, and in watercolors such as* West Church, Boston *(pl. 42), c. 1900–1901. One of his rare dated paintings, it helps to establish firmly the chronology of Maurice's work.*

Notre-Dame, Paris (pl. 69) and *Montparnasse* (pl. 70), both of 1907, are looser versions of the architectural motifs in the Venetian watercolors of eight years previous. They disclose a greater freedom of application of color and an even greater avoidance of illustrative detail. The arches of the Doges' Palace and the orchestrated fenestration of *palazzi* have become the casual shorthand dabs of the arcaded facade of Notre-Dame and the multistoried apartment buildings of Paris. In a sense, watercolors had begun to serve as a kind of recreation for Maurice, not necessarily less interesting in themselves but subordinate to the intensity that he progressively brought to bear on his paintings.

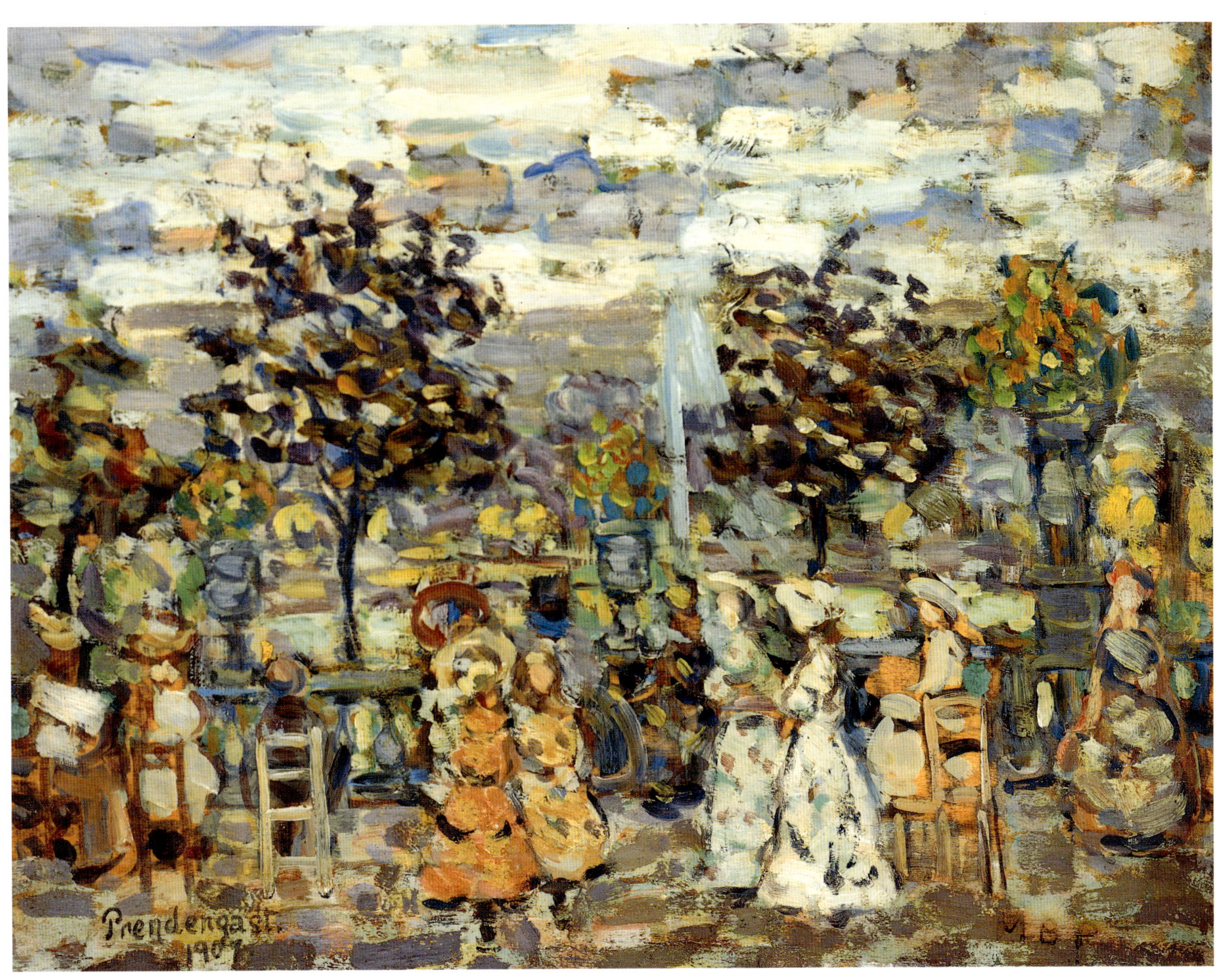

72. *In the Luxembourg Gardens*

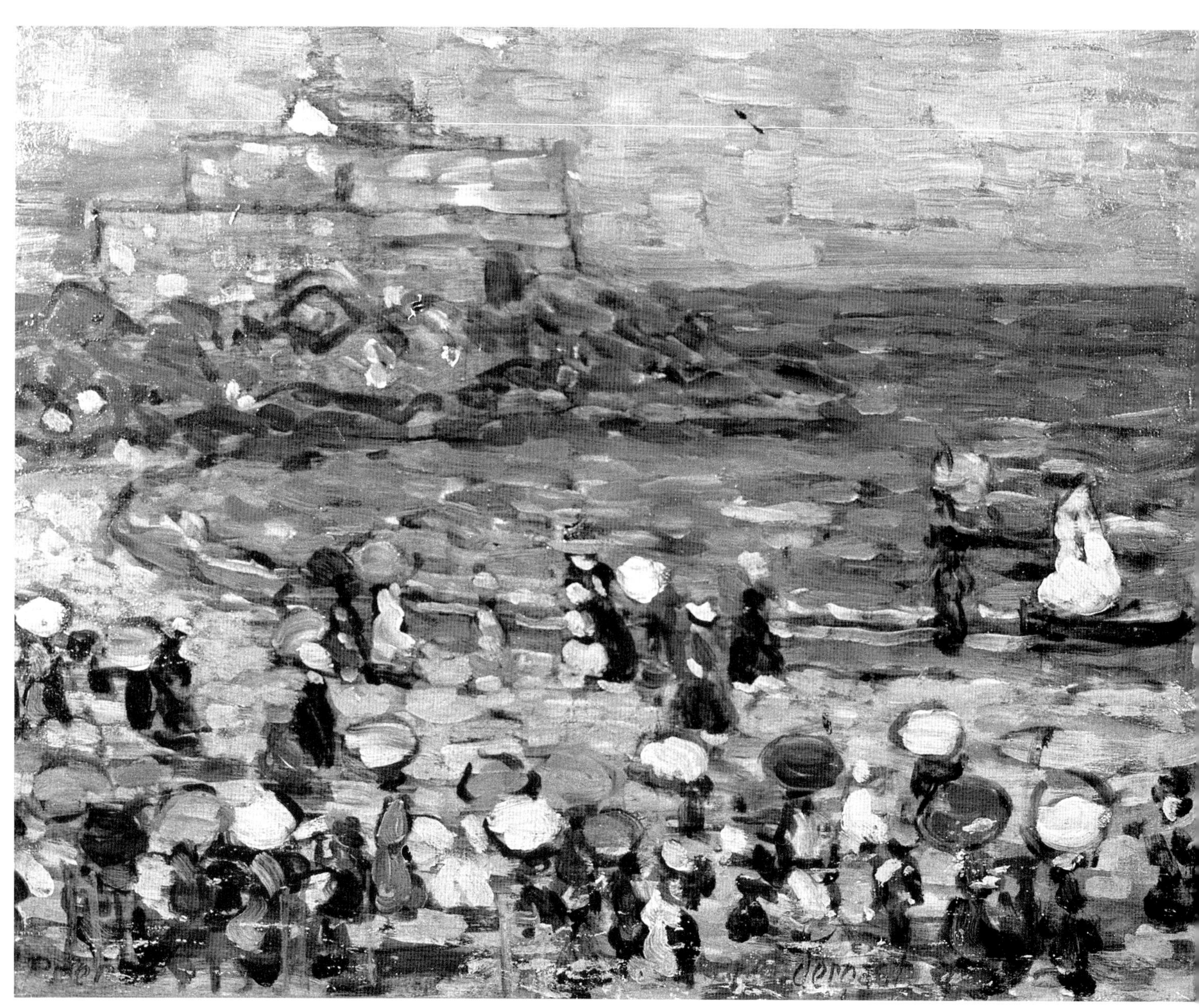

73. *Seascape (St. Malo)*

VIII. The Eight Show 1908

PRENDERGAST RETURNED HOME IN TIME TO PREPARE his entries for the forthcoming exhibition at Macbeth's. He planned to send seventeen pictures, at least ten of which were small panels painted at Saint-Malo. Toward the latter part of January, he wrote Mrs. Williams: "Our show comes off a week earlier than I expected and we are head over heels in working on the frames. . . . I have decided to throw out the girls playing and have substituted another. . . . I will bring all my St. Malo sketches and two or three frames so you can show them off well. . . . Your letter . . . set me working like Lucifer for the rest of the day . . . I am sending you *The Craftsman* with photos of all the Boys which will amuse you and a reproduction of the 'Promenade' "[82]—that is, *Salem Willows.* On January 30, Maurice wrote to Macbeth: "Greetings! I am sending you my pictures . . . two I have kept back, *The Park* 24—I started to paint on it and was unable to knock it into shape again. The other, *The Tower* No. 35 I will bring it on with me on Saturday Feb. 1st. when I hope I shall have the pleasure of seeing you. . . ." Maurice arrived from Boston in time to assist with the hanging. He included only sixteen of the seventeen pictures listed in the catalogue, numbers 20 through 36.[83]

The fuss surrounding the Macbeth show has received an inordinate amount of attention from historians, much of it distorted and sentimentalized. The publicity accorded the show, some of it created by journalists who were close friends of the artists, was enormous. Between the opening on the evening of February 3 and the conclusion two weeks later on the fifteenth, the galleries at 450 Fifth Avenue were mobbed.[84] While the modest catalogue brochure disappeared quickly, sales were meager—eight works for a total of only four thousand dollars—and Prendergast, Glackens, and Sloan sold not a picture. Arthur Hoeber, a conservative landscape painter and critic for the *Globe,* dished out some mild abuse: "Maurice Prendergast," he wrote, "sends nearly a score of modest sized canvases, full of spots of color, with many people mainly on the beach at the French St. Malo, obviously a place where the sun shines in a curious manner, where color is wonderfully made manifest, where the people are careless about their drawing and construction, and where everything is a jumble of riotous pigment, such as one does not see elsewhere. Hung in a group, these canvases of Mr. Prendergast look for all the world like an explosion in a color factory."[85] The last phrase of this review has been endlessly quoted out of context, although Hoeber was not the only observer to criticize the installation.

Each artist was allotted around twenty feet in one of two octagonal rooms. Joseph E. Chamberlain of the *New York Evening Mail* delivered himself of the following vituperation:

73. Seascape (St. Malo)

1907. Oil on panel, $10^{1/4} \times 13^{3/4}$"
The Barnes Foundation, Merion Station, Pennsylvania

The figures are aligned as a low screen completely covering the bottom band of the beach. In the middle ground are small interspersed units of sailboat and figures that curve around the shoreline to Chateaubriand's tomb in the far left corner.

The eight are the "radical" group whose collective demonstration of power has been awaited for some time. . . . The pictures of "The Eight" . . . certainly do not need any advertising. They advertise themselves. Macbeth's gallery scarcely opens in the morning before the crowd begins to arrive.

The pictures are startling to most people. Particularly those of Messrs. Glackens and Prendergast, which are in some respects more alarming than any of the others. . . .

They are all men who have felt an impulse, and they obey it. The impulse may be inspiration or it may be perversion, but anyhow the men feel it. . . . They all paint as they do because they must. They have "got the power," like the shouters and wailers in a negro camp meeting. Perhaps this impulse is as near to being inspiration as any artistic force the workings of which are to be noted at present in this community. . . . There are simply centuries of distance between a pure eccentric like Prendergast and a deep, antique idealist like Davies.

But Maurice B. Prendergast—let me confess that this artist is too much for me. Nothing is to be made out of him, unless you first acquire the taste—and it takes a long time to acquire it. The majority of these spotty canvases [they were, in fact, on panels] appear to me to be artistic tommy-rot. The best of them, the sanest, "The Tower," is the least like Prendergast. Though the exhibition would be stronger if it were the show of "the seven" rather than of "the eight," it is well worth while from any point of view, and just as it is. It represents originality, and native, instinctive power. There are ideas to burn here.[86]

Another writer stated: "Mr. Maurice Prendergast has some strange studies, in pink and purple paint of the beach at St. Malo. One of them is called decorative [no 34]. Another is called 'Young Girls at Play' [21]. There is what appears to be a tall birthday cake, which is called a tower [35]."[87] Not all of the critics were hostile, nor were they all uninformed: "Some of these men are termed extremists; some of them are all of that. Mr. Prendergast, for instance, would not deny the appellation. To some who saw his seventeen [*sic*] pictures his art suggested cloisonné work. Like much else in the galleries it is colorful and needs to be seen at a distance to get its true measure. And they are truly decorative."[88] James Huneker, cultural critic of the *New York Sun* and successor to FitzGerald as art critic, an urbane man familiar with the modern art being shown in France, took a more objective approach, expressing what Prendergast himself had written from Paris: "And now the writer must make a confession. He has been a frequent visitor at the Paris Autumn Salons of the Independents, and compared with the performances in paint he has witnessed there this show at Macbeth's is one decidedly reactionary. The truth is that New York in the matter of art is provincial. . . . Any young painter recently returned from Paris or Munich—the Munich of the secessionists—would call the exhibition of the eight painters very interesting but far from revolutionary. If some of us sit up now aghast, what will happen to our nerves when Cézanne, Gauguin, Van Gogh appear?"[89] In the body of the article he reflected, "Prendergast, with the delicate art of the Celt and a nimble touch, is really a neo-impressionist. He employs the *taches* according to the new men of the Independent Salons. His little panels are cunning mosaics, flowerlike arabesques, delightfully decorative." And he also criticized the hanging: "Mr. Macbeth did not hang the pictures. If he had we might have been spared some noisy contrasts, some glaring spots. . . . Maurice Prendergast kills his charming and joyous transcripts of St. Malo, of child life in gay little parks by the sparkling seaside, by hanging in juxtaposition sixteen of them. They are, thus grouped, whirling arabesques that tax the eye." And James B. Townsend wrote, "To Maurice B. Prendergast must be given the palm for handing out to the art public of New York, so-called pictures that can only be the product of the cider much drunk at St. Malo in Brittany, where his crazy quilt sketches were conceived and executed. Blotches of paint on canvas without harmony of color or tone—these are all that can be made out of these curious performances." He then hedged: "Prendergast may take heart, and who knows but these pictures may be the Monets of a quarter of a century hence."[90]

When the opportunity presented itself for a tour of the show, with some substitutions, additions, and deletions, to nine cities, Maurice made some suggestions for improvement. After John Sloan had arranged for the show to make its first stop on the itinerary at the Pennsylvania Academy of the Fine Arts, Prendergast wrote to Davies on February 12, before the end of the run in New York:

> *I received the art criticisms which you sent with many cordial thanks. I have not read them yet but after a while when things cool off I will read them carefully. Send some more and be sure and sign the names if you can.*
>
> *If anything important comes up during the meeting of the boys, please let me know, but we made two mistakes. The gallery should have been larger and got up more expensive catalogues and charge 10¢ a piece for them.* Comme ci comme ca. *I hope you are all satisfied with the experience. Send them my love and good luck.*
>
> *If I can judge from this remote neighborhood, we have made much more noise than the last show [National Arts Club 1904] and people will be looking for still greater things. But I hope we will give them more, an increased dose of art.*

Over the next year and a half, the show was seen in Philadelphia, Chicago, Toledo, Detroit, Indianapolis, Cincinnati, Pittsburgh, Bridgeport, Connecticut, and Newark. The critics in some locales had their say; some must have read the New York newspapers. Prendergast received some praise; a critic in Newark, New Jersey, probably having read Huneker, wrote: "But do not think that Prendergast has spoken the final word with his Cézanne technique. We will hear more of it when the influence of France upon the young artists studying there now becomes better known. Prendergast has sacrificed much in adopting it, but then, like his comrades, he has the satisfaction of being true to himself."[91]

Prendergast's recent work puzzled critics. In November, a writer remarked on Maurice's entries in the sixth annual watercolor exhibition at the Pennsylvania Academy: "Some of the groups of works would have been less interesting to the layman than to the painter, such, for example, as Mr. Maurice Prendergast's contributions, indefinite as they are in drawing, experimental in color."[92]

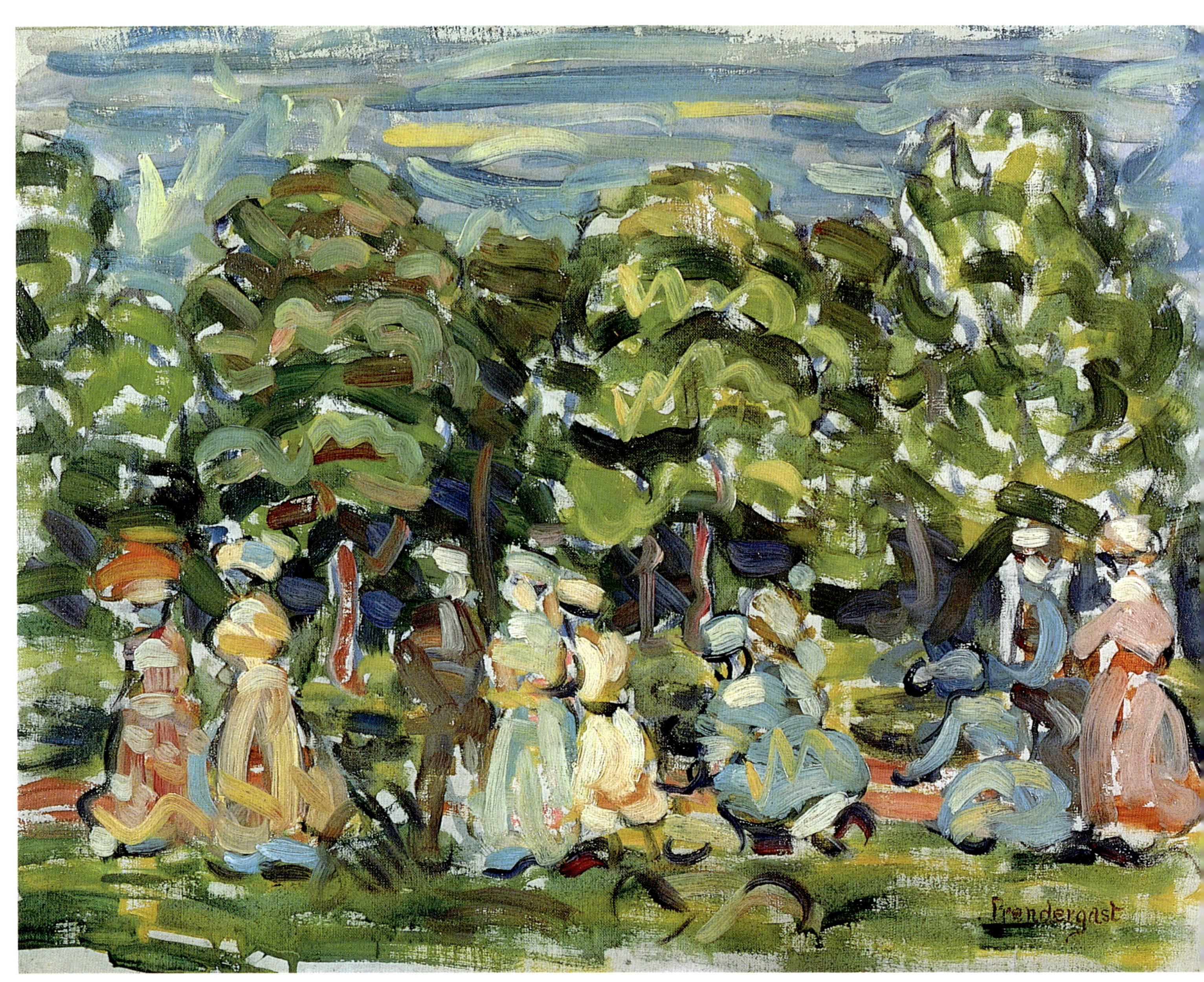

74. *Summer in the Park*

IX. Forging a New Style 1908–12

As was his long-established custom, Prendergast accepted invitations from organizations that would not necessarily enhance his prestige. Snobbism was not a part of his personality, and he wanted his pictures seen, particularly in New York. In May 1909, he entered several works in an exhibition at the Rand School of Social Science. Arthur Hoeber covered the event:

> *Under the auspices of the Rand School . . . at 112 East Nineteenth Street, there is held an exhibition . . . until June 1. It is explained by the amiable young woman in charge of the rooms that the object of this display is to make socialists acquainted with art and artists acquainted with socialism. . . . It is confided to the visitor that already several of the artists have seen socialist light. . . . To liven up the show there are landscapes by . . . Maurice Prendergast—who we are sure will keep these socialists guessing. . . .*[93]

Prendergast's development during the years following his return from France and the Eight show is characterized mainly by experimentation that built on and gradually extended the reach of the bright oil sketches done in Saint-Malo and Paris in the summer of 1907. Most of these landscapes, or figures in landscape—park or shoreline scenes—carry forward the compositional ideas first adumbrated in the Promenades painted since the turn of the century (see p. 75 and pls. 55, 56, 58, and 60). The motif seldom varies. Maurice appeared to be searching for ways of refining and adding substance to the spontaneous brushwork that makes these panels so appealing. By around 1908 and 1909 a discernible shift began to occur in the technique and scale of Maurice's compositions.

We have some insight into the process from a letter Maurice wrote to Walter Pach on December 6, 1909:

> *It is just now we saw the Cézanne. My brother telephoned to Mr. Sumner after you left and he told [us] not to come until his house was in good shape. The Cézanne [*Harvesters*, c. 1880, pl. 75] interested me extremely. It look[ed like] one of those pochades he [did] when he was [with] Pissarro. You are right about the beauty of the canvas; it is conscientious and absolutely sincere. He seems to be very careful with the quality of his canvas and lets the canvas show when it would give lightness to his colour. I noticed the same with some of the canvasses in his exhibitions. This sketch is done at the first wack and it made me jealous of his beautiful greys. I wish Mr. Sumner [would] secure one of his "nature mortes," fruit pieces where he painted one thin coat over the other. I am glad we have this Cézanne in Boston and it was*

74. *Summer in the Park*

c. 1908. Oil on canvas, 15½ x 20¼"
Santa Barbara Museum of Art, California.
Gift of Mr. and Mrs. Sterling Morton, for the Preston Morton Collection

Working rapidly, the artist reduced dark-light contrasts to a minimum, conspicuously leaving irregular patches of white canvas showing through the brushstrokes in order to intensify the pervasive light-saturated luminosity of the surface.

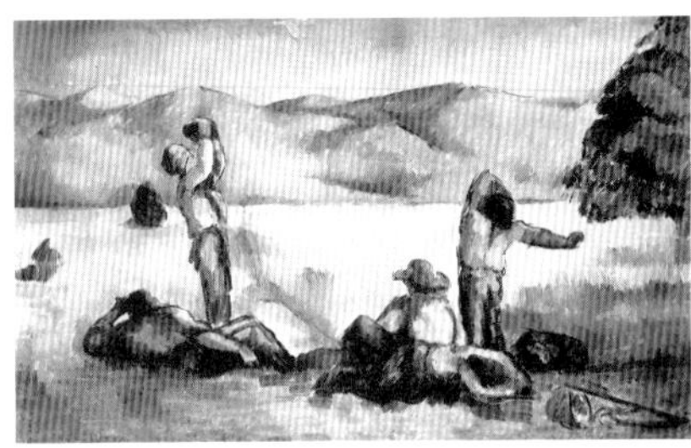

75. Paul Cézanne (1839–1906)
Harvesters

c. 1880. Oil on canvas, 10¼ x 16⅛"
Private collection, Paris

76. *Beach Road No. 2*

c. 1910. Watercolor and pencil on paper, 12⅜ x 17⅝"
Munson-Williams-Proctor Institute, Utica, New York. Edward W. Root Bequest

A rendition of Maurice's processional Central Park watercolors (pls. 46 and 47) of 1900–1902, replete with horse and carriage, figures and foliage screen, this sheet manifests a looser construction. The emphasis is placed on expressive decoration, related to contemporaneous oil compositions, rather than on an illustrative framework.

such a pleasure for me to see his work again and you cannot realize my gratitude for giving me this opportunity to see it.[94]

Pach had given the brothers an introduction to John O. Sumner, professor of art history at Massachusetts Institute of Technology, who owned the Cézanne canvas.[95] From the tone of his letter, it seems that the small canvas had assumed an almost talismanic character for Prendergast, so happy was he to reacquaint himself with Cézanne's work. According to Daphne Dunbar, Maurice "was so enthusiastic about Cézanne that whenever he mentioned the name he used the Gallic gesture of blowing a kiss into the air."[96]

An example of the brisk, summary brushwork that followed the color application of the Saint-Malo oil sketches of 1907 is *Summer in the Park* (pl. 74), c. 1908, in which green-pink-blue-yellow color notations were set down rapidly on a canvas of slightly larger format. Here, the regularity of the Manet-inspired stroke is deliberately varied, and the entire surface has an extremely high-key color intensity. Watercolors of this period are likewise experimental in their exploration of the Neo-Impressionist palette of Signac and Henri-Edmond Cross. *Beach Road No. 2* (pl. 76), c. 1910, is a typical example of this loose, irregularly spotted luminosity.

Maurice began to forswear the generally simple color surfaces of his small panels and, still employing the predominant beach scene motif that had fascinated him for a decade, gradually produced larger-scale compositions on canvas in which a distinct overlapping and building up of paint layers is clearly discernible. Although from time to time he briefly experimented with still life, flower piece, and even portrait subjects, the multifigure park and beachside motifs and groups of nudes preoccupied him for the next dozen years. He transformed the regularity of the glowing, rich spots and dabs of color into irregular and curvilinear shaped patterns, brushstroke overlapping brushstroke, and the surfaces gradually assumed a rougher texture and series of complex color harmonies, the basic elements with which his individual units and spatial organizations are constructed.

The Holiday (pl. 77), c. 1908–9, is a conscious reworking of the *Salem Willows* theme (see pl. 51). The figure groups of the earlier picture have been moved up, here restricted to a picket fence across the width of the canvas. This foreground alignment of figures is an extension of *Seascape (St. Malo)* (see pl. 73), 1907. The flat trees of *Salem Willows* here take on a Pissarro-like thickness and color-made solidity. The figure and tree units are now set against a large water-sky area that is pervasively pale and cool, and they are separated from each other by the narrow, purple strip of land. The color patterns have become more variegated, more luminous, some strokes scumbled so that their broken textures partially show the colors beneath in an effort to increase the sumptuous vibration of the surface. Gone is any hint of somberness; even the grass on which the figures are disposed is a layered mixture of pinks, yellows, blues, tans, and shades of green.

On April 1, 1910, an "immense throng," as the *New York American* exclaimed

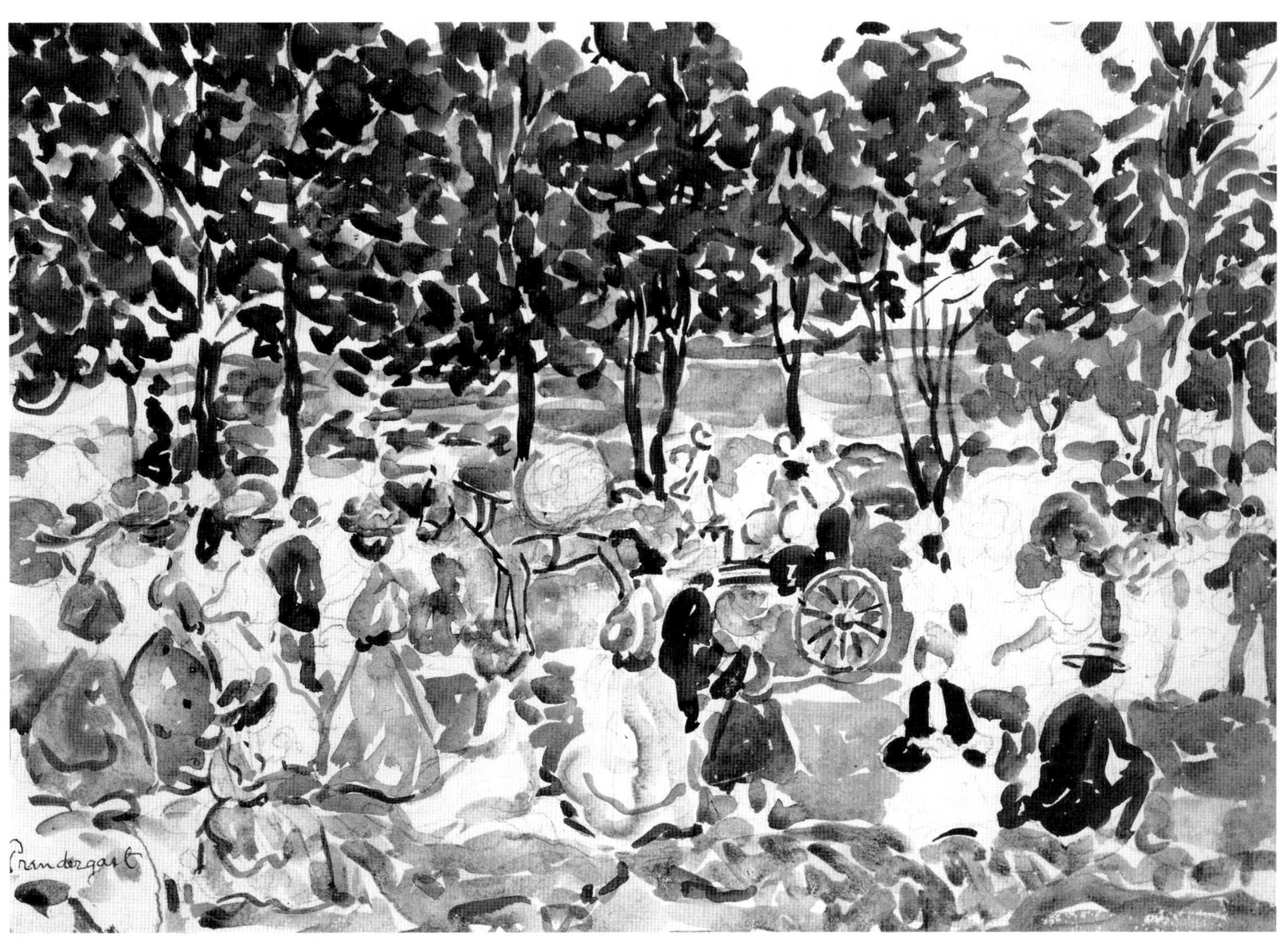

76. Beach Road No. 2

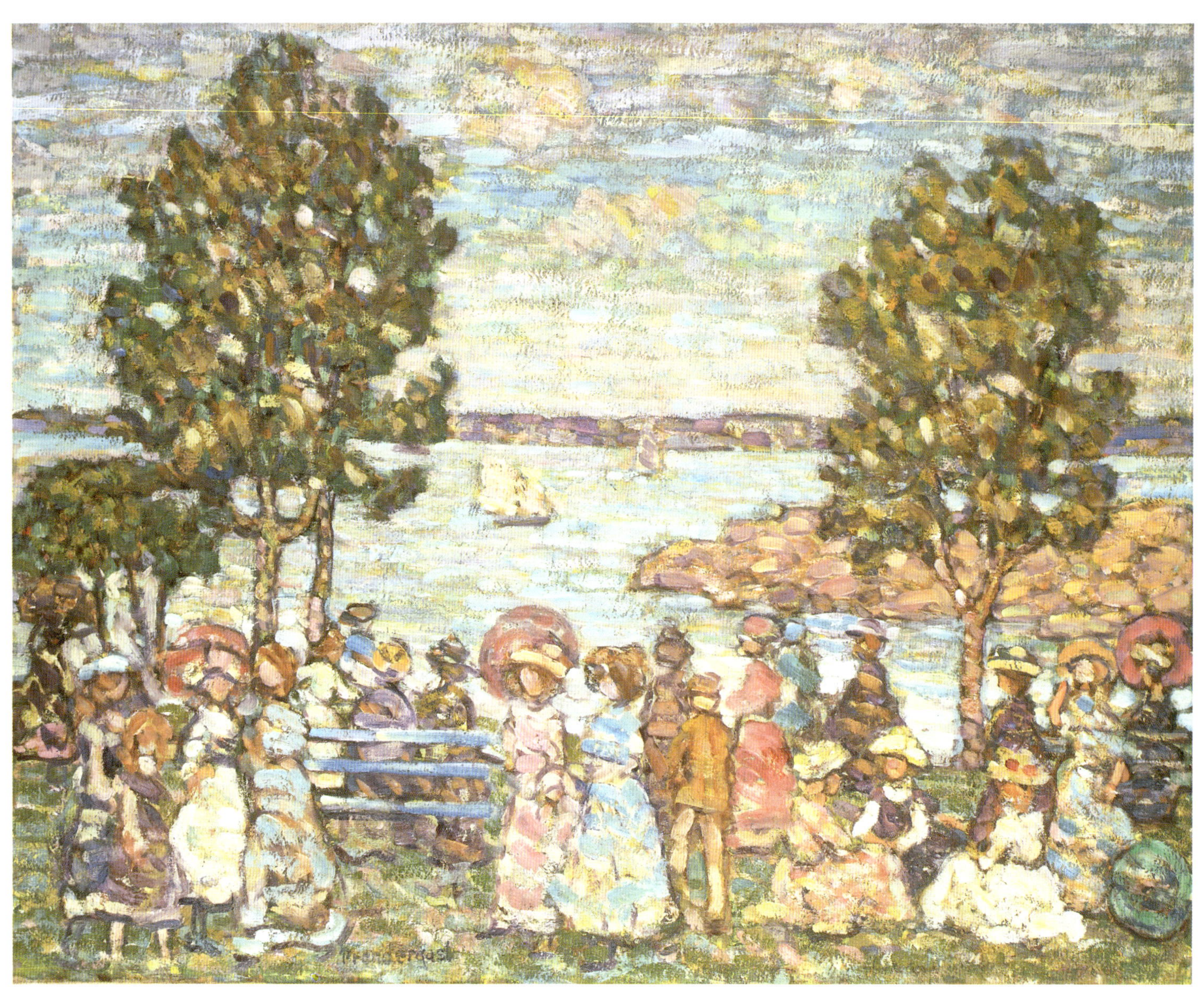

77. *The Holiday*

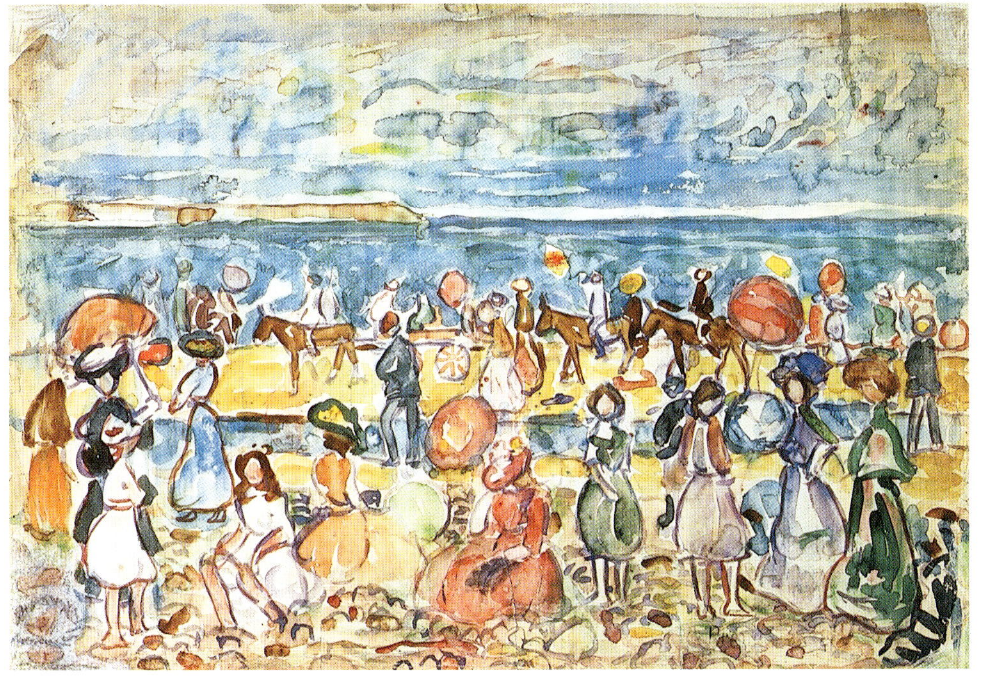

78. *Holiday in New England*

c. 1910–11. Watercolor, pastel, and pencil on paper, 15 x 21⅞″
National Museum of American Art, Smithsonian Institution, Washington, D.C.
Gift of Mrs. Charles Prendergast

The bright foreground figures and the bold horizon are bridged by the motif of donkeys with riders and a donkey pulling a wagon, a motif seen often in the artist's oil compositions from around 1910 on.

in its headline, of two thousand crowded the opening of the "Exhibition of Independent Artists," organized by Robert Henri, John Sloan, Jerome Myers, Arthur B. Davies, Walter Pach, Walt Kuhn, Rockwell Kent, and other artists who were opposed to the exclusionary policies of the academicians of the National Academy. The *New York Mail and Express* headlined "Panic Averted in Art Show Crowd . . . Police Preserve Order." The "Apostles of Ugliness" or the "Red Hots" understood up-to-date techniques of publicity. Prendergast entered five paintings, his typically titled *Seashore Nos. 1, 2,* and *3,* as well as canvases entitled *Autumn* and *Landscape with Nudes,* the nudes being the first such motif he had shown. On April 20, George Bellows wrote to Joseph Taylor,

> *I have been working night and day on the hanging committee of the Independent Exhibition. . . . Prendergast, whose pictures are often laughed at, are to me the most refined of decorations . . . surely one of this fellow's works gives a wonderful sense of quiet repose which would add dignity to any place where repose was in order. He is the only man I know except Chavannes, Davies, Botticelli and the Early Italians who has this quality to such a degree that one would love to have a place decorated by his paintings where he could go and rest. Where one could lose this internal nervousness!*[97]

Of 344 items in the catalogue, only one painting and two drawings—none by Prendergast—were sold on opening night.

Early in 1911 Rockwell Kent, a disciple of Henri, was offered free space for another Independents exhibition. Kent wanted to limit participation to artists who would guarantee not to submit their work to the National Academy that year. Henri responded negatively, but Davies, Luks, and Prendergast assented, along with others such as Alfred Maurer, Marsden Hartley, and John Marin.

77. *The Holiday*

c. 1908–9. Oil on canvas, 27 x 34⅜″
The Fine Arts Museum of San Francisco.
Gift of the Charles E. Merrill Trust with matching funds from the de Young Museum Society

Enlarging on the small Luxembourg Gardens oil sketches and intermediate-size canvases such as Summer in the Park *(pl. 74), with its broadly stroked blue-white-yellow sky, Prendergast created a marked buildup of layered units. The gaily colored figures reflect Maurice's interest in Watteau and Fragonard.*

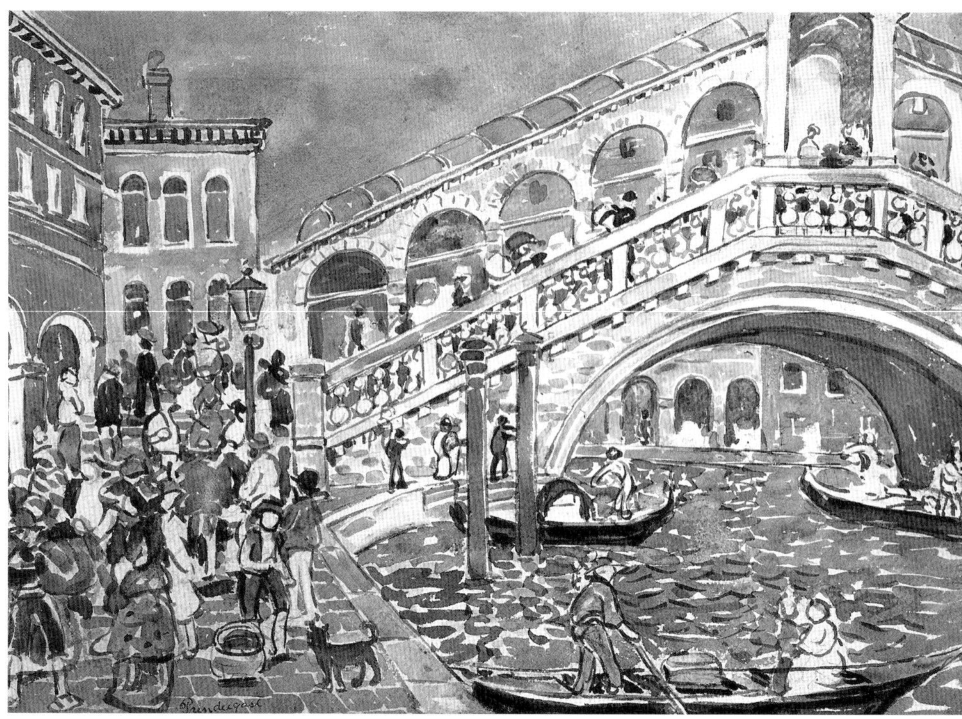

79. Rialto Bridge

1911. Watercolor and pencil on paper, 14½ x 22⅛"
The Metropolitan Museum of Art, New York. The Leslie and Emma Sheafer Collection, Bequest of Emma A. Sheafer, 1973

Rialto Bridge *presents the reverse view of* The Grand Canal, Venice *(pl. 32), painted some dozen years earlier. It is one of approximately two dozen watercolors dating from the summer and fall of 1911, some of which were left incomplete when Maurice was taken ill in late October.*

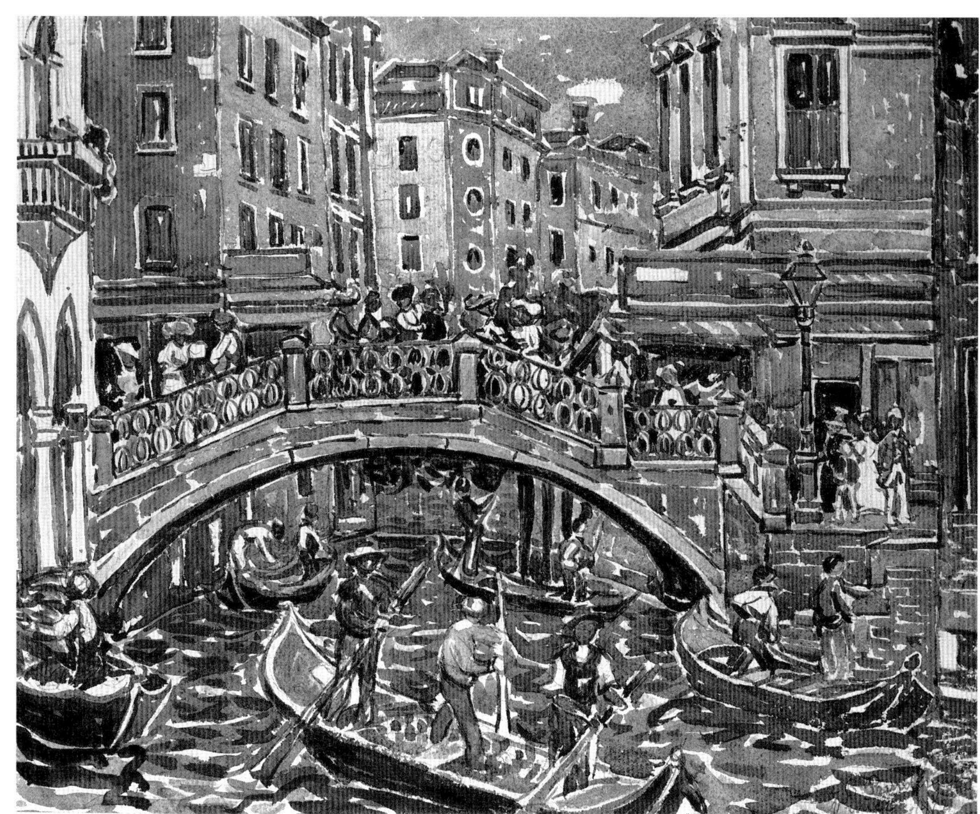

80. Canal

1911. Watercolor and pencil on paper, 15½ x 21⅞"
Munson-Williams-Proctor Institute, Museum of Art, Utica, New York. Edward W. Root Bequest

In December 1934, entrusting the Whitney Museum of American Art, New York, with this work, Edward W. Root wrote to its curator, Herman More, "The watercolor I bought as a result of its having been seen [with] George Luks at the American Water Color Society Show in April–May, 1912. George was very enthusiastic about it and told me to go and look at it and buy it. As a piece of color I have always thought it extraordinarily beautiful and subtle. I hope you give it daylight."

Prendergast wrote to Kent on February 23: "I am glad to hear of the forthcoming exhibition of the Independents and will give my best efforts towards making the exhibition a good one." On March 19, he wrote again: "I succeeded in getting my pictures off this afternoon, 4 oils and 12 water colors. . . . Some of the oils I have marked a thousand. Please make them $700.00. I have an exhibit running in Boston and I got some of the pictures mixed in regard to the prices."[98] "An Independent Exhibition of the Paintings and Drawings of Twelve Men" opened at the Society of Beaux-Arts Architects on March 26. Hoeber disparaged the show: "Here are a lot of young fellows—the older ones are in the minority—and their viewpoint is one of deep, impenetrable gloom. . . . A few bluebirds let loose in the gallery might make for happiness. . . . The oils and water colors by Maurice Prendergast . . . are very like color explosions, and are apparently made by receipt, for one resembles the other much like blades of grass."[99]

Before the show closed, Maurice wrote Kent,

> *I was up in the country painting the last three or four days and on my return home yesterday I found your letter introducing me to 191 dollars and 25 cents check, a solid appreciation which gives me an immense pleasure. I am glad the exhibition turned out so well and I hope the rest of the boys including yourself came out on the right side. I am glad I saw this exhibition. It is the first time since I left Paris that I was impressed. It had a touch of real art and I hope we will increase it.*
>
> *I am going to make an effort and get on to New York soon. If so, I will be sure to look you up.*
>
> *Give my best regards and congratulations to Mrs. Kent and tell her she has covered herself with glory.*
>
> *My best wishes go out to you. Artist Peintre Maurice Prendergast*[100]

In June Charles Prendergast sailed to Italy, and Maurice arrived there in August. On August 12, he wrote to Kent: "Your letter has followed me to Naples and I suppose you are surprised. My brother, who is staying with some people in Capri sent me an invitation to come over. I do not know how long I will be here. . . ." He gave a return address in Florence. In Venice by September 15, he wrote to Mrs. Williams:

> *We have been here for about four weeks taking in all the sights. It is the same Venice but it does not seem to have the attraction for me when I was here ten years ago. We stayed at the famous Casa Frollo for about a week (on the Guidecca). . . .*
>
> *I . . . will probably stay until the end of November and have another wack at the canals. We sometimes spend the evening at the Piazza [San Marco]. The same music, promenading and the fashionable crowd at Florians. The ladies wear black hats as large as parasols and smoking cigarettes seems to be on the increase among them.*

Maurice sketched and painted watercolors for a month, about twenty-five views of the Rialto and other bridges across smaller canals, which attracted him as a motif. Watercolors done in Venice in 1911, such as *Rialto Bridge* (pl. 79) and *Canal* (pl. 80), display the same kind of loose handling as the equivalent Paris and post-Paris sheets, such as *Montparnasse* (pl. 70), *Beach Road No. 2* (pl. 76), and *Holiday in New England* (pl. 78). *Clocktower, St. Mark's Square, Venice* (pl. 81),

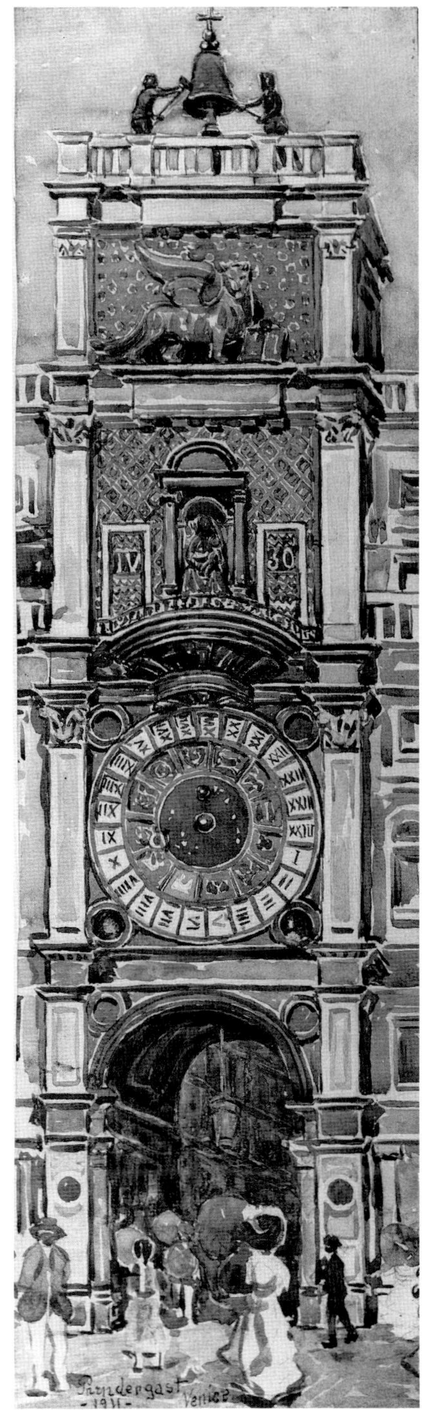

81. *Clocktower, St. Mark's Square, Venice*

1911. Watercolor and pencil on paper, 22½ x 6¼"
Stanford University Museum of Art, Gift of Janet Churchill Gould, Class of 1941

A simplified reprise of his earlier version (pl. 28), this watercolor displays the looser, broader technique Prendergast progressively developed as a result of his experiments with oils in the preceding decade.

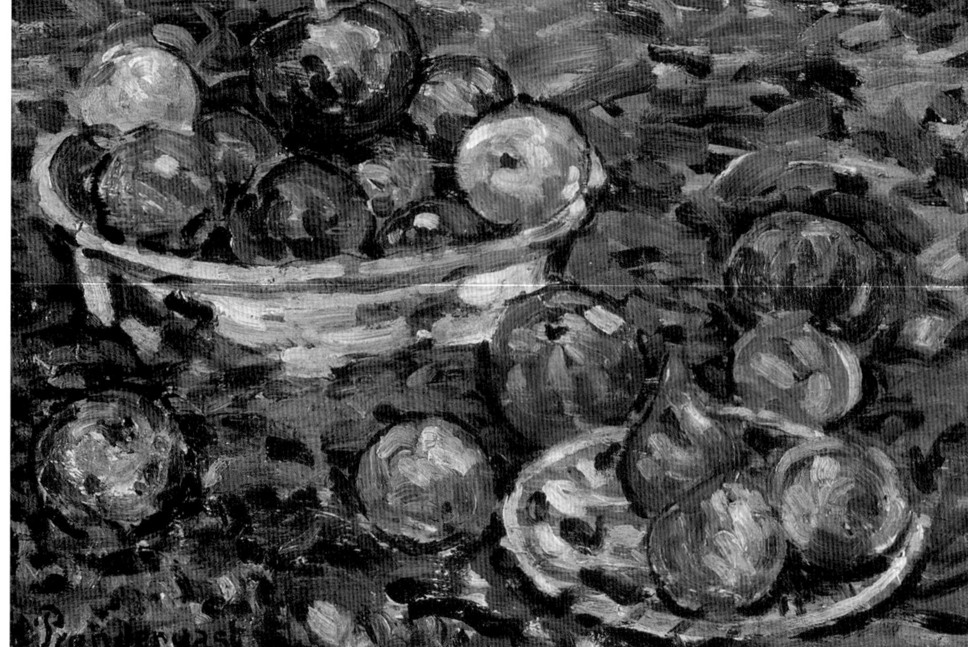

82. Apple and Pear on the Grass

1912. Oil on panel, 9⅞ x 13⅞"
Permanent Collection, Museum of Art, Fort Lauderdale, Florida. Bequest of Ira Glackens

Although Cézanne's still lifes appear to have directly inspired these experiments, as well as Paul Signac's watercolor still lifes painted around 1910, Prendergast's results are somewhat stiff, as if he had set himself a challenge. His still lifes, flower pieces, and portraits were likely part of his recuperation in the spring and summer of 1912.

83. Cinerarias and Fruit

c. 1912. Oil on canvas, 21 x 27"
Whitney Museum of American Art, New York. Purchase

Maurice never copied outright another artist in his oils and watercolors. This fact, plus the absence of any still life compositions in watercolor, indicate that the still lifes are deliberate experiments, more concerned with surface textures and decoration than compositional complexity and weight.

1911, incorporates the uppermost section of the tower with the two bell ringers striking the hour, a scene that had been truncated in the earlier version (see pl. 28). While the architecture's inherent specificity seemed again to concentrate Maurice's inclination to record carefully, a comparison of the two *Clocktower* sheets shows the diminished emphasis on detail that had taken place over the last decade.

Near the end of October, Maurice was taken ill and obliged to undergo prostate surgery at Venice's Cosmopolitan Hospital. The operation to remove a tumor was successful but recovery was slow, and he convalesced for three months, enjoying the winter in Venice, reading, buying frames, and gradually regaining his strength.

On November 13, he wrote to Charles, "I am feeling strong and healthy and with dutiful trust in God am ready for the other operation. . . . It is too bad for your sake I am sick. It would be so fine if I was home in the old studio and helping you along with the frames. We together were such a good team. If the work accumulates you can always get some means of shoving them through." Two days later: "I have concluded to let the operation go for the present and not have it done until I get home again. . . . The Dr. says I can take up my work again in a few days and that means the Steamer and home and it will be fine to take up the frames again and the brush. . . ." On the eighteenth: "I am once more up . . . and have been across on the little ferry boat . . . and walked down past the Academy. . . . I have been out in the Gondola twice and enjoyed it. . . . It was a delight to be able to go to my trunks again, rummage about them and look at the water colors." November 26: "I am keen on getting a hold of my water colors again for I would like to finish some of them while I am here. . . . The weather is beautiful, something like our Indian summer. . . . I tell you in spite of

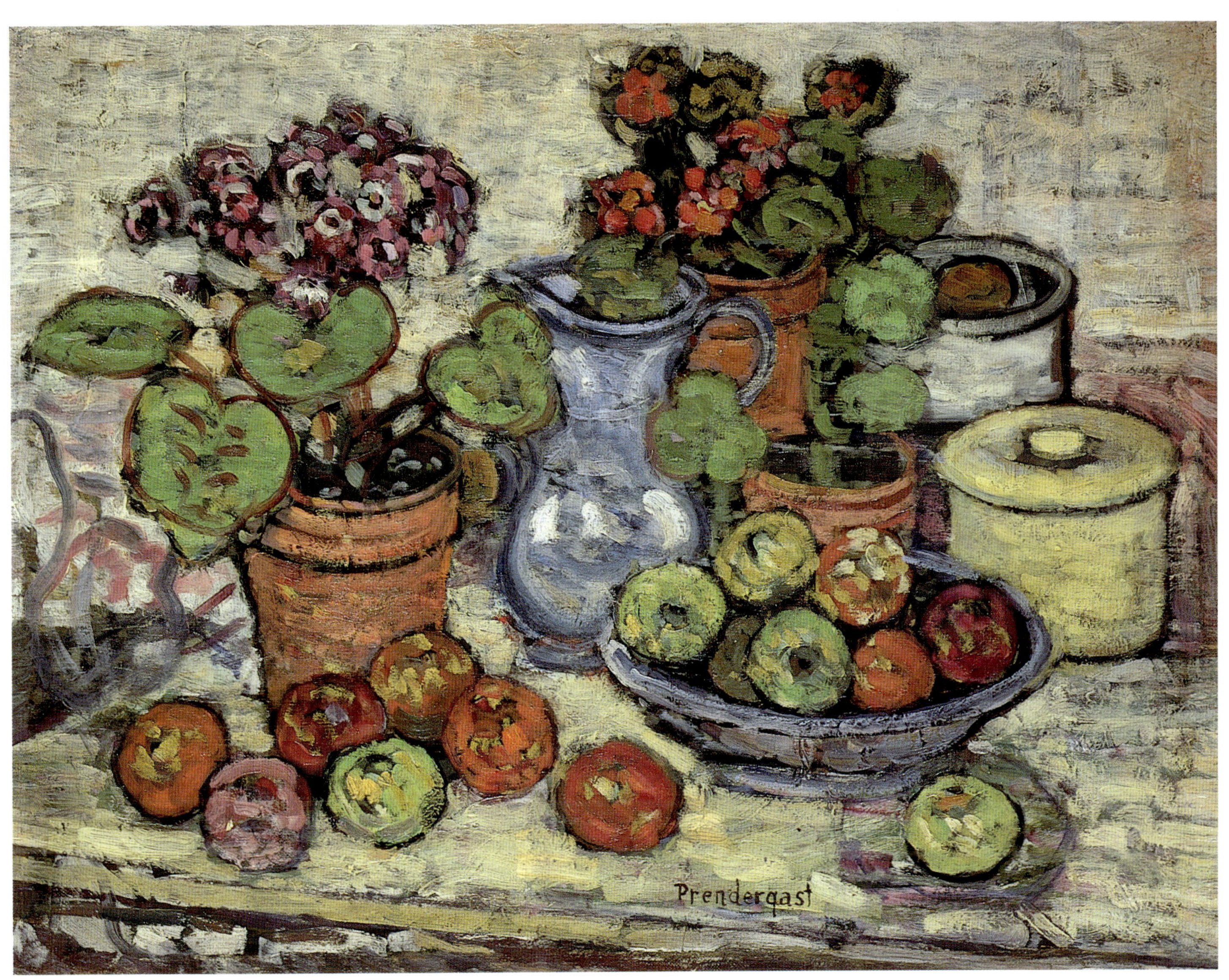

83. Cinerarias and Fruit

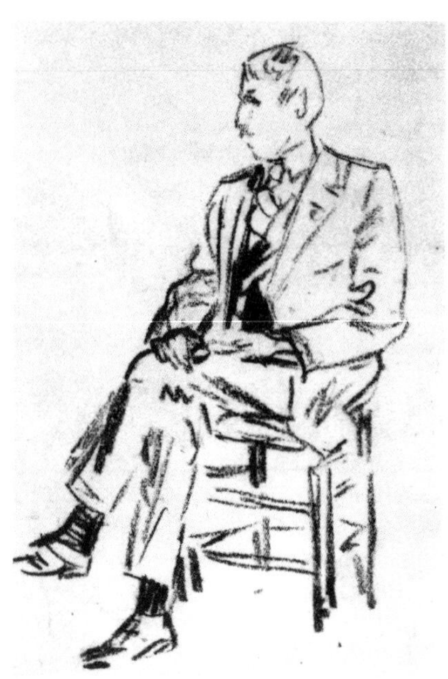

84. William J. Glackens (1870–1938)
Maurice Prendergast

1912. Pencil on paper, 10 x 6″
Location unknown
(formerly Collection Ira Glackens)

In the summer of 1912 Maurice visited the Glackens family at Bellport, Long Island, where Glackens made this sketch of his friend. Maurice painted a still life (pl. 82) and also started a portrait of Ira Glackens (CR 344).

everything (Italy is the place for Ideas)." November 28: "I will leave [the hospital] in a few days and get some of the sketches into shape. . . . I am feeling the old blood running through my veins." December 5: "I think I will buy a trunk and invest in some frames. . . . You will of course meet me with the cab and ho for 56 Mt. Vernon St. again. Try and keep the frames back as long as you can and we can put them through during February and March and have all the tools well sharpened. . . ."[101] December 14: "I am awfully glad to be all by myself again and getting out of the hospital the artist awakes at once. . . . I am commencing to like Venice immensely in the winter. [It] is so different and the color seems to get richer and deeper and on clear days you can see the surrounding mountains covered with snow. . . ." On the eighteenth he wrote to Mrs. Williams, who had been writing him in Venice:

> *I am now getting my things together for the homeward journey and expect to reach home again some time during the end of January. My sketching experience this time has been disastrous. . . . I am much taken with Venice . . . it . . . has a charm I do not feel in the summer time and one meets so many interesting people among the English and American residents. All the same I am never going to do my best work here. Boston for me with its surrounding green hills . . . I am looking forward to having a great handshake when I arrive and dance a high step on the paint box for I have not touched paint since last August.*

On December 23, Maurice again wrote to his brother, "Hope to find everything well and in apple pie order. . . . I don't think I will stay here much after New Year so for Genova and Smith's Hotel where I will sit tight until the boat sails. The boat . . . touches at Palermo. It will give me a chance to see Sicily. I am jumping wild to get on the start. I tried to do a little sketching but got chilled quickly. . . ."

A month after his return from Italy, Maurice wrote on March 8, 1912, to his neighbor and sometime pupil and painting companion, who, it seems, had been seriously ill. "My Dear Mrs. Williams, I was so glad when I heard from Charley that you were going to recover your health. . . . I am in capital health. The two months rest I had laying in bed reading books and newspapers seems to have done me a lot of good. I regretted leaving my painting to go. I am now glad I went for I have accumulated some fine ideas studying Giottos and the School of Ferrara painters. . . ." A month later on April 4, he wrote: "I am head over [heels] in work again in helping Charlie and getting pictures ready for an exhibition at the Women's Cosmopolitan Club on 33rd [St.] East [New York]. They have invited me to exhibit and I am sending seventeen canvases . . . [and] to come and see them on the walls. I suppose I will have to go. I am curious to see what kind of a reception they will give the pictures and how they will look. For this is the first exhibition of mine with collected canvases." A reviewer wrote: "Little can be said in description of the works, which are beautiful combinations of color, but incomprehensible as to form. . . . His aim seems to be to depict action, regardless of distinct form or facial expression. In fact, he pays no attention to features whatever, and all but the color is left to the visitor's imagination. It is to be regretted that such beauty of color could not be wedded to a more sane technique."[102]

At the same time he was showing at the Cosmopolitan Club, Maurice had work in the "Forty-fifth Annual Exhibition of the American Water Color Society" in New York. On May 7, he wrote to its secretary, Mr. Post: "Will you have the kindness to let Mr. Edward Root have my picture 'The Canal' No. 215 in the catalogue." The following day Maurice wrote to Root: "I have been away for a few days in the country. . . . You can have the water color for $100.00 for I would prefer you to have it. I will collect the two water colors you bought from the Independent Exhibition. I know it was you who bought them for Mr. Kent told me and I admire your selection especially 'The Beach.' It made an impression on me at that time for I considered your aid went towards helping the exhibition out. I am glad you mentioned George Luks for he is a good friend of mine and all his *friends are my friends.* I hope you will always like the water color and never put it in the dark corner." On May 16: "Your two water colors arrived this morning and also the water color from Macbeth. It was just as well you proposed having it come back to Boston for it was unsigned. When I came to look at it, though I [did] it myself, and looking at it with a fresh eye it struck me as a very interesting water color, miles ahead of the two I received. . . . [P.S.] I do not altogether care for bronze mats. I much prefer white of a certain quality for the water colors with slender gold frames. Of course everyone is guided by ones own taste and I just mentioned this as a personal matter. M.B.P."

Maurice's relations with the New York art world were becoming closer. His friends there were gently urging him to move from Boston, where the critical climate had been gradually proving less hospitable to his new work. Although he loved Boston, as is evident from his letters to Charles from Venice, it is also apparent that he was traveling to New York often.

At some point between 1910 and 1913, Maurice undertook to paint a series of still lifes and flower pieces. He had mentioned Cézanne's still lifes in his December 1909 letter to Pach, and his own canvases are so homogeneous in style that they must have been painted within a circumscribed time period. Moreover, Ira Glackens pinpointed the date of *Apple and Pear on the Grass* (pl. 82) as having been painted at Bellport while Prendergast was visiting the Glackens family in the summer of 1912.[103] He only painted a dozen, among which very few have any of the textural layering of the beach and park scenes, although they do use broad interlaced brushstrokes, ranging at times from a Gauguin-like paint surface to a cold blue/white conjunction reminiscent of Maurice Vlaminck's Fauve manner of about 1905–7. *Cinerarias and Fruit,* c. 1912 (pl. 83), however much it is superficially reminiscent of Cézanne, is indebted to Monticelli's still lifes in both composition and texture. In the corresponding number of flower pieces painted around the same time (pl. 85), Maurice was freer in varying his surface treatments, and it is likely that he looked at the atmospheric treatment of color in both Redon's flowers and mythological canvases. The same surface treatment is found in the individual figure studies and portraits (pl. 86).

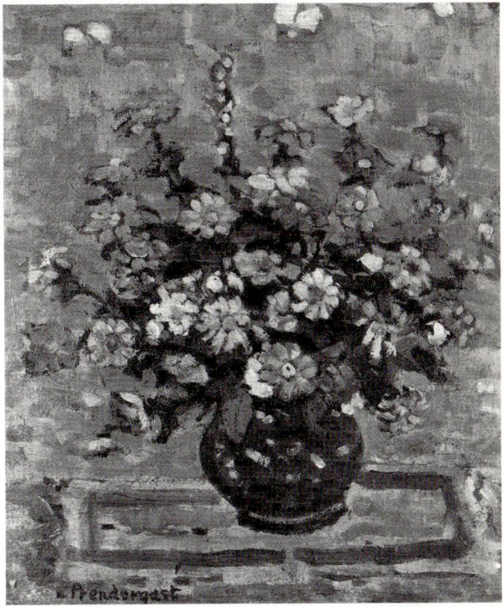

85. Flowers in a Blue Vase

c. 1912. Oil on canvas, 19 x 16"
Courtesy, Museum of Fine Arts, Boston.
Bequest of John T. Spaulding, 1948

This flower piece of zinnias, one of a half-dozen similar canvases, is more spontaneous than Maurice's still lifes and retains the Manet-like brushwork of the Paris and post-Paris landscapes.

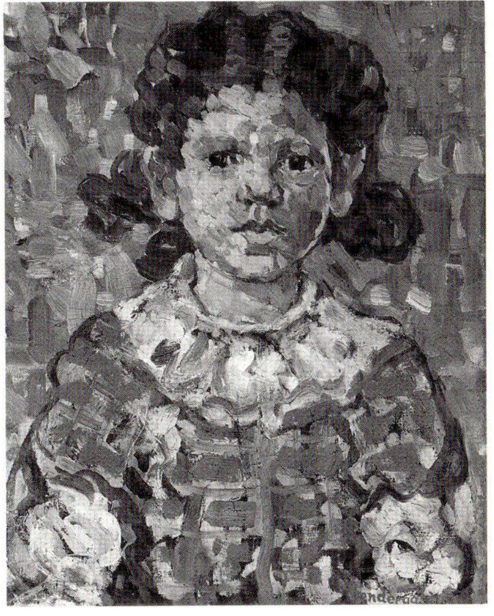

86. Girl in Blue

c. 1912. Oil on canvas, 13 3/8 x 11 1/4"
Hirshhorn Museum and Sculpture Garden,
Smithsonian Institution, Washington, D.C.
Gift of Joseph H. Hirshhorn, 1966

Girl in Blue *is one of the few completed half-length portraits. Its patterning of firm brushstrokes, a pervasively decorative expansion of the dense network of minute color patches in the* Sketches in Paris *panels (pl. 9), may reflect the influence of Vincent van Gogh's portraits.*

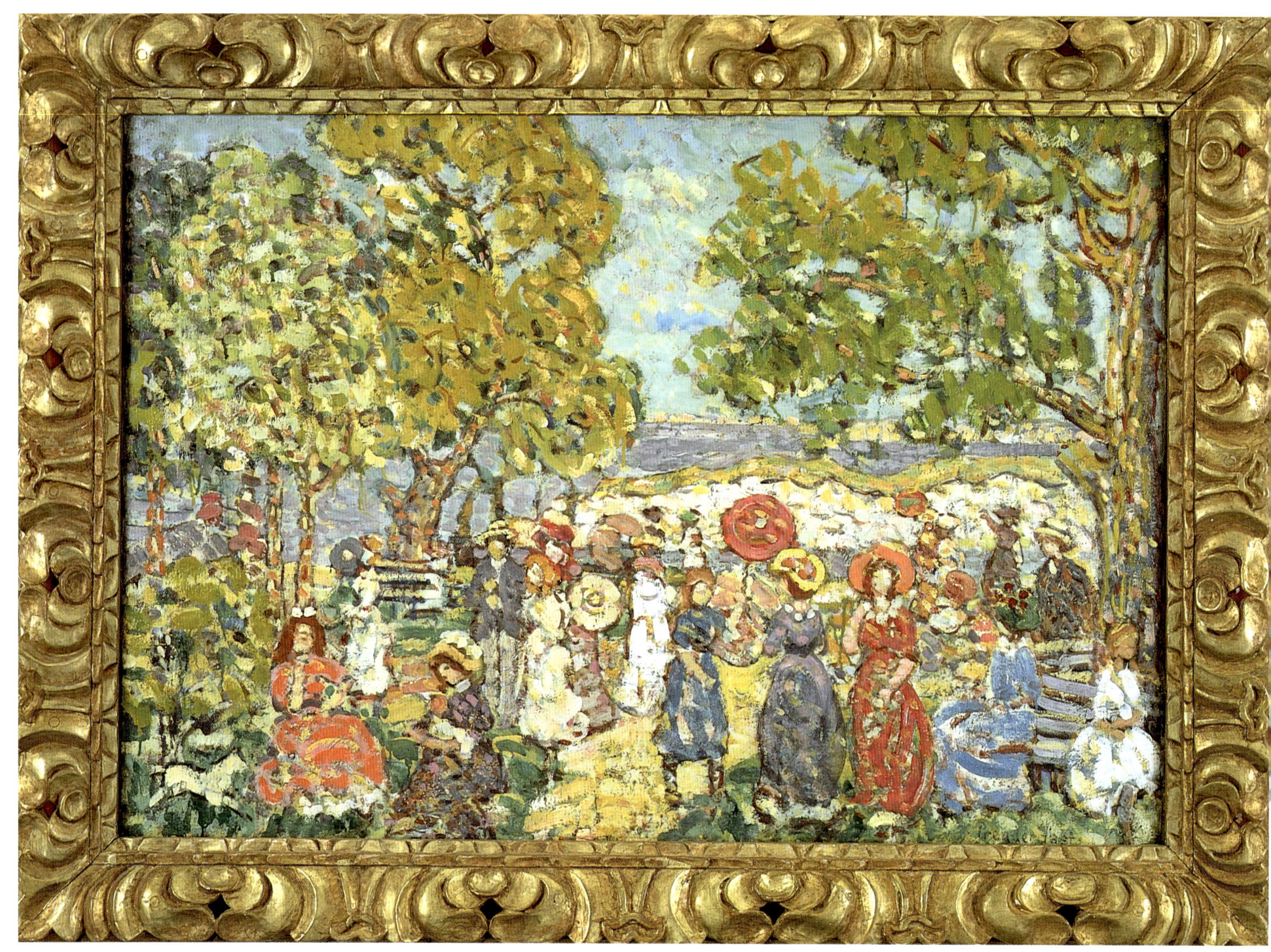

87. Landscape with Figures

X. The Armory Show 1913

AN ENTHUSIASTIC PARTICIPANT IN THE 1910 Independent Artists exhibition as well as the subsequent twelve-artist Independent show in 1911, Prendergast was a logical candidate to join the Association of American Painters and Sculptors, which began to organize the "International Exhibition of Modern Art" (known as the Armory Show), in 1912. Walt Kuhn, the association's secretary, wrote in early January 1912 to Maurice while he was still in Italy to invite him to join the group. Charles, on January 6, answered provisionally, "I know he will be delighted when he hears the good news." On February 23, Maurice wrote Kuhn: "It was a great pleasure to me reading your letter . . . announcing my election as a Member of the American Painters and Sculptors and I . . . promise I will give my best efforts to forward the interest of the Society." Maurice, who was very friendly with Davies and Pach, two of the prime forces behind the prospective exhibition, was appointed to the committees on Domestic and Foreign Exhibits, the only artist to serve on both. Kuhn kept Prendergast informed on the progress he and Davies were making with the organization of the show. On December 31, 1912, he wrote: "As I know that you are anxious to hear what's doing in the way of the coming show, I am sending you two important press clippings, as well as a general statement issued by our press committee, and a special statement by the President. . . . Davies and I have had a great time abroad, in fact a regular orgy of art. It is hardly possible to grasp the enormity of this undertaking, and we feel that it will be many years before a show of like import will be gotten together."[104] Prendergast's experience and knowledge of modern painting and his willingness to foster the work of young talents, such as Hartley, Max Weber, and Kent, as well as his steadfast support of older colleagues, especially Glackens, Luks, and Davies, made his counsel of special value. He had no enemies, did not countenance factions, and was on good terms with important collectors and dealers.

The exhibition, which Prendergast attended, opened on February 17, 1913, to great fanfare and controversy, mainly as the result of the public's reaction to Cubist works such as Marcel Duchamp's *Nude Descending a Staircase, No. 2* (1912), which was savagely ridiculed in the press. Prendergast exhibited seven works, three paintings and four watercolors (nos. 893–99), including *Landscape with Figures* (895) of c. 1909–12 (pl. 87), *Seashore* (894), c. 1910–12, and *Study* (899), c. 1912, a watercolor lent by Mrs. William Glackens. His pictures were juxtaposed with the great European masters from whose work he had repeatedly drawn sustenance, and seeing this must have given him immense satisfaction. An interview with William Glackens was published on the occasion of the show,

87. Landscape with Figures

c. 1909–12. Oil on canvas, 28⅝ x 42⅞"
Munson-Williams-Proctor Institute, Museum of Art, Utica, New York. Edward W. Root Bequest

In reply to a request to lend Landscape with Figures *to the 1934 "Maurice Prendergast Memorial Exhibition" at the Whitney Museum of American Art, New York, Root wrote in December of that year: "From 1920 until about 1927 it hung at the Metropolitan Museum. . . . I have dated the painting 1913 but it did not have the appearance of a new picture when I bought it. Charles Prendergast made the frame for me later at my request and from an earlier frame of his own make."*

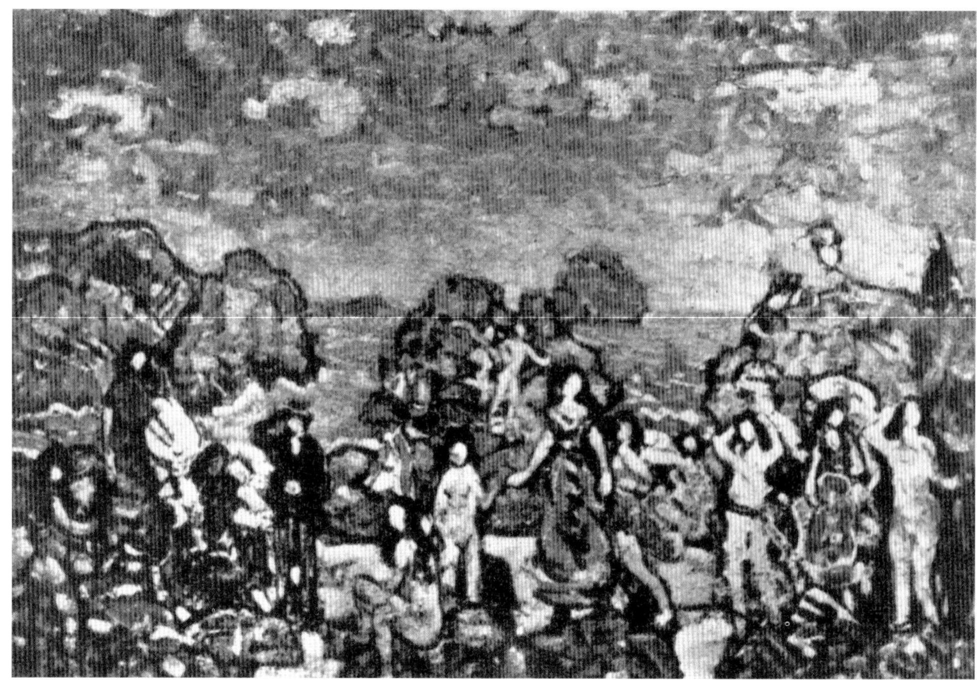

88. Seashore

c. 1910–12. Reproduced on a postcard published by the Association of American Painters and Sculptors, 1913. Archives of American Art, Smithsonian Institution, Washington, D.C. Walt Kuhn, Kuhn family papers, and Armory Show Records

The painting, an unconventional mix of nudes and clothed figures on a beach with rocks and clouds continuing their sweep through space, recalls compositions by Titian and Poussin.

ghostwritten, according to Ira Glackens, by Guy Pène du Bois, but certainly approved by Glackens. "Maurice Prendergast," it explained, "is prominent as one of the men who has been consistently and thoroughly modern. Years ago he was making patterns in joyous colors that gave delightfully the impression of the light, the happiness, the rhythm, the harmony of life."[105] Glackens understatingly added, "I am afraid that the American section will seem very tame beside the foreign section."

Tame or not, Prendergast's *Seashore* (no. 894 in New York and no. 296 in Chicago) was reproduced on a postcard by the association (pl. 88).[106] His friend Pepper had written to Macbeth (December 1912 or January 1913) referring to this now-lost canvas, "I have asked Prendy to hustle but he knows not the word. When he gets it done it will be done that is all. He is shocking good old Boston with a picture of ladies bathing in the garb of nature by a very dangerous craggy shore while gentlemen in black suits walk about. But a certain amount of shock is a good thing for this town of professional primness."

Jerome Myers recalled in his memoirs, "A rallying point for us [Myers and Prendergast] was the Armory Show, where we continued to meet through its duration. To him it was a huge circus, cramful of European novelties, of which the 'Nude Descending the Stairway' [*sic*] was but an outstanding item."[107] Du Bois seems to have caught Maurice's spontaneous reaction; to him he exclaimed, "Too much Oh-my-God! art here."[108] His more reflective observation was: "Now we must see what effect all this will have on us."[109] He wrote from Boston to Walt Kuhn on March 17, "Boston people coming back are full of the show—greatest thing they [have] ever seen."[110] Maurice studied the show carefully, both in New York and when 244 European works were transferred from Chicago and exhibited in Boston at Copley Hall from April 28 to May 19 without the American entries (pl. 89).[111] Prendergast made sketches in his note-

89. Postcard from Walt Kuhn to Mrs. Kuhn

April 23, 1913
Archives of American Art, Smithsonian Institution. Walt Kuhn papers. Inscribed:

[Kuhn:] "Just finishing a nice little dinner [signed] W."
[Davies:] "Don't mind them they are all drunk"
"from Boston Frederick James Gregg"
"Charles E. Prendergast"
"We all wish you the best wishes M. B. P. x x x"

Walt Kuhn, Arthur B. Davies, and Frederick James Gregg had gone to Boston to install the Armory Show in Copley Hall. In his catalogue introduction Gregg noted, "No works by Americans are shown in the Boston Exhibition because of lack of space. The members of the Association preferred to withdraw all of their own paintings and sculptures rather than make a choice. . . . They considered that the most important thing of all was to display the European section of the International Exhibition to the greatest possible advantage."

books of paintings by van Gogh and Gauguin and four works by Matisse, *Goldfish, La Coiffure* (pls. 90 and 91), *Still Life with Greek Torso,* and *Nasturtiums with "the Dance," II* (pls. 92 and 93).

In *Landscape with Figures* (pl. 87), Prendergast experimented with an intensely active surface pattern of saturated yellows, crimsons, blues, reds, and greens, flattening the figures so that they are only marginally distinguishable from the equally vivid multidirectional and -sized color patches. Layers of color are not built up into a thick impasto as they would be in subsequent canvases, many of them conceived and commenced around the same time as this but whose surfaces were painted on intermittently over a period of many years.

Landscape with Figures was purchased from the show by Edward W. Root. A letter on March 30 to Elmer MacRae, treasurer of the association, reveals Maurice's whimsical—or perhaps slightly sardonic—humor: "The check for $720.00 [eight hundred dollars less 10 percent] has been received all right. I will now buy a little villa on Lake Como and retire and be looking [for] you sooner or later." (A year later, at the end of April 1914, Maurice was elected president of the Association of American Painters and Sculptors. Alas, the position was honorary, since the association would never organize another exhibition.)

It was at this time that Albert C. Barnes began purchasing Maurice's paintings as well as Charles's carved and gilt gessoed panels and suggested to his associates that they do likewise. On August 4, 1913, John Quinn, who was a major force behind the Armory Show, wrote to Maurice Prendergast: "I talked to Walt Kuhn today and he gave me your address. I wondered whether your brother was coming to New York at any time during the summer. . . . I have about a dozen pictures that I should like to consider the frames of with him. I want good frames on them and Kuhn tells me that your brother is the best man on hand-made frames that we have. . . . I want sometime to own two or three of your things, but

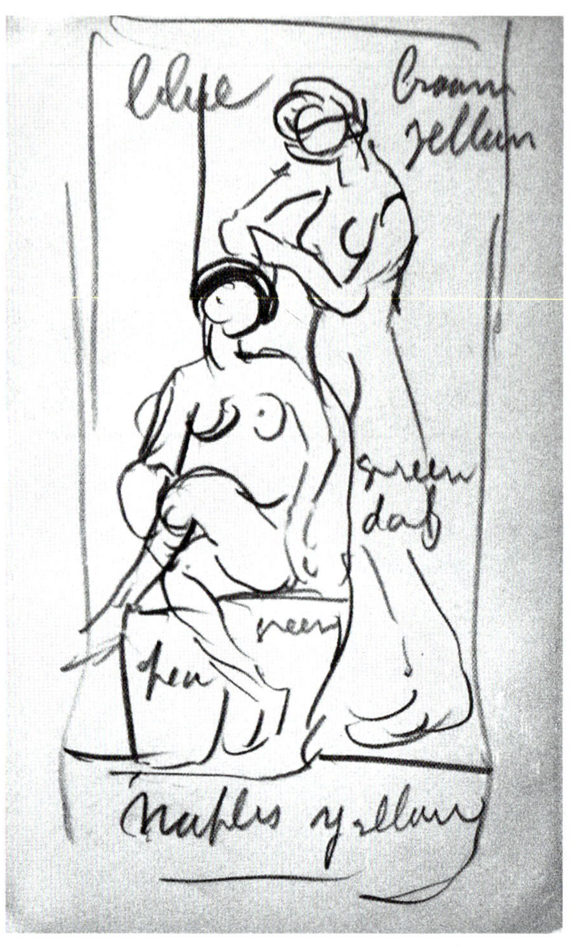

90. Sketch after Matisse's *La Coiffure*

1913. Pencil on paper, 7⅞ x 5⅛″
Courtesy, Museum of Fine Arts, Boston.
Gift of Mrs. Charles Prendergast in honor of Perry T. Rathbone, 1972, "Sketchbook #21" (CR 1509)

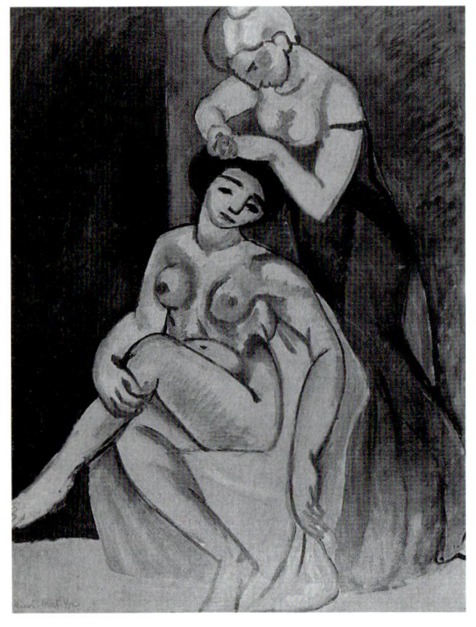

91. Henri Matisse (1869–1954)
La Coiffure

1907. Oil on canvas, 45⅝ x 35″
Staatsgalerie, Stuttgart

I should like to see them sometime at your studio in Boston, where I could make the selection."

On August 14, Maurice answered, "My brother expects to be in New York about the first week in September. . . . It will be extremely interesting and it will give him the greatest pleasure to frame some of your pictures. We had a very pleasant time in Maine—but did not do much painting—laid in a good stock of health instead. Whenever you want to see my canvasses I shall be glad to show them to you—and have a lecture on '*Art*.' "

A month earlier, following a second prostate operation at the City Hospital, Boston, Maurice wrote to Walter Pach on July 11 from 56 Mount Vernon Street,

> *I am sending you back the interesting post cards. It was a treat looking at them. They all had something in them—"Quelque chose là." Ingres especially; his drawings and painting of the Nudes* [The Turkish Bath?]. *I am coming along after my hospital experience and getting my strength back again, I am thankful to say. Both Charley and I leave for Brookville, a little place on the Maine coast to stay three or four weeks. . . . I have not started to do any work yet, just crawling around. P.S. If you hear of anything half studio half workshop let us know. There is trouble about renewing the lease of the studio here and it looks as if they are going to build. If we leave here it is New York for us. M.B.P.*

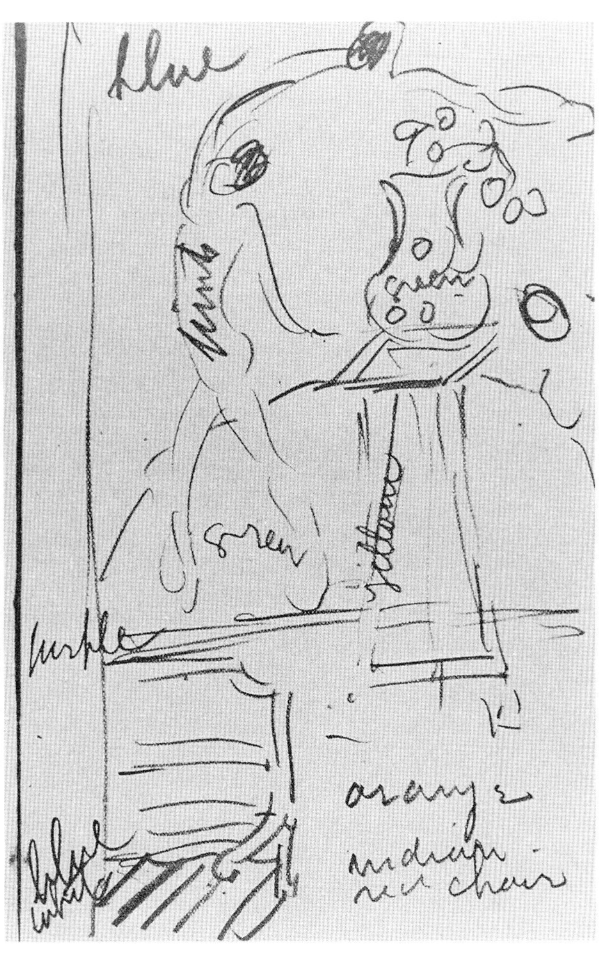

92. Sketch after Matisse's *Nasturtiums with "the Dance," II*

1913. Pencil on paper, $7^{7}/_{8}$ x $5^{1}/_{8}$"
Courtesy, Museum of Fine Arts, Boston.
Gift of Mrs. Charles Prendergast in honor of Perry T. Rathbone, 1972, "Sketchbook #21" (CR 1509)

In early December the brothers went to New York and Maurice wrote to Quinn to put him in touch with Charles. Amicable discussions took place throughout 1914, during which time the Prendergasts were occupied with finding accommodations in New York. At the end of 1913, Rockwell Kent introduced Maurice to a new dealer, Charles Daniel, who planned to exhibit contemporary American artists. Maurice accepted the suggestion and told his younger colleague, "In reply to your letter I will send a couple of pictures to your friend Mr. Daniel." He also exhibited again at the National Arts Club, from February 5 through March 7, 1914, where his work elicited a very enthusiastic commentary by James Huneker: "The new painting is beginning to look quite old-fashioned, the fate of all violent movements to escape the conventional. But what's good in the movement has come to stay. There's Prendergast with his paint which makes his canvases look like embroidery."[112]

After the brothers moved to New York in the fall of 1914, Barnes visited their studio weekly, as Glackens's studio was in the same building at 50 Washington Square South. By the end of the year, Maurice and Charles, together with the Glackenses, visited Barnes at his home in Overbrook, Pennsylvania. From the moment Maurice arrived in New York he also had access to Quinn's collection. Prendergast was thus on the best of terms with the two most advanced collections and collectors in America.

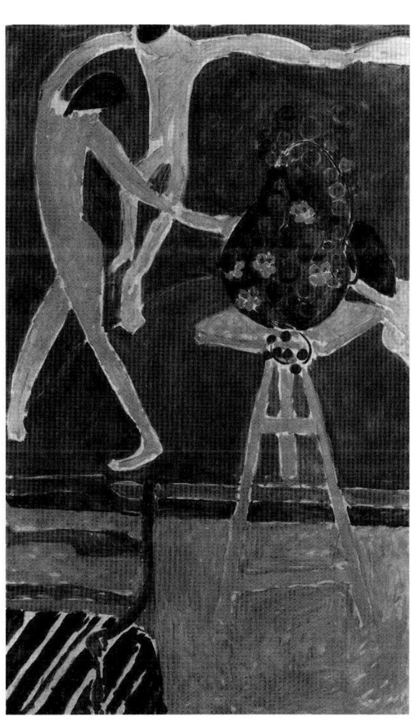

93. Henri Matisse (1869–1954)
Nasturtiums with "the Dance," II

1912. Oil on canvas, $75^{1}/_{2}$ x $45^{3}/_{8}$"
The Metropolitan Museum of Art, New York.
Bequest of Scofield Thayer, 1982

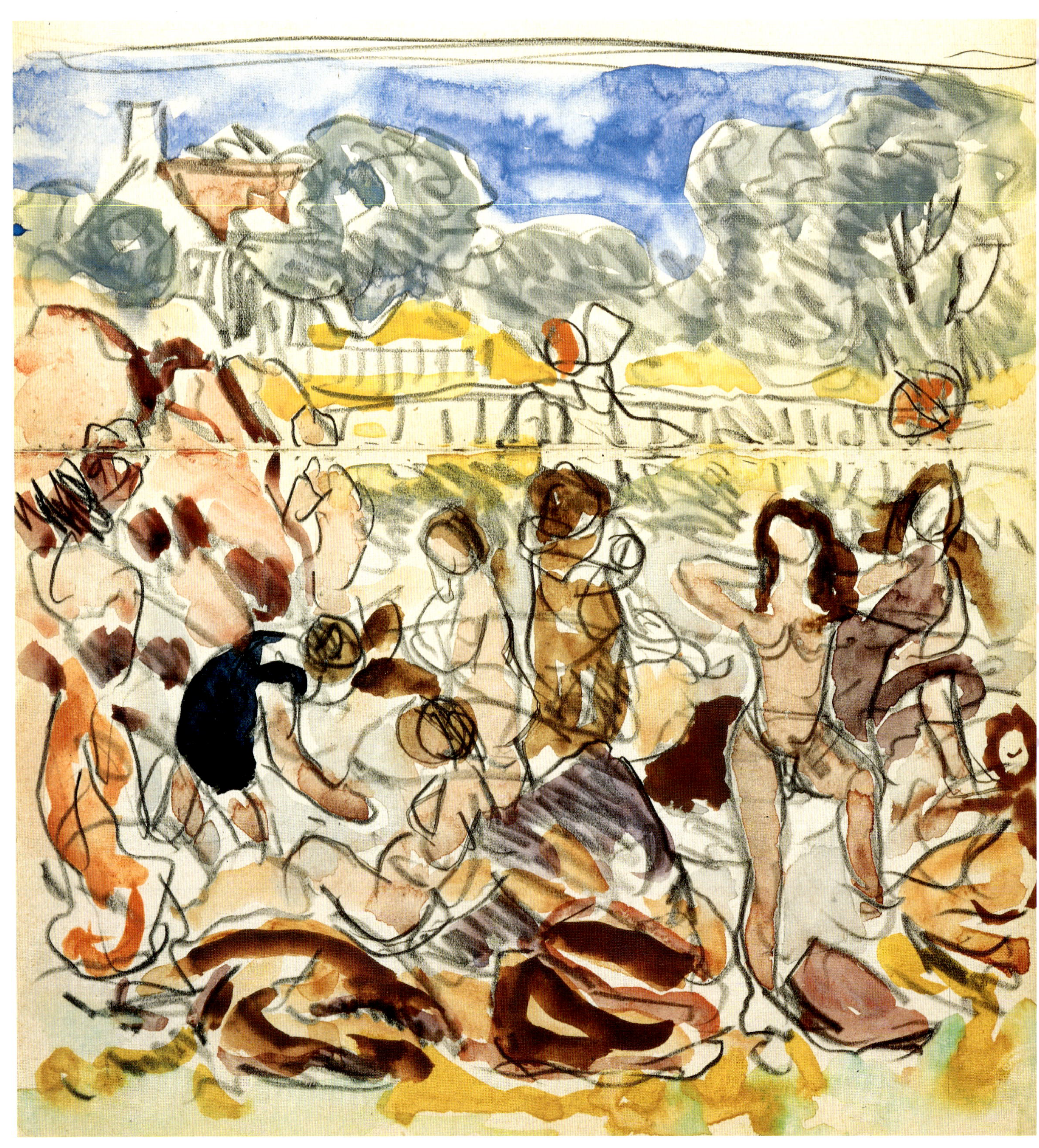

94. Figures on the Shore

XI. The Last Decade 1914–24

In April 1914, Maurice sailed on what would be his last trip abroad. His destination was the Emerald Coast of Brittany, from where on May 2 he wrote to Mrs. Williams on stationery of the Grand Café, Dinan:

> *I arrived early [April 22] at St. Malo this year and I have plenty of time to look around before the season opens. I have taken an excursion around Finistere, taken in Roscoff, Concarneau and Dinan. I am immensely [im]pressed here. It is a beautiful place; the walks with their noble trees and the fine old walls. . . . I will try and come here again late in the summer on my way home. I was not so much impressed with Paris this last trip. Everything is changing so much [that] in the next twenty years all the old Paris will have disappeared and it will be a great modern city. I saw the two exhibitions, the Champ de Mars and the Independents. Some of the canvases were very bad and childish in the last [latter] show [and] spoiled it just a trifle. For all that it stimulated me. . . .*

On June 8, he wrote to Elmer MacRae from Saint-Malo to acknowledge receipt of his dues for the Association of American Painters and Sculptors. "I expect to return in September. I have been here for six weeks. The season has not started yet. There is lots of wind and big blue ocean. I stay here four weeks more and return to Paris where I intend to study some of the exhibitions." Four days later he wrote to Pach:

> *I forgot to mention about your article and the reproduction of one of my pictures. My pictures looked immense and I am sending you my most hearty thanks for doing me so much honour. . . . I have changed my mind about staying here and am going home by the middle of August. . . . The weather has been so bad and I have been unable to get out with my box. There is a new collection opened at the Louvre, Isaac Camondo and I notice[d] by the papers [it] contains 3 or 4 Cézannes and several Degas. . . . Renoir is creating quite a stir. He is doing some small panels down at Cassis which are most delightful in color—a way ahead of his former landscapes.*[113]

In fact, Maurice painted perhaps as few as a half-dozen watercolors. It is not known whether he managed to sail before the outbreak of war. Charles, who wrote Quinn on June 24 from Boston that he expected Maurice to return in October, reported that he was "going to New York again soon, and try and find some place where we can work. We have been trying to do this for some time." By November, he wrote to Quinn: "I am afraid when I wrote you last about the

94. Figures on the Shore

c. 1916–18. Watercolor and pencil on paper, 7⅝ x 5"
Delaware Art Museum, Wilmington.
Gift of Helen Farr Sloan, Sketchbook (CR 1547)

Prendergast rarely made use of models in his studio. He preferred to sketch outdoors in the parks and at the seashore. Ideas from these drawings, made spontaneously from nature, were subsequently transferred to his watercolors and paintings. Frequently he "undressed" the bathers and placed them in animated poses and groupings, in the tradition of Delacroix and Cézanne. The drawings in this sequence are heightened with opaque touches of watercolor.

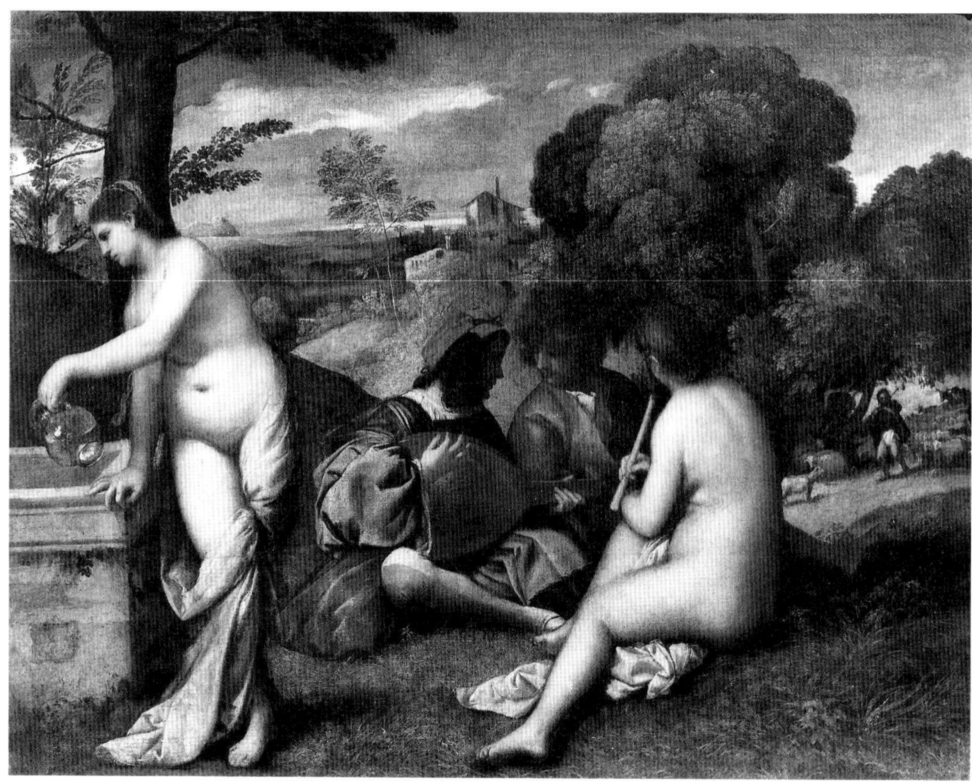

95. Giorgione da Castelfranco (c. 1477–1510). Alternately attributed to Titian (c. 1490–1576)
Le concert champêtre

c. 1508–10. Oil on canvas, 41½ x 53½″
The Louvre, Paris

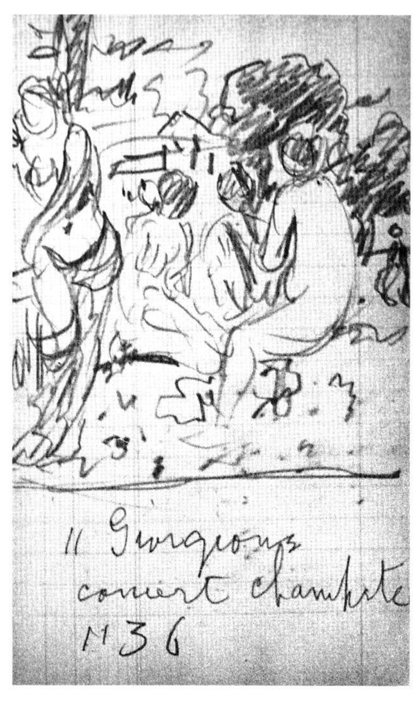

96. Sketch after
Le concert champêtre

1914. Pencil on paper, 6 11/16 x 4 5/16″
Courtesy, Museum of Fine Arts, Boston.
Gift of Mrs. Charles Prendergast in honor of Perry T. Rathbone, 1972, "Sketchbook #66" (CR 1518)

frames I did not comprehend what an undertaking it was finding a suitable place in New York City. And then after finding the place, packing and shipping all our things on. What an awful job. Well its all done and over. We are both very comfortably located at 50 Washington Square South. . . ."

Quinn replied the day after Christmas, "I am glad that you and your brother are comfortably located here and I hope you both like the change. . . . Perhaps you could come to my apartment some evening and I could point out to you what pictures I should like to have you make frames for. You might prefer to do frames for some over others." On January 8, 1915, Maurice wrote to Edward Root to tell him, "We have been located here since the first of last November. We occupy the whole of the second floor formerly the necktie people. Any time you feel like coming down it would give us the greatest pleasure to talk things [over] with you. We are in morning and afternoons except the couple of hours for lunch. We have been trying to get up to see Mr. and Mrs. Luks since we have been here and have not succeeded yet."[114]

Daphne Dunbar recalled the Washington Square studio: "It was almost a duplicate of Mt. Vernon Street, even the stove and the glue pot."[115] Ira Glackens has left the best firsthand description of the Prendergast brothers' workshop:

> *The place was furnished with the minimum necessities of life, but all about hung Maurice's paintings and Charles's panels. One of Charles's beautiful carved chests stood between the two front windows. These treasures, in all their glowing colors, made the place as rich as a palace. . . . A group of little Italian marionettes hung by their wires in a corner of the room. . . . Under a bench was a small wooden box con-*

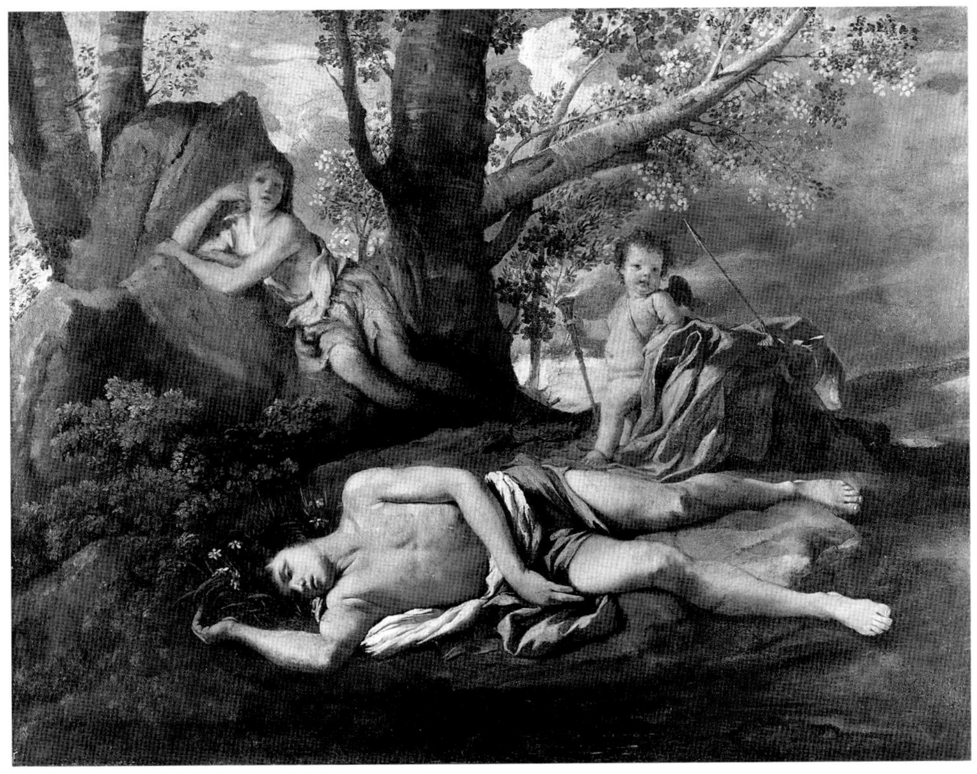

97. Nicolas Poussin (1594–1665)
Echo and Narcissus

c. 1630. Oil on canvas, $29\frac{1}{8}$ x $39\frac{3}{8}$"
The Louvre, Paris

taining ancient pieces of mosaic . . . a treasure found likewise in Italy. . . .

The Prendergasts' studio at 50 Washington Square, as remembered by a small boy, was a magic place. There was so little of it unconnected with art that the paintings, panels and chests (gold, silver, vermilion, viridian, cobalt), the Persian jars, the marionettes, the smell of paints and whiting and the faint aroma of rabbit glue, mingle in one wonderful pastiche.[116]

In Prendergast's subsequent arcadian, modernized versions of the *fête galante,* the artist sought sources in the traditions that carried him beyond the immediacy of Manet, the monochromatic tonalities of Whistler, and the naturalism and spontaneity of the Impressionists to more elaborate colorful spatial organizations. His attitude toward sources is best documented by remarks written in a notebook of about 1910:

The Signs of Genius is the power of recognizing and assimilating that which is necessary to the development of oneself. . . . We come into the world with nothing in our own right except the capacity for the acquisition of Ideas. We cannot invent Ideas, we can only gather some of those in circulation since the beginning of the world. We endow them with the color and form of our own time and if that color and form be of supreme quality the work is preserved as a representation of a period in the history of civilation. . . . Genius is the power of assimilation. Only fools think the[y] invent.

If the circumstances of a man's life admitted the acquisitions of only one set of Ideas his work would be thin. . . .[117]

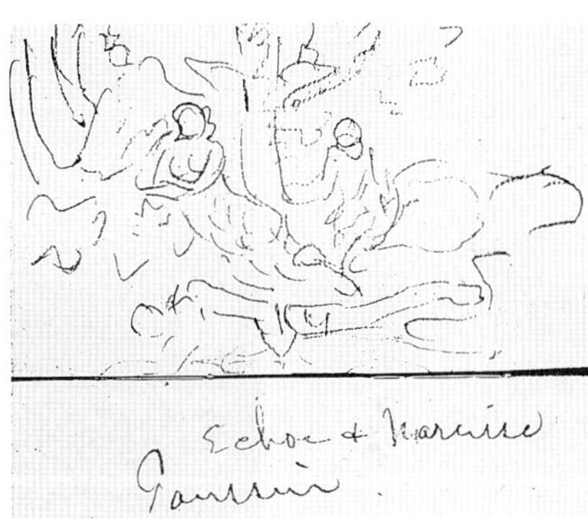

98. Sketch after Poussin's
Echo and Narcissus

c. 1914–15. Pencil on paper, $3\frac{3}{4}$ x $4\frac{3}{8}$"
Courtesy, Museum of Fine Arts, Boston.
Gift of Mrs. Charles Prendergast in honor of Perry T. Rathbone, 1972, "Sketchbook #54" (CR 1518)

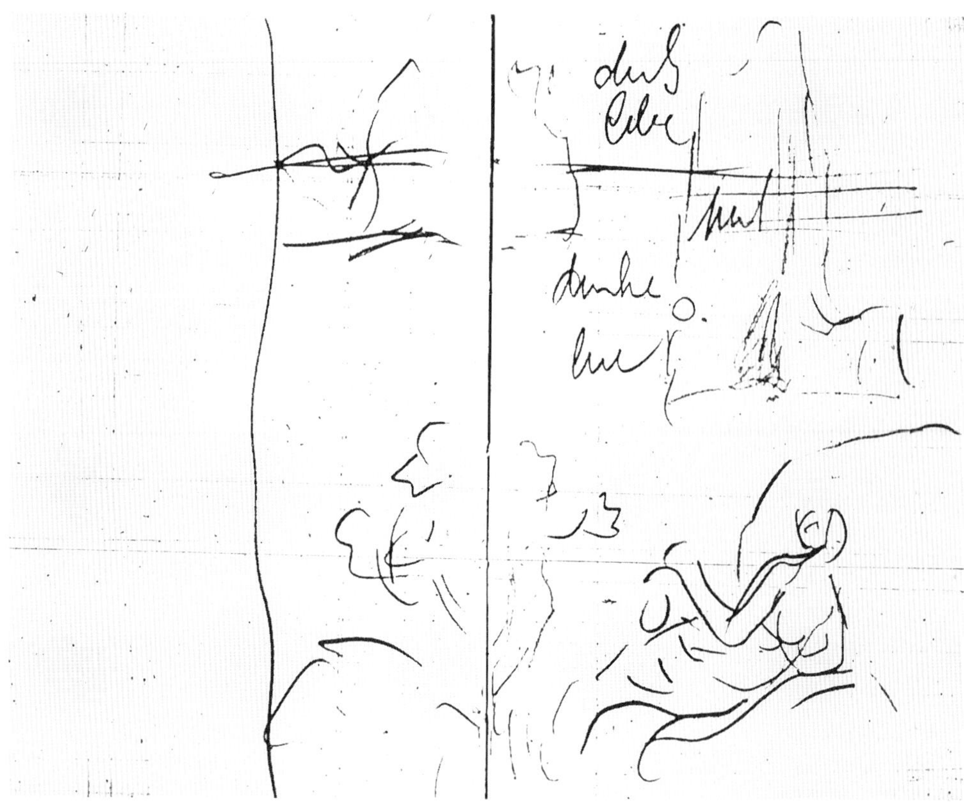

99. Sketch after Pierre Puvis de Chavannes's *Dramatic Poetry*

c. 1912. Pencil on paper, $6\frac{1}{16}$ x $7\frac{7}{8}$"
Courtesy, Museum of Fine Arts, Boston.
Gift of Mrs. Charles Prendergast in honor of Perry T. Rathbone, "Sketchbook #51" (CR 1506)

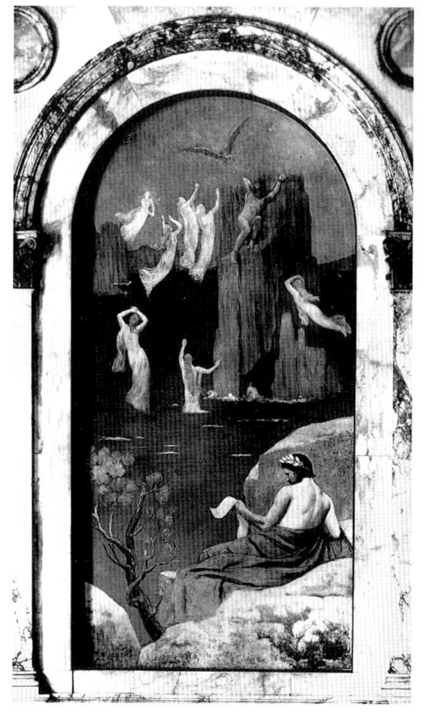

100. Pierre Puvis de Chavannes (1824–1898) *Dramatic Poetry*

c. 1895. Oil on canvas, $164\frac{1}{2}$ x 86" (rounded at top)
Courtesy of the Trustees of the Public Library of the City of Boston

The lessons of the early watercolors and oils were merged and culminate in the majestic, expressive multifigure compositions, which represent Prendergast's creativity at its highest level. For these new compositional formats he sought classical models, and he did not invest his preferred motif with symbolic or mythological meanings; his references are specific and in no way esoteric: Trecento and Quattrocento frescoes, Carpaccio, Giorgione, Poussin, Watteau, Puvis de Chavannes, Cézanne, Renoir, Gauguin, and Maurice Denis among the classicists, and others such as Monticelli, Conder, Cross, K.-X. Roussel, Bonnard, and Charles Guérin. This unbroken tradition nourished Prendergast—as it had Cézanne and Matisse—and he freely adapted and explored his own ideas; his color relationships took on an intricacy and depth distinct from mere Impressionism, formulaic Neo-Impressionism, or any of their dependents.

Prendergast drew incessantly from nature, and in his pencil sketches he sought to preserve the immediacy of the moment observed and to transfer some of this fresh, spontaneous liveliness into the sparkle and fluidity of the paint surfaces done in his studio. Maurice's sketchbooks are filled with nude studies, in many cases figures in parks or at the seashore, which he considered inserting into his paintings (pl. 94). Moreover, in his search for pastoral figure compositions taken from nature or classical models, Prendergast knew exactly what type of source he was looking for. Between his drawings of teeming outdoor scenes at the beach or in the park are interspersed more formal figure groupings freely copied from such pictures as Giorgione's *Le concert champêtre* (pls. 95 and 96),[118] Nicolas Poussin's *Echo and Narcissus* (pls. 97 and 98),[119] and Pierre Puvis de Cha-

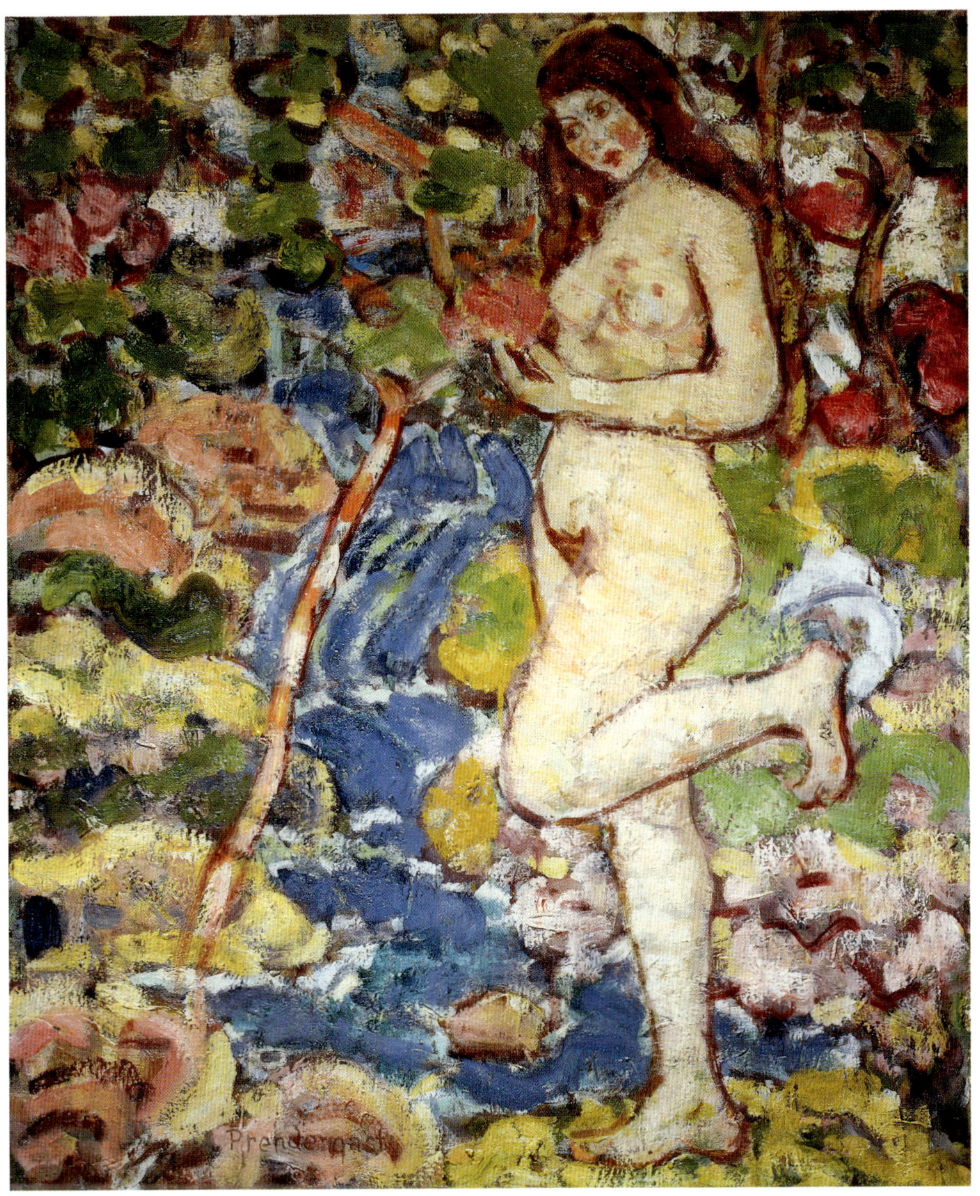

101. Waterfall

c. 1911–12. Oil on canvas, 23¾ x 19¾"
Private collection, courtesy of R. H. Love Galleries, Inc., Chicago

The collector John Quinn originally owned this painting, showing a single nude reminiscent of similar figures in the work of Pierre Puvis de Chavannes set against a decorative background. The nude also reveals Prendergast's awareness of Renoir. The unusual illustrative focus on facial features recalls similar effects in a number of Maurice's early monotypes.

vannes's three compositions *Pastoral, Dramatic,* and *Epic Poetry* (pls. 99 and 100) on the north wall of the Boston Public Library,[120] among numerous others.

From around 1909 onward, the multifigured park and seashore compositions became the main focus of Prendergast's art. His convalescence in Venice in 1911, during which he was obliged to do very little painting—no oils whatsoever—gave him time to read and reflect. "Italy is the place for ideas," he had written to Charles, and studying the old masters, particularly Giotto, made him eager "to dance a high step on the paint box." This was an abbreviated version of his 1898–99 Italian experience with, of course, the accumulated work of more than a decade to build upon. After his return from Italy, early in 1912, Maurice continued to experiment with nudes, both individually and in groups, in his watercolors and paintings. It appears that he also prepared for these compositions by working from a model in the studio. The results of these sessions, like the still lifes and portraits, are somewhat stiff and artificial. Once, however,

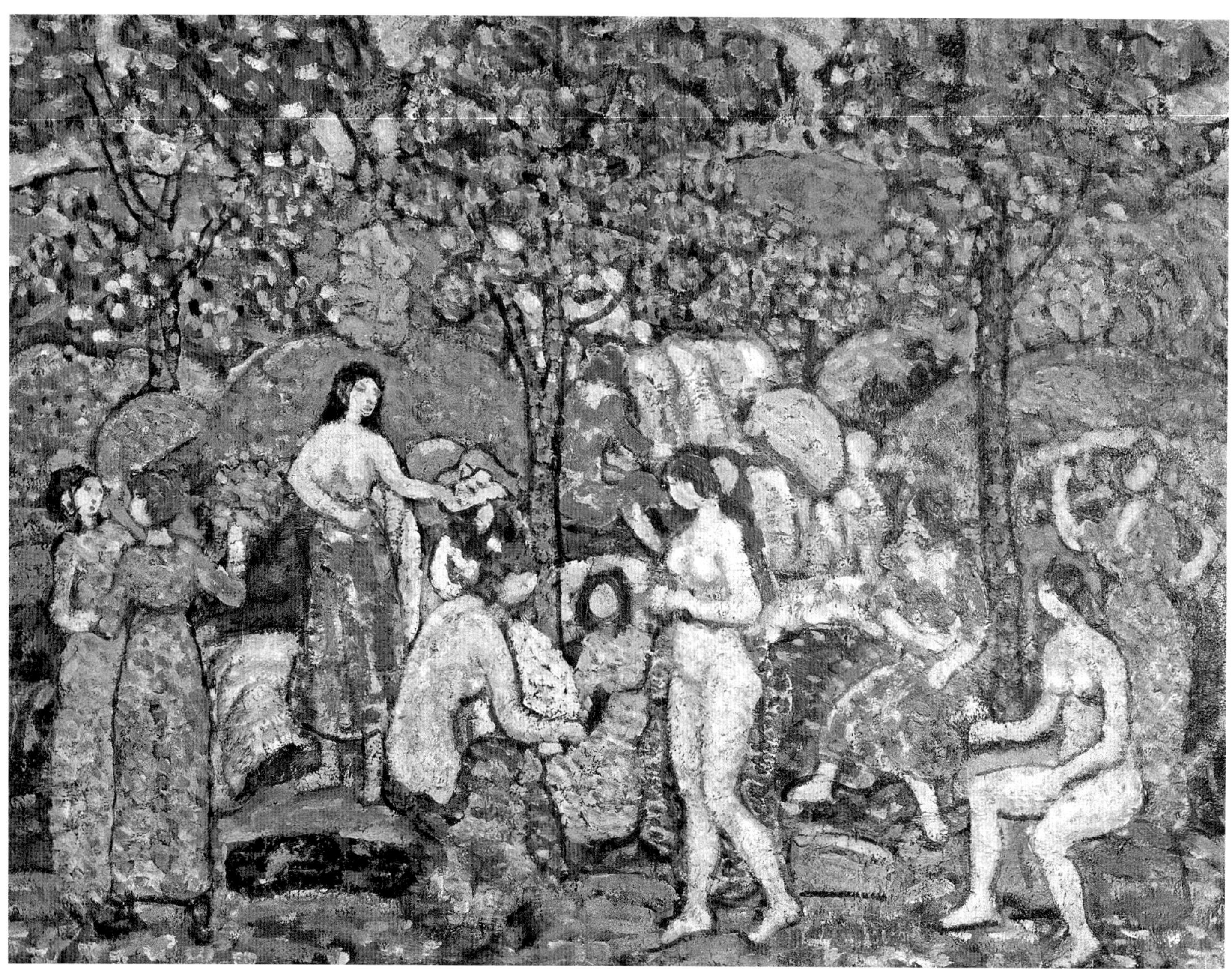

102. Idyl

c. 1912–14. Oil on canvas, 24 x 32″
The Barnes Foundation,
Merion Station, Pennsylvania

This composition, with its undulating waterfall, has an internal color and textural diversity that complements the seated and standing figures. Dark tree trunks break the rolling hills and frame the figures, clothed and unclothed, back views and front, facing left or right within a luminous landscape tapestry screen.

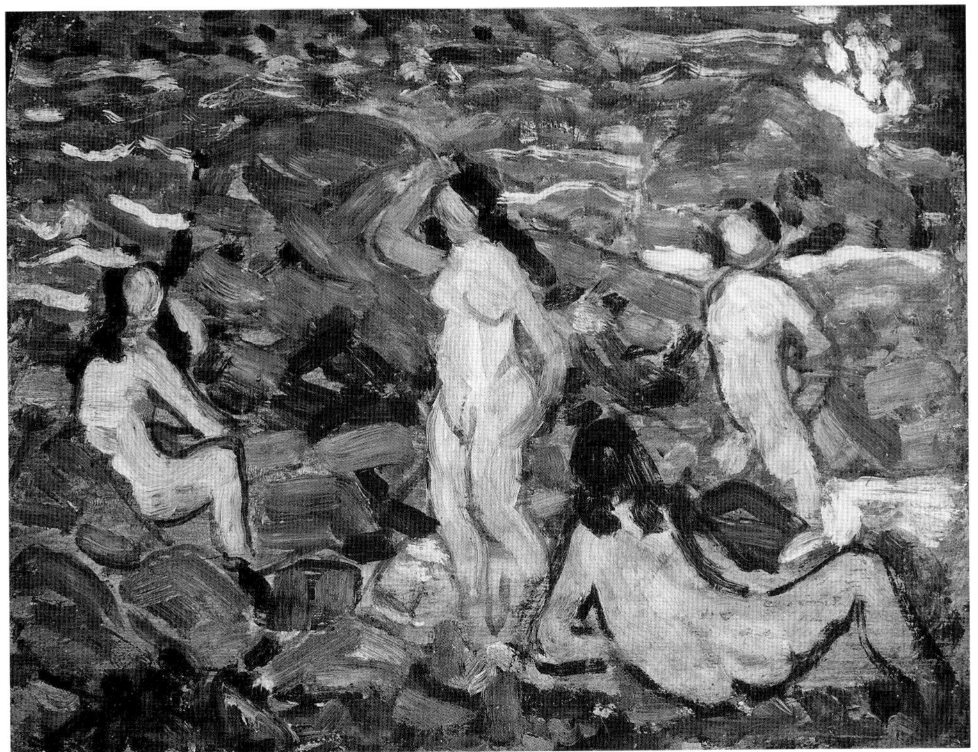

103. Four Nudes at the Seashore

c. 1910–13. Oil on panel, 10½ x 13¾"
Williams College Museum of Art, Massachusetts.
Gift of Mrs. Charles Prendergast

Maurice replaced the angular drama of Cézanne's Five Nudes *(pl. 104) and other works with a simplified sweep to the bodies, retaining the subtle rhythms of placement and repetition found in that master's compositions.*

he integrated the figures into a landscape or landscape/shore setting, a concept that had been reinforced by seeing the sweeping landscapes with nudes and mythological figures of the old masters, Maurice found his own unmistakably personal direction, completely transforming his style from the 1907 panels exhibited at Macbeth's in 1908.

Waterfall (pl. 101), c. 1911–12, provides an overall decorative setting for the Eve-like nude, firmly outlined in purple and brown, with luscious bits of pink, lavender, blue, ocher, and green surrounding her, as if the spots and patches of a monotype such as *Summer Day* (see pl. 57), c. 1900–1902, had been expanded and made into a richer network of irregularly overlapping patterns. In *Idyl* (pl. 102), c. 1912–14, Prendergast translated his understanding of Florentine frescoes, Giorgione, Gauguin's elegant Tahitian versions of the Greeks, Renoir's nudes and nude groups, and Puvis de Chavannes[121] into a graceful frieze, combining clothed, semiclothed, and nude figures in a rhythmic sequence recalling but not resembling Gauguin's *Where Do We Come From? What Are We? Where Are We Going?* of 1897. The dry, frescolike sparkle of color, the emphasis on rich, granular built-up pigment, such as that found in Cézanne's bathers and landscapes that Maurice had scrutinized, merged its rugged texture with an appealing, almost anticlassical "awkwardness" of drawing, with its compact, unconventional placement of three-dimensional figures against a screenlike background. Indeed, the small *Four Nudes at the Seashore* (pl. 103), c. 1910–13, and other closely related multifigure compositions that Maurice would paint for the next several years were the result of this renewed and in-depth contact with the art of Cézanne (pl. 104).

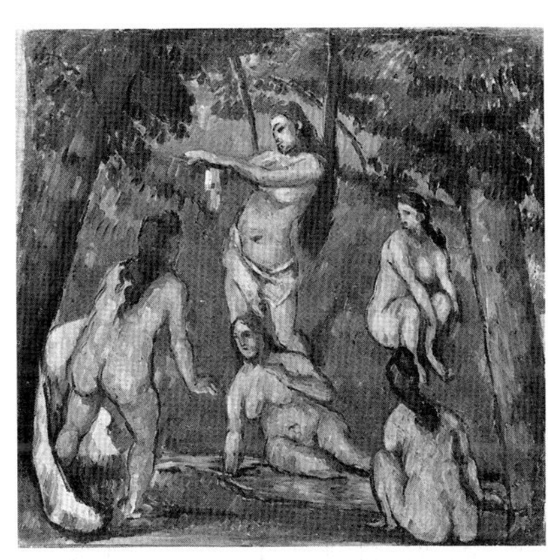

104. Paul Cézanne (1839–1906)
Five Nudes

c. 1877–78. Oil on canvas, 15½ x 16½"
The Barnes Foundation, Merion Station, Pennsylvania

A related composition, Four Bathers, *c. 1877–78 (V. 384), was exhibited in the Armory Show (no. 216) and was therefore also known to Prendergast.*

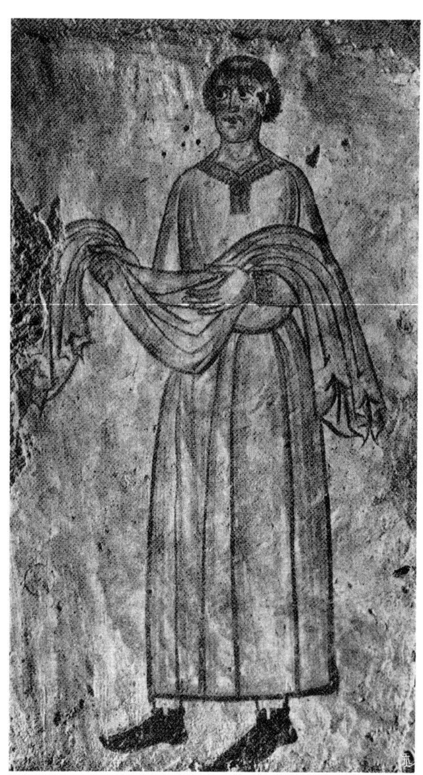

105. Fresco

11th century
Church of San Ambrogio, Milan. Fig. 58, page 87, from *La pittura e la miniatura nella Lombardia* by Pietro Toesca. Milan: Hoepli, 1912

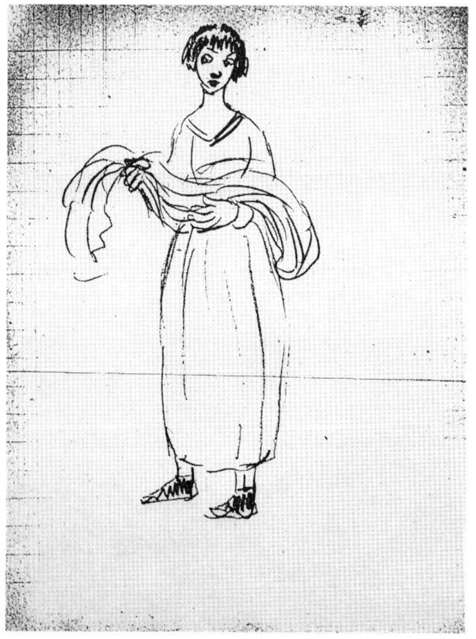

106. Sketch after Toesca Fig. 58

c. 1912–13. Pencil on paper, 7⅞ x 6⅛"
Courtesy, Museum of Fine Arts, Boston. Gift of Mrs. Charles Prendergast in honor of Perry T. Rathbone, 1972, "Sketchbook #46" (CR 1502)

During these years Maurice read and/or scanned the reproductions in such books as Charles Diehl, *Manuel d'art Byzantin* (1910); Bartolomeo Nogara, *I mosaici antichi* (1910); O. M. Dalton, *Byzantine Art and Archeology* (1911); Pietro Toesca, *La pittura e la miniatura nella Lombardia* (1912); and Carl Robert, *Die Antiken Sarcophagreliefs* (1890, 1898, 1904), whose subjects disclose archaic alternative or parallel sources that extend the ideas of the Renaissance masters and Post-Impressionists. The standing seminude figure third from the left in *Idyl* may appear conspicuously Gauguin-like, but it also derives from an earlier source in the traditions, a deliberate archaism seen in such figures as those Maurice freely sketched from illustrations in Toesca of Romanesque frescoes (pls. 105, 106, 107, and 108). At the same time, Charles was carving panels utilizing adaptations of the Byzantine, Etruscan, Persian, Hindu, Coptic, and Oriental traditions.[122]

However much Prendergast studied and was influenced by the color constructions of Cézanne, his figures and figure groupings have something distinctly idealized, pastoral, gentle, as opposed to the thumping rhythmic force of Cézanne's compositions. The fact that Maurice's were made up primarily of color relationships links him to Cézanne. All of the familiar and exotic sources he brought into play would mean little were it not for the evidence of the paintings themselves, their format, color tonality, texture, mood, pattern, and spatial organization. Barnes, in 1925, described Prendergast's color scheme as including "lilac pinks, yellow, pale blue, chalky whites, pale greens and roses."[123] These color qualities, so reminiscent of Puvis de Chavannes, Redon, and Denis, tone down the Impressionist and Neo-Impressionist colors that are dominant in the Saint-Malo panels, in the interest of uniting the figures into a one-piece tapestry effect. As we can see from the pictures themselves, as well as the sources Prendergast chose to study, this immersion in the ancient, medieval, and Renaissance traditions was deliberate and prolonged, and it had a profound impact on the conception and execution of Maurice's art.

In his pastorals Prendergast pursued color harmonies as musicians shift key settings. Just as one writes music in the key of C Major or G Major, Maurice painted in blue or red or yellow as the dominant harmony, and this stress on harmonies led him into intricate, subtle relationships akin to what musicians have found in their manipulation of major and minor keys. Whether Prendergast's deafness played a role in leading him to discriminate such a remarkable range of elusive color harmonies remains intriguing speculation. For Prendergast, one picture has its blues, reds, and yellows shot through and dominated by a pale blue-purple; another controls the primary colors by emphasizing a pale pink-purple; a third offers harmonies of a delicate lemon yellow. Prendergast stressed the tertiary blending of colors for their infinite variety of grays, tans, and browns. The Impressionists used a wide range of secondary blendings but in general avoided mixing three colors together, believing that this would bring them too close to the brown tonalities they were trying to avoid. Prendergast found that the broken tertiary tones weave shifting color harmonies throughout the picture. He had learned by looking carefully at Cézanne the importance of controlling warm and cool colors in both large areas of contrast and the most subtle of juxtapositions. In 1907, of course, these were used in a more obvious Signac-influenced mosaic pattern of application. As he accumulated experience, he came to overlap and interweave colors and drag the stroke with a deliberate buildup of tangible paint, which results in a flickering, broken, crusty, opulent surface of warm and cool bits and pieces, clusters of microharmonies that can be controlled and distributed across the surface and that lead to a nuance of atmosphere. These atmospheric harmonies, coupled with gracefully choreographed processions of elongated figures and donkeys, successors to the earlier horses, trees, water, boats, and houses, are unified by a gentle, rhythmic flow of line and pattern across and into space in countless configurations, which lend a contrapuntal diversity to the compositions. Maurice worked and reworked his surfaces, often over a period of years, to gain his interwoven webs of paint and atmospheric space that are at the core of his art.

Although Quinn had yet to buy any paintings by Maurice, he was instrumental in arranging for Harriet C. Bryant, director of the Carroll Galleries, New York, to organize an exhibition of twenty-nine paintings and thirty-one watercolors in 1915, a presentation of the artist's work dating from after the Eight show in 1908. Quinn, who owned the gallery, purchased seven oils and nine watercolors for a total of $4,700. Prendergast wrote Quinn on February 21, "I am deeply grateful to you for giving my exhibition such a fine start and also for the great interest you have shown in my work right along. . . . Your letter gives me confidence and pleasure and will pave the way for the future." Quinn continued to collect Charles's panels and commissioned frames for such paintings in his collection as Duchamp's *Chess Players,* Redon's *Roger and Angelica,* works of Augustus John, and, of course, Maurice's oils.

The catalogue essay for the Carroll Galleries show was written by Frederick James Gregg, former critic of the *New York Evening Sun,* tireless publicist for the Armory Show, close friend and adviser to Quinn, and staunch supporter of modern art.

> *Prendergast's eminence has been accepted for years as a matter of course. . . . At home he is revered, particularly by the younger men. This, his first really comprehensive exhibition, ought to convince the public that does care for art that in him it has to do with a great master. . . . He has superb courage, consistency and determination never to be moved from his own chosen path. He has never condescended to make his art easier for the public. . . . The work of Prendergast as exhibited here ranks easily with that of the most modern Frenchmen. . . .*[124]

The reviewer in the *New York Times* wrote:

> *The catalogue tells us that . . . he is essentially part of "the new movement" in capital letters. He is really better than all this. He is a serious and humble student of design, and marshals line and color into patterns of some intricacy. . . . When he paints a "decorative composition" with a background of waving lines and a fore-*

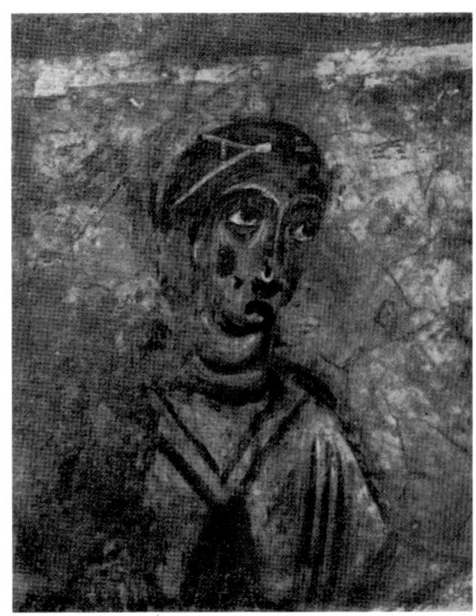

107. Fresco

11th century
Church of San Vincenzo, Galliano. Fig. 33, page 51, from *La pittura e la miniatura nella Lombardia* by Pietro Toesca. Milan: Hoepli, 1912

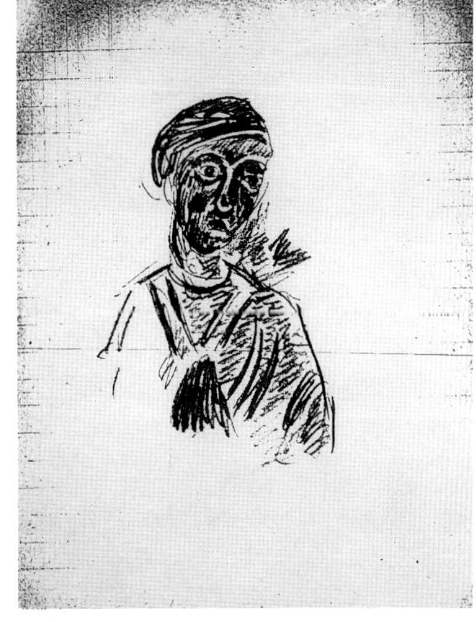

108. Sketch after Toesca Fig. 33

c. 1912–13. Pencil on paper, 7⅞ x 6⅛"
Courtesy, Museum of Fine Arts, Boston.
Gift of Mrs. Charles Prendergast in honor of Perry T. Rathbone, 1972, "Sketchbook #46" (CR 1502)

ground of domestic animals and a middle distance of home-going youth with a basket he simply spells "sampler" to the middle-aged public, and they delight in him. Thus they can bear it not quite to understand his bathers and very distinguished nudes. He is one of the painters who paint for the honest fun and toil of painting and the public sooner or later will be his friend.[125]

Charles Caffin in the *New York American,* who had first written about Prendergast sixteen years earlier, enthused:

I suspect his own style was completely formed before he became acquainted with Cézanne. If . . . you regard it as in a general way representing the claim of the artist to his own vision and expression, and his courage to assert it consistently, then by all means include Prendergast among the new movers. . . . His work has the stamp of personality that makes it, like all original work, new. It is an expression of quiet exhilaration, of pure refreshment, akin to that subtle satisfaction, so devoid of effort, that permeates one's sensations. . . . These paintings . . . are irresponsibly gladsome yet their make-believe is a serious preoccupation with the artist.[126]

In a sidelight to the show, Maurice found himself caught in the middle of an acrimonious dispute between Dr. Barnes and Quinn. Barnes, who had been buying paintings and panels directly from Maurice well before the Carroll show, and who became his most perceptive critical supporter, did not want to buy from the gallery and indirectly pay Quinn a commission. Harriet Bryant and Barnes exchanged vituperative letters, Bryant's drafted by Quinn. Both collectors wrote directly to Maurice, counseling him on how to conduct his business affairs. Barnes urged Maurice not to make Carroll his exclusive agent, which Prendergast had indicated to Quinn he would. The issue remained unresolved between Quinn/Bryant and Barnes, but the artist never again exhibited at the short-lived gallery. Nevertheless, he maintained excellent relations with both collectors, telling Charles Daniel: "They're both my friends, what can I do?"[127]

A month before Maurice's show, the Carroll Galleries staged its "Second Exhibition of Works by Contemporary French Artists." Assembled by Walter Pach, it showed seventy works in various mediums by Redon, Georges Rouault, Raoul Dufy, Cross, André Derain, Duchamp, Raymond Duchamp-Villon, Seurat, Signac, Roger de La Fresnaye, and Valtat, among others. Pach corresponded with some of the artists in order to arrange the show. It was less than a year into the war, and French artists were eager to find an outlet in America for their work. In the spring, Dufy sent Pach one of his recently illustrated books, *Les Alliés: Petit panorama des uniformes,* inscribed to Prendergast "Souvenir du Paris en 1915."[128]

On July 7, 1915, Maurice wrote to Pach to ask him to thank Dufy for his gesture: "I was deeply touched when I received from you Dufy's little book on the soldiers. Please tell Monsieur Dufy when you write him I felt more pleased than if I got a gold medal, and I shall always treasure it in remembrance of him and his work. It brought up that nice dinner we had at the Romano and the pleasant evening at your friend's studio. . . ." He continued in a different vein: "I must say Boston is an interesting place in summer. . . . I don't think I should care about living here again. It has a local side the same as Quebec and Halifax. They lack the great stimulus of New York." Dufy wrote to Pach from Paris, September 18, 1915, to acknowledge Prendergast's thanks and asking Pach to send a book with reproductions of Prendergast's work: "Je suis bien heureux de savoir que M. Prendergast a aimé mon petit souvenir. J'irais heureux si vous pouviez m'envoyer un ouvrage et des reproductions de ses oeuvres afin que je le connaisse mieux. . . ."

In July, Maurice went to Ogunquit, Maine, stopping to visit the Williamses in Annisquam, also paying a call on Walt Kuhn in nearby York, with a stop in Portsmouth. Early in September he wrote to Quinn: "I am back again in New York. I passed my vacation going from one place to another . . . nothing but rain and fog. Quite a lot of painters there. . . . As a painter I like the surroundings of Boston the best. Cohasset, Marblehead and Salem especially appeal to me. . . . As soon as the foliage commences to turn I will go up to the Catskills and see what it looks like."

Maurice continued his busy exhibition schedule, showing at the Panama-California Exposition in San Diego, at the Maxwell Gallery in Los Angeles, and at the Panama-Pacific International Exposition in San Francisco. Nor did he neglect the opportunity to include his latest work in the exhibitions of lesser-known organizations. For example, in June 1916 he joined the People's Art Guild, a Socialist cooperative educational organization that between 1915 and 1918 organized art exhibitions in which many of the leading modern painters—Abraham Walkowitz, William and Marguerite Zorach, Leon Kroll, as well as his friends from the Eight, among many others—participated.[129]

In October, he wrote to Mrs. Williams, "Enclosed is the little book on Cézanne."[130] He invited the Williamses to New York: "I hope you will find time to come on . . . sometime this winter and take in the museums." In later years Mrs. Williams would recall to Charles: "One could feel the breath of life you and Maurice always imparted to the stodgy atmosphere of Boston. Yes, I never pass that sacred spot on Mt. Vernon St. where you and Maurice carved and painted and dreamed of art (and France) and the sun poured in from the little garden behind, without a quiver of warmth and lively reminiscence coming over me. It was from you two that I first became acquainted with Cézanne and got most of my inspiration in art."[131]

In *Figures in a Park* (pl. 109), c. 1914, the elongated distortions in the drawing of the figures, the dusky, scumbled impasto, the chalky tonality of the paint, and the fixed poses of the figures all point to origins in Puvis de Chavannes, the later canvases of Conder (pl. 110), and their own early Florentine and eighteenth-century French origins. The subtle grays, tans, pinks, and blues within a restricted chromatic spectrum recall the gentler scope of harmonies of these sources.[132]

As Maurice's pictorial conceptions progressed, the patterns of his paintings became less attached to specific illustrative sources, until the surfaces grew vir-

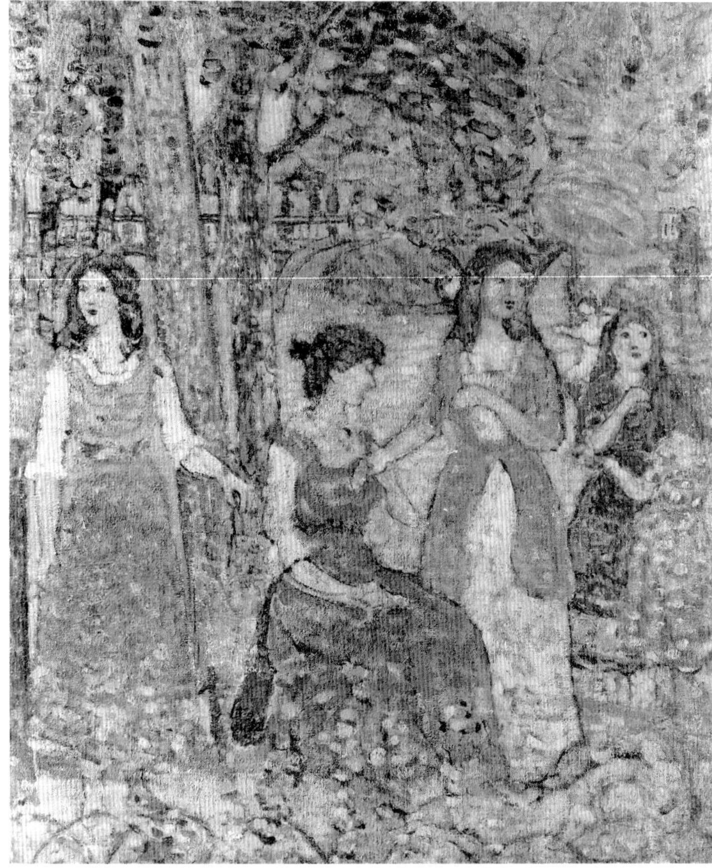

109. Figures in a Park

c. 1914. Oil on canvas, 58 x 49″
The Chrysler Museum, Norfolk, Virginia

Prendergast toned down the Impressionist and Neo-Impressionist color in the interest of uniting the figures into a one-piece monumental sampler effect. The distinctly placid mood is derived from not only Puvis de Chavannes and Conder but also artists who in varying degrees were influenced by Puvis de Chavannes, such as Maurice Denis, Edouard Vuillard, and K.-X. Roussel.

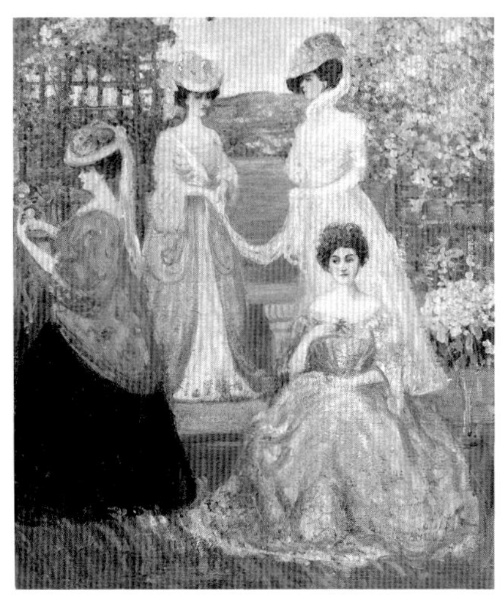

110. Charles Conder (1868–1909)
Four Ladies on Terrace

c. 1905. Oil on canvas, 30 x 25″
Private collection, courtesy Davis & Langdale Company, New York

tually seamless, their glowing, scumbled textures thoughtfully stroked, daubed, and dragged, sensuous, saturated by the piling of pigment, building up unexpected juxtapositions that pull the eye over the canvas, imparting a crusty tapestry quality recalling the work of Ryder, Monticelli, Pissarro, Cézanne of the mid- and late 1870s, and Rouault, all artists with whom Prendergast was familiar. *The Swans* (pl. 111), c. 1914–15, densely knit together with a silvery, pearly opalescence of ivories, greens, lavenders, yellows, and beiges, is a variation on a compositional theme that Prendergast employed on several occasions. He included three standing figures grouped closely together, a three graces motif that the artist often repeated, and which is also found in numerous panels by Charles, including the mural size 55-by-80½-inch panel *The Spirit of the Hunt* (pl. 112), c. 1917. The strong blue draws the eye to the patterns on the far left and far right, playing against the tertiary tones of the center and the note of surprise that the blue hair of the silhouetted figure with arms raised then evokes. In *The Swans* the one-piece tapestry effect of the picture's surface is reminiscent of Monticelli and Ryder, but in a different key and with a more variegated complexion to the colors that make up the patterns. There is a distinct sense of the individual gestures that echo the tree branches and swans. The seated figure in the right corner with arms raised above her head, ultimately based on classical poses and frequently used by Renoir, is a motif that Maurice inserted to anchor the corner of his composition.

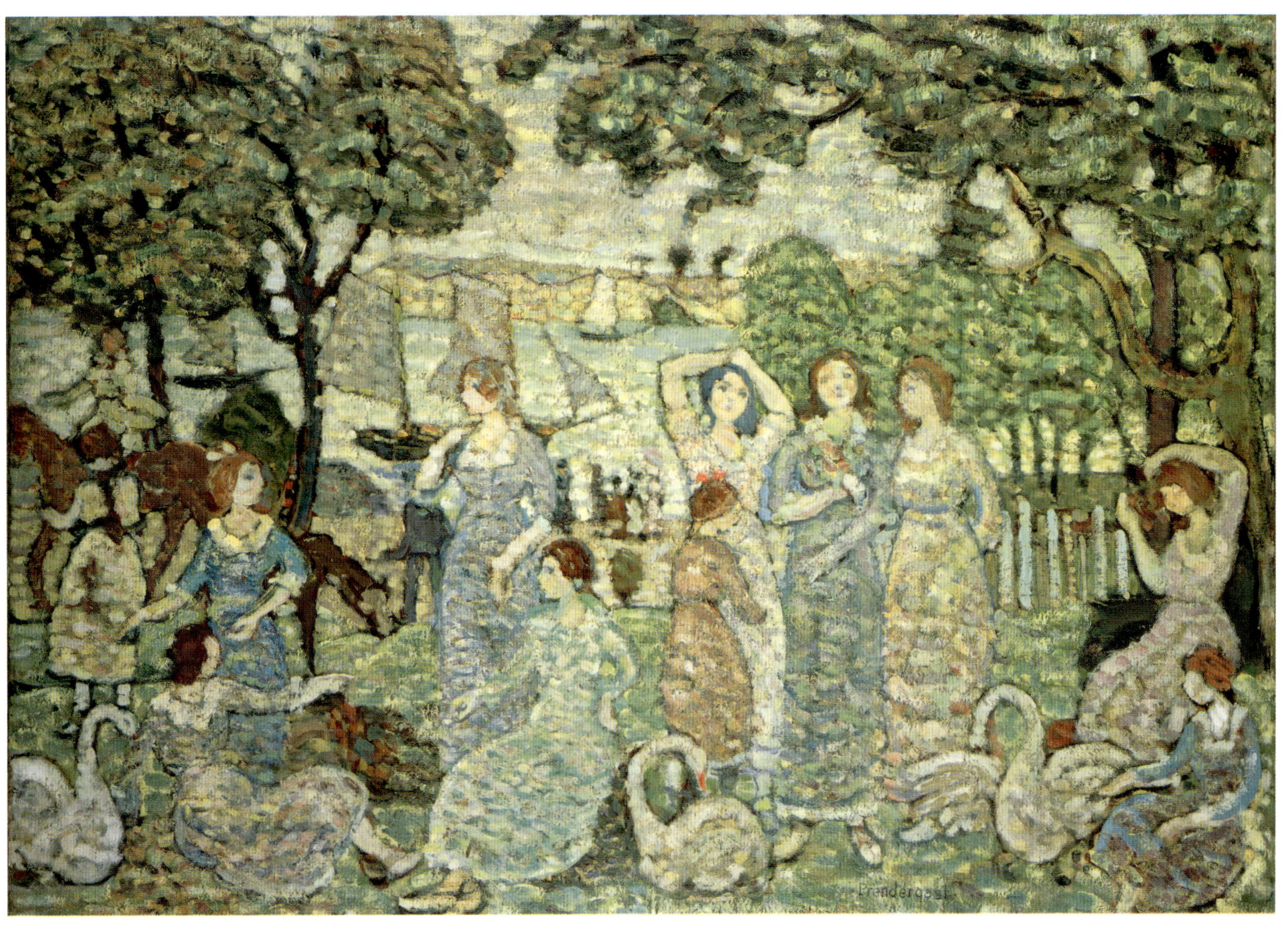

111. The Swans

c 1914–15. Oil on canvas, 30¼ x 43⅛″
Addison Gallery of American Art,
Phillips Academy, Andover, Massachusetts.
Bequest of Miss L. P. Bliss

Nearly all the figures of The Swans *retain vestiges of Degas's poised ballet dancers, many of whom served as models for Prendergast's monotypes of dancers and circus themes. Similar figures in other compositions, such as the closely related composition* The Picnic *(National Gallery of Canada, CR 388), are nude or seminude.*

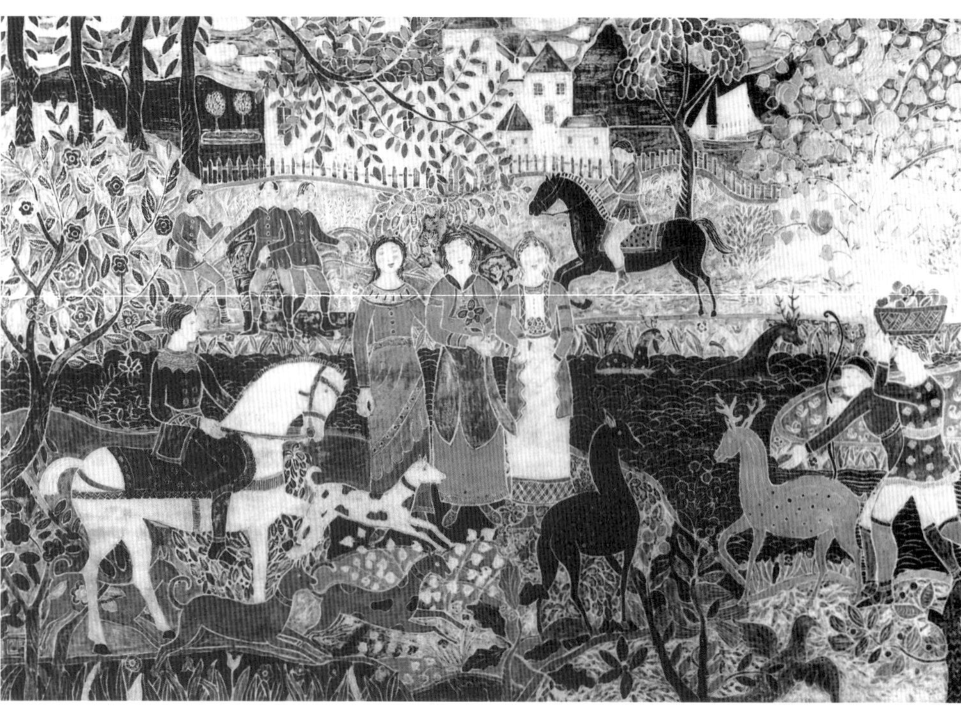

112. Charles and Maurice Prendergast
The Spirit of the Hunt

c. 1917. Tempera, gold and silver leaf, and pencil on incised gessoed panel, 55 x 80½″ Courtesy, Salander-O'Reilly Galleries, Inc., New York. Jon and Barbara Landau Collection

This large panel was commissioned by Lillie P. Bliss and hung over the mantelpiece in the Bliss home at 29 East Thirty-seventh Street in New York. It is the only known work, other than frames, on which Maurice acknowledged his collaboration by a signature.

Along the Shore (pl. 113), c. 1914–15, in a smaller format than *The Swans,* has twice the number of figures. Inserting only a branch in the upper right, which recalls Cézanne's similarly Japanese-inspired repoussoir units, Maurice replaced its leafy foliage in favor of an interlaced layering of volumes and space; three Giottoesque donkeys are threaded among the compact atmospheric warp and weft of stately simplified figures. The entire surface is painted in a brilliant high key; the figures are varied in scale, held in place by the Poussin-like gridwork of vertical color patches receding toward the horizon. Strong colors are used as stabilizing horizontal and vertical bands, binding the composition, while orange umbrellas, spatial accents that zigzag in rhythmic syncopation from front right to back left, open the space around intervening figures. Mottled mahogany accents that bounce through the picture, pegging the space like bossed nail heads, provide an eye-catching asymmetry. The elongated figure in white in the center with intense blue coat is a daring focal point, with the donkey's head on one side and body with rider on the right intersecting with the man with blue coat and yellow hat.

113. Along the Shore

c. 1914–15. Oil on canvas, 23¼ x 34″ Columbus Museum of Art, Ohio. Gift of Ferdinand Howald

Color in Along the Shore *is unusually rich in its variety and diversity of tertiary tans, gray-greens, and ivories, all of which coalesce in a pale, suffused glow. Ferdinand Howald (1856–1931), who originally owned this painting, was an important collector who acquired works by Prendergast from the dealer Charles Daniel (1878–1971).*

While water and sky recede into space in *Along the Shore, Donkey Rider* (pl. 114), c. 1914, treats the theme of figures and donkey with rider on the shore by bringing the procession up close and creating a conspicuous patchwork curtain–like foil. The eye is further brought forward by the bright yellow, green, brown, and purple dabs and squiggles in the immediate foreground and the distinct outline of the donkey's profile. The two tall, elegant strolling figures on the left, with their multicolored dresses, long coats, and hats, recall Whistler's *Tanagra* figures of c. 1867–70 (pl. 115), with their loosely brushed pale pinks, whites, lavenders, and disklike Japanese fans. The foreground is made even more intense by the pervasively blue-green background. The man who holds the don-

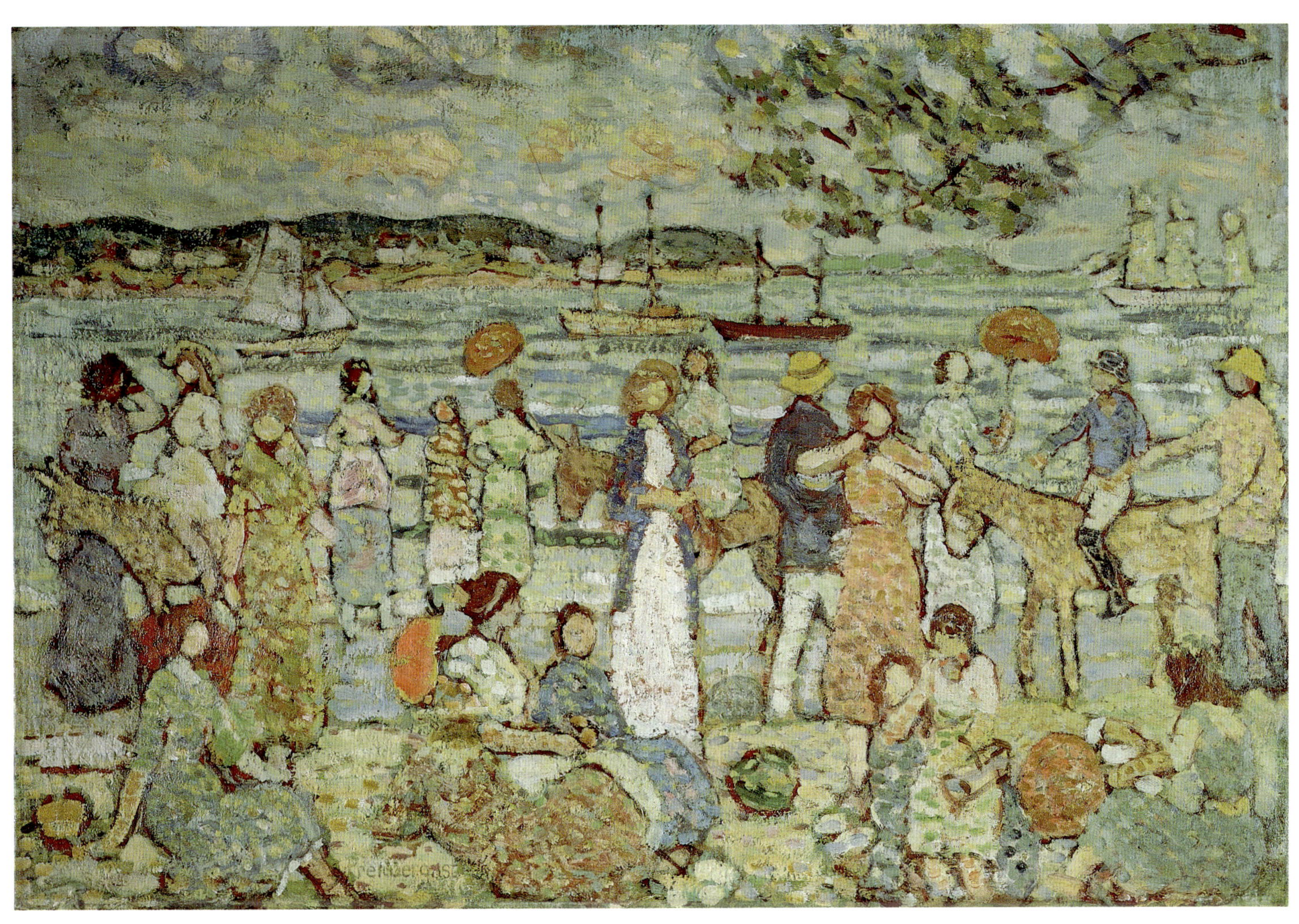

113. Along the Shore

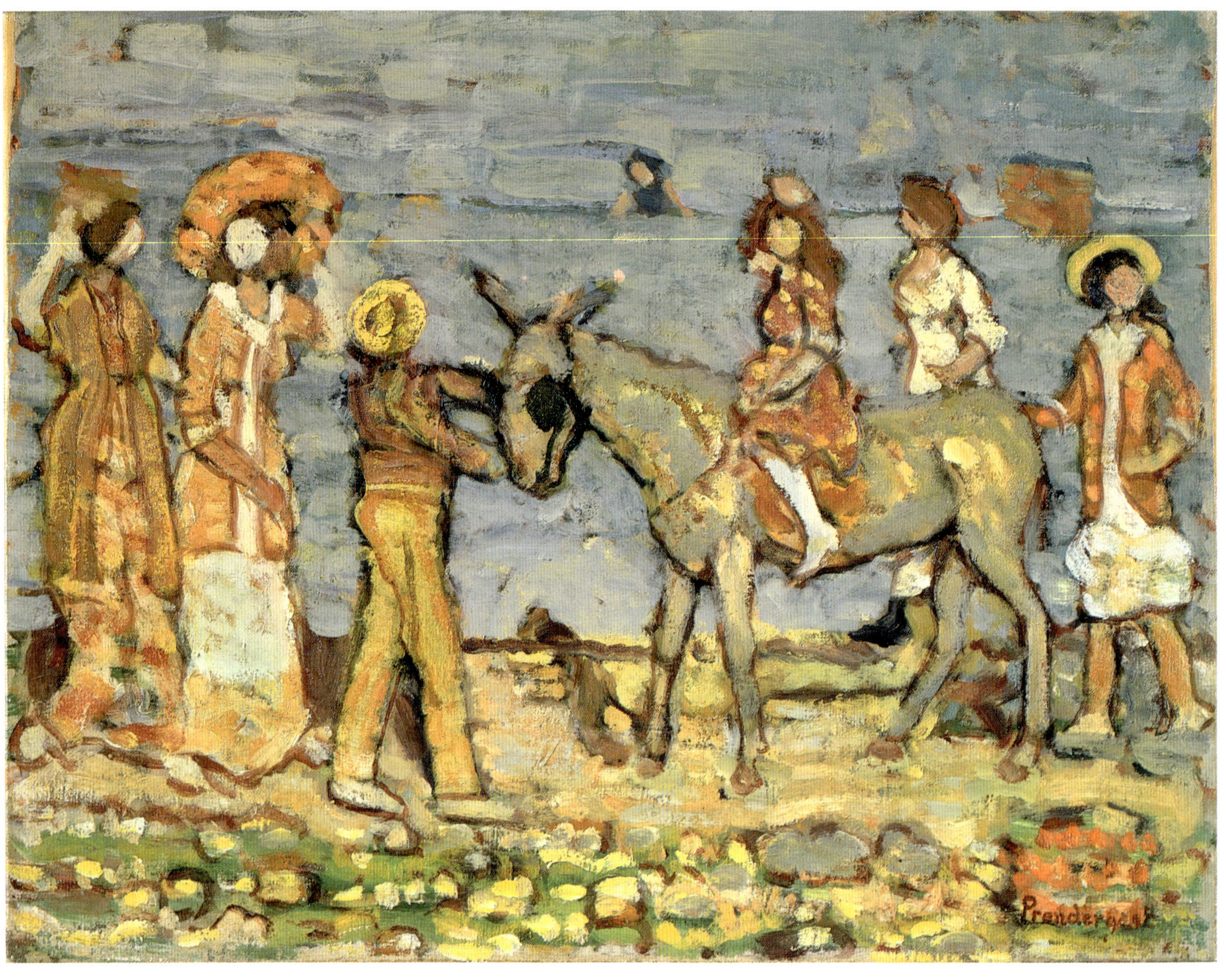

114. Donkey Rider

c. 1914. Oil on canvas, 18½ x 24"
The London Collection

This canvas represents a close-up vignette of Prendergast's larger beach scenes. Its dramatically arranged relief-like frieze of figures is enhanced by the area of blue-green water that sets a high horizon. This compression of space skillfully reinforces Donkey Rider*'s monumentality.*

key is balanced by the figure to the animal's right, creating a friezelike sequence of legs; the woman in white behind the donkey, with decisively placed black shoe, and the corresponding patch of the donkey's blinder mark out the space on the narrow band of beach on which the seven units are placed. The contrast of subdued background and richly spotted figures is further enlivened by the bather half submerged in the water at the horizon line, which opens out the space of the screen. *Beach Scene with Donkeys* (pl. 116), c. 1914–15, virtually a pendant to *Along the Shore,* sets a firm, pyramidal group of figures in front that joins with the branch units in the upper third of the picture to make a dense, rich, warm foreground.

The Beach (pl. 117), c. 1915, makes use of some watercolor ideas of the 1890s, such as *Low Tide, Beachmont* (see pl. 23) of about 1897. For example, it echoes the earlier watercolor in the round rocks in the foreground and the young girl in white dress walking in the center foreground, simply turning its figures from frontal to three-quarter poses. In addition, the detailed shoes of the watercolor are picked up again here as the soles and heels of the kneeling figure left of the girl in white. Such illustrative detail also appears in the carefully rimmed jar directly above the shoes, which here functions as a hub in the center of a group of seated and kneeling girls. Watercolor devices to hold the eye, such as decorative borders of skirts, are still used, as in the red border on the white dress at left, though now it is echoed in the white shoulder stripe in the man's red sweater in the foreground, which helps create a dramatic spatial anchor for the corner. The high horizon is another early watercolor device, though here the playful detail of the watercolor is simplified into a strip of land with a variant of Cézanne's Mont Sainte-Victoire in the center. The faces resembling Japanese masks, apparent in the watercolor, reappear with bolder curves, and the note of Japanese kinship is expanded in the rhythmic accent of the trees with a *matsu-no-ki* (pine tree)–type arabesque quite different from the large, blurred flowing branches of *Beach Scene with Donkeys.*

Growing out of such compositions as *Along the Shore* and *Beach Scene with Donkeys, The Beach "No. 3"* (pl. 118), c. 1915, has a complex, lateral polyphonic rhythm, at once friezelike and layered in atmospheric space, that fully reveals Prendergast's grasp of Poussin's figures in landscape, which he had studied and sketched. The pageantry of the New England and Venetian watercolors and the processional decorativeness of Carpaccio, Monticelli, and the Impressionists culminate in a luminous, dappled seaside panorama. The measured cadences of figures standing, sitting, riding, with graceful introspective gestures, are set out with a beguiling complexity that belies the carefree, uncomplicated festiveness of the scene. But the movements embody a sophisticated knowledge of ancient sarcophagi, their pale bas-reliefs translated into a color-saturated, embroidered sequence of gentle decorative patterns recalling a complete chapter, as it were, of the Bayeux tapestry. Maurice's absorption of sources in the traditions is so impeccably mastered, his improvisations so commandingly embedded, and his personal lyrics so daringly yet disarmingly arrayed that we might mistake the intensity in his exploration of color and color relations for what some have referred to as a "childlike" quality. His sophisticated transformation of a uniquely complex selection of color and figural sources, from the Byzantine and Coptic traditions to Cézanne, Gauguin, and the Neo-Impressionists, demonstrate that this is a misconception. The ravishing spontaneity of his color and its application reveal that nothing was left to chance.

The Inlet (pl. 120), c. 1916, organizes within its small dimensions a developed compositional sequence comparable to the larger beachside scenes of similar and later date.

In *On the Beach No. 3* (pl. 119), c. 1916–18, pronounced sculptural friezelike figures, like the Florentine painted and gilded marriage chests that Prendergast found so stimulating, dominate the lower half of the canvas. These provide a deliberately paced, monumental compositional geometry, while the landscape recalls Constable's vistas with their large massive trees. Maurice's stately tall figures move in a broad circular flow around the central group, creating a spatial

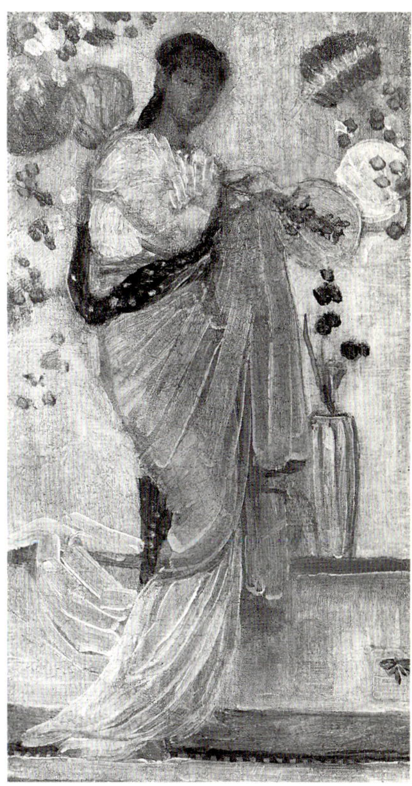

115. James McNeill Whistler (1834–1903)
Tanagra

c. 1867–70. Oil on canvas, 12¼ x 6⅞"
Maier Museum of Art, Randolph-Macon Woman's College, Lynchburg, Virginia

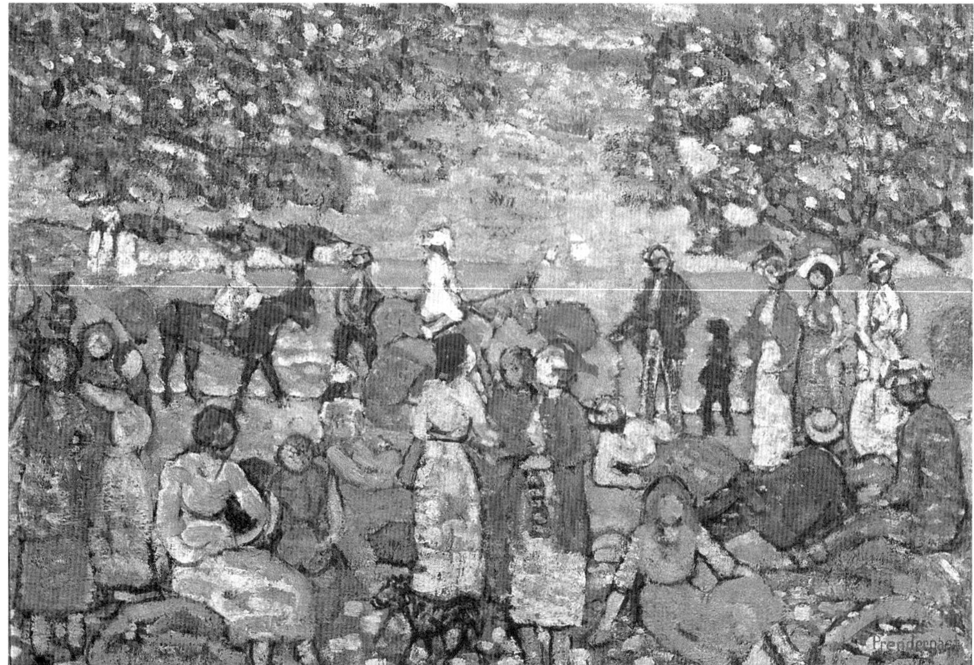

116. Beach Scene with Donkeys

c. 1914–15. Oil on canvas, 22½ x 32″
The Barnes Foundation,
Merion Station, Pennsylvania

Prendergast used the silhouettes of donkey, girl in white on a donkey, man with cane, and child to reinforce and spread a distant atmospheric glow along the edge of the shore, in contrast to the stepped effect of Along the Shore *(pl. 113).*

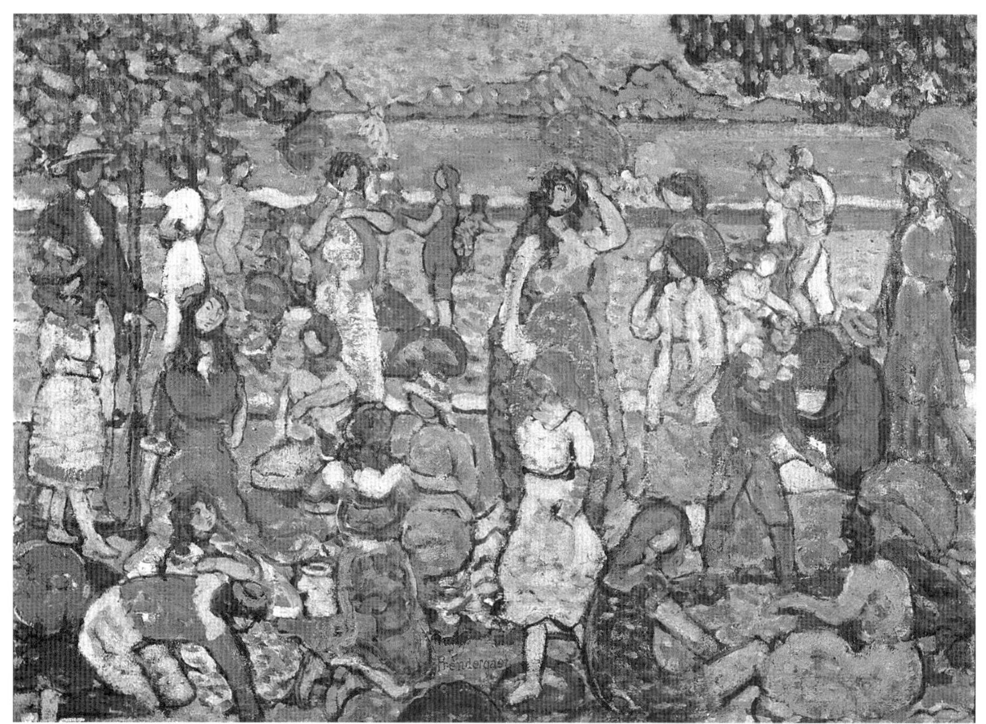

117. The Beach

c. 1915. Oil on canvas, 24¾ x 34″
The Barnes Foundation,
Merion Station, Pennsylvania

This composition is a veritable encyclopedia of the compact, gentle bending and turning figure movements Prendergast developed over the years. Among these figures, the large standing woman in the center, behind the girl in white, is given added emphasis by her robelike surround of color. The combination of the woman, her parasol, and the mountain above makes a bold central column that divides the canvas in half and anchors the inverted pyramid that binds the spatial groupings together.

depth that provides an effective complement to the landscape setting. This general type of composition was already in use in *Salem Willows* (see pl. 51) of 1904. In *On the Beach No. 3,* the landscape is no longer muted, flat, and silhouetted but rather light-filled, grass and leaves glowing with a broad brilliance that also suffuses the figures. These figures are fewer and widely spaced, enabling Maurice to increase their modeling and flowing linear movement. The particularly

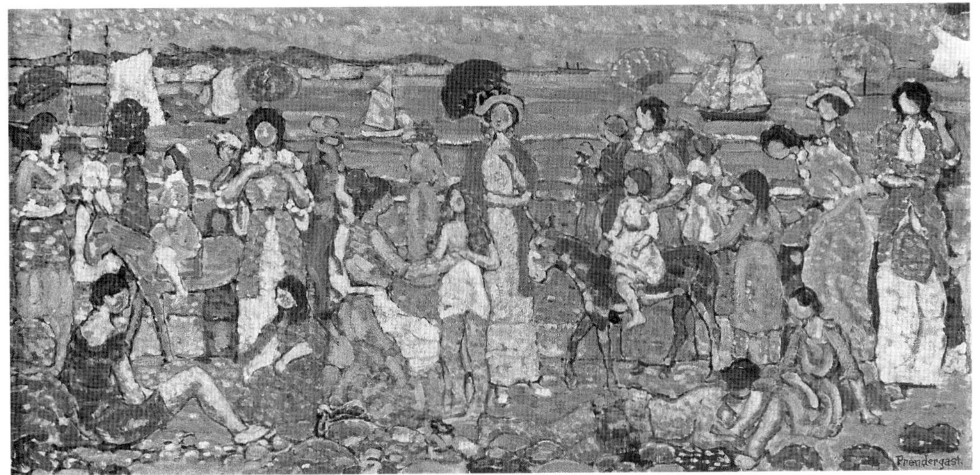

118. The Beach "No. 3"

c. 1915. Oil on canvas, 24 x 49"
The Barnes Foundation,
Merion Station, Pennsylvania

The horizontal pull across the picture surface, with a perspective depth having vanishing points beyond the frame, serves as the compositional container for Prendergast's color experiments. The intricate grouping of figures, in addition to its friezelike aspect, acts as a cat's cradle balancing solid sumptuous color-made figures in space.

weighty quality of both landscape and figures reinforces the daring and unconventional color harmonies and textures that make Prendergast so important as an innovator in twentieth-century painting. For all his innovation, he delighted in subtly introducing allusions to old masters, recasting ideas such as those of Piero della Francesca, whose triumphal wagon pulled by horses from *The Triumph of Battista Sforza*[133] Maurice transformed into a cart and donkey with diminutive red and blue driver on top.

Maurice and Charles were included in an exhibition, "Fifty Pictures by Fifty Artists," at the Montross Gallery, New York, in February 1916, their work hanging alongside that of Cézanne, van Gogh, Seurat, and Matisse. A reviewer remarked, "Prendergast shows a tapestry-like canvas which recalls both Guérin and the earlier K.-X. Roussel."[134] A month later at the Bourgeois Galleries Maurice showed two paintings and three pastels in the "Exhibition of Modern Art Arranged by a Group of European and American Artists in New York," organized by Walter Pach, in which Seurat's *Final Study for "A Sunday Afternoon on the Island of La Grande Jatte"* (now in the Metropolitan Museum of Art) was also on display.

Occasionally, Maurice would shift keys, as in the autumnal *In the Park* (pl. 121), c. 1914–16. Here, the paint is applied with a breadth and ruggedness, resulting in a pristine dry surface; the eighteenth-century French delicacy seen initially in the Central Park watercolors and subsequently in such canvases as *The Holiday* (see pl. 77), of c. 1908–9, is conveyed by means of figures arrayed against trees of varying shapes and hues. Several trees become not merely a frame or setting but also serve as a multipatterned screen device in the picture organization. The figures, dressed in yellow, white, blue, and a range of tawny brown oranges, are placed in a park setting that matches them in its uncluttered spacing and flowing arabesque rhythms. The cool blue water, seen between the trunks of trees, not only opens the pleasing spatial recession but, coupled with the blues, grays, and purples of the sky, sets off the golden tones of trees and people, revitalizing the Fragonard-Monticelli-Manet fête, the last's *Music in the Tuileries* of 1862 transformed into a lyrical arcadian poem.

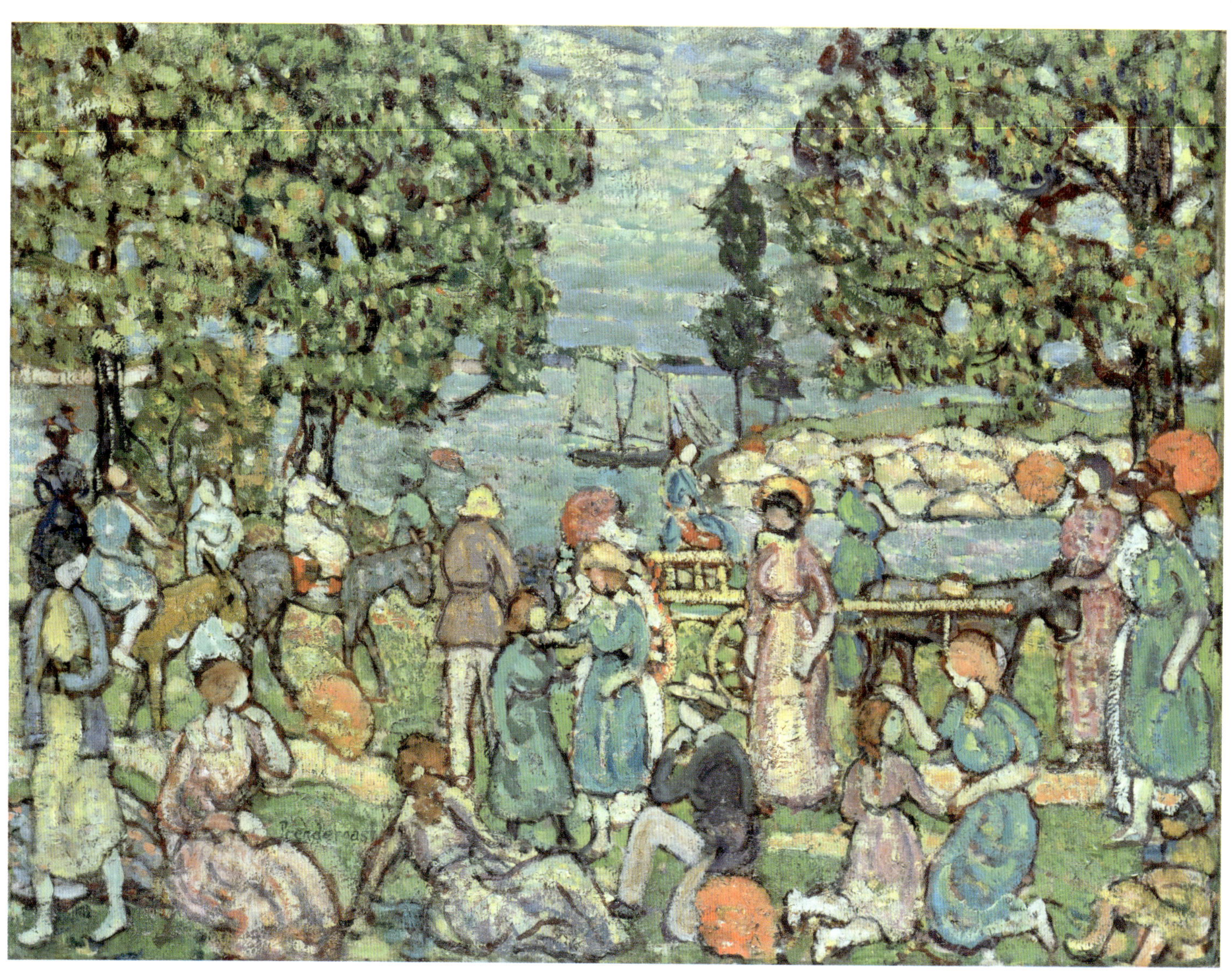

119. On the Beach No. 3

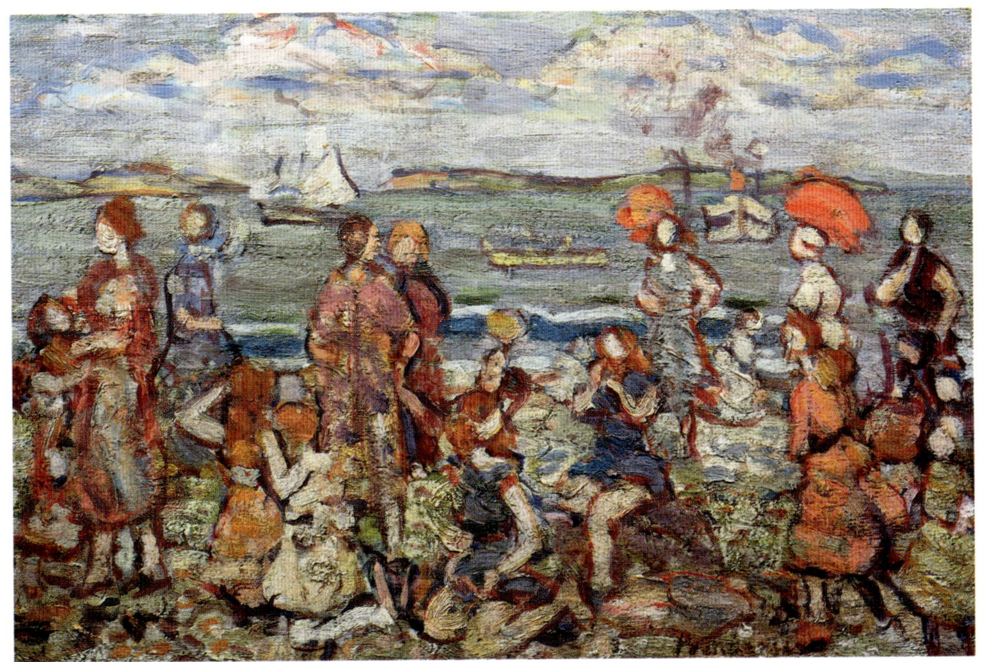

120. The Inlet

c. 1916. Oil on panel, 10¼ x 16⅛″
Altman/Burke Fine Art, Inc., New York

Since executing the park scenes on panel of about 1908–10, Maurice preferred to work on fine linen canvas. This panel departs from the dry, frescolike surfaces of the previous canvases and offers a deeper, internally glowing unctuousness that had been hinted at in the Luxembourg Gardens panels of 1907 but had not been dominant in his subsequent color schemes.

In *Holidays* (pl. 122 and p. 2), c. 1915–18, the architectonic frame is expanded, eliminating the middle-ground detail of *The Swans* (see pl. 111) and centering the three graces deeper in space, posed in a looser triadic alignment of delicate pale white, gold, and pale blue. Above this, the dense tan-green leaves cut off a central funnel into deep space and divert that recession to either side of the trio. While the frieze motif is retained, it now arches through the space, and in this deeper, Raphaelesque arena the trunks of the trees function like narrow columns in supporting a spacious canopy of foliage. Prendergast applied broad horizontal strokes of russet to the women on either side of the composition to fix the side-to-side alignment of standing figures. The seated women in the foreground and the lounging nude in the right middle ground are contained by this broad sequence of elongated figures. Although the general organization of large compositions such as *Holidays* is similar, Prendergast imbued each with a particular balance of distinct color harmonies. Pepper, who was one of those, including Glackens and Forbes Watson, who observed Prendergast at work, described how Maurice addressed the canvases, which were never tightly stretched: "When he hit one with his brush it would go flop, flop."[135] His description of those canvases has the firsthand authority of one who fully understands the process: "This is the art of Prendergast. The photograph gives the design, the holiday gaiety, but loses the color. Such color. Now the opal . . . now a topaz, now a lapis. Trays of jewels. Rich brocades from eastern looms. And with all this beauty, and quality and joy, variety and downright individuality."[136]

Landscape—Figures, Cottages and Boats (pl. 123), c. 1916–18, has a crusty surface of pitted and scumbled paint, centered on the striding woman with her disklike orange-yellow parasol and further anchored by the blue strokes of the skirt below, around which the interspersed hills, cottages, water, boats, penin-

119. On the Beach No. 3

c. 1916–18. Oil on canvas, 26 x 33⅜″
The Cleveland Museum of Art.
Hinman B. Hurlbut Collection

Maurice Prendergast was the American artist who made the most creative personal use of the ideas on color, texture, and light developed by the French Impressionists and Post-Impressionists. On the Beach No. 3, *with its posed figures, seemingly awkwardly articulated like colorful rag dolls and assembled in groups to a well-planned ensemble, represents the artist's oil compositions at their most complete stage of development.*

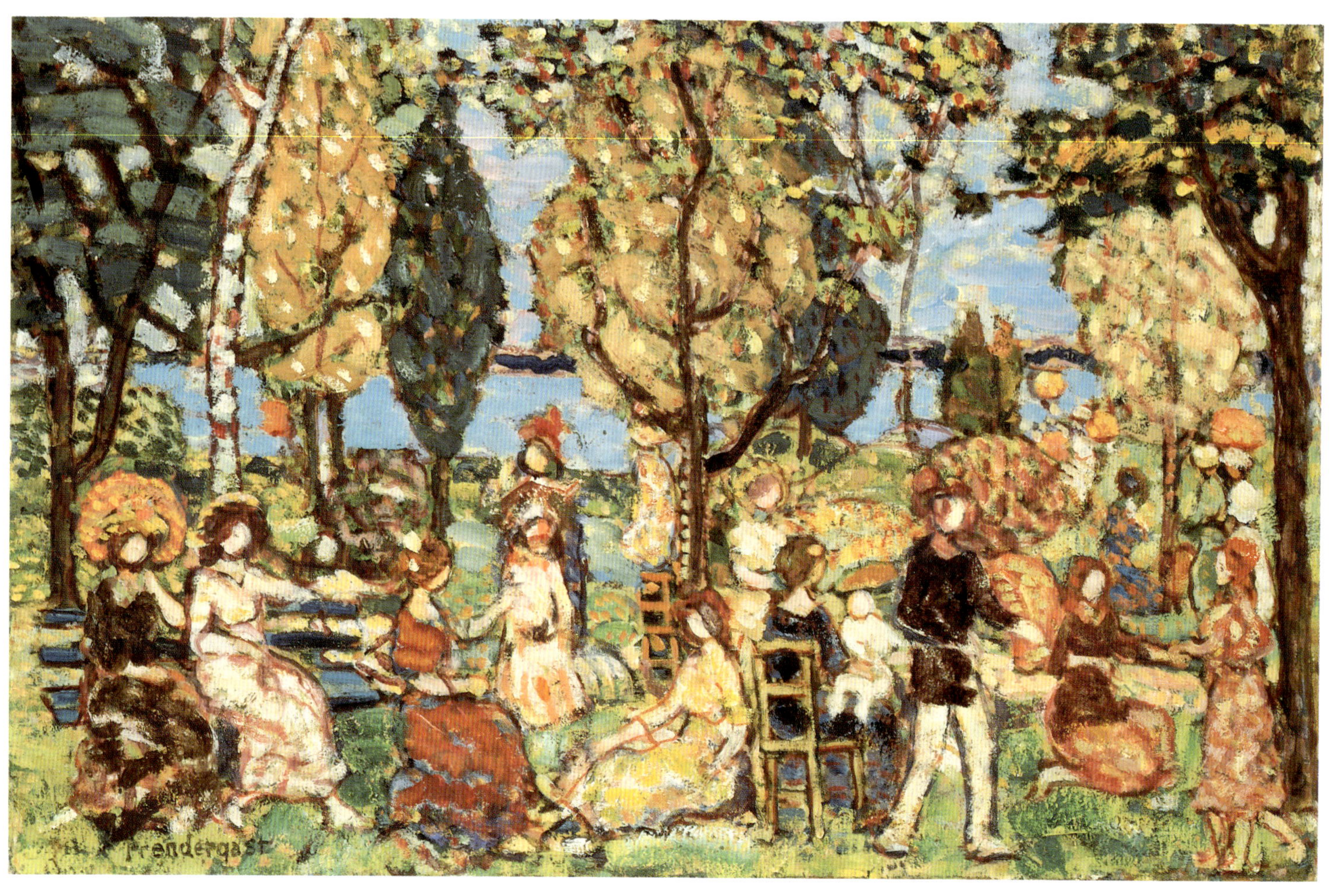

121. In the Park

c. 1914–16. Oil on canvas, 25 x 36″
Private collection, Washington, D.C.

An outgrowth of the Paris scenes of 1907 (see pls. 71 and 72), this canvas was photographed at two earlier stages: c. 1908–10, in a photograph in the possession of C. H. Pepper (CR 197), and before February 1914 (CR 270), when it was partially reworked. Van Wyck Brooks, longtime friend and admirer of the Prendergasts, observed in his book New England: Indian Summer 1865–1915 *of 1940, "The Yankee Giorgiones, Maurice Prendergast, Winslow Homer, Ryder. The innocent eyes that perceived these wore no veils."*

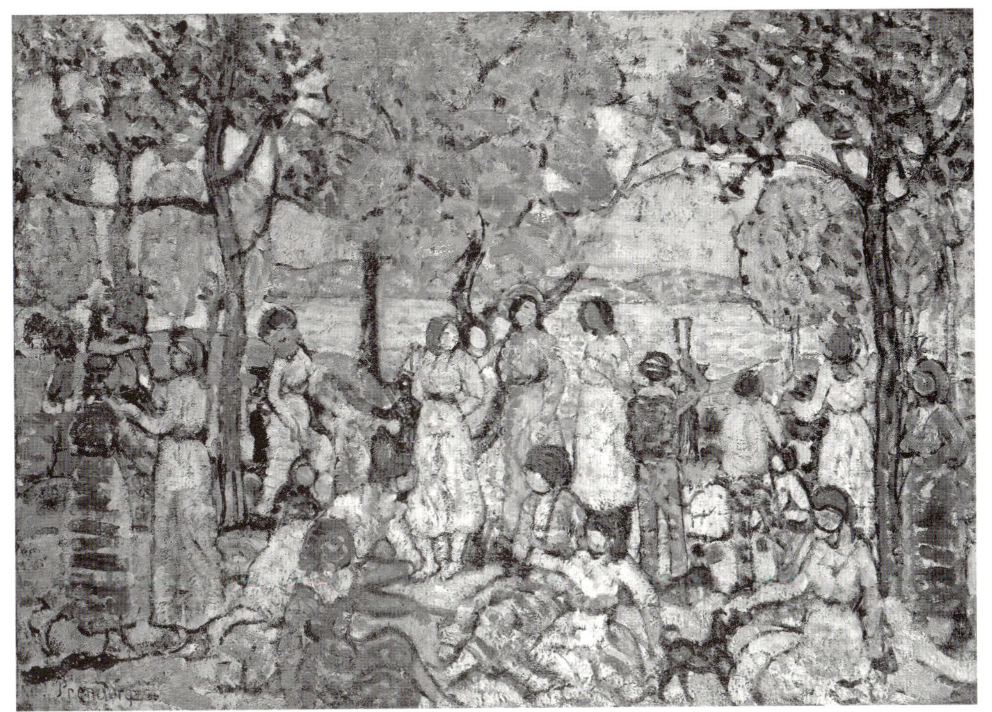

122. Holidays

c. 1915–18. Oil on canvas, 30 x 43¼″
Minneapolis Institute of Arts.
The Julia B. Bigelow Fund by John Bigelow

Charles Hovey Pepper wrote in 1910 ("Is Drawing to Disappear"), "Prendergast. What does that name bring to the mind? Trees and silver skies. Deep blue sea and orange rocks. People in movement, holiday folk in their saffron, violet, white, pearl, tan. Quaint design. Color powerful, but not crude. Canvases built up with overpainting—color dragged on color. A paint quality as delicious as an old tapestry."

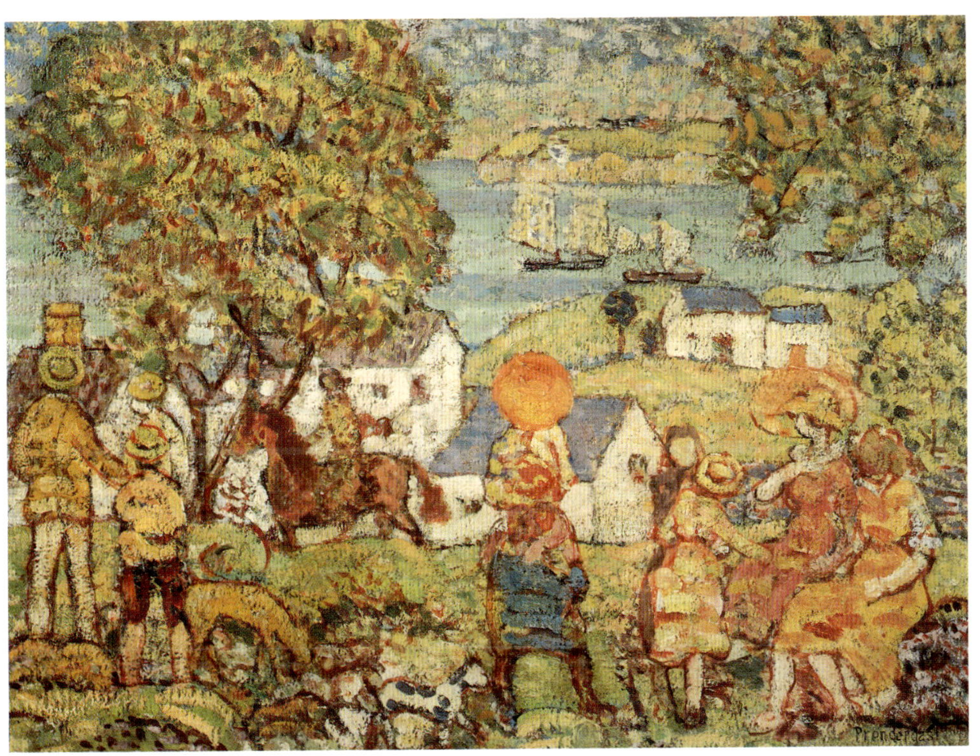

123. Landscape—Figures, Cottages and Boats

c. 1916–18. Oil on canvas, 24⅛ x 32⅛″
Private collection

The range of colors, from the warm sorrels, tawnies, russets, and oranges to cool purple and blue roofs and lavender, pale blue, pink, and yellow spots in the background units, as well as the dense substantiality of the walls, ivory tinged with yellow, imparts an unusually rich surface treatment to the masses throughout the composition.

sula, and sky beyond weave a recession into space, amplified by the chunky foliage on either side. From the blue spotted dog in the foreground to the minute color specks of the sails, from the quartet of girls in the lower right to the sequence of standing men, chimney, horse and rider on the left, the color saturation and variety go a step beyond the paintings of Monticelli, van Gogh, and even the rugged surfaces of the late 1870s work of Pissarro and Cézanne—

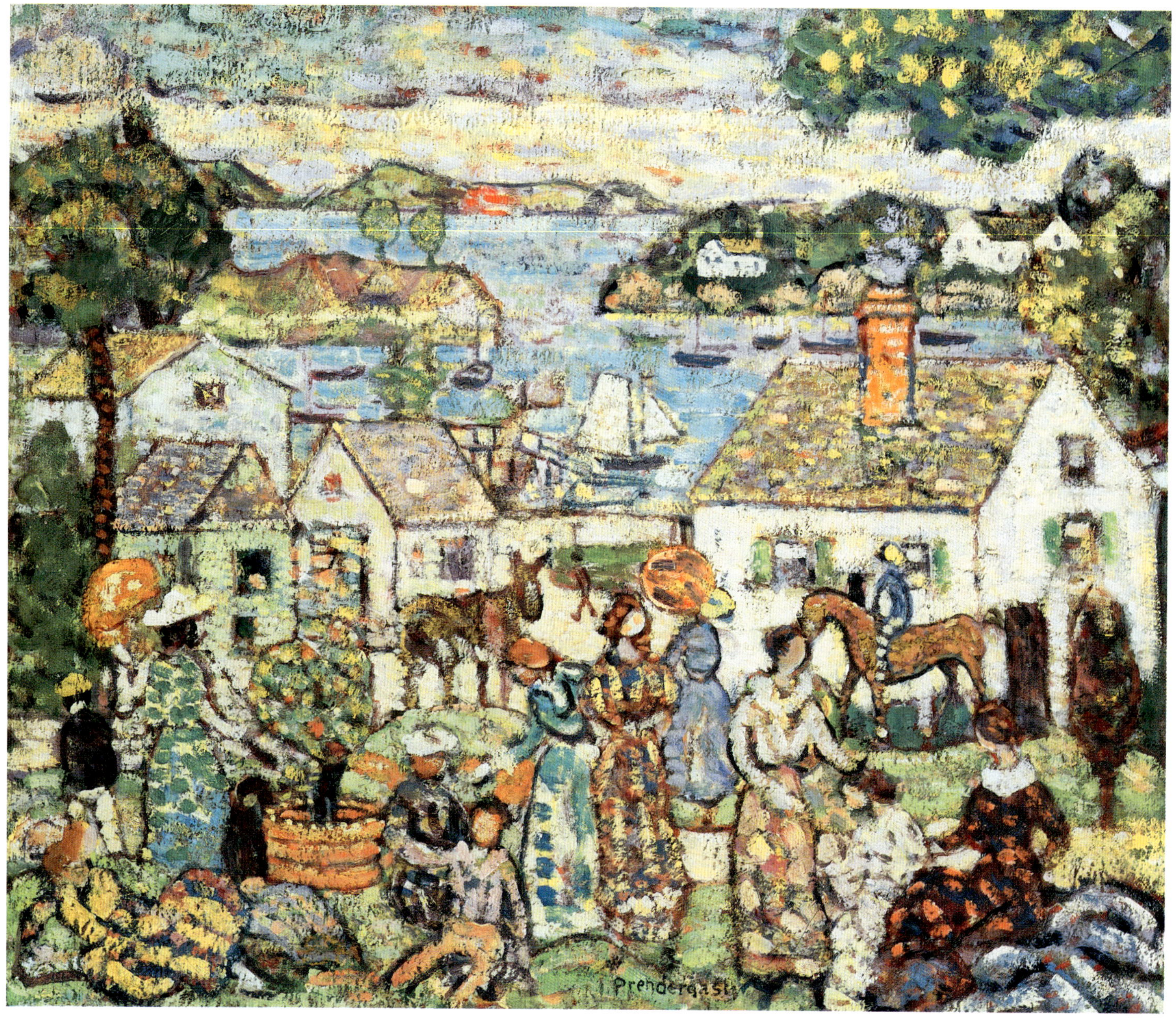

124. New England Harbor

c. 1918–21. Oil on canvas, 24 x 28"
Cincinnati Art Museum.
The Edwin and Virginia Irwin Memorial

Gently articulated planes of roofs and walls under a particularly luminous sky convey a different effect than the friezes set within backdrops of leafy foliage. The inherent geometric angularity of the architectural masses organizes the setting for the fore- and middle ground figures and subsidiary units by the shore.

truly a greater tour de force than the engaging, masterful color sequences of the 1897–1902 watercolors. The sense of vibrating texture, adapted from the unevenly reflected surfaces and dimensions of the mosaics Maurice so loved and found in the oils after about 1909–10, establishes a new and powerful level of color relationships not approached by any of his contemporaries, including Bonnard and Rouault.

New England Harbor (pl. 124), c. 1918–21, balances figures and architecture in a succession of peninsular outcroppings that dovetail and lock the deep composition together. Not as brilliant as *On the Beach No. 3* (see pl. 119), the multidirectional dashes, spots, and patches of pigment have a restrained luminosity that springs from Maurice's contemporary pastels over watercolor, which in turn are based on numerous annotated drawings in his sketchbooks.

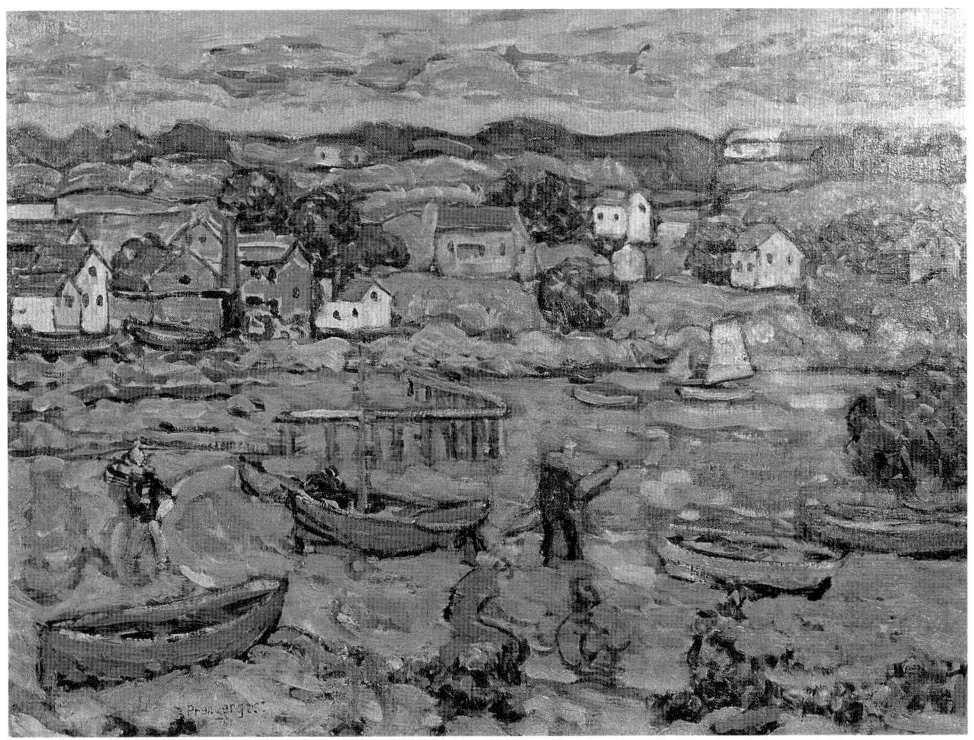

125. Landscape (Rowboats)

c. 1918–20. Oil on canvas, 18¼ x 24″
The Barnes Foundation,
Merion Station, Pennsylvania

In his book The Art in Painting *of 1925, Albert C. Barnes described* Landscape (Rowboats): *"The whole canvas is a succession of contrasts of line, color, mass and spatial relations, that give rise to a series of rhythms comparable to those of a Bach fugue. . . . In every part there are an infinite number of minor variations . . . which correspond to the internal variations of contrapuntal music."*

Prendergast varied his motifs more than is generally recognized. *Landscape (Rowboats)* (pl. 125), c. 1918–20, is based on a rough compositional sketch in a notebook of about 1916–19 and a watercolor of Gloucester.[137] This painting has a number of areas of bare canvas with loose purple drawing notations still visible and does not develop into the thick biscuit surfaces he ordinarily cultivated. While the work is thin in paint layers, the color and light qualities merge in a very bright atmosphere seen earlier in embryo with a darker spectrum of colors in such works as *Seascape (St. Malo)* (see pl. 73) of 1907.

When *The Idlers* (pl. 126), c. 1918–20, was exhibited by Daniel early in 1920, its saturated Renoiresque effulgence was admired by the reviewer for the *New York Times*:

> *Mr. Prendergast's remarkably handsome and personal patchwork of greens and blues and pinks and yellows is spread over a foundation design so sturdy in its unpretentious vigor as to make us very comfortable about the strength of his composition. If one looks too casually at these "decorative" canvases there is an impression of a lack of cohesion, the bits are so detached and fragmentary that they seem quite likely to fall about like an unsolved picture puzzle. But the slightest second glance shows the superficiality of such a notion. Each blot of color has its place in a fabric woven in the usual way with an almost commonplace regularity. The combination of great originality with this simple directness is very enticing always.*[138]

Landscape with Figures (pl. 128), dated 1921, one of Maurice's favorite crepuscular compositions, employs a verdant architectonic setting for the sinuously out-

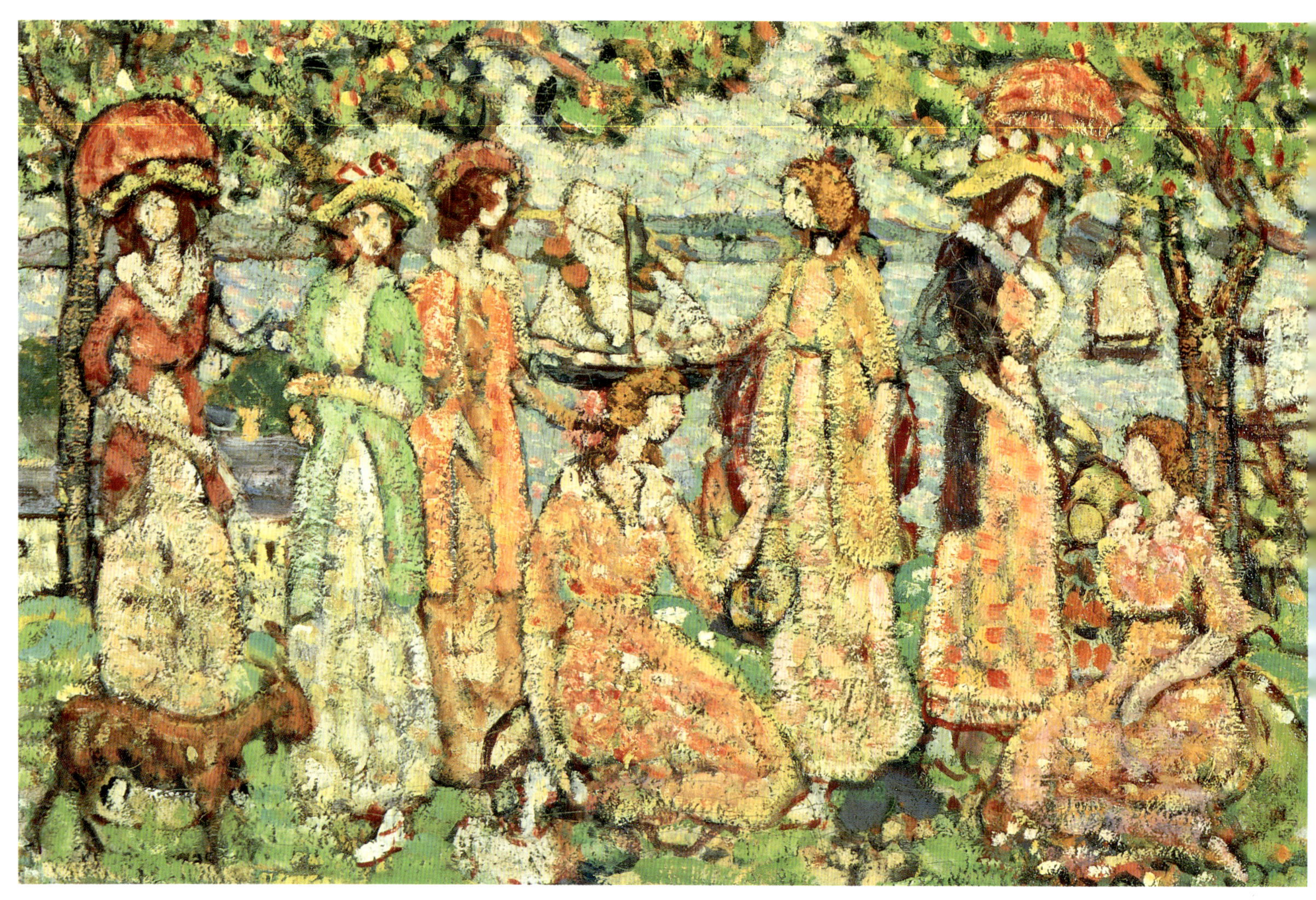

126. The Idlers

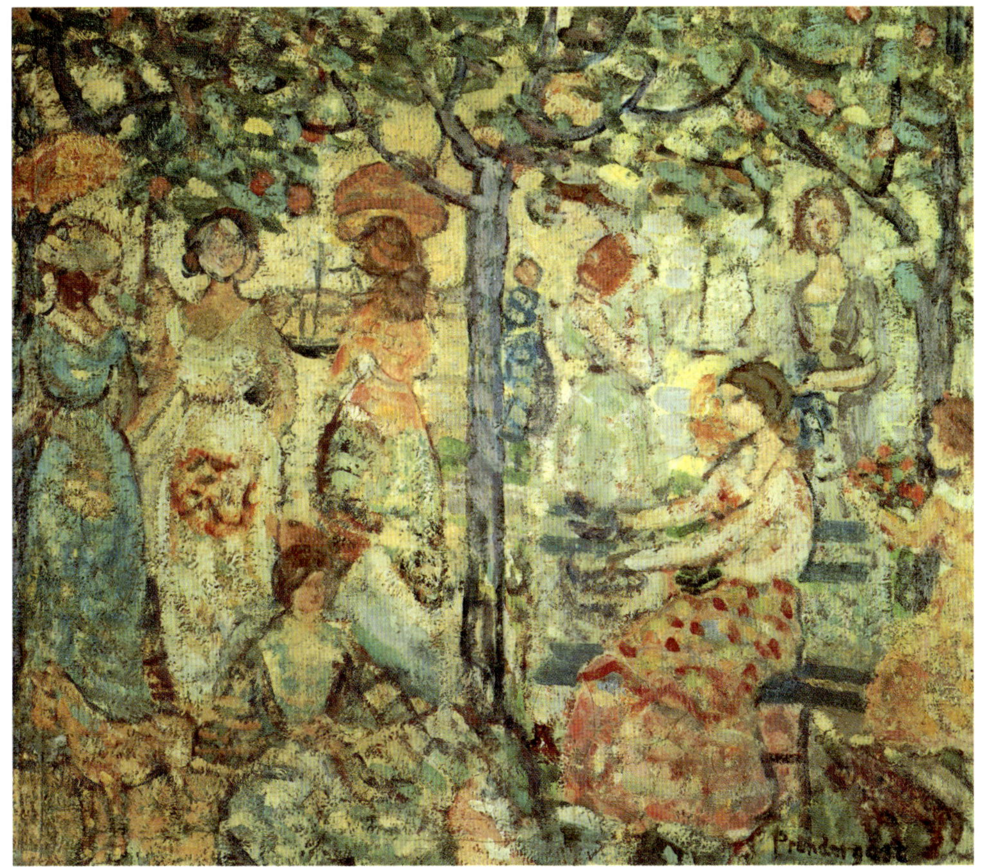

127. Acadia

c. 1922. Oil on canvas, 31¾ x 37½"
Collection, The Museum of Modern Art, New York. Gift of Abby Aldrich Rockefeller, 1945

One of Maurice's last canvases, Acadia *was signed, although possibly not completed at the time of his death. The scumbled textures, dragged and dabbed in endless variations, create bursting areas of color that saturate the surface, effects reminiscent of late Renoir and Bonnard.*

lined players in its rustic drama. The expanded network of branches, building on that of *Holidays* (see pl. 122), lends a monumentality and power to the multidirectional rhythms they create. There is a rare instance of backlit cast shadows in the left foreground, which, for all their obliqueness, emanate from the sun directly behind. Instead of mere shadow, the scumbled golden-yellow strokes achieve with pure color relations what colorless light and dark shadows illustrate in the figures in landscapes of conventional painters. Since Prendergast's objective has little to do with illustration for its own sake, the color orchestration is the primary subject of the picture. Related thematic material is found in *Acadia* (pl. 127), c. 1922, but with the emphasis on large figures bathed in colorful shadows with warm russets and ambers, played against the cool silvery sheen of filtering light, the nearly abstract color variations bursting within the borders of a single area, textures extended beyond the frontiers of late Titian.

These fully realized majestic oils of Prendergast's last decade are the culmination of more than thirty years of patient and determined exploration, trial and error, wholly personal variations on subjects that have captivated the most subtle and sophisticated minds of the Western tradition since the dawn of the Renaissance. Prendergast's comprehensive experiments within this humanistic tradition bring to bear his unique adaptations of ideas from both East and West. If modern painting is primarily about extending the boundaries of color and color relations, Maurice Prendergast has a stature that guarantees him an

126. The Idlers

c. 1918–20. Oil on canvas, 21 x 32"
Maier Museum of Art, Randolph-Macon Woman's College, Lynchburg, Virginia

Elongated figures loom up and nearly fill the vertical plane of the horizontal composition. This feature of Prendergast's later style is combined with an opulent, rugged impasto, which heightens the one-piece effect of the color-saturated surface.

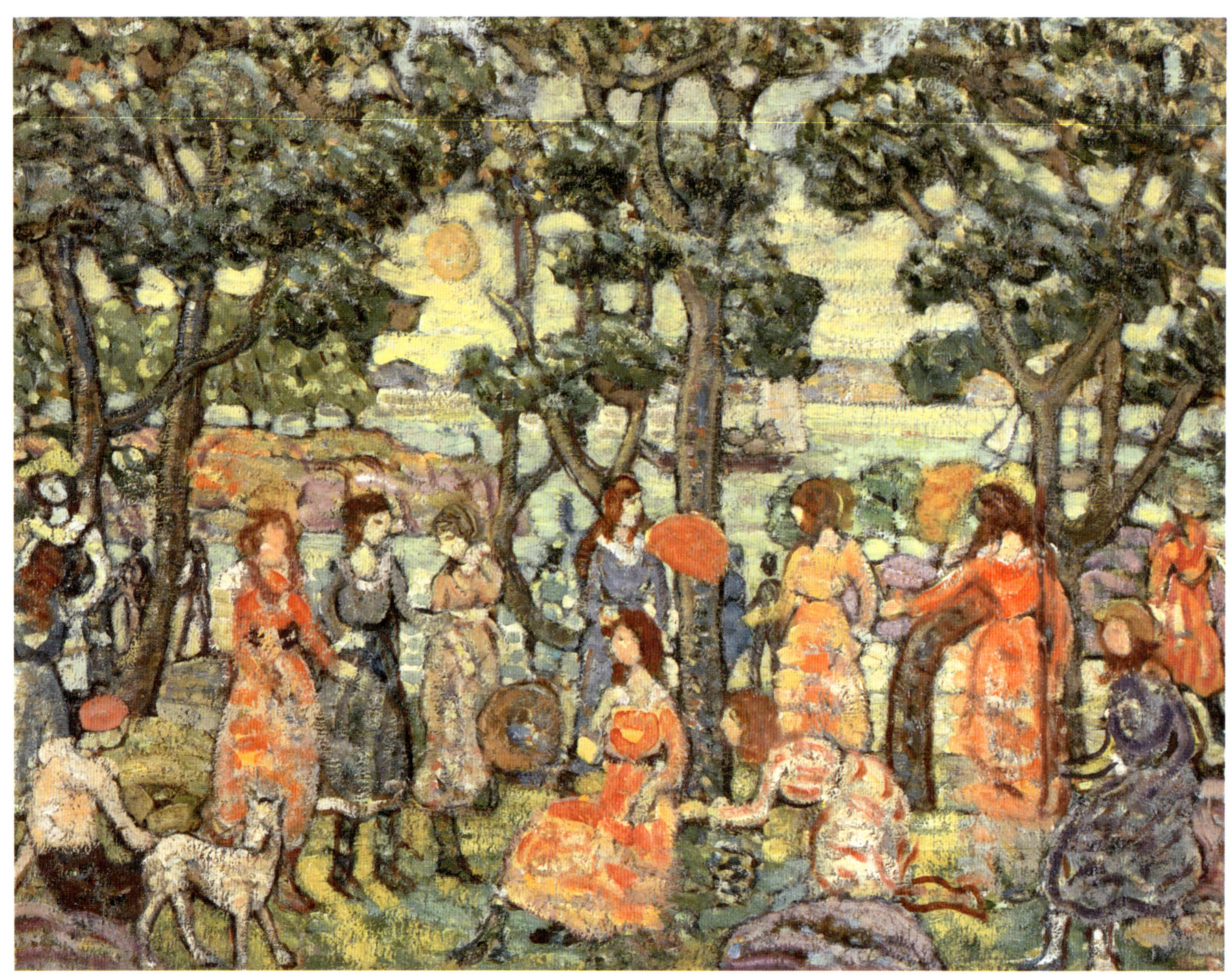

128. Landscape with Figures

important place in the pantheon with the masters he so admired and whose ideas he so richly repaid.

Early in 1921, Walter Pach introduced Joseph Brummer to the Prendergasts, and the dealer offered the brothers an exhibition to inaugurate his new gallery at 43 East Fifty-seventh Street. Maurice wrote to Pach on February 28, "First and foremost I want to tell you how much I enjoyed your visit on Sunday with Mr. and Mrs. Brummer. Both Charlie [and I] found the Brummers extremely interesting and I am glad we have them in New York. He is going to give us an exhibition of our works. . . . We both want to thank you for bringing this meeting about."[139] Maurice wrote to John Quinn on March 29 to inform him of the show: "We are having another exhibition, this time a joint & Charlie with his carving and I with my painting. Mr. Brummer has offered us his gallery. He likes our things which is one for us. You were such a great assistance to me in my first exhibition. Of that I am deeply sensible and you may be sure I am never going to forget it. P.S. Since I had my first exhibition I am a much richer man Voila!" John Quinn replied to Maurice on April 11 while the show was on, "I received your letter of March 29th. I also received from Mr. Brummer a catalogue of the joint exhibition of your work and Charley's. I have not been able to go to see the exhibition yet but I intend to. I am sure it is very delightful, like walking into a corner of a poet's garden." He ended his letter, saying, "I wish you not only good luck but length of days and years and continued joy in your work, for one of the chief notes in your work is the note of joy in its creation."

Maurice was represented by thirty paintings and seven watercolors dating back to his Venice compositions and Charles by eight panels and one carved and decorated chest. Reviewers were universally ecstatic: "In choosing the Prendergasts for his opening exhibition, Mr. Brummer has shown both taste and judgment. The paintings show off the beauty of his galleries and are an excellent foil to the antiquities which Mr. Brummer has in the rooms on the ground floor, wonders from Greece, from Egypt and gothic works from France."[140] Visiting the show a few days before the opening, Lewis Mumford walked through the galleries with Maurice.

> *As I looked, my . . . spirit lightened as Saul's did at the sound of David's harp. I have been told that Mr. Maurice Prendergast is the greatest living American artist; I know that Mr. Brummer . . . considers him so. . . . I have seen no finer work by any contemporary painter. . . . Here in these canvasses one sees an untrammelled expression of the creative spirit. . . . Its supreme honesty precludes all thought of yielding to the clamour of public taste, and its earnest preoccupation with real values saves it from the contamination of influences which are real in nothing save the mere fact that for the passing moment they exist—and then the artists themselves entered the room and I was convinced that I was right. Mr. Maurice Prendergast has the outward appearance and the years of an old man, but his spirit is not a day over twenty. . . . I walked around the gallery with Mr. Maurice Prendergast and we talked about this or that picture. I remember looking at the tiny gem called "Charenton Boat": "Ever been in Paris?" he said. "You can ride in that boat for three cents."*

128. Landscape with Figures

1921. Oil on canvas, 32⅝ x 42⅝"
The Corcoran Gallery of Art, Washington, D.C.
Museum Purchase, William A. Clark Fund

This painting was awarded the third William A. Clark Prize of one thousand dollars and the Corcoran bronze medal in December 1923—two months before Prendergast died. The jury, chaired by Gari Melchers, consisted of Rockwell Kent, Daniel Garber, Ralph Clarkson, and Lilian Westcott Hale.

Again, before a landscape: "Green is the hardest colour in the world to paint. It looks easy, but it's very hard; it took fifteen years to learn to paint a tree."[141]

Another reviewer wrote: "Besides the beauty of the display, it has additional interest from the fact that Maurice B. Prendergast is the oldest of the American 'Modernists.' This veteran painter was doing his tapestry-like landscapes, in which he cared not a rap for exactitude of form, before Modernism was dreamed of in this country. . . ."[142]

January 26, 1922, Maurice wrote to Walter Pach, who was preparing an important article for the magazine *Shadowland*: "The Shadowland man brought the two pictures back this morning and showed us two reproductions. I was curious and I must say they exceeded my expectations. They were perfectly charming in color. . . . If you are going to write an article I will give you all the assistance I can. I think those reproductions are worth backing up. . . . The English was so well written and you got all the spirit of the writer. I take off my hat to anything '*that is first class.*' "

In "Maurice Prendergast," published in April, Pach wrote,

The man of the preceding generation who first claimed his homage was Cézanne, and . . . it is still that master to whom he looks most often for pleasure and for counsel. . . . A casual observation may not reveal what he has meant to Mr. Prendergast. And that is a healthy sign, for it indicates a genuine absorption by the American painter of the great Frenchman's principles, instead of that copying of externals. . . . What he had learned at different times had been assimilated and made a source of growth in the art he already possessed. . . . Having kept his own vision . . . he was strong enough to come into contact with the great mind that has its expression in Cézanne's pictures. Probably the first American to realize the importance of the master of the modern school, able to do justice to the broad scope of Cézanne's qualities, Mr. Prendergast did not make over his own art completely. Instead he deepened it along its own lines, with the logic he recognized in the older painter. . . .[143]

Prendergast approved of the ideas advanced in the article. On February 2, he returned the manuscript to Pach and said, "It was a pleasure reading it and you expressed a lot which I feel and you are right about Cézanne; his work strengthened and fortified me to pursue my own course."

By the end of 1921, the Prendergast brothers established relations with John Kraushaar, whose gallery would represent Maurice and Charles for forty years. In the spring, Duncan Phillips, who had been collecting Maurice's work since 1917, indicated that he wished to purchase the oil version of the *Ponte della Paglia*. Maurice, who, like Degas and Bonnard, could rarely refrain from touching up—"improving"—his canvases, wrote on April 1922 to the dealer: "When you find it convenient will you send the Venetian picture down. I would like to have it here when framing it." On April 30, he wrote again to Kraushaar: "I am sorry to cause you any inconvenience but I do not want the picture to go yet. I must be thoroughly satisfied with it before I let it go." Then he added, but crossed out: "It is coming on and I am more satisfied with it." Marjorie Phillips recalled a lunch at this time (1921–22) in New York with Prendergast: "Maurice, who was stone deaf when we knew him, lunched with us one day at the apartment . . . shaggy haired, with a kindly face and keen eyes. We communicated by passing around slips of paper with our written thoughts or observations. His were largely about his utter pleasure in the flowers of our centerpiece, from which he could not take his eyes."[144]

Around this time, Pach recalls in his memoirs, Prendergast's thoughts were more and more directed to the work of the great Renaissance masters.

> *Most of all he loved the fantasy of the early Italians and their summing up of form by a firm contour. There was always a photograph or two of their work on the wall of his studio, and their art was in his mind from his early years till that of his death. . . . As if in preparation for the gravity of that time, his thoughts were constantly upon Giotto in the last months of his life, and it seems to me as if each time when I called on him in those days, he would have a volume of Giotto reproductions across his knees.*
>
> *I thought to round out this study of his with a Brueghel book I had lately bought, and I took it along to his studio one day. The northern master was almost unknown to Mr. Prendergast. . . . He was taken aback to find that so great an artist had escaped him all those years, and I can still hear the tone of his voice, admiring and yet defending, as he said again and again, "He ain't no Giotto; no that ain't yet Giotto."*
>
> *But as the lovable figure of my old friend comes back before my eyes it is not as I saw him toward the end: I think of him as the man before his easel, "pecking away" as Charlie Prendergast would call it, eager and exhilarated as he "punched up" a canvas that might have seemed perfect before but in which he saw possibilities of greater depth, a hardier build, or more of light and richness.*[145]

Landscape with Figures (see pl. 128), dated 1921, was entered in "The Ninth Exhibition of Contemporary American Oil Paintings" at the Corcoran Gallery of Art, Washington, D.C., which opened on December 16, 1923. Prendergast had been a regular exhibitor there for many years. Maurice, who had been suffering from progressive circulatory problems, was gravely ill. At the time of the Brummer exhibition nearly three years earlier, a reporter had asked Mr. Brummer, "Which is the younger?" "Charles," responded the dealer, "He is only sixty—Maurice is eighty."[146] At the time, Charles was fifty-eight, Maurice not yet sixty-three. C. Powell Minnigerode, director of the Corcoran, and Charles C. Glover, president of the board, telegraphed Maurice on December 6: "Third William A. Clark Prize of One Thousand Dollars and Corcoran Bronze Medal awarded to you on your picture. . . . Accept warmest congratulation. Earnestly hope that you will without fail make special effort to be present for opening of exhibition on December 15." Tradition has it that when handed the telegram announcing his prize, Prendergast said, "I'm glad they've found out I'm not crazy, anyway."[147]

The following day Maurice wrote to the president in a shaky hand: "With all honor to the Corcoran Gallery and the $1000 prize with the bronze medal which is awarded to me. I am afraid I will not be able to go down as I am sick in the New York Hospital, but I hope to be out in a few days. . . ." The director replied on December 8: "I write to extend to you our deepest sympathy in your temporary confinement to the Hospital. . . . Our warmest congratulations on the honor awarded to you, and our warmest good wishes for a speedy and complete recovery. . . ." This was followed on the fourteenth by another formal letter. On December 16 Prendergast wrote the director: "I received the medal . . . for my painting Landscape with Figures. . . . I shall prize it very much. I am getting along and feeling much better. Thank everyone most cordially from the Bottom of my heart. Yours very faithfully." On the seventeenth, the director wrote again: "The Committee on Works of Art of this Gallery has asked me to ascertain from you the lowest price at which this Gallery might acquire for its permanent collection your picture entitled 'Landscape with Figures.'. . . As our funds for purchases are at present in a depleted condition . . . it is necessary that we should know the rock bottom price which you would be willing to accept for this picture." On the eighteenth Maurice wired: "My picture . . . is now three thousand dollars. I will take off one thousand which will make two thousand for the Corcoran Gallery." A letter of December 19 confirming the reduction added: "I hope this will be satisfactory for I prefer Washington to have it." Minnigerode replied on December 20, accepting the "concession of 33⅓ in the price," asking Prendergast to sign a typed release relinquishing the picture and all copyright privileges. This was done on December 23, twice, in a very weak hand.

Maurice's condition worsened dramatically, and toward the end of January he was operated on. On the night of January 31, William Glackens visited Maurice at his bedside and the two friends bid farewell to each other. Prendergast died on February 1. Following his expressed wish, he was cremated the next day.

On February 6, the *New York Telegram and Evening Mail* published du Bois's unsigned editorial, "Maurice Prendergast":

> *Those who take the rather unusual view that passing from this life is a private matter will be encouraged in their theory by the case of Maurice Prendergast, who slipped out of existence so quietly the other day that his funeral was over before most of his friends had even heard of their loss. Yet here was a man accounted in his later years one of the half dozen most interesting of living American painters, whose pictures were to be found in most big exhibitions of any importance and who was represented in such noted New York collections as those of Miss Lizzie Bliss, Mrs. Havemeyer and John Quinn.*
>
> *When the much talked of International Exhibition of Modern Art, better known as "the Armory Show," was held in this city in 1913 Prendergast said: — "Now we must see what effect all this will have on us."*
>
> *As a matter of fact, it had no effect on him, for the very good and simple reason*

that he had been an art "modernist" before Cézanne and his successors, Seurat, Matisse, Picasso and the rest, came into their own.

Maurice Prendergast was not only a fine artist, but a keen critic. He never hesitated through any false politeness about saying to even the most distinguished of his contemporaries if the occasion called for it.— "Well, you didn't quite do it that time." It was because of this that his enthusiasm for some other work really meant a great deal.

The oldest in years of his group, he was in many ways the youngest and an interesting example of the combination of New England caution, Irish alertness and French intelligence.[148]

Four days later, an article appeared in the *New York Herald*: "The sudden taking off of Maurice Prendergast shocked a large portion of the community, for, though this artist appeared but seldom in the public places, there was something in the quality of the man that endeared him generally."[149] The *Herald* then took the extraordinary step of reprinting the entire *New York Telegram and Evening Mail* editorial.

The *New York World* published its obituary, written by Forbes Watson, on the tenth: "The position which Maurice Prendergast occupied in American art was unique. Although his name is known to every close follower of the painting that is going on in our midst, the general public seemed less aware of his rare quality. The artists, on the other hand, who gathered to pay a final tribute to Prendergast, included a distinguished group of the leaders of American art, men who knew well what the passing really meant. For Prendergast was a man who cannot be replaced."[150]

Notes

Letters from Maurice Prendergast to his brother Charles are all located at the Prendergast Archive and Study Center, Williams College, Williamstown, Massachusetts, and are on microfilm at the Archives of American Art, Smithsonian Institution, Washington, D.C. (AAA). Unless otherwise noted, all other letters cited are held in the personal papers or in the institutional records listed in the Bibliography. In addition to those papers identified as in the collections of the Archives of American Art, microfilm copies of the Elmer MacRae Papers, Hirshhorn Museum and Sculpture Garden, Smithsonian Institution, the John Quinn Memorial Collection at the New York Public Library, the Archives of the Cincinnati Art Museum, and the Edward W. Root Papers, Munson-Williams-Proctor Institute, Utica, New York, are available at the Archives of American Art. *Maurice Brazil Prendergast, Charles Prendergast: A Catalogue Raisonné* is abbreviated throughout as *Catalogue Raisonné* or CR.

1. Charles Hovey Pepper, "Is Drawing to Disappear in Artistic Individuality?: A Sketch of the Work of Maurice Prendergast," *The World To-day* 19 (July 1910): 716–19.
2. Daphne Dunbar, quoted in Fred Brady, "Anonymous Friend Reveals Prendergast's Love of Life," *Boston Herald,* November 27, 1960, sec. 4, p. 3.
3. Daphne Dunbar, quoted in Hedley Howell Rhys, "Maurice Prendergast: The Sources and Development of His Style" (Ph.D. diss., Harvard University, 1952), 10, n. 39.
4. Max Weber, quoted in Rhys, "Sources and Development," 10, n. 40.
5. Notes for an unpublished article on the Armory Show, Jerome Myers Papers, AAA.
6. Marsden Hartley, "Somehow a Past," unpublished autobiography, 1933–42. Yale Collection of American Literature, Beinecke Rare Book and Manuscript Library, Yale University, New Haven. A variant holograph version describes Maurice as "lovable—and if ever there was a flaming enthusiast it was Maurice for whatever he liked. He was one of the first to like Cézanne in this country and he was the first artist in this country to speak enthusiastically of me."
7. Compiled from multiple holograph and typed drafts, Forbes Watson Papers, AAA.
8. Ira Glackens, *William Glackens and the Ashcan Group* (New York: Horizon Press, 1957), 131–32.
9. Walter Pach, *Queer Thing, Painting* (New York: Harper & Brothers, 1938), 226.
10. From Newfoundland Archives, Saint John's, Saint John's Basilica Baptismal Records.
11. Information courtesy Ellen M. Glavin.
12. Although Charles Prendergast told Hamilton Basso that both he and his older brother attended Rice Grammar School and specified that his art teacher in the seventh grade was Mrs. Crocker (Hamilton Basso, "A Glimpse of Heaven," Part 2, *New Yorker* 22 [August 3, 1946]: 28), Glavin has discovered that Mrs. Sarah E. Crocker taught in the Dwight school district. See Ellen M. Glavin, "The Early Art Education of Maurice Prendergast: Art Education in Boston in the 1870s," *Archives of American Art Journal* 33, no. 1 (1993).
13. Louis H. Sullivan, *The Autobiography of an Idea* (New York: Dover, 1956), 107. See also Robert Twombly, *Louis Sullivan: His Life and Work* (New York: Viking, 1968), 5–17, 470, n. 29.
14. See Van Wyck Brooks, "Anecdotes of Maurice Prendergast," in *The Prendergasts: Retrospective Exhibition of the Work of Maurice and Charles Prendergast,* exhib. cat. (Andover, Mass.: Addison Gallery of American Art, Phillips Academy, 1938), 36–37.
15. Ellen M. Glavin, "Maurice Prendergast: The Boston Experience," *Art and Antiques* 5 (July–August 1982), 64–71. Some color theory was part of the grammar school instruction.
16. Glavin has discovered that in 1871 a whittling school was conducted at the Hollis Street Church in the South End two evenings a week to instruct boys in the use of woodcutting tools, thus confirming that, as Charles told Basso, he received such training. It is likely that Maurice also attended classes at the whittling school. In "The Early Art Education of Maurice Prendergast," Glavin documents in depth the professional instruction Maurice received in draftsmanship at the Starr King school on Tennyson Street.
17. See Brooks, "Anecdotes," 33, and Basso, "A Glimpse of Heaven," Part 2, 28, wherein Charles refers to "store cards."
18. CR 509, 510, 1475.
19. Ibid., 512, 513, 514, 515.
20. Arthur H. Jameson, letter of February 1951, quoted in Rhys, "Sources and Development," 16, n. 57.
21. Wm. H. Harvey [pseud.], "A Week at Colarossi's," *The Quartier Latin* 1, no. 2 (August–September 1896): 55.
22. From Archives of the Académie Julian, Archives Nationales, Paris, Cote 63 AS 4. Prendergast registered as a part-time—or "*matin*"—student from October 12, 1891, paying in twice-monthly installments. He continued on a regular basis through June 6, 1892, reenrolling January 23, 1893, to February 20, 1893.
23. Maurice Prendergast to Edgar L. Hewett, n.d. [fall 1914], Alice Klauber Papers, AAA.
24. Pepper, "Is Drawing to Disappear," 718–19.
25. Ibid., 719. Pepper owned three watercolors dating from this early period (CR 545, 571, and 575). Maurice's formal training may have been more intermittent than Pepper allowed. Also see note 22.
26. George Thompson, "The Sketch Book in the Street," *The Studio* 1 (1893): 187–90. See also Brooks, "Anecdotes," 35–36, and *Catalogue Raisonné,* p. 636.
27. Brooks, "Anecdotes," 45. See also Carol Clark, *American Drawings and Watercolors in the Robert Lehman Collection* (New York and Princeton, N.J.: The Metropolitan Museum of Art and Princeton University Press, 1992), 7–59.
28. Pepper, "Is Drawing to Disappear," 719. A *pochade* is the French term for a rapid sketch in oils, usually done from nature on a small wood or cardboard panel.
29. For example, CR 520, 534, 535, 536, 539, and 541.
30. CR 555, 564, 576, 578, 592, 594, and 595.
31. "Local Information," *The Quartier Latin* 4, no. 20 (March 1898): 740.
32. Mrs. Oliver E. Williams, quoted in Rhys, "Sources and Development," 75, n. 75. Also see Brooks, "Anecdotes," and the *Detroit Journal,* October 19, 1901: "[In] the monotypes of Maurice B. Prendergast of New York . . . the pictures are painted first on copper plates, and then put through a press and the impression taken on the paper."
33. See Glavin, "Boston Experience," 69–71. Pepper was an authority on Japanese art who had his first solo exhibition of watercolors at Siegfried Bing's gallery L'Art Nouveau in Paris in December 1897. He traveled to Japan in 1903 and published *Japanese Prints* (Boston: Walter Kimball, [1905]). Also see Julia Meech and Gabriel P. Weisberg, *Japonisme Comes to America* (New York: Harry N. Abrams, 1990).
34. C. O. Elliett Gallery, Oak Grove, Malden, Mass., *Artists' Exhibition and Sale in the Gallery of C.O. Elliett, Oak Grove Malden by H.R. Burdick, S.L. Brackett, G.L. Noyes, M.B. Prendergast,* sales cat. (April 21–May 4, 1897 [sale, May 3–4]), no. 28.
35. "Boston Notes," *Art Interchange* 41 (December 1898), 136.
36. *Detroit Journal,* October 19, 1901.
37. Due to the difficulty in precisely dating Morrice's panels, it is virtually impossible to posit a cause and effect relationship between the early work of Prendergast and Morrice.
38. C. O. Elliett Gallery, *Artists' Exhibition and Sale.*
39. "New Books," *New York Evening Sun,* January 2, 1896, 5. The text continues: "These, which are frequently used as head and tail pieces, are always clever and *spirituel.* The cover of the book is quaint and original. . . . Altogether this ought to be a very popular edition of a popular book. The next book illustrated by Mr. Prendergast will be looked forward to with interest."
40. "The Boston Art Club's Fifty-second Exhibition," *Boston Sunday Herald,* April 7, 1895, 33.
41. William H. Downes, "The Fine Arts," *Boston Evening Transcript,* April 15, 1895, 6. As late as 1935, Downes wrote a biographical sketch of Maurice, which appeared in the 1935 edition of *Dictionary of American Biography* (15:186).
42. William H. Downes, "The Fine Arts," *Boston Evening Transcript,* April 3, 1897, 7. The text continues: "Modern art, since the advent of Fortuny, has found one of its distinctive expressions in pure and bright and positive color. This example is extraordinary. It is a splendid bouquet of flowers or a cluster with figures by Fortuny that were no better." Quoted in Dominic Madormo, "The 'Butterfly' Artist: Maurice Prendergast and His Critics," in *Catalogue Raisonné,* 62.
43. Pepper, "Is Drawing to Disappear," 719.
44. William Dean Howells, *Venetian Life,* 2 vols. (Cambridge, Mass.: Riverside Press, 1892). See *A Regatta,* vol. 2, frontispiece, and compare *Gondoliers* (2: 160) to Prendergast's *Fishing Boats, Normandy* (CR 529), dated 1892. The original watercolor, *A Venetian Regatta* of 1891, is illustrated in Christie's, New York, *Important American Paintings,* sales cat. (December 4, 1992), sale no. 7544, no. 77, p. 21.
45. The Wallace Collection, London.
46. CR 725. He is known to have brought back glass tesserae, which, according to Ira Glackens, he probably assembled into the mosaic after his return to Boston (*Ashcan Group,* 117). *Fies-*

ta Grand Canal, Venice (CR 725) was probably a collaboration between Charles and Maurice.

47. Prendergast to Walter Pach, February 2, 1922, Walter Pach Papers, AAA.
48. Maurice Prendergast, CR 1497.
49. Barbara Novak, "American Impressionism," *Portfolio* 4 (March–April 1982), 76.
50. Maurice Prendergast, quoted in Ellen M. Glavin, "Maurice Prendergast and Central Park," *Archives of American Art Journal* 31, no. 4 (1991): 20–26.
51. Prendergast to Pach, December 6, 1909. The letter is quoted on page 99.
52. William H. Downes, "Twelfth Annual Exhibition of the Water Color Club," *Boston Evening Transcript*, March 4, 1899, 10.
53. Hermann Dudley Murphy to William Macbeth, [October, 1899], Macbeth Gallery Records, AAA.
54. Lorado Taft, "Famous Artists in Town," *Chicago Record*, January 6, 1900, 4.
55. William H. Downes, "The Murphy and Prendergast Exhibition in Chicago," *Boston Evening Transcript*, January 3, 1900, 11. See Madormo, " 'Butterfly' Artist," for a full discussion.
56. William H. Downes, "Gallery and Studio Notes," *Boston Evening Transcript*, January 17, 1900, 11.
57. "Rare Exhibit at Local Art Gallery: Collection of Interesting Watercolors by Maurice B. Prendergast, the Boston Impressionist," *San Francisco Chronicle*, May 13, 1900, 11. The critic also noted that the watercolors had "flat frames, which have been made to suit the coloring of the painting. The dull gilts used are copper, brass and bronze hued." Actually, they were burnished bronze powder, for which the trade term was *Roman gilding*.
58. Charles H. Caffin, "The Picture Exhibition at the Pan-American Exposition," *International Studio* 14 (September 1901): 21–28.
59. The catalogue priced by Prendergast is in the Archives of the Detroit Institute of Arts.
60. A photographic portrait of Prendergast appeared in the *Detroit News Tribune*, November 17, 1901.
61. See Richard J. Wattenmaker, *The Art of Charles Prendergast*, exhib. cat. (Boston: Museum of Fine Arts; New Brunswick, N.J.: Rutgers University, 1968), no. 73, ill. p. 110. For another illustration also see Fred Lockley, "A Westerner at Tom Lawson's Dreamworld," *Pacific Monthly* 26 (December 1911): 644. Two similar frames of differing dimensions were carved by the Prendergasts for Lawson in 1908 and 1912. The second version included incised French spaniels as well as bulldogs. Illustrated in William Adair, "Forgotten Frames as Works of Art," in *The Regilded Age*, exhib. cat. (Newark, N.J.: The Society of Gilders at The Newark Museum 1991), 26, 27.
62. Another frame, commissioned by Mrs. Jack Gardner, signed "Prendergast" and dated 1903, was created for Sargent's portrait of *Charles Martin Loeffler*. Other dated frames from this period are also known. See Carol Derby, "Charles Prendergast's Frames: Reuniting Design and Craftsmanship," in *The Prendergasts and the Arts and Crafts Movement*, exhib. cat. (Williamstown, Mass.: Williams College Museum of Art, 1989), 31 and n. 18.
63. Maurice Prendergast, "Sketchbook of Frame Studies," c. 1903 (CR 1481).
64. Maurice Prendergast, "Sketchbook No. 47" (CR 1528).
65. Charles Hovey Pepper, quoted in Joseph Coburn Smith, *Charles Hovey Pepper* (Portland, Me.: Southworth-Anthoensen Press, 1945), 41.
66. Prendergast wrote to Macbeth after the close of the Society of American Artists exhibition in early May 1901: "Would you like to take charge of the oil I have in the Society 'Salem Willows' and try to sell it. Get anywhere near $300.00 and you can have 33 1/2%. . . . Can you keep it until [next year]. . . ." The painting found no buyer and apparently Maurice was satisfied enough with it not to ask that it be returned at that time for retouching.
67. The *fête galante* is a French term, untranslatable into English, associated with the outdoor scenes of Jean-Antoine Watteau (1684–1721), which represent gatherings of elegantly dressed figures in a pastoral park setting.
68. CR 49 and 700. The original invoice, dated May 4, 1899, is in the Esther Baldwin Williams Papers, AAA.
69. Although dated 1904, it is possible that the canvas was retouched between April 1904 and October 31, 1905, when it was finally delivered to Mrs. Williams, who made a payment of four hundred dollars for it. On the receipt, however, Maurice wrote "one oil painting 'The Promenade' Salem Harbor Painted in 1904." In a letter to Mrs. Williams five days later he sent "many sincere thanks for your prompt check. . . . It is a great pleasure to me you like it so well. You are so truly appreciative that if I could afford [it] nothing would [give] me more pleasure than to present the picture to you. . . . About framing the picture my original idea was one of those mysterious empire frames not exactly an empire but a flowing frame but I gave up on account of the time and expense" (Esther Baldwin Williams Papers, AAA).
70. Maurice Prendergast, CR 1483.
71. See the National Arts Club, New York, *Loan Exhibition of Pictures by Eminent American Painters*, exhib. cat. (1904), nos. 10, 17, 20, 33, 34, 37, and 38.
72. Charles DeKay, "Startling Works by Red-Hot American Painters," *New York Times*, January 20, 1904, 9. Charles FitzGerald wrote, "Mr. Prendergast['s] delightful series of 'Promenades,' [are] marked by that science and inimitable delicacy of perception of which he holds the secret" ("A Significant Group of Paintings," *New York Evening Sun*, January 23, 1904, 4).
73. Maurice Prendergast, CR 1482.
74. Charles FitzGerald, "The Society and the Ten Deserters," *New York Evening Sun*, April 3, 1902, 4.
75. Charles DeKay, "French and American Impressionists," *New York Times*, January 31, 1904, 23.
76. An accommodation must have been reached, for the Macbeth Gallery records indicate three panels were sold to Breckenridge. See CR 1864. Davies informed Prendergast that Breckenridge was also interested in *Salem Willows* (Prendergast to Esther Williams, November 10, 1905). Also see note 101.
77. Maurice Prendergast, CR 1483.
78. Harriet Monroe, "Fine Water Color Exhibit," *Chicago Examiner*, May 13, 1905.
79. "Eight Independent Painters," *New York Sun*, May 15, 1907, 5.
80. See Galeries Georges Petit, Paris, *Exposition Chardin et Fragonard*, exhib. cat. (Paris: Imprimerie Georges Petit, 1907). The exhibition ran from June 11 to July 12.
81. He was probably provided a copy by Walter Pach, who had also seen the Salon d'Automne and who mentions Bernard's article in his own article "Cézanne—an Introduction." Pach wrote: "At the Salon d'Automne of last year there was a wonderful retrospective exhibition of some sixty Cézannes. . . . Had it not been for the enterprise and perseverance of one of his most impassioned admirers, Emile Bernard . . . we should be practically without information about . . . Cézanne's most remarkable accomplishment. The record of his several visits to 'his master,' as he loves to call him, is published in *L'Occident*, for July, 1904" ("Cézanne—an Introduction," *Scribner's* 8 [December 1908]: 766).
82. The article referred to is Giles Edgerton [Mary Fanton Roberts], "The Younger American Painters: Are They Creating a National Art?" *The Craftsman* 13, no. 5 (February 1908), 512–32. The article includes photographs that Gertrude Käsebier took of the members of the Eight in the spring of 1907.
83. The canvas held back, *The Fête* (CR 47) is the only Prendergast illustrated in the catalogue; it was reproduced again in 1910 by Charles Pepper but is now lost, perhaps "disappeared" under another composition. The photograph was not necessarily taken by Pepper in 1910; it may have been one taken earlier and supplied to him for his article "Is Drawing to Disappear."
84. See Gwendolyn Owens, "The Legacy of the Eight: Independent Exhibition and the 'National Salon,' " in *Painters of a New Century: The Eight & American Art* by Elizabeth Milroy, exhib. cat. (Milwaukee: Milwaukee Art Museum, 1991), 58, n. 109, documenting the extension of the exhibition.
85. Arthur Hoeber, "Art and Artists," *New York Globe and Commercial Advertiser*, February 5, 1908.
86. Joseph E. Chamberlain, "Two Significant Exhibitions," *New York Evening Mail*, February 4, 1908, 6.
87. Review of the Eight show, *New York Herald*, February 4, 1908, Macbeth Gallery Records, AAA.
88. Review of the Eight show, unidentified newspaper clipping, Macbeth Gallery Records, AAA.
89. James Huneker, "Eight Painters," *New York Sun*, February 9, 1908, 8 (the first of two articles, of which only the first mentions Prendergast).
90. James B. Townsend, " 'The Eight' Arrive," *American Art News* 6 (February 8, 1908): 6.
91. " 'The Eight' Stir Up Many Emotions," *Newark Evening News*, May 8, 1909, sec. 2, p. 4, quoted in Judith Zilczer, "The Eight on Tour, 1908–1909," *American Art Journal* 16, no. 3 (Summer 1984): 20–47.
92. *International Studio* 37, no. 146 (April 1909): 165.
93. Arthur Hoeber, "Art and Artists," *New York Globe and Commercial Advertiser*, May 22, 1909, 10.
94. Pach had lately published "Quelques notes sur les peintres américains" (*Gazette des Beaux-Arts*, October 1909), which men-

tioned but did not illustrate Prendergast, whom it described as "M. Prendergast, amoureux de la vie joyeuse et de la lumière" (Mr. Prendergast, lover of the joyful life and light, 334).

95. John Rewald described *Harvesters* as "executed thinly in fairly luminous though not vivid colors, showing how the artist began to dilute his paint and to abandon the heavy impasto as well as the accumulation of square, parallel strokes, in favor of a more homogeneous coat of almost transparent pigment without insistence on separate, apparent brush strokes" in *Cézanne and America* (Princeton, N. J.: Princeton University Press, 1989), 196; also see pp. 173, 196–98.
96. Daphne Dunbar, interview with Hedley Rhys, 1950. See his "Sources and Development," 120.
97. Bellows to Taylor, April 20, 1910, transcription in Frank Seiberling, Jr., Ph.D. diss., "George Bellows, 1882–1925: His Life and Development of an Artist" (University of Chicago, 1948), Appendix, 1–2. Papers, Archives of American Art, Smithsonian Institution. Research material on George Bellows. Taylor was Bellows's former English professor at Ohio State University.
98. The show referred to was a three-man exhibition of work by Prendergast, Charles Hopkinson, and Charles Hovey Pepper at the Copley Gallery, March 13–25, 1911.
99. Arthur Hoeber, "Art and Artists," *New York Globe and Commercial Advertiser*, March 28, 1911, 14. Maurer's paintings were termed "absolutely without any meaning . . . and . . . even offensive in their crudity."
100. See Garnett McCoy, "The Rockwell Kent Papers," *Archives of American Art Journal* 12, no. 1 (January 1972): 4; and David Traxel, *An American Saga: The Life and Times of Rockwell Kent* (New York: Harper & Row, 1980), 61–62.
101. Probably a reference to the commission received by the Prendergast brothers in the spring from the Insurance Company of North America, Philadelphia (CIGNA), to frame portraits belonging to the company, which was founded in 1792. The Committee on Portraits was appointed on April 4, 1911. Hugh Breckenridge, who had painted the portrait of the company's president Eugene L. Ellison around 1909, undoubtedly suggested Prendergast for the job. The elaborately carved frame for the Ellison portrait (37 1/4 by 31 1/4 inches) is signed and dated "Prendergast 1912." Approximately eighteen additional frames were made for these portraits over the next several years, none of them signed and possibly not all of them carved by the Prendergasts. Also see note 76.
102. "Prendergast at Cosmopolitan," *American Art News* 10 (April 13, 1912): 2.
103. Glackens, *Ashcan Group*, 120.
104. Walt Kuhn to Maurice Prendergast, December 31, 1912, Walt Kuhn, Kuhn family papers, and Armory Show Records, AAA.
105. "The American Section: The National Art," *Arts and Decoration* 3, no. 5 (March 1913), 159–67.
106. *Seashore* was the sole contemporary American painting reproduced (under the title *Summer*) in the preopening publicity, opposite van Gogh's *Mountains of Saint-Rémy*, 1889, F622 ("The New Idea: 'Cubists and Futurists,'" *The Evening Post Saturday Magazine*, February 8, 1913).
107. Jerome Myers, *Artist in Manhattan* (New York: American Artists Group, 1940), 108.
108. Guy Pène du Bois, *Artists Say the Silliest Things* (New York: American Artists Group, Duell, Sloan, and Pearce, 1940), 175.
109. Guy Pène du Bois, *New York Telegram and Evening Mail*, February 6, 1924, 12.
110. Maurice Prendergast to Walt Kuhn, March 17, 1913, Walt Kuhn, Kuhn family papers, and Armory Show Records, AAA.
111. See Garnett McCoy, "The Post Impressionist Bomb," *Archives of American Art Journal* 20, no. 1 (1980): 12–17 for a discussion of the Armory Show in Boston.
112. James Huneker, "The Seven Arts," *Puck* 75, no. 1936 (April 11, 1914). As early as 1911, Charles DeKay described Maurice's work in the following terms: "Prendergast is pursued by a dream of decorative combinations of colors to which he subjects the groups of city folks, until they look like figures on old faded samplers or wall papers." Charles DeKay, in *Schools of Painting* by Mary Innes (New York: G. P. Putnam's Sons, 1911), 386.
113. The article in question is Walter Pach, "The Point of View of the Moderns," *Century Magazine* 87 (April 1914): 851–64. Prendergast had seen five Renoirs at Bernheim-Jeune's exhibition "Le Paysage du midi" in June. See also William C. Agee, "Walter Pach and Modernism," *Archives of American Art Journal* 28, no. 3 (1988): 2–10.
114. Root took painting lessons with Luks.
115. Daphne Dunbar, quoted in Brady, "Anonymous Friend."
116. Ira Glackens, *Ashcan Group*, 116–17.
117. CR 1483.
118. CR 1522 (France, 1914).
119. CR 1518 (c. 1914–15).
120. CR 1506 (c. 1912–14).
121. For example, Puvis de Chavanes's *Pleasant Land* (Musée Bonnat, Bayonne), of which Maurice had made a drawing (CR 1487), and *A Vision of Antiquity* (The Carnegie Museum of Art, Pittsburgh).
122. CR 2217. See Wattenmaker, *The Art of Charles Prendergast* (Boston: Museum of Fine Arts; New Brunswick, N.J.: Rutgers University, 1968), p. 41, no. 3 (colorplate on p. 18). The composition is based directly on a mosaic in San Apollinare Nuovo, Ravenna.
123. Albert C. Barnes, *The Art in Painting* (New York: Harcourt, Brace, 1925), 298–99.
124. Frederick James Gregg, *Maurice B. Prendergast: Paintings in Oil and Water Color*, exhib. cat. (New York: Carroll Galleries, 1915). The exhibition ran from February 15 through March 6, 1915.
125. "Prendergast's Paintings," *New York Times*, March 4, 1915, 8.
126. Charles H. Caffin, "Prendergast Shows His Happy Art," *New York American*, February 22, 1915, 9.
127. Unpublished memoirs, Charles Daniel Papers, AAA.
128. See Eleanor Green, et al., *Maurice Prendergast: Art of Impulse and Color* (College Park, Md.: University of Maryland, 1976), 26.
129. See Gail Stavitsky, "John Weichsel and the People's Art Guild," *Archives of American Art Journal* 31, no. 4 (1991), 12–19, and John Weichsel Papers, AAA.
130. *Cézanne's Studio* (New York: Washington Square Gallery, 1915), introduction by Robert J. Coady. The translation is from Ambroise Vollard's *Paul Cézanne* (Paris: Vollard, 1914).
131. Esther B. Williams to Charles Prendergast, November 3, 1946, Prendergast Archive and Study Center, Williams College, Williamstown, Mass.
132. Ellen M. Glavin has pointed out the debt this composition owes to the arrangement of figures in an ancient Greek grave relief reproduced in Irene Weir's *The Greek Painter's Art* (Boston, 1905). See Glavin, "Maurice Prendergast: The Development of an American Post-Impressionist, 1900–1915," Ph.D. diss. (Boston University, 1988), 142–43 and nn. 35, 36. The attribution of this source in ancient Greek sculpture is reinforced by a photograph in Prendergast's possession of a similar relief representing Juno and Jove from the temple of Selinunte, Sicily, in the Museo Nazionale, Palermo (now in the Maurice and Charles Prendergast Archive and Study Center, Williams College, Williamstown, Mass.). Maurice visited the museum in January 1912, when he stopped in Palermo on his way home from Venice.
133. At the Galleria degli Uffizi, Florence.
134. "The Fifty at Montross," *International Studio* 58, no. 229 (March 1916): 34. Charles Guérin (1875–1939), whose surprisingly bright scenes of women in park settings were reminiscent in their imagery of both the works of Conder (see pl. 110) and the *fêtes galantes* of Monticelli, was well known as an instructor at the Académie Moderne in Paris, where many Americans studied in the years before World War I. Roussel's name was actually noted in a sketchbook—CR 1520—Prendergast used on the trip to France in the summer of 1914.
135. Charles Hovey Pepper, quoted in Smith, *Charles Hovey Pepper*, 41.
136. Charles Hovey Pepper, "Is Drawing to Disappear," 719.
137. CR 1546 and watercolor CR 1333, *Gloucester Beach*.
138. "Notes on Current Art: A Strong Exhibition," *New York Times*, January 11, 1920, sec. 9, p. 3.
139. Joseph Brummer (1883?–1940) was a student in Matisse's class in 1908 and knew Pach, who was not enrolled but who also attended from time to time.
140. Review of the exhibition of Maurice and Charles Prendergast at Brummer Galleries, *Brooklyn Daily Eagle*, April 10, 1921, 3–4.
141. Lewis Mumford [Journeyman, pseud.], "Miscellany," *The Freeman* 3, no. 59 (April 27, 1921) 159–60.
142. "Prendergast First American Modernist," *American Art News* 19 (April 9, 1921): 3.
143. Walter Pach, "Maurice Prendergast," *Shadowland* 6 (April 1922): 74.
144. Marjorie Phillips, *Duncan Phillips and His Collection*, rev. ed. (New York: W. W. Norton, 1982), 19–20.
145. Pach, *Queer Thing, Painting*, 225.
146. "Her Vagaries," *International Studio* 73, no. 290 (May 1921): 77.
147. Charles Prendergast, quoted in William W. Milliken, "Maurice Prendergast, American Artist," *The Arts* 9, no. 4 (April 1926): 192.
148. *New York Telegram and Evening Mail*, February 6, 1924, 12. Mrs. Havemeyer did not own any work by Maurice Prendergast.
149. *New York Herald*, February 10, 1924, sec. 7, p. 13.
150. *New York World*, February 10, 1924, 8.

Biographical Outline

1857 Marriage of Mary Malvina Germaine (1833–1883), daughter of Thomas Hutchinson Germaine, M.D. (1779–1862), to Maurice Prendergast (1820–1901), February 23, 1857, in Saint John's, Newfoundland. Her brother, Charles Napoleon Germaine (b. 1824 in Boston), had graduated Harvard Medical School in 1850.

1858 Maurice Brazil Prendergast and twin sister Lucy Catherine are born October 10 and baptized in Saint John's Basilica. Lucy dies approximately eighteen to twenty years later. Maurice's godfather is Patrick Brazil.

1863 Charles James (later changed to Edward) Prendergast is born May 27 and baptized June 24 in Saint John's Basilica. Charles is named after his mother's brother.

1864–65 Maurice, Sr., is listed as a grocer at 138 Water Street in Saint John's, according to *Hutchinson's Newfoundland Directory*. Maurice attends school in Saint John's, c. 1864–68.

1868 The Prendergast family moves to Boston in September.

1868–72 Maurice attends public school in Boston. His formal education ends after four years, and he is employed wrapping packages at a dry-goods store, Loring and Waterhouse, Boston.

1872–77 Maurice, Sr., residing at 86 West Dedham Street, Boston, is listed as "laborer" in the Boston directories of 1872, 1873, and 1874 and as "confectioner" in those of 1875, 1876, and 1877.

1877 Charles completes his schooling and obtains a job as an errand boy for Doll & Richards Gallery, where he stays for three years. Maurice completes classes at the Free Evening Drawing School, held at the Starr King School on Tennyson Street, which he began in 1873.

1878 Maurice Prendergast is listed as "clerk" in the Boston directory.

1879 Maurice Prendergast is listed as "designer" in the Boston directory. He works at the firm of J. P. Marshall, producer of show cards, 266 Washington Street, Boston.

1880 Census records list Maurice as "painter," age nineteen. Charles E. is recorded "at home," age sixteen.

1880–93 Prendergast family resides at 119 Center Street, Roxbury.

1882 Maurice listed as "decorator" in Boston directory. Charles Napoleon Germaine dies June 12 and is given a Masonic funeral.

1883 Mary Malvina Prendergast dies November 27.

1886 Maurice accompanies Charles to England and Wales, traveling on a cattle boat.

1886–90 Maurice Prendergast gives his business address as 1 Province Street, Boston, the firm of Peter Gill, designer of show cards.

1891 Maurice and Charles are in Paris by January. Both brothers study at Colarossi studio. Maurice enrolls at Académie Julian in October, resides 9 rue Campagne-Première.

1892 Charles returns to Boston and forms a partnership with Lars F. Peterson & Co. to produce architectural woodwork.

1891–94 Maurice works in Paris and on the Normandy coast.

1894 Maurice returns from Liverpool in September.

1895 Exhibits watercolor in "Fifty-second Exhibition of the Boston Art Club" (April). Designs posters, book covers, and illustrations for W. A. Wilde and Co. and Joseph Knight Co., Boston.

1896 Exhibits watercolors for the first time at Pennsylvania Academy of the Fine Arts, Philadelphia, and at the Jordan Gallery, Boston, to very positive reviews.

1897 Last illustration commission published for L. C. Page and Co., Boston. Exhibits for the first time at Art Institute of Chicago and New York Water Color Club.

1898 Exhibits in Boston, New York, Philadelphia, and Chicago. Sails for Italy in July.

1898–99 Stays sixteen months in Italy, primarily in Venice. Visits Padua, Florence, Siena, Assisi, Orvieto, Rome, Naples, and Capri. Returns home around November 30 via Berlin and London.

1900 First show at William Macbeth's gallery in March, showing watercolors and monotypes. From mid-July to mid-September goes on a sketching trip, possibly to Quebec. Resides in Winchester with Charles.

1901 Maurice Prendergast, Sr., dies September 23. Maurice wins bronze medal for *The Stony Beach,* c. 1897, at Pan-American Exposition, Buffalo. In spring and fall, works in New York City.

1902 Exhibits in Boston, New York, Chicago, Cincinnati, and Philadelphia. Creates last dated monotype.

1903 Takes studio with Charles at 56 Mount Vernon Street, Boston.

1904 In January, exhibits paintings with William Glackens, George Luks, Robert Henri, Arthur B. Davies, and John Sloan at the National Arts Club.

1905–6 Sells *Salem Willows,* 1904, to Mr. and Mrs. Oliver Williams (October 31, 1905). As his loss of hearing begins to concern him, joins L Street Brownies bathhouse, trying swimming and sunbathing to improve his health.

1907 Arrives Le Havre, May 28. In Paris, impressed by Cézanne watercolor exhibition (June) and Salon du Champ de Mars. Paints in Saint-Malo and Paris. Sees fifty-six Cézannes at Salon d'Automne (October). Arrives home early November.

1908 Exhibition of the Eight, Macbeth Galleries, February 3–15. Displays mainly small Saint-Malo panels but no Paris compositions. Glackens visits 56 Mount Vernon Street in June. Maurice visits Glackenses at Yarmouth, Cape Cod. Meets Marsden Hartley.

1909 Sends Hartley to show work to Glackens, Davies, and Ernest Lawson in Glackens's studio in New York. Visits Professor Sumner in December to see Cézanne's *Harvesters.*

1910 In April, shows five canvases in "Exhibition of Independent Artists." Article by C. H. Pepper appears in *The World To-Day* (July). Around this time, Pepper paints Maurice's portrait.

1911 Charles sails to Italy in mid-June. Maurice joins him in Capri in August, stopping in Rome and Florence en route to Venice. Maurice is taken ill and has a prostate operation at the Cosmopolitan Hospital, early November.

1912 Sails from Genoa on January 31, via Palermo. Elected member of the Association of American Painters and Sculptors and appointed to both foreign and American selection committees for the Armory Show. Visits Glackens family at Bellport, Long Island.

1913 Exhibits seven works in Armory Show. In June, he has a second prostate operation at City Hospital, Boston. Summers in Brooksville, Maine. First sales to Dr. Albert C. Barnes.

1914 Last trip to France. Visits Saint-Malo, Roscoff, and Concarneau, Brittany. Sees Salons and Camondo bequest at Louvre. He and Charles move to 50 Washington Square South, New York, by November 1.

1915 An exhibition of sixty works is given at Carroll Galleries, February 15–March 6. First sales to John Quinn. First sale to Ferdinand Howald.

1916 Exhibition at St. Botolph Club, Boston, with Glackens. Charles is appointed vice-president of the Society of Independent Artists (William Glackens, president).

1917 Exhibits at the Society of Independent Artists and the Whitney Studio Club. First sales to Duncan Phillips.

1919 Appointed to Advisory Board of Society of Independent Artists. Exhibits in Boston, Chicago, Detroit, Buffalo, Washington, D.C., Philadelphia, Saint Louis, Toledo, Rochester, N.Y., and at the Musée du Luxembourg, Paris.

1920 Exhibits two paintings at the Venice Biennale (commissioner Forbes Watson). Shows at Daniel, Montross, and Knoedler galleries.

1921 Retrospective exhibition at Brummer Galleries, of thirty-seven works by Maurice, nine by Charles. One canvas, *Figures on the Beach* (CR 2013?), included in "Exposition d'un groupe de peintres américains," Galeries Georges Petit, Paris, organized by Mrs. Harry Payne Whitney. Show travels to Venice, London, and Sheffield, England.

1923 Awarded bronze medal and third William A. Clark Prize of one thousand dollars by Corcoran Gallery of Art, Washington, D.C., for *Landscape with Figures* (1921). Corcoran purchases painting for two thousand dollars.

1924 Maurice dies February 1. Funeral service held February 2 at Broadway Tabernacle Church, New York.

Selected Bibliography

BARNES, ALBERT C., AND VIOLETTE DE MAZIA. *The Art of Cézanne.* New York: Harcourt, Brace, 1939, 138–40.

BARNES, ALBERT C. *The Art in Painting.* New York: Harcourt, Brace, 1925.

BASSO, HAMILTON. "A Glimpse of Heaven." Parts 1, 2. *New Yorker* 22 (July 27, August 3, 1946): 24–28, 30; 28–32, 34, 36–37.

BRADY, FRED. "Anonymous Friend Reveals Prendergast's Love of Life." *Boston Herald,* November 27, 1960, sec. 4, p. 3.

BROOKS, VAN WYCK. "Anecdotes of Maurice Prendergast." In Addison Gallery of American Art, Phillips Academy, Andover, Mass., *The Prendergasts: Retrospective Exhibition of the Work of Maurice and Charles Prendergast,* 1938, 33–45.

CAFFIN, CHARLES H. "Prendergast Shows His Happy Art." *New York American,* February 22, 1915, p. 9.

CLARK, CAROL, NANCY MOWLL MATHEWS, AND GWENDOLYN OWENS. *Maurice Brazil Prendergast, Charles Prendergast: A Catalogue Raisonné.* Munich and Williamstown, Mass.: Prestel-Verlag and Williams College Museum of Art, 1990.

CLARK, CAROL. *American Drawings and Watercolors in the Robert Lehman Collection.* New York: The Metropolitan Museum of Art; Princeton, N.J.: Princeton University Press, 1992.

DE MAZIA, VIOLETTE. "Subject and Subject Matter: Part II. Instrumentalism." *Vistas* 2 (1981–83): 2–58.

GENGARELLY, W. ANTHONY. "Maurice Prendergast's Applied Graphic Art." In *The Prendergasts and the Arts and Crafts Movement* by Anthony W. Gengarelly and Carol Derby. Williamstown, Mass.: Williams College Museum of Art, 1989.

GLACKENS, IRA. *William Glackens and the Ashcan Group.* New York: Horizon Press, 1957.

GLAVIN, ELLEN M. "Maurice Prendergast: The Boston Experience." *Art and Antiques* 5 (July–August 1982): 64–71.

———. "The Early Art Education of Maurice Prendergast: Art Education in Boston in the 1870s." *Archives of American Art Journal* 33, no. 1 (1993).

———, and Eleanor Green. "Chronology." In *Maurice Prendergast.* College Park, Md.: University of Maryland, 1976.

LANGDALE, CECILY. *The Monotypes of Maurice Prendergast.* New York: Davis & Long, 1979.

———. *Monotypes by Maurice Prendergast in the Terra Museum of American Art.* Chicago: Terra Museum of American Art, 1984.

MADORMO, DOMINIC. "The 'Butterfly' Artist: Maurice Prendergast and His Critics." In *Maurice Brazil Prendergast, Charles Prendergast: A Catalogue Raisonné,* by Carol Clark, Nancy Mowll Mathews, and Gwendolyn Owens. Munich and Williamstown, Mass.: Prestel-Verlag and Williams College Museum of Art, 1990.

MATHEWS, NANCY MOWLL. *Maurice Prendergast.* Munich: Prestel-Verlag, 1990.

——— et al. *The Art of Charles Prendergast from the Collections of the Williams College Museum of Art & Mrs. Charles Prendergast.* Williamstown, Mass.: Williams College Museum of Art, 1993.

MILLIKEN, WILLIAM M. "Maurice Prendergast, American Artist." *The Arts* 9, no. 4 (April 1926): 180–92.

MUMFORD, LEWIS. [Journeyman, pseud.]. "Miscellany." *The Freeman* 3, no. 59 (April 27, 1921), 159–60.

OWENS, GWENDOLYN. "The Legacy of the Eight: Independent Exhibition and the 'National Salon.'" In *Painters of a New Century: The Eight & American Art,* by Elizabeth Milroy. Exhib. cat. Milwaukee: Milwaukee Art Museum, 1991.

PACH, WALTER. "Maurice Prendergast." *Shadowland* 6 (April 1922): 10–11, 74–75.

———. *Queer Thing, Painting.* New York: Harper & Brothers, 1938.

PEPPER, CHARLES HOVEY. "Is Drawing to Disappear in Artistic Individuality?: A Sketch of the Work of Maurice Prendergast." *The World To-Day* 19 (July 1910): 716–19.

RHYS, HEDLEY HOWELL. "Maurice Prendergast." In *Maurice Prendergast: 1859–1924,* by Hedley Howell Rhys and Peter A. Wick. Exhib. cat. Cambridge, Mass.: Harvard University Press, 1960.

SMITH, JOSEPH COBURN. *Charles Hovey Pepper.* Portland, Me.: Southworth-Anthoensen Press, 1945.

WATTENMAKER, RICHARD J. *The Art of Charles Prendergast.* Exhib. cat. Boston: Museum of Fine Arts; New

Brunswick, N.J.: Rutgers University, 1968.
———. *Puvis de Chavannes and the Modern Tradition.* Toronto: Art Gallery of Ontario, 1975; rev. ed., Toronto, 1976.
———. "Maurice Prendergast." *Allen Memorial Art Museum Bulletin* 40, no. 1 (1982–83): 25–37.
———. "Maurice Prendergast at the Whitney." *The New Criterion* 9, no. 3 (November 1990): 33–40.
WICK, PETER A. "A Critical Note." In *Maurice Prendergast Water-Color Sketchbook 1899.*: Boston: Museum of Fine Arts; Cambridge, Mass.: Harvard University Press, 1960.
ZILCZER, JUDITH. "The Eight on Tour, 1908–1909." *American Art Journal* 16, no. 3 (Summer 1984): 20–47.

Unpublished Sources

Private Papers

DANIEL, CHARLES. Papers. Archives of American Art, Smithsonian Institution, Washington, D.C. (hereinafter cited as AAA).
HARTLEY, MARSDEN. "Somehow a Past." Unpublished autobiography, 1933–42. Yale Collection of American Literature, Beinecke Rare Book and Manuscript Library, Yale University, New Haven, Conn.
KENT, ROCKWELL. Papers. AAA.
KLAUBER, ALICE. Papers. AAA.
KUHN, WALT. Kuhn family papers, and Armory Show Records. AAA.
MACBETH GALLERY RECORDS. AAA.
MACRAE, ELMER. Papers. Hirshhorn Museum and Sculpture Garden, Smithsonian Institution, Washington, D.C.
MYERS, JEROME. Papers. AAA.
MURPHY, HERMANN DUDLEY. Papers. AAA.
PACH, WALTER. Papers. AAA.
QUINN, JOHN. Memorial Collection. New York Public Library, New York.
ROOT, EDWARD W. Papers. Munson-Williams-Proctor Institute, Utica, New York.
SEIBERLING, FRANK, JR. Papers. AAA.
WATSON, FORBES. Papers, AAA.
WEICHSEL, JOHN. Papers. AAA.
WILLIAMS, ESTHER BALDWIN (Mrs. Oliver E.). Papers. AAA.

Institutional Records

Kraushaar Galleries Archives, New York.
Archives of The Barnes Foundation, Merion Station, Penn.
Archives of the Carnegie Institute, Pittsburgh.
Archives of the Cincinnati Art Museum.
Archives of the Detroit Institute of Arts.
Archives of the Corcoran Gallery of Art, Washington, D.C.
Archives of the Pennsylvania Academy of the Fine Arts, Philadelphia.
The Maurice and Charles Prendergast Archive and Study Center, Williams College, Williamstown, Mass.

Articles and Dissertations

RHYS, HEDLEY HOWELL. "Maurice Prendergast: The Sources and Development of His Style." Ph.D. diss., Harvard University, 1952.
GLAVIN, ELLEN M. "Maurice Prendergast: The Development of an American Post-Impressionist, 1900–1915." Ph.D. diss., Boston University, 1988.

Index

Page numbers in *italics* refer to illustrations and their commentaries. Unless otherwise noted all works are by Prendergast.

Photograph Credits

The author and publisher wish to thank the museums, galleries, and private collectors named in the captions for supplying the necessary photographs. Other photograph credits are listed below by page number.

Art Resource, New York/National Museum of American Art, Washington, D.C.: 103; Ball State University Photographic Services: 28, 30, 31; © 1994 The Barnes Foundation, Merion Station, Pennsylvania: 36 below, 76, 94, 122, 123 right, 134, 135, 141; Geoffrey Clements: 71, 75, 109 below, 128 below; Tibor Franyo: 54; © Musée National d'Art Moderne, Paris: 87 above; Edward Owen: 49; Photocraft, Muncie, Indiana: 57; Service Photographique de la Réunion des Musées Nationaux, Paris: 86 above, 118 right, 199 left; Lee Stalsworth: 88; © Daniel J. Terra Collection, Terra Museum of American Art, Chicago: 10, 24 left, 32, 50, 55, 73 above, 80.